TACIT SUBJECTS

TACIT SUBJECTS

Belonging and Same-Sex Desire

among Dominican Immigrant Men

: : :

Carlos Ulises Decena

Duke University Press   : : :   Durham & London   : : :   2011

© 2011 Duke University Press

All rights reserved

Printed in the United States

of America on acid-free paper ∞

Designed by Amy Ruth Buchanan

Typeset in Scala by Achorn International

Library of Congress Cataloging-in-

Publication Data appear on the last

printed page of this book.

Para Alfredo,
compañero al andar,
por enseñarme que lo
que más importa
es la gente.

CONTENTS

ACKNOWLEDGMENTS

Completing this book would not have been possible without the informants' willingness to share anecdotes and opinions drawn from their experiences. I am grateful to all the persons who spoke to me as participants, as advisors at various stages of this process, and as interlocutors and critics. Special thanks to Julio Dicent Taillespierre, Bruno Aponte, Richard Camarena, Jimmy Herrera, Luis Nieves-Rosa, Francisco Lazala, Leonardo Sánchez, E. Antonio de Moya, and Francisco Díaz for their friendship and insights and for inspiring and challenging me. I am also grateful to Heriberto Sánchez-Soto at the Hispanic AIDS Forum, Andrés Duque, and the Latino Commission on AIDS for their support.

My dissertation committee in the American Studies Program at New York University supported this project from the earliest stages. Phillip Brian Harper and Arlene Dávila set the highest standard with their scholarship and encouraged me by the care, generosity, and critical eye with which they engaged with this project at various stages. I am particularly grateful to my dissertation advisor, George Yúdice, for his incisive readings of this text and for his unwavering support. I feel privileged to have counted on the perceptive feedback of dissertation reader Richard Parker, whose pioneering scholarship I admire. I thank Lisa Duggan for her unswerving support of my work, for becoming a reader in my committee on short notice, and for giving me invaluable advice throughout my years at NYU. I thank Alyssa Burke and Madala Hilaire for helping me navigate the NYU bureaucracy and for advocating for me when needed.

Patrick McCreery, Kitty Krupat, Lisa Maya Knauer, Sujani Reddy, Marcelo Montes Penha, Khary Polk, and Laura Harris were colleagues at NYU who honored me with their friendship, challenged me with their smarts, and inspired me. I am especially grateful to the members of the Queer Dissertators Group, the single most important group providing me with critical feedback and encouragement throughout the dissertation-writing process:

Christina Hanhardt, Alison Redick, Mireille Miller-Young, Richard Kim, Tanya Saunders, Warren Hoffman, and Noah Ben-Asher.

At Rutgers University, I have the good fortune of rubbing shoulders with the best minds of my generation: Robyn Rodriguez, Ana Yolanda Ramos-Zayas, Aldo Lauria-Santiago, Ben Sifuentes-Jáuregui, Ethel Brooks, Nikol Alexander-Floyd, Jasbir Puar, Ed Cohen, Louisa Schein, Sonali Perera, Allan Isaac, Julie Livingston, Edlie Wong, and Nicole Fleetwood have all interacted with my research as it has evolved. The result is much richer because of their contributions. The former women's and gender studies chair Joanna Regulska has always been a strong advocate of my work. Special thanks go to outgoing chair Mary Hawkesworth, for her mentorship and friendship. Suzy Kiefer and Joanne Givand, administrative coordinators in women's and gender studies, are models of professionalism and good humor, and their assistance has a value beyond measure to me. Feedback from members of the 2005–2006 Faculty Seminar at the Institute for Research on Women and from colleagues at the Tepoztlán Institute for the Transnational History of the Américas in 2009 have enriched this study.

I have been lucky to count on the generosity of various interlocutors. Thanks to Mark Padilla, Shauna Ahern, Miguel Muñoz-Laboy, Caridad Souza, Susana Peña, José Fernando Serrano, Nick Mai, Gabriel Araujo, Licia Fiol-Mata, Arnaldo Cruz-Malavé, Marysol Asencio, Katie Acosta, Ginetta Candelario, and Julian Carter for their insights and unforgettable conversations. I am particularly grateful to Salvador Vidal-Ortiz for his friendship, for his generous yet probing readings of my work, and for making me laugh.

Strong supporters of this work volunteered crucial and productive final readings of the whole text. Edgar Rivera-Colón has my eternal gratitude for being a genuine comrade every step (and word) of the way and for inspiring me to be a better writer with his gorgeously written dissertation. Milagros Denis, I am your fan. Yolanda Martínez-San Miguel read every word and demanded the rigor that she demands of her own admirable scholarship. Carlos Vásquez-Cruz caught me off guard with his imagination, passion, vision, and unparalleled editorial skills. Gracias. Nicole Guidotti-Hernandez's scholarship is a model of courage, vision, and integrity; her probing critiques enriched what you now read. She rocks my world.

I was able to pursue graduate studies through the support of the Andrew W. Mellon Fellowship in Humanistic Studies as well as the Henry Mitchell MacCracken Fellowship and the Dean's Fellowship from the Graduate School of Arts and Sciences at New York University. The Center for the Study of Gender and Sexuality at NYU, through the Joan R. Heller Dissertation Award in Gender and Sexuality Studies, and the Center for Lesbian and Gay Studies at CUNY, through the James D. Woods III Fellowship, supported my work at crucial stages. Thank you.

The Mellon Mays (formerly Minority) Undergraduate Fellowship Program and the Social Science Research Council—MMUF—have been crucial sources of financial support at the undergraduate, graduate, and postgraduate levels and have provided me with the precious gift of intellectual community with other scholars of color. I am grateful to my mentors and friends within the Mellon Program: Valarie Swain Cade-McCoullum, Patricia Ravenell, Herman Beavers, Lydia English, and the late Beverlee Bruce. The presence of Maurice Stevens, O. Hugo Benavides, Ernesto Martínez, Ebony Coletu, Mendi Obadike, and Ruby Tapia (among others) in my universe became possible through Mellon; your voices make mine possible. The Career Enhancement Fellowship for Junior Faculty from the Woodrow Wilson National Fellowship Foundation, together with a Rutgers University Faculty Fellowship Leave grant, allowed me to concentrate on the completion of this book during the 2009–2010 school year and afforded me the gift of the presence of my cherished mentor, Arnaldo Cruz-Malavé. Madhavi Bhojraj, my research assistant during the summer of 2008, deserves special thanks for the hard work and good humor she put into helping me find many of the scholarly sources I needed to move the writing forward. Lisabeth Matyash, my research assistant during the summer of 2010, also has my gratitude for her patience, good humor, and strong judgment about written communication as we reviewed the copyedited version of this manuscript. Bhojraj and Matyash are the kind of dedicated students I feel blessed to have encountered in my journey at Rutgers. Small Research Grants from the Office of Research and Sponsored Programs at Rutgers, and from the Office of the Vice President for Research and Graduate and Professional Education (Michael Pazzani) have made it possible to undertake and complete important parts of this research.

Alex Carballo-Diéguez taught me much about working within public health to improve Latinos' lives. Michele G. Shedlin is one tough cookie and a gifted social scientist; she listens harder than anyone I know, and whatever I know today about facilitating interviews and focus groups, I have learned from Michele. Gracias, doctora. I also thank Gary Dowsett for the

"Qualitative Research Methods" class that helped me think through this project at its earliest stages and for giving me permission to borrow from his interview instrument to design my own.

Ken Wissoker has been consistently supportive and patient with me; I thank him, Leigh Barnwell, Rebecca Fowler, and everyone at Duke University Press who went above and beyond the call of duty to move this manuscript toward publication. Two anonymous reviewers provided excellent critical feedback on this manuscript. My wonderful copyeditor, Leonard Rosenbaum, together with the Duke copyeditor Lynn Walterick, provided invaluable assistance in polishing this text. Thank you.

I have been blessed by caring mentors and friends. Joseph Wittreich and Stuart Curran provided me with models of scholarly accomplishment. I am honored and grateful to have become a part of their family and to have enjoyed unforgettable meals spiced by Stuart's wit and by Joe's incorrigible humor. Michael Gamer provided me with a model of scholarly rigor. Alan Filreis, who met me when I was a senior at Edison/Fareira High School in Philadelphia, has enriched me as a person and scholar in more ways than he knows.

Evelyn Bender, my mentor, closest friend, partner in many a crime, and toughest critic, has been with me since the time I could hardly articulate myself in English, let alone dream of a pursuing graduate education. I thank her for seeing potential in me when I could not see it myself, for the ways in which her extraordinary intellectual curiosity has enriched my life, and for the love and care with which she read and offered comments on this manuscript.

Close friends to whom I owe gratitude for their feedback and presence in my life include Cicelia Acevedo, Shauna Ahern, Yrsy Núñez, Richard Camarena, Jimmy Ariza, Max Greenhut, Jenny Fernández, Lenny López, Madeleine López, Tomás Maireni Silverio, Chad Williams, and Pilar Peña.

A mis padres y a mis hermanos, Carlos Darío, Xiomara Altagracia, Edwin Alexander, y Carlos Omar Decena, doy gracias por la vida que me han dado y por el apoyo incondicional que me han ofrecido, muchas veces sin saber cómo proporcionarme los recursos que necesitaba. Este logro es tanto mío como de ellos.

Joaquín Alfredo Labour me enseña todos los días que amar está en el placer de compartir con los demás. Por eso, y por compartir mi vida con él, me considero el hombre más afortunado del planeta.

Sections from individual chapters have appeared previously, and I am grateful to the presses for granting permission to reproduce them here. An earlier version of chapter 1, "Tacit Subjects," appeared in *Gay and Lesbian Quarterly* (2008) 14, nos. 2–3: 339–59. The section on Latoya Mejía in chapter 2 appeared in slightly altered form as "Surviving AIDS in an Uneven World: Latino Studies for a Brown Epidemic," in *The Blackwell Companion of Latino Studies*, edited by Juan Flores and Renato Rosaldo (Malden, Mass.: Blackwell, 2007), 276–88.

INTRODUCTION

:::

ESTA OBRA HA SIDO IMPRESA EN
UNA EDICIÓN DE AMIGOS QUE
CONSTA DE SÓLO VEINTICINCO
EJEMPLARES, NUMERADOS DEL
1 AL 25 Y CINCO EJEMPLARES
NUMERADOS DEL I AL V, CON LA
FIRMA DEL AUTOR.

THIS WORK HAS BEEN PRINTED
IN AN EDITION FOR FRIENDS
MADE UP OF TWENTY-FIVE COPIES,
NUMBERED FROM 1 TO 25 AND
FIVE COPIES NUMBERED FROM
I TO V, WITH THE AUTHOR'S
SIGNATURE.[1]

In 1943, barely a decade into the bloody regime of Rafael Leonidas Trujillo
Molina, the established editor, poet, and essayist Pedro René Contín Aybar
published the first Dominican novel with a male homoerotic theme: *Biel, el
Marino*. As far as examples of the genre go, Contín Aybar's piece is short for
a novel: in fourteen pages, the narrator recounts his relationship with Biel,
a seaman. The specifics of the story and the lyrical prose the author uses
to tell it deserve literary critical treatment, but my interest in *Biel* resides
in its distribution and the scandal it provoked. As the prefatory comment
above says, an edition of twenty-five copies and five extras, all numbered and
signed by the author to his "friends," made up the first edition of this literary
work. Nevertheless, the novel and its subject matter titillated the imagina-
tions of many who did not read it. As Andrés L. Mateo explains, "Todavía
en los años sesenta duraba el resplandor del escándalo asordinado que le-
vantó" (The muted scandal it caused lived even into the sixties).[2] Mateo suggests that the scandal was provoked mainly by Biel, a character "que muchos
decían conocer" (whom many claimed to know) and by a piece of writing
that "todos . . . conocía[n] de oído, pocos lo había alcanzado a leer" (many . . .
knew by ear, few had the chance to read).[3] In 1982, an edition of Contín
Aybar's *Poemas* was published and edited by Víctor Villegas. A reproduction of the last of the copies with roman numerals (*Ejemplar V*) was made

available in this compilation thirty-nine years after the novel's initial pub-lication. Villegas provided no commentary or reference to *Biel*'s controver-sial history. Though Mateo suggests that *Biel* caused a scandal because of its topic, what may be ultimately most scandalous is the way this short piece of writing, which was accessible only to a select group of people, worked its way into literary circles of writers and critics who gossiped about it, won-dered who the characters were, claimed they knew one of them, and claimed they knew the novel's contents "by ear" without having read it.[4]

We will never know who Contín Aybar's twenty-five (or thirty) readers were, what they were like, or what linked them to him, just as most of this book's readers will not know who were the twenty-five participants in the research leading to the study you now read. After all, the first and last names settled in these pages are pseudonyms, and details about the men's lives have been modified to protect them from adverse effects from their involve-ment with this project.

This book describes and performs connections that cannot be said. It is about what words say, but also about the way words produce circuitries of sociality. To the degree that it participates in that which it describes, this book is an invitation to continue a conversation.

Tacit Subjects is a study based on autoethnography, participant observa-tion, and twenty-five retrospective life-history interviews with Dominican immigrant men in New York City. It argues that when they moved to New York, they moved into a site in an increasingly transnational Dominican society, and they continued to juggle their proximity with fellow compatriots in the city with the advantages and challenges of pursuing a life as men who love and have sex with men.[5] The participants offer great insight into the worlds they straddled and struggled with, and the book develops concepts informed by feminist, queer, ethnic, and cultural studies to aid in under-standing how invested these men were in stretching, refashioning, and re-producing the structures of possibility and constraint in their lives.

This study is composed of seven chapters. The first, which bears the title of the work, is its point of departure. The Spanish-language grammatical concept of *sujeto tácito* draws attention to the informants' negotiation of in-formation about their lives with families, friends, and associates before and after migration. It foregrounds the importance of unspoken bases of connec-tivity for the making and sustenance of socialities. While sexuality is often implicated in what I call "tacit subjects," this chapter stresses a key insight this book will develop: what binds people to one another and what makes networks, solidarities, and resource sharing possible and sustainable are forms of connection that cannot be fully articulated but can be shared, intuited, and known. The informants in this book are astute readers of the worlds they traversed, and this book makes it possible for me to share some of what I learned from their stories.

The book explores different aspects of the narratives, and readers will encounter moments when what is tacit is central to a given situation. Sometimes I stress its importance, but my overall interest is in drawing out the implications of what these men said and thought for the choices they made, the values they challenged, and the values they upheld. Thus, the analytical work that the book performs and the concepts it develops aid in understanding what is at stake for the interlocutors in any given interview exchange. My narrative voice shifts in emphasis, sometimes focusing on migration and survival, and sometimes underscoring what was at stake in self-presentation in daily life or in narrated sexual encounters. This movement in focus refuses the title of this book as a closed frame. Concepts may help us think through life, but we are always more; we always exceed what can be said about us. I follow these men's preoccupations to highlight how much more they are than any of the categories that attach to them. Indeed, the central theme of this book is the intensity and unease with which these men grappled with their identities and their refusal to let any category or imperative rule their choices, despite how limited they may have been.

The six chapters that make up the rest of the study are divided in pairs, organized following three insights: (1) moving to New York means moving to another part of a Dominican world, and these men juggled their continuing connections to fellow Dominicans after migration to critique and rethink their identities; (2) in their past socializations and present negotiations of daily life, the body and the regulation of its significations functioned to communicate, demand legitimacy, and create boundaries with others; and (3) narrating sexual practices allowed these men to elaborate on their values, revisions of traditional Dominican identity, and erotic investments in masculinity and power.

I appear in this study as narrator, social analyst, translator, and participant. But the translation happens long before I put English and Spanish side by side, as I do at the beginning of this introduction; the selection and recounting of specific aspects of a person's life history are acts of interpretation and translation. As a Dominican immigrant man who self-identifies as gay, as someone who experienced firsthand the subordination and denigration of his native language in the United States, and as a person linked to the networks about which I write throughout this book, I soon realized that writing it demanded a different kind of social and cultural analysis, one for which I could draw inspiration from decades of writing by artists and critics of color.[6] All of the translations are mine, but having the Spanish original and the English translation side by side illustrates the cohabitation of these languages in what the men said and in how I analyzed what they said. It also gives readers access to the materials to evaluate on their own, which may lead them to disagree with my translations or capture interpretive nuances in the movement between languages that escape me. To the degree that exposure to both languages allows the reader more than one way to access what the informants said, *Tacit Subjects* is an open text.

Each part of the book begins with an introductory section that is either autobiographic or autoethnographic and that acts as counterpoint to the chapters that follow it. A counterpoint emerges from the interaction of several voices and registers. They may momentarily repeat or invert what another voice has presented, but contrapuntal music is not bound to strict repetition; its richness derives from the densities of sound with unexpected points of pressure, contact, release, and silence. By including these alternative ways to enter this project, I insert my voice and parts of my history in the ongoing conversation and thus position research as an activity that is embedded in dynamics of power, legitimation, and professional mobility, but also one that partakes of belonging, and that uses language to open up possibilities of connection. This polyphony of voices, which includes mine, constitutes *Tacit Subjects* as an expressive and critical artifact that relishes in the ability of words to establish and sustain affective and political networks as well as to open up possibilities of transit between different forms of being—words as worlds.

Tacit Subjects is about the messiness of daily life and the joys, laughter, struggles, and possibilities of connection, belonging, and complicity with social hierarchy that we can glimpse if we remain vigilant of the ways research is embedded in power. The analysis of the stories these men shared with me attends to the dynamics of the interview encounter itself: to the moments when they positioned me and the project, letting me know that they knew how the interview fit my career aspirations; to the moments when they conveyed the closeness of friendship through jokes; and to the moments when they enlisted (or hailed) me in their criticism of fellow Dominicans. Throughout this study, the interview encounter is an event that makes it possible to interpret individual lives, but it also becomes a mechanism for the informants to critique me, themselves, their friends, their networks, gay communities, and Dominican society. In short, constructing a self was part of the project, but it was, like all self-making in this study, a collaborative project possible given the conditions of where we were.

Tacit Subjects stages, performs, and interrogates interlocution through its analysis of the interview encounter, that quintessential moment of apparently totalizing revelation of the self before someone else. Its protagonists have a lot to teach us with their words, with stories, with insights, and with the bits and pieces of their lives that they narrated. This study promotes intellectual activism committed to think with what people say as much as it might think with self-designated theory. The aims are to point to the richness and complexity of what happens when people encounter someone in an interview; to demonstrate that what people say merits as much careful attention as any other form of literary and artistic expression, performance, or piece gathered in the historical archive; to model a critique that listens to how people view the world and that never assumes language to be transparent. To borrow Arnaldo Cruz-Malavé's words, this book "was born from the commotion that is to listen—to truly listen—to someone else's voice."[7] It is an initial step toward a critique on the move,[8] an agile hermeneutic that draws insight from the way everyday people interpret and theorize their own lives, from the ways they transit through the world and from their quotidian contestation and complicity with structures of oppression.

::: Answering Hamlet

The impulse to write about these men sprung from living in New York City from 1997 to 2009. Although the bulk of the research for the book was conducted between 2001 and 2002 (and the majority of the interviews were completed before 9/11), many of the men with whom I spoke were friends or acquaintances of mine long before and after our interview exchange. I experienced and engaged the city through the networks of (mostly) Dominican self-identified gay and bisexual men I was meeting, men whose lives, loves, and struggles I shared and learned from. An important turning point for me was becoming involved in federally funded studies on HIV/AIDS among Latino gay and bisexual men. As a sex interviewer, outreach worker, and project director, I was educated in the conceptualization, design, implementation, and administration of public health research while being schooled in the challenges Latino men faced in their lives and with the spaces of sociality available in the city. I learned about the experiences of men like myself through one of the few mechanisms that made access to financial and institutional support available for such work. For me, as for other Latino/a intellectuals emerging out of the HIV/AIDS research industry, the perception of risk and the experience of marginality in these communities became a condition of possibility for my work, for the networks I built, and for the coalitions that supported the research I conducted.

While being involved in HIV/AIDS research and activism, I learned about the degree to which many of the positions about identity and sexuality adopted by men like those I interviewed were seen as suspect or pathological. For the participants in this study, living was about dealing with conditions stacked up against their survival and success as immigrants, as men who love and have sex with other men, and as parents, sons, brothers, friends, and providers in the lives of those whom they loved. Yet their candor in relegating information about their lives to the realm of the tacit, or calibrating their bodies as they moved or interacted with others to achieve relative masculine normativity, were initially challenging for me as a scholar, an activist, and a gay man. After all, wasn't it precisely this inability to come out, this inability to own their sexualities, that was holding these men back from organizing and possibly even putting them at risk for HIV/AIDS?

My initial interpretations of what these men were saying found their echo in the voices of colleagues at conferences, some of whom went so far as to question these men's politics, as well as mine. Some argued that the informants' not wanting to say that they were gay and their degree of investment in normative masculinity signaled denial. These men had psychological problems. By presenting their views without registering my disapproval, I was echoing and possibly espousing these strategies.

I listened to my colleagues, listened to interviews repeatedly, and reread transcripts. By letting these voices live in my ears and mind, I realized that my interpretive praxis had to change. As long as I let my own investments in existing models of normative gayness color my interpretations, I would see these men only as failures. But these men survived, and I was a witness to that survival as they faced me as well as themselves and their pasts, presents, and futures. They spoke.

As I listened more and more, the lives of these men began to resonate with larger themes in Dominican history and culture. After all, they had been born in the Dominican Republic, and their plights were in many ways similar to those of other immigrants in the United States. Could the lives of these men, gay or bisexual identified, Dominican, and immigrant (who may appear to be so particular as to be of interest only to a specialist like me), speak to all Dominicans, or speak to everyone?

I began to formulate the question differently, inspired by feminist intersectional analysis:[9] when one straddles so many worlds, demands, investments, expectations, and communities, what are the conditions of possibility for being? Antonio E. de Moya, a social psychologist and pioneering analyst of Dominican sexuality, shared the following insight with me:

> If Shakespeare presents Hamlet's dilemma as "to be *or* not to be: that is the question," Dominicans seem to have resolved it when they say: "to be *and* not to be: that is the answer." We don't seem to believe in a disjunction but in a conjunction. If you offer me A and B, why not give me both? Why choose only one of the two?[10]

This statement speaks to many of the paradoxes of Dominican history: a country that yearned for independence in the nineteenth century but had elites who did not believe in the viability of that autonomy and sought protection from more powerful nations; a society openly admiring of everything foreign ("xenophilic," as de Moya told me once) but ambivalent or disdainful toward everything Haitian; an independent society living under the economic and political influence of the United States, an "unsovereign state" somewhere between the Cuban revolution and the commonwealth status of Puerto Rico;[11] and a people whose history oscillates between the rebellion of Caliban and the servility of Ariel in Shakespeare's *The Tempest*.[12]

De Moya's provocative framing of a Dominican answer to Hamlet's dilemma echoes the way this study responds to that earlier self who sought pride and visibility but found something else altogether when he encountered the men whose thoughts fill these pages: if one is so much more than the labels one uses to define oneself, then although the mandate to be something versus something else may be justified by political necessity, labels cannot fully define anyone, let alone dictate how anyone should live. It is not hypocritical to navigate and work through the contradictions of living in and through various identities, positionalities, and commitments. But it is totalitarian to demand one choice versus another, or to suture moral imperatives to identities. To the degree that the analysis in this book registers

that individual choices, decisions, and interpretations were for-
(given conditions these men could not control), the realities with
hese men wrestled individually resonate with the limited choices
....ggle for self-determination of other Dominicans and of Dominican
society as a whole.

:: : *Razón de estar*: Bodies in Places

Tacit Subjects argues that identities are lived in their partiality and polyva-
lence but that living is centrally about contestation among differently situated actors who claim one category. Though they reproduce hierarchy and
division, identities also have the potential to be "enabling, enlightening, and
enriching structures of attachment and feeling."[13] "Razón de estar" refers
to an interpretive praxis that insists that self-making is based on the construction of positionalities that emerge from interlocking, interarticulating
structures that function as situated conditions of possibility and constraint
for the protagonists and narrators of the stories I analyzed.

Capturing the partiality and relationality of identities as they are lived and
narrated demands that we capture "being" as a movement without end, as
an enabling transitivity. This study pushes against the expressive and political limitations of the English language by arguing that English misses a distinction between forms of the verb "to be" that are crucial to capture being
as movement. The literary and cultural critic José Quiroga offers an astute
distinction that helps articulate the analytic strategy of this book:

> Spanish makes a distinction between two forms of the English verb "to be":
> *ser* implies a permanent essence, whereas *estar* is a verb of position. It is the
> verb of position that interests me here. Spaces portrayed in Latino art . . . are
> not marked with their own specific borders—they are all (*están*) in constant
> interrelation with each other. Static definitions of culture clash with a sexuality
> mobilized by different positionalities. This negotiation allows us to see charac-
> ters in a state of "becoming" . . . possibilities and not fixed identities.[14]

"To be" will not do anymore, for the structures of signification of the English language may be part of the problem of capturing identities as forms of
"becoming," as always relational and always in process. *Tacit Subjects* offers
an analysis that takes to heart Quiroga's emphasis on the verb of position.
We do not need to abandon identities but rather need to better grasp the

mediations and intersubjective conditions of their emergence. The proposal this text makes is to pursue a radically contextual analysis of the mediations of identity as the transit between *ser* and *estar*.

The argument repeatedly highlights the transitivity of subjectivity. The anthropologist and philosopher Rodolfo Kusch articulated the dichotomy of *ser* and *estar* as an "American" dialectic,[15] one that refuses synthesis or transcendence and insists on the cohabitation and co-presence of different forms of being.[16] He explains:

La intuición que bosquejo aquí oscila entre dos polos. Uno es el que llamo el ser, o ser alguien, y que descubro en la actividad burguesa de la Europa del siglo XVI y, el otro, el estar, o estar aquí, que considero como una modalidad profunda de la cultura precolombina. . . . Ambas son dos raíces profundas de nuestra mente mestiza.

The intuition I am sketching here moves between two poles. One is the one I call to be [*ser*] or to be someone, which I discover in the activity of the European bourgeoisie of the XVI century and the other, the to be [*estar*], or to be here, which I consider a deep modality of pre-Columbian cultures. . . . Both are two deep roots of our mestizo mind.[17]

Living and working in the Argentina of the 1950s and 1960s, Kusch was a forerunner of critiques of "the politics of location" that circulated internationally in the 1980s,[18] but he was not a North American or European writing about Asia, Latin America, or Africa. Kusch was an Argentine of German ancestry, writing about indigenous populations in his own country and in other parts of South America. As the semiotician Walter Mignolo writes, "The people and communities he contacted, both historically and at that time, were simultaneously 'they' and 'we' vis-à-vis himself. . . . And Kusch's 'selfsame' was also his 'other,' in that he had grown up amid the fragments of the European tradition at the colonial periphery."[19] The conditions for the production of Kusch's work led him to an intellectual project to explore "'America' as a locus of enunciation," a project summarized in its early stages by the coexistence of "cognitive patterns of dealing with new situations, allowing for creativity, resistance, and survival very much shaped by the colonial difference."[20] The idea behind Kusch's early formulations is not that one cognitive pattern takes over for or annihilates a second one but that the forms of thinking and being that emerge from the aftermath of the colonial encounter in the Americas are necessarily split, and that no pure "being someone" (*ser*) is possible without accounting for one's being somewhere, for its location (*donde está*).

Mapping the circuitry that compels or impels movement, toward becoming something different from what a person has been taught he is, points to the way in which *Tacit Subjects* transforms existing narratives of queer migration and is in dialogue with emerging scholarship on this topic.[21] For the informants, moving to New York City is part of a larger process of pluralization in the possibilities for being ironically provoked by the historical desire of the U.S. and the Dominican states to appease the political turmoil that threatened to make "another Cuba" of this country in the 1960s.[22] The choice to move to New York City to find oneself in another site of a Dominican transnational world points to these men's investment in being part of ethnoracial networks, to transit in worlds where the expansion of a person's erotic, social, cultural, and economic prospects are possible without rupturing these contested and conflicted but cherished and necessary connections. For this reason, *Tacit Subjects* wrestles with the ways gay and bisexual men continue to critique, reformulate, and practice belonging in Dominican worlds. In an ironic twist in the story of U.S. empire in Latin America, the transnationalization of Dominican society prevented "another Cuba" but pluralized, exploded, and continued to put pressure on the national polity through the disarticulation of *dominicanidad* (Dominican identity) from the geopolitical space of one nation and one state. Thus, the multiplication of sites for "being" Dominican undermined the hegemony of official and nationalist subject forms. In other words, the escape valve to brewing tensions and social conflicts, which was the massive exodus of Dominicans beginning in the 1960s, has ironically lessened the grip of the Dominican state over the projects of being of its populace.

Written by someone living in an officially (and stubbornly) monolingual country, *Tacit Subjects* borrows from Spanish to challenge, expand, revise, and present alternatives to the accepted geopolitics of feminist and queer knowledge production by fashioning concepts that attend to the specificity of the experiences being narrated. But this is no naive celebration of the Spanish language. Spanish, like English, has been and continues to be a language of conquest and colonization in the American continent. Nevertheless, the subordinate structural position of the Spanish language in U.S. society at large and in the academy gives an edge to *Tacit Subjects* as a political intervention that is (*está*) in the United States.

Students of Dominican cultures will recognize this study as one of emerging efforts to add nuance and complexity to the study of migration and transnationalism among these populations.[23] For a long time, Dominicans appeared to be the quintessential transnationals, but as Silvio Torres-Saillant has put it in his trenchant critiques of this trend, there is "nothing to celebrate" about Dominican transnationality.[24] This book is also part of ongoing and emerging feminist and queer Dominican criticism.[25] It contributes to U.S. Latino studies by addressing and analyzing at length the conflicted ways in which immigrant men who self-identify as gay or bisexual deal with their fellow Dominicans and official notions of national identity and society. The study goes beyond adding sexuality to the intersectional analysis of Latina/o experience: through the stories these men tell, this book explores the ways that differences in class, race, and education shape their relations with their compatriots; instead of taking dominicanidad as a given, *Tacit Subjects* focuses on the ways these men contest, reproduce, and reformulate it in New York.[26] Though it values the impulse of Latino studies scholarship to document the experiences of these populations, *Tacit Subjects* does so and interrogates critically the technologies used to produce this knowledge. Furthermore, this book bridges Latin American and U.S. Latino studies by addressing the afterlife of the nineteenth- and twentieth-century Latin American nation-state in contemporary immigrant lives. Moreover, it bridges ethnic and area studies as it brings the geopolitics of U.S. imperial designs to bear on the daily lives of immigrant men whose racialization in the United States has everything to do with encountering and learning to interpret their lives through linkages and exchanges with African Americans and Puerto Ricans.

Tacit Subjects contributes, offers alternative ways of seeing and producing knowledge for intellectual labor at the crossroads of transnational feminist and queer studies,[27] and promotes intersectional analyses that honor and build on decades of activist scholarship by illustrating the ways immigrant men negotiate interlocking and interarticulating oppressions and sometimes uphold them because of their investment in patriarchal privileges. It extends feminist transnational critiques and feminist-inspired masculinity studies into a consideration of immigrant men's investment in male privilege while also demonstrating what investments in masculinity have to do with power and legitimacy, as well as with establishing, sustaining, and regulating socialities. *Tacit Subjects* also contributes a critical social scientific account of transnationalism within the United States to emerging scholarship on transnational queer sexualities.[28] It offers another view of "gay New York"[29]—one that sees the struggles for respect, belonging, and survival within immigrant communities at the center and the dazzle and pride of the gay metropolis out of the corner of its eye or, as Rafael Damirón put it so admirably, "de soslayo."[30]

::: The Study

The analysis in this study draws from twenty-five semi-structured retrospective life-history interviews conducted between May 2001 and May 2002 with self-identified Dominican gay and bisexual men.[31] It also draws selectively from an interview with an informant who self-identified as transsexual; excerpts from this interview are highlighted in chapter 4 because they are relevant to that discussion. Given the specificities of this informant's experience, however, extended analysis of this narrative will be published separately. The interviews ranged from forty-five minutes to two hours. I conducted most of them in Spanish, though informants and I also used English, code switching, and Spanglish. Each participant and I discussed a consent form, which they signed. Participants received a small monetary compensation. In addition, I conducted archival work at the Dominican Studies Institute at City College, City University of New York. Finally, I complemented these interviews and archival work with ethnographic observations at general Dominican community events and at formal and informal events attended by Dominican and other Latino homosexual men in New York City during the research period. These events included gay and Dominican Pride Day parades, poetry readings at Alianza Dominicana, organizing meetings, and informal gatherings among informants, friends, and acquaintances. As I explained earlier, in the course of data analysis, autobiography and autoethnography were also integrated into the study.

The men ranged in age from their early twenties to their late fifties, though most were in their mid-thirties. Most had immigrated to the United States as adults, except for one informant who had migrated at age fifteen. Some participants came from the capital city of Santo Domingo. However, most of them were originally from other parts of the country and migrated to either Santo Domingo or Santiago (the second largest city in the Dominican Republic) when they began their university studies. All participants had graduated from high school, more than half had earned a college degree, and a few had advanced degrees in areas such as medicine and education. These

attainments characterize this sample as possessing higher educational levels than those that appear in Dominican communities in the United States
in general, where almost half of all people above the age of twenty-five had
not completed high school as of 2000.[32] Socioeconomic backgrounds varied. Most informants described themselves as middle class, a term that in
the Dominican Republic accounts more for social than for material capital,
for one might have an education, values, and aspirations of upward mobility without the financial security to sustain it. A few informants described
themselves as working class. Others described themselves as upper class.

Most participants described a deterioration of their class position upon
arrival to the United States, partly due to their experience as undocumented
immigrants. Many of them arrived in the United States with either tourist
visas or work permits that expired after their arrival. About two-thirds were
undocumented. The lack of documents made it difficult to work in jobs
with benefits or union protections. Indeed, most of the undocumented (and
even some of the documented) men had to work independently or work
in restaurants, retail and sales, or jobs in the ethnic economy in Washington Heights. A few men with advanced degrees fared better than others.
Still, most informants with professional credentials had not been able to
work in their fields of expertise, even after changing from undocumented
to documented status. Some had not been interested in continuing their
careers. Others were unable to pass the examinations required to have their
advanced degrees validated. The characteristics of the job participation of
these men are consistent with findings about Dominican populations in
general in 2000, where only 17.3 percent of all members of this population
worked in high-skilled, technical, or professional occupations.[33]

Being a member of this community and being known already as an HIV
researcher influenced who agreed to participate in the study. Having worked
as an HIV researcher shaped the characteristics of the men I approached for
interviews and the men who agreed to be interviewed. I was acquainted with
most of the men interviewed because they were friends or acquaintances of
mine, community activists, or frequent attendees at community events. I
also met informants through my work in AIDS-prevention research. Finally,
I established connections with informants through people who had already
participated in the study and who volunteered to recruit their friends.

The chapters in part I of the book explore the men's existing linkages
with fellow Dominicans and with Dominican identity. Providing an alternative to accounts that view gay men as having to "choose" between biological

kin and other kinship formations, chapter 2, "Moving Portraits," argues that biological families, as well as gay and other non-kin Dominican social networks, made possible the migration and survival of the informants in New York City. To the degree that these men, in their stories about arriving and settling in Nueva York, accounted for their circulation between two sites in Dominican transnational cultures, the three case studies analyzed point to the ways these men experienced, participated in, traversed, and negotiated the regulation of their bodies on multiple and often disparate discursive registers. Although their telling of the stories that follow attests to the many obstacles they overcame, their ingenuity in the face of adversity, and ultimately their success, their stories are not the stories of young men unshackled from the binds and pains of biological family by the vicissitudes spawned by transformations in the capitalist world economy. Instead, the stories in the chapter illustrate the ways these men wrestled and straddled multiple and conflicting demands, prohibitions, intimacies, and affective investments. Apart from introducing the reader to some of the men I interviewed, these narratives offer portraits of the relations of individuals and collectivities in order to demonstrate that self-realization as a man who loves men does not require moving away from the biological family. Indeed, these narratives show that as individuals move and evolve, so do their families.

Migration, settlement, and ongoing interactions with Dominicans and other populations in New York City set in motion a process of recognition, evaluation, and self-fashioning premised on the vibrancy of and need for transnational networks of support and the informants' growing awareness of themselves as racialized subjects. Geographical displacement and the immediacy of racial and class subordination provoke a *desencuentro*, or failed encounter, with dominicanidad in New York City. This failed encounter is the focus of the third chapter, "Desencontrando la dominicanidad," which explores what Kusch calls "la continuidad del pasado americano en el presente" (the continuity of the American past in the present).[34] In this case, I am interested in untangling the cohabitation of past and present visions of modernity, culture, and progress expressed by the informants in relation to the work of late-nineteenth- and early-twentieth-century nationalist intellectuals to envision the Dominican nation's move toward the future through the concepts of *progreso* and *cultura*. In many ways, the negative light these men cast on Dominican identity in New York makes it antithetical and irreconcilable with gayness and modernity. However, the language of race plays a key role in resuscitating older discourses about the Dominican national question in ways that make possible these men's trenchant critiques of the racism, sexism, classism, and homophobia they associate with Dominican society.

Part II focuses on the body and its stylizations as signifying practices the informants remember learning through their collaboration with relatives (as children) and sustained in their ongoing regulation of themselves and others. Chapter 4, "Eso se nota," uses childhood narratives to illustrate how important it was for these men to calibrate the movements of their bodies through coaching with their mothers and other relatives. Embodying masculinity was about recognizing the disjuncture between the way they carried themselves as children and the men they had to become, a form of labor coordinated through transfers of knowledge and collective evaluation and coaching. The figure of the effeminate homosexual (la loca) makes an initial appearance here not as an abject but as a proximate "other" who cohabitates with "serious" masculinity. I theorize la loca as a performative utterance, which I call gynographic to reference the staging of stereotypes of femininity on a male body instead of communicating that effeminate men "want to be women," as they are traditionally perceived. By figuring masculinity as a straightjacket, an apparatus of collective surveillance and regulation of what is supposed to be a male body, the chapter argues that the opposition in Dominican patriarchal regimes is not between masculinity and femininity but rather between masculinity and locura, an opposition that stresses the need to keep vigilance and to control bodies always already imagined as feminized and excessive. Conceptualizing locura in this way helps locate "serious" masculinity in opposition to the figure of la loca and also in relation to other suspect forms of masculinity that may not be "effeminate" but that are structurally subordinate to "seriousness." My analysis shows that structurally, some ubiquitous and privileged forms of masculinity are ultimately other forms of locura that need controlling: the key example explored in this chapter is that of the Dominican tíguere.

Chapter 5, "Code Swishing," brings the narratives of negotiating masculinity in daily life to the present to suggest that la loca has negative as well as positive valences and that we miss a lot of its richness if we imagine it only as a figure of homosexual abjection. In this way, the chapter offers an alternative to established and influential interpretations of queer subject constitution that overemphasize abjection while ignoring the multiple meanings of identities. Through an investigation of the conditions that make la loca instrumental in the expression of closeness and intimacy, the chapter analyzes the way it operates in the making and regulation of networks of self-identified Dominican gay and bisexual men. My conceptualization of "code swishing" borrows from scholarship on bilingualism and code switching. But it revises this work to implicate the body and gender dissent as communicative practices and to make clear that these men established and sustained networks with one another so long as camaraderie and connection did not threaten their legitimacy in daily life and their investments in normative masculinity. For them, surviving and being respected was more important than any sense of community they may have felt toward one another.

Part III explores the narrations of sex practices and relationships as mechanisms for these men to further articulate their values and continue to revise and express their investments in proximity with fellow Dominicans. Chapter 6, "Virando la dominicanidad," explores sex as a site of continuing regulation and discipline. The sexual also appears here as a space to work through one's relationship with dominicanidad, personified in the figure of the macho. The ideal of versatility, which several of these men presented as important to them in relationships, is ideologically connected with the idea of reworking dominicanidad toward what they envisioned as sexual cosmopolitanism. But this ideal, as the case studies central to this chapter show, is often frustrated by the expectations other men had of the informants—expectations that (I suggest) are connected to broader perceptions of Dominicans within New York City's transnational sexual cultures.

The final chapter uses narratives of return to further explore the ways power and mobility are implicated in the formation and sustenance of hierarchies of desire of which Dominican gay and bisexual men (along with other traveling men of color) participate. Using autoethnographic accounts of my return to Santo Domingo and informants' commentaries on return, this chapter suggests important dynamics of power, male privilege, and mobility that obtained among men of color. Instead of continuing to center the white-gay-male traveling body of the sex tourist as the antagonist of our critiques, "To Be Someone, To Be Somewhere" argues that the time has come to grapple with what it means for people of color to establish and sustain sexual relations where money is explicitly implicated. The point is not to condemn or pass judgment on these practices but rather to understand what they might mean to the men and their partners and to grasp better the ways men of color negotiated power and the erotic with one another.

CHAPTER 1

Tacit Subjects

I did not tell them anything. They did not ask me anything. I know that they know.—DANNY, Filipino.[1]

Basically, you know, she doesn't like my way of life so we don't talk about it. She respects me, she loves me, she spoils me. But it's something we just don't discuss. I think I don't do it out of respect for her, and she doesn't do it out of respect for me.—ALICIA B., Puertorriqueña.[2]

They know, I mean, parents know. . . . I've had relationships . . . and when I've been with these guys, they [his parents] always refer to me as like you in plural. . . . And if there's like a family gathering or whatever, they'll always invite that particular friend that I'm going out with. So, you know, it's understood but it's never discussed.—PATRICIO, Puerto Rican.[3]

What is funny is I think they know. . . . I have been living with a man for 13 years and so how can they not . . . so I think my family is just living in denial, but I think that they know but they don't want to deal with it and I think it is safe not to discuss it.—UNNAMED, Latino.[4]

You know that's very interesting because I know they know. But my family is like this. They don't discuss it. . . . My older sister, she and I get along best of all. She loves me to death. But she doesn't discuss it. And if someone tries to discuss it in a demeaning way or something, not about me but just about gay people, period, she will immediately attack or whatever. But no, they don't discuss that.—D.C., African American.[5]

I imagine that my whole family knows, but not from my mouth or because they've asked me. I think that they intuitively know. They prefer not to ask me and prefer that I don't tell them. It's not necessary, it's only my sexual preference.—MARCOS, *mexicano* interviewed in Guadalajara.[6]

:: :

Conventional views of *coming out* in the United States celebrate the individual, the visible, and the proud. Given the growing legitimacy of predominantly white and middle-class lesbians and gay men in this country and of models that presume and uphold individual decision making, refusals of speech, pride, and visibility have been generally interpreted as suspect, as evidence of denial or internalized homophobia, or as outright pathology.

These standard interpretations stayed with me as I talked to Dominican self-identified gay and bisexual men who were my friends or acquaintances and, in some cases, who became participants in this study. Much of what I heard in these conversations paralleled the comments excerpted above from the work of other scholars: the men with whom I spoke described their sexuality as something present yet not remarked upon, something understood yet not stated, something intuited yet uncertain, something known yet not broached by either person in a given exchange. The sites where this presence, understanding, intuition, or knowledge mattered were invariably those of family and close interpersonal relationships. I began to realize that to become an apt interpreter of what I heard required me to listen carefully to what people said for what I could learn from them.

As the diversity of the men and women cited above illustrates, other scholars have remarked on this tendency to be present, be understood, or be known as lesbian or gay in several communities of color in the United States without statements or declarations.[7] In the case of the Dominican immigrant gay men with whom I worked, the analysis of them as "in the closet" was consistent with existing views about the way Latinos and other populations of color deal with their sexual identities. These men were at best cast as indifferent to the development of a gay Dominican community and at worst were seen as immigrants whose physical displacement had not helped them overcome the internalized homophobia that supposedly characterized their lives in the Dominican Republic.[8]

A neoliberal interpretation of coming out characteristic of the contemporary United States takes for granted that all LGBTQ people should come out of the closet. Instead of being the beginning of a project of social transformation—as coming out was understood in the early days of gay liberation—individual self-realization through speech has been severed from collective social change. Today, one comes out not to change the world but to be a "normal" gay subject.[9] From this perspective, some queers of color have an uneasy relationship with the closet because they resist the depoliticized "liberation" that coming out promises, which currently resides in a gay identity as a sociocultural formation and as a niche market. Critiques of coming out in its current form have been and continue to be made partly because of the persistence of this way of thinking about gay subject formation and the racial and class biases obscured by this dominant model.[10]

Some individuals who do not explain their sexual identity to others are *not* silent about it, as can be seen in the quotes from the work of other scholars at the beginning of this chapter.[11] Drawing from Spanish grammar, I propose comparing (1) the way some of the informants in this study inhabit a space that is both "in" and "out" of the closet with (2) the tacit subject—an analytic framework that is attentive to the range, interaction, and intersection of the meanings and contexts involved in whether or not informants present their sexual identity in public. Negotiations of information about a person's sexual identity, as I will show, teach us about the forms of knowledge and complicity that structure and sustain hierarchical social relations.

In Spanish grammar, the "sujeto tácito" (tacit subject) is the subject that is not spoken but that can be ascertained through the conjugation of the verb used in a sentence. For example, instead of saying "*I* go to school," in Spanish one might say, "Voy a la escuela" without using the pronoun "yo" (I). Since the conjugation "voy" (I go) leaves no doubt that one speaks in the first-person singular, whoever hears this sentence knows that the subject is built into the action expressed through the verb.[12] Using this grammatical structure as a metaphor to explain how the informants interpret the way others view their lives, the "sujeto tácito" suggests that coming out may sometimes be redundant. In other words, coming out can be a verbal declaration of something that is already understood or assumed—tacit—in an exchange.[13] What is tacit is neither secret nor silent.[14]

My formulation of "tacit subjects" is partly inflected by my reading of the work of the philosopher Michael Polanyi, in particular his idea of *tacit knowledge*. For Polanyi, tacit knowledge refers to forms of expertise and ways of carrying oneself in the world that cannot be taught to others by way of verbal information exchange. When we think about skills, "there are things that we know but cannot tell,"[15] by which Polanyi refers, for instance, to the coordination of motor skills with balance and other factors that produce a competent bike rider. Another example might be that of a musician who learns to play a piece of music correctly not only by reading notes on a pentagram but also by learning to "hear" how a piece of music is supposed to sound through interaction and collaboration with a music teacher. In *The Tacit Dimension* and *Personal Knowledge*, Polanyi elaborated on this conceptualization as a way to challenge what he perceived as a problematic and dangerous scientific emphasis on logic and rationality. He put forward a view that emphasized the importance of learning that takes place through apprenticeship and interpersonal exchange because of how much of knowledge and expertise are developed through learning that goes beyond what is written or "taught" verbally.[16] Although "tacit subjects" might include forms of "tacit knowing," Polanyi's conceptualization has a positivistic end that is far from what I am interested in underlining through "tacit subjects." Whereas Polanyi's "tacit knowing" will ultimately yield an adequate competence (you will get to play the piece "properly") "tacit subjects" cannot be grasped in consistent or totalizing ways. My formulation points to zones of complicity that may include (but are not limited to) shared knowledge. "To know more than one can tell" (to borrow from Polanyi)[17] involves the impossible project of "telling" overlapping layers of collaboration and complicity that structure and sustain sociality.

This is particularly relevant when addressing the question of family knowledge about a person's sexual orientation. How tacit one's sexual identity is to others is a matter of interpretation and requires that the others interacting with the informants recognize and decode the self-presentation of bodies and the information about them that circulates in families. In thinking that their homosexuality is knowable in a tacit way to the people close to them, the informants in this book assumed that many people had the requisite skills to recognize and decode their behavior. Some people may not get the signs, but these men understood that there was a distinction between their intentional manipulation of their self-presentation and impressions that they unintentionally gave to others. Following Goffman, I argue that the men I interviewed understood that there was a difference between "the expression that [they] *give*, and the expression that [they] *give off*."[18] They understood that their own bodies traversed the social world and signified in ways that exceeded (and often betrayed) the intention of those who inhabited them. Thus, it was always possible that someone might "get" their gayness despite all effort put into concealing it.

Instead of focusing on an explicit definition or categorization of individuals, "tacit subjects" helps us get at the various complicities that structure social relations. As the examples presented below will show, the tacit subject in specific situations included but ultimately exceeded individual subjectivity and sexuality. Indeed, what materializes in these examples are the power dynamics that shaped the way individuals negotiated information about their sexual identities. In the case of the informants, the concept shifts the analysis away from self-definition toward an investigation of the way they refused the reductionism gayness engendered in the public sphere.[19] Avoiding this reductionism is paramount when the very conditions of one's migration, survival, or (real or imagined) upward mobility depend on people's continuing reliance on the resources that facilitated one's geographical displacement in the first place, as will be documented in the chapters that follow.

However, there is more at stake than just the way individuals made choices to tell or not to tell others about their sexual identity. Some of the examples offered below illustrate potential or real confrontations that actualized, through the verbal utterance of tacit subjects, the way people were linked to one another in asymmetrical power relations that they were invested in maintaining. There is a meaning of the word *sujeto* in Spanish that is not immediately derived from its pairing with *tácito*, but that points to a slippage I want to keep between "tacit subjects" (topics) and "tacit *subjectivity*."[20] When seen as the adjective form of the verb *sujetar*, *sujeto* is someone under the power of someone else (as in the English *subjected*). Yet one of the meanings of *sujetar* in Spanish, according to the Real Academia de la Lengua Española, is "poner en una cosa algún objeto para que no se caiga, mueva, desordene, etc." (to put an object inside something so it will not fall, move, get disordered, etc.).[21] In this sense, something or someone is *sujeto* if they are held by someone or something else that prevents them from "falling," from producing disorder.

An incorporation of this meaning of *sujeto* into my discussion of tacit subjects illustrates the complicities that constitute social relations. The tacit subject not only holds a person or topic from "falling" by bringing shame on those it concerns; the tacit subject holds the social formation as a whole from falling, moving, getting disordered. In the various exchanges and confrontations that I will discuss, at stake were the terms in which people addressed or interacted with one another. When the terms were violated and people confronted one another, what were most exposed and threatened were the social relations established. A *sujeto tácito* in this context might be constituted by the unaddressed yet understood knowledge (of individuals or issues) that linked together people within specific social groupings. What may fall, break, or get disordered was the very glue of sociality that made survival possible for these men and the people they loved.

The informants' negotiations of coming out illustrate that ambiguity and shared understandings are crucial to the sustenance of individuals and collectivities. Interviews suggest that the main pattern was the refusal of disclosure to others. Indeed, part of their coming out involved taking ownership of their lives. Most of these men saw accepting their gayness as a private matter. This can be seen in their frequent references to personal privacy, especially when it concerned their sexual and romantic attachments. Their understanding of "personal privacy," though echoing the traditional distinction between public and private spheres that characterizes liberal democracies, referenced individuals and contexts where such distinctions were tenuous at best. As will be shown in the chapters that follow, many of these men migrated and survived in New York *through* the resources within or connected to their families. Thus, they exercised ownership of their sexual identities by negotiating the degree to which their sexual and romantic lives became (or not) points of discussion in family settings. In this way, the informants referenced the public and private realms as "indexical signs that are always relative" and that depended on the context in which they were invoked for their deployment, meaning, and communicative effectiveness.[22]

In some situations, the absence of a family dialogue about an openly lived homosexuality reveals the legitimacy that informants enjoyed, a legitimacy that allowed them to refuse to make their homosexuality a point of discussion. Máximo Domínguez, a light-skinned, forty-five-year-old informant who was unemployed but who came from a family that enjoyed ties to the Trujillo regime, did not like to talk about his life with his relatives. Because of what he characterized as his "strong personality," relatives did not broach the topic with him.

"Nadie se atreve a preguntarme nada" (Nobody dares ask me anything), he said.

"¿Cómo tú sabes que ellos saben?" (How do you know that they know?)

"Ellos no son estúpidos. Mi hermano ha ido conmigo a las discotecas. Y yo me he besado con mi novio alante de ellos." (They are not stupid. My brother has gone to gay discos with me. And I have kissed my boyfriend in front of them.)

This example is, undoubtedly, that of someone who was out to his family while remaining protective of his personal space. Having relationships with men was a part of Domínguez's life that did not need to be discussed. Most readers will probably agree in thinking that this informant was out of the closet even though there had never been a discussion with his family about the issue.

That Domínguez's relatives had seen him kiss his partners shows the degree of openness he enjoyed within the family while he remained protective of the issue to a point where they did not "dare" raise it. This was far from representative of what happened to others. Although some informants integrated partners into their family lives in New York, kissing and other expressions of affection were uncommon. More common were situations in which informants introduced partners as "amigos" (friends) to relatives. The case of Pablo Arismendi's dealings with information about his sexual identity illustrates the ways some informants handled these questions.

¿Quiénes en tu mundo saben que a ti te gustan los hombres? ¿Cómo tú se lo has hecho saber?

Donde vivo, mi tía lo sabe. No porque yo se lo haya dicho. Ella lo intuye y se hace la loca. Pero ella sabe, por la manera en la que yo me visto y las salidas extrañas. Mi prima, se lo dije, porque una vez recibí una noticia de una persona muy allegada a mí que murió de una manera trágica. Entonces, yo me puse, como que me descontrolé en ese momento. Y le bombié el asunto. . . . Y ya después de ahí es historia. Somos cómplices. Mi mamá es otra que lo sabe. No porque yo se lo haya dicho, sino que porque lo intuye como madre y también se hace la indiferente. Los demás familiares se lo imaginan, pero no se atreven a hacer comentarios ni a decir nada.

¿Tu familia se ha enterado de que tú has tenido pareja?

Who in your world knows that you like men? How have you let them know?

Where I live, my aunt knows. Not because I have told her. She perceives it and acts as if nothing is going on. But she knows because of how I dress and the strange outings. I told my cousin because one time I received the news that a person very close to me died in a very tragic way. Then I kind of lost control in that moment. And I spilled out the issue. . . . And then after that the rest is history. We are accomplices. My mother is another one who knows. Not because I have told her but because she perceives it as a mother and also acts like nothing is happening. The other relatives can imagine it, but they do not dare make comments or say anything.

Has your family found out that you have had partners?

Bueno, mis dos novios . . . yo los integré a la familia. Iban a los cumpleaños y a algunas reuniones.	Well, my two boyfriends . . . I integrated them into the family. They went to birthday celebrations and other gatherings.
Y ¿cómo tú los presentabas?	And, how did you introduce them?
Como amigos. Pero, lo que te digo. Ellos saben quién es.	As friends. But that's what I'm telling you. They know who it is.

Extreme circumstances resulted in Arismendi informing his cousin of his homosexuality. As a consequence of Arismendi's coming out, the relationship with his cousin strengthened. Far more typically, the relationships Arismendi had with his aunt (in whose household he resided) and mother (living in Santo Domingo) point to the ambiguities with which he worked. On the one hand, it was clear to Arismendi that his aunt may have had a sense of what was going on because of the signs Arismendi gave of living a "gay" life. On the other hand, the mother's perception of Arismendi's homosexuality was more a matter of "intuición de madre" (mother's intuition) than of anything else. Arismendi's insistence on the visible signs of his gayness and his bringing partners into family gatherings point to the many traces of his life he consciously brought into these settings without resorting to a verbal declaration of his gayness. His sense that they "know" what was going on was based on speculation, though it was also possible that his aunt and mother themselves gave him signs that they knew. Regardless, whether or not and to what degree it was shared is something that cannot be known or expressed explicitly in this situation. Access to the support and resources his mother and his aunt provided him depended on the doubt exhibited in these negotiations. A confrontation about his gayness, providing a definitive answer to traces that remained relegated to spaces of epistemological uncertainty, could have ruptured the bonds Arismendi had and needed.

The example of Javier Acuña, a light-skinned, forty-four-year-old college counselor from an upper-class background, shows that some informants sought to bring their homosexuality to the family table to breach their emotional distance from their parents. Acuña was born into an established family of professionals in a tourist town in the Dominican Republic. He enjoyed an education in a private school, along with other benefits that class status conferred to a young man in a small town. Acuña had access to individuals with cosmopolitan aspirations. Pursuing an education degree at the Universidad Católica Madre y Maestra in the city of Santiago gave Acuña the opportunity to develop gay friendships and sexual and romantic relationships away from his parents.

However, Acuña was falsely accused of drug possession and spent time in jail. The ostracism he experienced after being released forced him to leave the Dominican Republic. After completing an English-language program in a public university in a city in the Northeast United States, Acuña moved to New York. His father bought him an apartment in Brooklyn, where Acuña lived for more than fourteen years. He visited his relatives in the Dominican Republic several times a year.

It was evident from the pain in Acuña's voice, and the frequency with which we returned to this theme during the interview, that dealing with "el asunto gay" (the gay matter) in his family had been difficult. This excerpt shows Acuña's sadness over not being able to come out. It also reveals his hope that a discussion of his homosexuality would help him breach the emotional distance he felt from his father:

Por ejemplo: un día estaba comiendo en mi casa y estábamos hablando de algo . . . Hablábamos de problemas y mi cuñada . . . habló algo como de problemas económicos, asuntos de esos. Y yo dije, "Los problemas míos no son económicos. Los problemas míos son problemas del alma." Y cuando yo lo dije así . . . Porque yo pensaba que lo que venía después de eso era mi papá que me dijera, "Yo quiero que tú cruces por la oficina esta tarde." A ver un hijo mío que se exprese de esa manera, que diga "Yo no tengo problemas económicos. Mis problemas son problemas del alma." Yo creo que yo . . .

Lo llamaría para . . .

For example: one day I was eating at home and we are talking about something . . . We were talking about problems and my sister-in-law . . . said something about economic problems, things like that. And I said, "My problems are not money problems. My problems are problems of the soul." And when I said it like that . . . Because I thought that what was coming after that, was that my father would say, "I need you to come by my office this afternoon." To see a son of mine express himself like that, that says "I don't have money problems. My problems are problems of the soul." I believe I . . .

Would call him to . . .

"Ven acá. Vamos a hablar. ¿Qué es lo que pasa?" Entonces no. Eso pasa. Y precisamente ese es uno de los motivos por los cuales a esta altura del juego, cuarenta y cuatro años, yo no he hablado con mis padres sobre el asunto gay nunca en la vida.

"Come here. Let's talk. What's going on?" But no. They let it pass. And it's precisely because of that, that at this point, I'm forty-four, I have not ever talked to my parents about the gay issue.

Acuña had opportunities to begin a conversation about "el asunto gay" (the gay issue) with his parents. Nevertheless, the inability (or unwillingness) of his mother and father to engage in that conversation made Acuña's visits strained and frustrating. When asked about his relationship with them, Acuña contextualized the lack of discussion of his homosexuality within the larger issue of his parents' inability to provide emotionally for him and his older brother. At the time when men and women of the generation of Acuña's parents formed families, he explained that "el que una familia fuera buena o fuera mala era más que nada por la responsabilidad . . . y el soporte económico que los padres . . . le daban a uno" (whether a family was good or bad was basically because of the responsibility . . . and the economic support that parents . . . gave you). Acuña contrasted his parents' attitude with that of younger parents: "Pero en cambio en el aspecto afectivo yo considero que ahora los padres tienden a ser mucho más afectivos con los hijos . . . no había tanta comunicación a nivel de sentimientos" (But on the other hand, emotionally speaking, I think that now parents tend to be much more affectionate with their children . . . there did not use to be a lot of communication at the level of feelings).

Other informants took as a given that their homosexuality was sufficiently understood or assumed by those around them so as to render its revelation redundant, and being considered a family's provider helped these men command respect in their families to a degree that made intrusions into their "private lives" problematic for the intruders rather than the informants. Underlining the redundancy of what was tacit, in the example of someone like Sábato Vega, could be used as a weapon to ridicule attackers. Vega shared an anecdote with me concerning a family gathering he attended with his partner. During the gathering, one of Vega's cousins tried to show him up by asking, in front of the whole crowd, when Vega was going to get married. Unfazed and without skipping a beat, Vega replied: "Pero ya yo tengo marido. ¿Tú no sabes que yo tengo marido? Míralo aquí [*Señalando al compañero*]" (But I already have a husband. Don't you know that I have a husband? He's right here [*Pointing to his partner*]).

By responding to his cousin in this manner, Vega turned on its head a situation meant to shame him in public. His cousin was the one shamed for making an issue of something everyone else knew or should have known. What is important about Vega's response was not that the utterance "Don't you know I have a husband?" actualized a truth about him (his homosexuality) so much as that it made evident that the cousin should have known something Vega assumed everyone else knew. One might say, following Michael Taussig, that this was a situation where the assumed character of what Vega said did not become evident until Vega pointed it out. What the realization of this tacit subject effected was to underline everyone's complicity. As Taussig puts it, "knowing what not to know" in public secrets demonstrates "not that knowledge is power but rather that active not-knowing makes it so. So we fall . . . aghast at such complicities and ours with it, for without such shared secrets any and all social institutions . . . would founder."[23]

The ability Domínguez and Vega had to present themselves before relatives in the daring ways that they did can be partly explained by their geographical proximity with their immediate family (most of their parents and siblings also lived in New York). But it was also related to their economic independence. Their independence from relatives was evident even though Domínguez and Vega struggled financially. Whereas Vega's transition between jobs was punctuated by periods of unemployment, Domínguez sustained himself through disability benefits as an HIV-positive person. Their class backgrounds did not translate into easy upward mobility in the United States, a difficulty shared by most of the informants. Still, these two men learned enough English and had enough experience to act as brokers between their family members and local institutions. Their proficiency at representing their families before institutions and persons with social power came either because of their professional accomplishments (Vega held a BA and worked as a civil servant when I interviewed him) or their ability to navigate the system (living with HIV for over a decade and having lost a partner to AIDS taught Domínguez to be aggressive with providers of health and social services). Thus, the fact that others "did not dare" confront them (or face possible ridicule for trying to out them) tells us much about the privileges Domínguez and Vega enjoyed within their families. Family was important for Domínguez and Vega, but relegating the "public secret" of their homosexuality to the realm of what was tacit helped sustain kin relations that also depended on the knowledge, experience, and resourcefulness that Domínguez and Vega contributed. In other words, all relatives were complicit in the tacit subject precisely because they were invested in the sustenance of an institution that made them socially viable.

The structural location of Domínguez and Vega as male providers (perhaps not always economically but most often in terms of resources) in their families suggests that the degree of authority and legitimacy they enjoyed was also inflected by male privilege. Like their fathers before them, Domínguez and Vega enjoyed less scrutiny of their lives precisely because their private lives were severed from the spheres most relevant to the sustenance of their families. What mattered was not which bodies populated their fantasies and their beds but that they helped sustain their family units. Although Dominican or Latina lesbian-identified women might also enjoy certain respect when they become providers in their families, the socialization of Dominican and Latina women and the regulation of their bodies in the domestic sphere suggest that, even as important and respected resources in their respective families, they might negotiate these dynamics differently.[24]

Acuña's frustration over his father's inability to embark on a conversation about the son's troubles stemmed, perhaps, from family dynamics that did not change drastically after migration. Although Acuña may have experienced a longing to address the gay issue with his parents, geographical distance and a relatively unaltered family scenario—the father continued to be the provider, and Acuña was the only one of the children who migrated at the time of the interview—made the possibility of a discussion of this issue difficult. Also, there may have been fear in what Acuña perceived as his father's lack of "sensitivity" to what the conversation about the gay issue may ultimately trigger. Indeed, in Acuña's case, the gay issue might have been a point of entry for a larger discussion about the role of emotional support in parenting, and his father (and mother) may not have been ready or willing to have that conversation.

Pablo Arismendi's situation was more typical of participants who were undocumented, whose immediate families lived in the Dominican Republic, and whose relatively low level of education limited their prospects for upward mobility as well as their becoming a resource to their loved ones. Although Arismendi left enough traces of the life he led to let others know what was going on, the ambiguity of his situation—at least in front of the aunt who provided him with a place to live—made him shy away from a more confrontational style.

Although there are differences in the ways these informants handled information about their sexual orientation, Domínguez, Arismendi, and Vega were all involved in gay politics from the time they arrived in New York. For a brief period, Vega was involved in the creation and leadership of a New York–based organization for Latino gay men. As an HIV-positive gay man, Domínguez was involved in projects ranging from support groups to activist initiatives among LGBTQ Latinos in New York. Arismendi's activities included volunteering for a social service organization serving LGBTQ Latinos as well as conducting outreach for agencies promoting safer sex. These participants may be exceptional within a broader Latino gay male population. Nonetheless, the way in which these men dealt with information about their sexual orientation within their families suggests that they were familiarized with normative models of coming out.

Situations where circumstances beyond a participant's control forced him out of the closet constituted a disruption in the boundaries the informant established with his parents and relatives around the family's handling of his sexual orientation. In other words, parents and children agreed not to talk about questions of sexuality in general and questions of homosexuality in particular. But what made that agreement possible was the understanding that one's sexuality was a private matter best kept away from scrutiny outside of one's immediate family. Rogelio Noguera's outing, by the publication of his arrest in a police raid of a bar frequented by homosexual men in the Dominican Republic, points to the violence, challenges, and frustrations that accompany the state's shaming of homosexuals. This illustrates the ways that in the Dominican Republic, being outed can make homosexual subjects vulnerable to ostracism and closes almost all possibilities of social legitimacy, let alone upward mobility.

At its core, Noguera's case points to the costs of public scandal to upper-class informants. A man whose skin color would qualify him as "white" by Dominican standards, Noguera was one of three children of a renowned family living in a city in the Cibao region. Noguera's father was a civil engineer, and his mother was a housewife. Members of his family were farmers and generals during the Trujillo dictatorship. He described his father and grandfather as "machos of the land," men whose life revolved around working the land, taking care of animals, gambling on gamecocks, and visiting

prostitutes. Although Noguera's parents were invested in making professionals out of their children, they did not send young Noguera to pursue a medical degree by himself in the capital. Instead, the whole family moved to Santo Domingo to support young Rogelio's studies.

Living in Santo Domingo and attending the university brought Noguera in contact with other gay-identified men. But he insisted throughout his interview that this was not a topic of conversation in his family. "El asunto de mi sexualidad no está claro" (The issue of my sexuality is not clear), he explained, "La familia y yo, tú sabes, nadie habla. Nadie pregunta. Tú sabes cómo es con los dominicanos. Nadie pregunta. Nunca . . . nunca se ha casado. No tiene muchachos. Pero no preguntan nada" (The family and I, you know, nobody talks. Nobody asks. You know how it is with Dominicans. Nobody asks. Never . . . he's never been married. He doesn't have children. But they don't ask anything).

When I asked whether he had ever encountered problems with the authorities because of his homosexuality, Noguera recounted a scandal that estranged him and his father for two years. While he was meeting up with some friends at a bar, the establishment was raided, and Noguera was jailed for a few days. He recounted the following:

Después de los tres días de estar preso, parece que la publicación [en el periódico] . . . se realizó el mismo día o al día siguiente. Mi papá ya lo había leído y nadie me iba a visitar. . . . cuando yo salí de la cárcel, que fui a mi casa, mi papá me llamó y me dice, "Mira. Ve eso." Y yo leí el periódico y ahí estaba . . . "fueron detenidos por uso de drogas y los clientes homosexuales" . . . Entonces, él me dijo, "Saca toda tu mierda y te largas de la casa."

[Llora] [Pausa]

Y entonces lo agarré y le dije, "Bueno ¿Terminó? Ahora yo quiero decirle a usted algo. Primero, no fumo ni cigarrillo. Segundo, si aprendí a ir a

After three days being locked up, it seems like the publication [in the newspaper] . . . was done the same day or next day. My father had read it and nobody was visiting me . . . when I came out of jail, that I went home, my father called me and said, "Look. Look at this." And I read the newspaper and there it was: "they were arrested for drug use and the homosexuals . . . in this bar." Then, he said to me, "Take out all of your shit and leave this house."

[He cries] [Pause]

Then I took this opportunity and said to him, "Well. Are you [uses the formal pronoun] done? Now I want to

las barras y a los sitios, fue con usted. ¿O usted no se recuerda cuando me llevaba a . . . ?" Era una loca, este, que . . . parece que era reformista.[25] Entonces ahí se reunían generales, ingenieros y vainas para hablar disparates . . . "¿O usted no se recuerda las veces que yo iba a donde Cambumbo[26] a buscarlo temprano a las siete de la mañana? Bastante veces yo fui y usted estaba tan borracho que tenía una draga sentada al lado suyo." Se paró y me dio una trompada. Eso fue el resultado de eso. [Señala su mandíbula desencajada] Esto está arrancado. No me lo han podido poner más para atrás . . . Este ahí él me tiró unos puños. Yo no le tiré . . . Entonces de ahí me fui para Puerto Plata después que duré dos años sin verlo.

tell you something. First, I don't even smoke cigarettes. Second, if I learned how to find . . . the bars and other places, it was with you. Or don't you remember when you took me to . . . ?" There was this queen there that . . . must have been a reformista. Then at that place generals, engineers, and other people gathered to talk nonsense . . . "Or don't you remember the times that I went to fetch you at Cambumbo's at seven o'clock in the morning? I went there plenty of times and you were so drunk you had a drag queen sitting next to you." He got up and punched me. [Points to his sunken jaw] This is torn up. They haven't been able to put it back . . . Then he threw a few punches my way. I did not punch him back . . . Then after that I went to Puerto Plata and then I did not see him for two years.

This anecdote reveals the pain of Noguera's confrontation and estrangement from his father. But it is hard to tell whether the blow that altered Noguera's jaw was produced by his father's anger at the son's public shaming, at the son's homosexuality, or at the son's outing of the father's habit of frequenting bars where generals, government officials, prostitutes, drag queens, and other figures of dubious repute congregated. In other words, the recounted anecdote may substantiate Noguera's claim that his sexuality itself has not been a subject of discussion. This messiness suggests slippages that can help further elaborate the meaning of the tacit subject. A tacit *subject* might be an assumed and understood, but not spoken, aspect of someone's subjec*tivity* as well as a particular theme or topic. The difference between father and son, apart from the newspaper outing that interpellated this child of the upper class as a social outcast (possibly a drug addict or a homosexual), was that the father could enter and leave social spaces of "deviance" as attributes of his social power so long as his activities were "known not to be known," as Taussig might put it. Active not knowing—after all, Noguera knew where to go pick up his father even though it is doubtful that he and the rest of the family talked about it—transformed into expressed knowledge must have given bite to Rogelio's recrimination. In this sense, Noguera's sexuality itself was not the tacit subject of the exchange. Nor was Noguera suggesting that his father was gay. Rather, Noguera suggested that his father did not have a steady moral ground on which to stand and judge his son. Apart from actualizing the "truth" of social difference (homosexuality, drug addiction), this exchange actualized the complicities constituting the social power of differently situated actors. The father's violent response was, in short, a response to the destabilizing force of an utterance by the son that revealed that the ability to dabble in marginality was also a function of power.

::: Playing with *lo tácito*

The closet is a collaborative effort. Keeping the closet door ajar is accomplished only to the extent that the gay subject and his others coproduce the closet when they interact with one another. Francisco Paredes, the dark-brown-skinned professional son of a Dominican business leader and of a mother with an advanced degree in biology, articulated eloquently the meanings informants gave to coming out. His observations echoed the uneasiness Latin Americanist critics have voiced with the metaphor:[27]

Cuando tú te sientas con una gente a aclarar tu vida sexual, estamos yendo con este estigma social de que "tú eres raro y tienes que explicarlo." De que "tú estás mal y tienes que explicarlo." ¿Por qué yo me tengo que defender si yo pienso que es normal? Sobre todo para que vengan a decirte, "Yo lo sabía." Entonces, ¿qué sentido tienes tú en discutirlo si yo ya lo sabía?	When you sit down with someone, to clarify your sexual life, we are going along with the social stigma that "you are queer and you have to explain it." That "there is something wrong with you and you have to explain it." Why do I have to defend myself if I think it's normal? And then somebody comes and says to you, "I knew it." Then, what's the point of your discussing it if I already knew?

Paredes articulated some of the concerns other informants expressed in interviews. Paredes rejected disclosure because he associated it with confession. His was a rejection of the confessing subject as the guilty subject. Saying no to the confession meant that Paredes repudiated the religious resonance that made a sin of what was being confessed. Instead of confronting others with the revelation of his sexuality, Francisco Paredes assumed its normality. Because being a homosexual was as normal as being a heterosexual, there was nothing for Paredes to talk about with others.

As a result of owning his sexuality without the guilt associated with confession, Paredes positioned himself within the discursive register of the liberal-democratic right to privacy. At the same time, he revealed an awareness of the tenuousness of his access to privacy, for that which he considered private may already have been accessible to the people who knew him. Paredes's statement reveals that his sense of ownership of his own sexuality was predicated on the exercise of the right to not tell, to let others figure out what was going on if they could pick up the signs. Jason King's discussion of men "on the down low" (DL)—predominantly African American men who have sex with other men without identifying as gay and while continuing to have female partners—resonates with what I have found among the informants: "Whether they pass as playas, [or] blend into the skateboard scene . . . young people of every race and class are responding to something in the air. It may seem like a retrenchment—and in some ways, it is—but their demand for self-determination extends a core value in gay liberation."[28] Like the men on the DL whom King writes about, Paredes's emphasis was on the necessity to respect individual self-determination.

Paredes's comments reveal his understanding that he did not ultimately control the reception of his insertion in the public sphere. In other words, he thought it was likely that his friends would figure out that he was gay because he was only seen with men and because he may "let out a feather or two" every once in a while.[29] This is why, in gathering his friends to "tell them," Paredes feared he would be stating what was already a tacit subject to them. His comments suggest his awareness of the ways his body could be read by others as gay despite his own intentionality. Apart from avoiding the confession, stating what was tacit could be read as if Paredes underestimated his friends' ability to interpret his behavior.

Francisco Paredes attended and graduated from a Catholic school. He then pursued studies in a private university. Before immigrating to the

United States, he established himself in the Dominican Republic's engineering business community as an independent contractor. Being able to work independently as Paredes did was rare at the time. In addition, Paredes had spent a year in Germany living with the man who was then his partner. His decision to move to New York came when he learned of the failure of a business opportunity he had pursued in Puerto Rico. After moving to New York and meeting his current partner, Paredes chose to stay.

Even though he came to the United States on business, Paredes arrived with a six-month tourist visa. Unable to obtain employment in his area of specialization because of his undocumented status, Paredes looked for jobs where his immigration status would not be a problem. A friend helped him get a job in a restaurant, which made it possible for Paredes to earn some money and work on his English. He eventually befriended a woman who agreed to marry him to help legalize his status, and their successful application helped him begin to find work closer to his professional expertise. Nonetheless, the scarcity of available work and his precarious position as a newly arrived professional put him at a disadvantage in the job market.

When the interview turned to the theme of disclosure, Paredes insisted that his mother and all of his relatives knew everything they needed to know, even though he had never discussed his sexuality with them. I asked him to elaborate:

El único derecho que tú no puedes dejar que nadie te arrebate es el derecho de compartir lo que tú quieras compartir de tu vida. De ejercer ese derecho de decir, "Yo no quiero hablar de esto." ¡Y eso no quiere decir esconderlo! Porque yo nunca lo escondí.

The only right you cannot let anyone take away from you is the right to share what you want to share from your own life. To exercise the right to say, "I don't want to talk about this." And that doesn't mean to hide it! Because I never hid it.

Háblame de eso.

Tell me about that.

Todos los novios que yo tuve yo los llevé a la casa.

All of the boyfriends that I had I took home.

Pero hay personas que pueden decir que son amigos tuyos . . .

But there are people who might say that they were friends of yours . . .

Mi hermana mayor llevó a todos los de ella a la casa y nunca le dijo—mi

My oldest sister brought all of hers and she never said to my mother—

mamá nunca se enteró que ella tuvo. ¿Por qué yo le tengo que decir que ese es el mío?

Dicen que uno de los problemas que tienen estas comunidades en particular es que la gente no sale. ¿Qué le responderías tú a ese tipo de crítica?

Una de las cosas en las que yo tengo que estar claro es que yo nací en un lugar, en un país que está colocado en una parte del globo terráqueo. Y dependiendo de donde está ese país colocado en esa parte del globo terráqueo, yo ya nací con ventajas y desventajas. Entonces, yo tengo que jugar con mis ventajas y mis desventajas, que son a nivel mundial, que son a nivel nacional, que son a nivel social, que son a nivel familiar. Tú tienes que decidir si jugar a ganar o jugar a perder.

Háblame de tu relación con tu mamá y de tus parejas.

Tú tienes que empezar diciendo que tu mamá te dio a luz a ti, ¿eh? Y te viene observando. Entonces, tu mamá tiene un Ph.D. en ti. ¡Y yo no puedo subestimar la inteligencia de mi mamá! Ahora, ella hizo su trabajo y lo hizo muy bien. Excelentemente bien. Ella lo hizo bien porque ella quiso a todos mis amigos y los incorporaba en la familia. . . . Y esos novios durmieron allá muchas y otros vivieron allá otras veces. . . . Y ella iba a las 5:30 de la mañana y

my mother never found out that she had. Why do I have to say that that one is mine?

It has been said that one of the problems that these communities have in particular is that people do not come out. What would you say to that kind of criticism?

One of the things that I have to be clear about is that I was born in a place, in a country that is located in a certain part of the globe. And depending of what part of the globe that country is located in, I was already born with advantages and disadvantages. So I have to play with my advantages and disadvantages, at a global level, at a national level, at a social level, at a family level. You have to decide if you want to play to win or to lose.

Tell me about your relationship with your mother and your partners.

You have to start saying that your mother gave birth to you. Eh? And she has been observing you. Therefore, your mother has a Ph.D. in you. And I can't underestimate my mother's intelligence! Now, she did her job and she did it well. Excellently well. She did well because she loved all of my friends, she loved all of my boyfriends very much. . . . And she incorporated them into the family. . . . And those boyfriends slept there many times and others lived there other times. . . . And she went at

abría la puerta de la habitación que nunca estuvo cerrada a llevarme el café . . . y ella lo que veía ahí eran dos hombres abrazados. Entonces, ella hizo su trabajo muy bien.	5:30 in the morning and opened the door of the room, which was never locked, to take coffee to me . . . and what she saw there were two men hugging. Then, she did her job well.

Paredes was explicit in using the right to privacy to frame the decision of whether or not to disclose. In his case and that of other informants, Paredes's class privilege did not protect him from being accused of marriage fraud, for instance, should information about his homosexuality have reached immigration authorities. Along with Noguera's experience of a public shaming by having his name published in a newspaper in connection with the raid of a bar frequented by drug users and homosexuals, the possibility of being outed as a homosexual in immigration court demonstrates the importance of attempting to control how and where information about one's sexuality circulates. Keeping one's sexuality in the realm of what is tacit is also a strategy for the management and circulation of information that, if expressed explicitly in the wrong context, could hurt a person's real (or perceived) possibilities of legitimacy or social mobility. Paredes's experience may be particular, but it reveals ways in which he wrestled with his disadvantages within structures of inequality.

One advantage that informs Paredes's conviction of the need to respect individual self-determination and his access to privacy with an ease not shared by other informants was that he could perform normative masculinity. Paredes's ability to pass as a heterosexual man allowed him access to a respect that may not be as accessible to informants whose self-presentation was considered effeminate and whose gender nonconformity got conflated into their sexuality. Though it is hard to guess what his mother thought when she brought in the coffee and saw two men hugging in bed—and asking such a question of his mother would probably do violence to the agreement between mother and son not to talk about what was tacit between them—the ability of this family to share in this tacit subject was probably facilitated by Paredes's gender conformity and male privilege. In other words, Paredes's masculine self-presentation probably helped avoid external pressures (from distant relatives and neighbors) his family could have experienced around his sexuality.

In addition, class position shaped Paredes's views on coming out. Apart from the respect his mother and other relatives showed toward his privacy while he was growing up, Paredes had resources and enjoyed privacy in ways that were not accessible to informants such as Pablo Arismendi. Other informants could not afford living with a partner independently from relatives in New York, especially shortly after their arrival in the United States. What set Paredes apart from most of the informants was that he had that independence *before* he ever migrated to the United States. Although he brought partners to live at his mother's house, he had rented his own apartment and moved in with his partner for a number of years before traveling to the United States. This was rare among the men I interviewed. Thus, other informants might share in Paredes's conviction that every individual has the right to not tell, but it is not simply about whether or not one tells. Informants like Pablo Arismendi would have to consider not only whether or not to tell. Arismendi had to consider whether he wanted certain things to be visible to people who might say something to his mother in Santo Domingo or his aunt in New York.

There is a game of advantages and disadvantages being played, Paredes suggested. The challenge becomes making decisions about the way one chooses to play. It is not hypocritical or unethical to wrestle with this complexity. On the contrary, it is authoritarian to suggest that everyone needs to decide his or her identity, no matter the complexity. Paredes's comments about his own location at various levels (family, local, national, and global) suggest that while in some ways aware of his own class privilege, he understood the risks and benefits of disclosure for someone of his situation. He understood the ways in which disclosure might curtail an individual's chances to occupy certain social positions. While these comments point, once again, to mobility and aspirations possible because of a social status he already enjoyed, Paredes's comments also suggested that, in the case of working-class men, disclosure versus nondisclosure may have little to do with upward mobility in New York. Being undocumented forced Paredes to take up the same kinds of work that men with fewer years of education and professional experience continued to perform. Yet his not telling, coupled with his level of education, might have allowed him to move up the social ladder in ways that may have been inconceivable for other informants.

This chapter has focused on interpersonal relationships between informants and their relatives. Nonetheless, my argument relies on the critic's ability to contemplate varying contingencies as he or she investigates the operations of the tacit subject across locations (e.g., home, family gatherings, public settings, institutions), actors (e.g., parents, relatives, police), and publics (e.g., parents and relatives, friends and colleagues, institutions, marketers, researchers). Just as I do not use tacit subjects to generalize about the experiences of all of the informants, I am also wary of assuming that this strategy works in the same way across the different locations of which a particular subject may partake daily. The boundaries of what is tacit, what is silent, and what is secret are harder to define in some instances.

The image of the individual white gay subject "liberated" through migration to the metropolis may make New York attractive to men like the informants. Nevertheless, the experiences they recount present us with people able to make decisions and assert a sense of autonomy while being deeply cognizant of the social relations that make it possible for them (and for those linked to them) to survive. By underscoring these implicit and shared linkages and understandings that cement social relations, the concept of *tacit subjects* begins to move us toward more relational accounts of the social construction of identity in queer studies. In a neoliberal world that exalts the atomized and unmoored individual and in LGBTQ communities that celebrate self-making by clinging to the promise of coming out as the romance of individual liberation, tacit subjects may make us more cognizant that coming out is always partial, that the closet is a collaborative social formation, and that people negotiate it according to their social circumstances.

As I stated in the introduction, *tacit subjects* is more a point of departure than a frame for the overall discussion that follows. The next sections and chapters will illustrate and analyze dimensions of the lived experiences of the informants, which shape the way they lived and narrated their lives. Discussions of their geographical displacement and settlement, their relationship with other Dominicans (with gay-identified Dominicans and with Dominicans in general), their investment in masculinity for the production of legitimacy, and the ways in which nationality and mobility inflect narratives of sex and return will demonstrate how important it is to understand how these men are much more than their sexuality. We now turn to an analysis of the messiness of their lives and the place that being men who love other men occupies in their stories.

PART I

~~LEAVING~~ LIVING IN
THE MENTAL ISLAND

:::

Words as worlds. Worlds as words. Speaking English, at first, was like gargling with sound. Spanish sounds jump off the tongue, through the roof of one's mouth, and out by the movement of one's lips. It took me months to hear and then produce the distinction between *word* and *world*. It finally sunk in when I realized how involved the lower part of the mouth has to become in producing the *r* sound; far from the rattle of the rolled *r*. The tongue sinks in and lets the space it opens up be occupied briefly by the air coming through the throat and moving between the upper and lower lips. *R. Are. Arc. Art.* Then come the ends: a light touch-and-go of the tongue and the roof of the mouth to produce the *d* in *word*, or a longer caress and then a sudden letting go to produce the *ld* in *world*. What a whirl of words in this world.

My high school librarian, mentor, and best friend in Philadelphia took it upon herself to help me polish my pronunciation, a labor of love that complemented the novels by Baldwin, Kafka, and Dostoyevsky I was reading at the time. I was eager to work on (i.e., eliminate) the traces of Spanish in what was coming out of my mouth, until one day when she asked if we wanted to continue with the "polishing." Our collaborative efforts had brought me to a point where only a few signs of a native tongue other than English persisted in my speech. My friend's emphasis had always been clarity of diction, to ensure that the way I spoke did not cause me to be misunderstood. As far as she was concerned, that part of the work was done. My choices now were either to continue working on my accent or to "sound interesting," as I recall.

I chose the latter.

This decision brought to a provisional conclusion work that must have taken place during most of 1990. I remember these as arduous sessions, where I would speak about any topic and exchange phrases back and forth with her until we came to a word, phrase, or sentence she could not make out. Puzzled, she asked me to repeat and rephrase it until signs of comprehension washed over her face. At other points, she would pronounce the words, and I would imitate those sounds. If I still did not get them right, I asked her to imitate my mispronunciation so I could hear what was coming out of my mouth. Then she would utter the "correct" sound. We did this until I approximated the proper pronunciation.

Leave. Live. Living to leave. Leaving to live. After a few years of immersion in life in English, I was still baffled by the distinction between the *i* and the *ea* sounds. One day, walking to class with a fellow student and wanting to know where she lived, I asked, "Where do you leave?" She stopped and looked at me for three uncomfortable beats before making out what I meant. "Oh," she said, "I live in the dorms."

Straddling between worlds and words, between leaving and living in the Dominican Republic and New York City, are central themes in the chapters in this section. One of the men used the phrase "the mental island" to refer to the inability of his fellow Dominicans to part ways with what he perceived as the more problematic aspects of social life back in their home country. No matter how far from the Dominican Republic the men went, they still felt that their compatriots continued to keep the insular and close-minded mentality they had before migrating. But as these chapters illustrate, even those most eager to depart did not definitively do so. They never left any of the worlds they transited through, but their living and narrating themselves in these worlds attests to their efforts to fashion and refashion themselves given conditions that were stacked up against them.

CHAPTER 2

Moving Portraits

"I began to run before he [Sábato's father] opened the closet. When
he opened the closet and began to see all that was there [cards from
the hotels where Sábato had been with lovers, marijuana joints], he
only said, 'Find her!' [We laugh] and the girl [Sábato addresses himself
in the third person] went far [ran as far from his father's reach as he
could]. She was going so fast her legs brushed against her ears, honey:
run run run run."

Sábato Vega ran, but only across the street, where he was protected by a gay
neighbor.

: : :

Many migration stories, especially when they also tell of the person's growth,
have the narrative arc of an epic: young heroes hungry to learn the ways of
the world and figure out their place in it bump again and again into the obstacles to opportunity, learning, and self-realization where they were born.
Displacing oneself to another country promises unknown adventures and
hardships, but heroes are guided by the sense that no matter how hard their
lives become, they will be better off than settling for the familiar, the comfortable, and the known. Telling the story of problems solved, tears shed,
and wounds healed (or not healed) signals arrival and success, which are no
mean feats: the narrator steps out of the anonymity of the "huddled masses"
and uses a retrospective lens to inject the quotidian gesture, the act of solidarity or abjection with meanings these gestures and acts could not have
had when they were first experienced.[1]

Yet the narratives I present here document lifelong, daily, and ongoing
struggles to define a self in relation to the worlds one lives in and moves
through. That Vega's outing (literalized by his father's "opening of the closet"
where Vega kept the evidence of his trysts and marijuana) prompted him

to run across the street suggests that departures are anything but definitive in these narratives. Biological families, as well as support from gay or other non-kin Dominicans, made possible the migration and survival of the informants in New York City. To the degree that in their stories about arriving and settling in Nueva York these men accounted for their circulation between two sites in Dominican transnational cultures, the case stories that follow point to the ways three of these men experienced, participated in, traversed, and negotiated the regulation of their bodies on multiple and disparate discursive registers. Their telling of their stories attests to the obstacles they faced, their ingenuity in the face of adversity, and, ultimately, their success. However, their stories were not stories of young men unshackled from the binds, pains, and joys of biological family by the vicissitudes prompted by transformations in the capitalist world economy.[2] Instead, the stories here illustrate the ways these men wrestled and straddled multiple and conflictive demands, prohibitions, intimacies, and affective investments. Apart from introducing the reader to some of the men I interviewed, these narratives demonstrate that self-realization as a man who loves men does not require moving away from the biological family. Indeed, these narratives show that as individuals moved and evolved, so did their families.

Moving portraits, the title of this chapter, appears to be a contradiction. How can portraits move? Isn't portraiture about arresting the image of a moment, the conjunction of eye, mediating technology (e.g., the camera), and object? The contradiction is not inherent to the conjunction of the words *moving* and *portrait*. Rather, the title obtains from the idea of the portrait as a window into a reality out there, available for display through mediating representations. Nevertheless, the perspective advanced throughout what follows resulted from a series of mediations, movements in between technologies and bodily organs (through the tape recorder, the ear of the transcriber, the fingers that typed) to produce the words you are reading.[3] Roland Barthes explains what he realized when he encountered a photograph of a relative of Napoleon, taken in 1852: "I am looking at eyes that looked at the Emperor."[4] Strictly speaking, what a reader sees in a text such as this book are words resulting from mediation processes that are easily erased when we think of what appears on the page, especially when attributed to someone other than the author and submitted as evidence, as real or raw material. Even those words produced by men such as those who speak in this book are the result of mediations and intentionalities that get lost in the shuffle from voice to word but that nevertheless matter to the analysis at hand.

Moving portraits points to the incompleteness of knowledge production itself, if we take the research interview to be one important technology through which such knowledge is produced. One assumption that has been foundational to projects that document who marginalized populations might be and the way they experience specific social ills is the idea that once what people say is documented, "the subaltern speaks," even though critics such as Gayatri Spivak have suggested that "speaking" is not possible given the layers of mediation and symbolic violence in the construction of the archives where such voices might be found.[5] Nevertheless, speech is part of what this book engages while recognizing that to take on the speech of others suggests a false sense of intimacy and mastery. This chapter and this book insist, like the literary and cultural critic Doris Sommer, that whatever knowledge emerges from it results from engaging the words the informants produced in the interview encounter. As Sommer explains when talking about ethnic literatures in the Americas, "a variety of rhetorical moves can hold readers at arm's length or joke at their pretense of mastery, in order to propose something different from knowledge. Philosophers have called it acknowledgment. Others call it respect."[6]

Respect for the boundaries established by one's interlocutors (instead of the easy slip into a false sense of intimacy or false grasp of what the other experiences because of interpersonal proximity) is particularly important in situations where the interviewer is a member of the population being studied. *Moving portraits* also suggests (1) that no one's life can be reduced to the hour they shared with an interviewer and (2) that the perspective of the one listens, transcribes, and writes is far from dispassionate or impartial.

::: Moving Up in the Family: Aníbal Guerrero

Migration to New York, in the accounts of some informants, allowed them to renegotiate their relationship to their biological families. Aníbal Guerrero, a thirty-five-year-old, working-class, light-skinned man, explained in our interview that he did not have an urgent need to migrate to the United States. But when the right opportunities presented themselves, he pursued this option. During the process of obtaining the paperwork to travel, his three-year relationship with a Filipino medical student in the Dominican Republic entered a crisis that did not survive Guerrero's migration. Soon after arriving in Dallas, Guerrero connected with a friend in New York. This friend gave Guerrero the help he needed to move to the city. After his arrival, Guerrero moved several times chasing after jobs, from Philadelphia to Virginia, then back to New York. Until our meeting, most jobs he pursued were in restaurants. Guerrero worked as the assistant to a photographer in New York when I interviewed him. He was undocumented.

Guerrero's recollections of his childhood reveal pressures with which Dominican families struggle. He was the youngest of three boys and a girl. The Guerrero children were well acquainted with the neighboring children, families, and relatives who surrounded them. However, they faced the constant threats, blows, and prohibitions inflicted by a father Guerrero remembered as authoritarian.

Nosotros no tuvimos una niñez muy buena que digamos porque el papá de nosotros era muy recio, muy de mano dura, y nosotros no tuvimos como esa conexión, cuando éramos niños, de que estábamos jugando. El papá de nosotros siempre nos paraba y nos maltrataba mucho.	I wouldn't say we had a very good childhood because our father was too rough, very much of an iron fist, and we didn't have that sense of connection when we were children like when we were playing. Our father always stopped our games. He mistreated us a lot.

No trips to the river in their hometown, a small village in the northern province of María Trinidad Sánchez. No visits with neighborhood friends, at least while Mr. Guerrero was around. No sports. They were not even allowed to go to church because, as Guerrero explained when I asked if his mother was religious,

Ella se metió a la iglesia católica. Yo sé que a nosotros nos bautizaron y todo, pero nosotros nunca practicamos religiones. Mi papá era muy comunista y él no quería nada de eso.	She became a Catholic. I know we were baptized and all, but we never practiced religions. My father was very much a communist and he didn't want any of that.

Still, the Guerrero children had opportunities to explore their surroundings. When his father's occupation as *chofer* (chauffeur) took him away from the village, Guerrero and his siblings visited with neighbors and friends.[7] There were also occasional visits to relatives, mostly on Mr. Guerrero's side of the family. Nonetheless, Aníbal Guerrero characterized life with his father as asphyxiating. His mother, whose occupations were childrearing and all matters related to the household, intervened frequently to protect the youngsters. The frequency of Mr. Guerrero's violence toward his children strained the couple's relationship.

¿Cómo era la relación entre ellos?

Problemática. Siempre uno veía los problemas porque mi mamá estaba en disgusto [de] cómo el papá de nosotros nos trataba. Pero ella no podía hacer nada porque ella tenía cuatro muchachos y no podía mantenerlos. Entonces [ella] tenía que soportarle todo eso a mi papá.

How was the relationship between them?

Problematic. You always saw the problems and all that because my mother did not like how my father treated us. But she could not do anything because she had four kids and could not sustain them on her own. So [she] had to put up with my father and all that.

Perhaps as an effect of the retrospective frames through which Guerrero narrated his childhood, an account of the relationship between his parents centered on the children and not the marital relationship. In other words, Guerrero's narrative identified the treatment of the children as the central problem between Mr. and Mrs. Guerrero. Though his characterization of the issues left little doubt that paternal violence must have concerned Mrs. Guerrero, what this excerpt makes most obvious is the force that the gendering of their living conditions had on Mrs. Guerrero's (in)ability to change the plight of her children. As a married housewife and mother of four children living in a small town far away from her own relatives, she could do little other than deal with Mr. Guerrero's temper.

Years later, in New York, away from his family, Guerrero pointed to an issue in his family situation that might have contributed to his father's behavior. When I asked if the relationship between father and son had changed over the years, Guerrero said,

Bueno, ahora sí, él ha cambiado porque él ahora es una persona más adulta y él es una persona que nunca ha podido tener un trabajo estable porque tiene sus ideales. A él le gusta ayudar a la gente, pero mi pensar es:

Well, nowadays, he has changed because he is more of an adult and he is someone who has never been able to keep a job, you know, because he has his political ideals. He likes to help people, but what I think is:

¿cómo tú vas a ayudar a una gente si	how are you going to help somebody
tú no tienes con qué ayudar a nadie?	if you don't have what you need to
Tú tienes que ayudarte a ti primero	help? You have to help yourself first,
y después tú ayudas al otro. Pero no:	and then you help others. But no: he
él no es así. Entonces él ahora tiene	is not like that. So now he has all of
todos estos problemas económicos, y	these financial problems and I help
eso, yo lo ayudo a él cuando puedo.	him when I can.

Guerrero described his father as someone who never kept a job. Working as a chofer in a small city like Guerrero's hometown was not particularly profitable. Obviously, job insecurity did not excuse a father's abuse of his children. But it gives a sense of the financial instability in which Mr. Guerrero asserted his authority. As he was an unreliable breadwinner, his outbursts might have been a response to feeling that his authority was constantly threatened.

Aníbal, on the other hand, presented himself as relatively successful as a worker since he left his household. He even contributed to the family's finances. His comments on his father—remarking on the way his father seemed more of a "grown-up" and pointing out how Mr. Guerrero never held steady employment—signaled a shift in Guerrero's position in the house, even if from a distance. This rearrangement of family dynamics because of the children's increased ability to provide financially for relatives is consistent with Lionel Cantú's findings with Mexican immigrant gay men.[8] What is striking about Guerrero's account of this shift in the context of the interview was that it helped cast him as a "mature" man vis-à-vis his father's failure to hold on to a steady job—a small gesture, perhaps, but one that located the father figure symbolically in an infantilized position. In other words, the retrospective lens and Aníbal's newfound role of "provider" of the family unit, within which he grew up, allowed him to rewrite the family romance in a transnational context. According to Aníbal's characterizations, as "mature" and responsible breadwinner, he came to occupy the role of father/provider that his father was never competent enough at performing.

The strain between father and son was palpable throughout Guerrero's account of his relationship with his family. When sending contributions, Guerrero did so through his mother. He generally avoided talking to Mr. Guerrero:

Cada vez que yo hablo con él, él busca una forma u otra de sacarme dinero. Yo le dije a mi mamá, "No le des mi teléfono. Porque yo aquí no estoy sacudiendo la matica para buscar cuartos. Yo no tengo dinero aquí."

Every time I speak with him, he finds one way or the other to get me to give him money. I told my mother, "Don't give him my telephone number. Because here, I am not shaking trees to get money. I don't have money here."

Apart from suggesting the shift in family dynamics because of the children's ability to provide, Guerrero's alliance with his mother may have impacted the setting of priorities and decision making in the household. In other words, some of the money may still end up in Mr. Guerrero's hands, but Aníbal's account of his exchanges with his mother suggested that the flow of remittances into the household, when it took place, did not happen to please the father's wishes or fulfill the household priorities Mr. Guerrero set.

After learning about his father's behavior, I expected Guerrero to focus his growing awareness on what behaviors were acceptable for a man within the range of things his authoritarian father controlled. But that was not the case. Guerrero recalled being told what being a man did and did not mean by family members (older siblings, parents, and other relatives) and by neighbors.

Cuando tú estabas creciendo, ¿cuáles eran las cosas que los adultos alrededor tuyo decían que un hombre debía y no debía hacer?

When you were growing up, what were the things that the adults around you said a man could and could not do?

No jugar con muñecas. No hacer oficios de la casa porque eso no era de hombres. No vestirse de mujeres. No ponerse maquillaje. Cosas así. Que debemos andar con hombres. No debíamos juntarnos tanto con las mujeres. Que por la manera de sentarnos: deberíamos sentarnos de una forma. Las mujeres se sientan de otra.

Not to play with dolls. Not to do household chores, because that was not for men. Not to dress up as women. Not to wear makeup. Things like that. That we have to hang out with men. We weren't supposed to hang out with women too much. The way we sat: we were to sit one way. Women sit in another way.

This list of things "not to do" was partly a response to the framing of the question. Yet it is striking the way in which masculinity emerged in Guerrero's describing a list of things not to do rather than the reverse. Indeed, the only do's in the list were to hang out with men and to sit as men should sit. Furthermore, the not to do's were generally framed in relation to practices associated with women. Be it through avoiding Barbie or other generic dolls associated with young girls or avoiding signals of femininity on the body such as dresses or makeup, the notion of masculinity as "not to do" may signal the threatening feminine lurking inside each man. Thus, Guerrero's words gave the impression that masculinity was the "straightjacket" that controls the symbolic woman inside.[9]

In his own account of it, "acting like a man" was not a problem for young Guerrero. Even though he was scolded a few times for playing with his sister's dolls, Guerrero quickly learned the body language of proper manhood and made sure he did not deviate from it. Guerrero also had a few girlfriends and a few secret erotic encounters with boys before leaving his home in 1987. One of his older brothers, who had already married and left the household for Santo Domingo, hosted Guerrero initially in the capital. After Guerrero landed a job in a hotel, he began to enjoy his newly won independence and started frequenting bars. A few months after arriving in Santo Domingo, he moved in with an acquaintance he had made during his outings. Guerrero then met, fell in love, and moved in with his first boyfriend, a Filipino foreign student.[10] Through his partner's connections, Guerrero was able to obtain papers with which he could travel.

The linkages mobilized for Guerrero's migration were connected to a non-Dominican man with whom he shared affective ties. Nevertheless, Guerrero's circulation within the United States was linked to his ability to associate with people across the homo/heterosexual binary. Indeed, all but the most recent of the job opportunities available to Guerrero in different U.S. cities were connected to friendships he established within heterosexual networks. By "heterosexual networks," I mean groupings in which there might be queer people but in which people assume that everyone else is heterosexual. Guerrero's English-language skills also played a role in creating these linkages, as most of his connections were made with non-Dominican Anglos. Thus, Guerrero may not have experienced upward mobility as a consequence of migration, but his survival depended on his ability to circulate between gay and straight and between Dominican and non-Dominican worlds.

Guerrero's ability to slip in and out of heterosexual networks had its requirements, however. Behaving like a man for a straight audience—something that made Guerrero avoid straight environments for socializing—also required having a girlfriend. Guerrero may have escaped the surveillance of his family and neighbors by moving to Santo Domingo and later to the United States. But he continued to have girlfriends in the capital and, later, throughout the time he spent circulating in cities in the United States. He stated that having a girlfriend was a way of dealing with peer pressure. Like speaking English and behaving like a man, Guerrero's ability to date women and navigate these environments demonstrates that he understood that survival would be possible if he performed masculinity and made it work to his advantage.

One might be tempted to conclude that this migration narrative imagines displacement as movement away from the eye of surveillance of the biological family toward a "liberated" space. However, reading Guerrero's account this way ignores the suggestion that there were eyes watching for Guerrero to "act like a man" inside and outside of the family environment. It also ignores that developing the competencies to perform proper masculinity has helped Guerrero establish and sustain interpersonal relations that are generally out of reach of some of the other men I interviewed. Thus, upward mobility was not at stake in Guerrero's situation, but a reading of him as the liberated queer man would ignore that adhering to certain norms was a precondition to his survival.

Finally, seeing Guerrero as the liberated queer subject ignores the fact that Guerrero's group of friends has been shaped by the attention he paid to the gendered behavior of its members, as the following exchange makes evident:

¿Y qué tipo de gente no te gusta tener como amigos? Descríbelos más o menos.	And what kind of people you do not like to have as friends? Describe them more or less.
No me gusta tener amigos que sean chismosos. Que les guste estar llevándole vida a nadie. Personas escandalosas.	I don't like to have friends who are gossipy. The busybody types. Scandalous people.
	Scandalous. How so?
Escandalosas. ¿En qué sentido?	

Like a flaming queen. Porque como yo me comporto como yo soy, que aparento ser straight, pero no lo soy. A mí no me gusta andar con una persona que esté partiéndose al lado mío. Cuando uno está caminando, uno no sabe bien quién lo está mirando. Y a mí no me gusta que me estén catalogando de que "mira una loca ahí donde va." Porque yo ande con él a mí me van a catalogar de loca también.

Like a flaming queen. Because given that I behave the way I am, that I look straight but I am not, I do not like to hang out with someone who's letting out feathers next to me. When you are walking, you do not know who is looking at you. And I don't like it for people to be categorizing me, like "look at a loca walking over there." Since I am walking with this person, they will categorize me as a loca also.

Guerrero's unease with effeminate men was typical among the informants, as I discuss in chapters 4 and 5. I also revisit and fully analyze this exchange in chapter 5. Guerrero's main concern was that being seen with an effeminate man on the street would bring into the public realm what he considered a private matter. These comments illustrate the ways in which Guerrero policed his behavior and the behavior of his friends. Indeed, he selected friends partly on the basis of their ability to perform "proper" masculinity. Furthermore, Guerrero was invested in preserving "normative" behavior as the characteristic of the group. Conformity to these expectations not only determined who entered or not but also who was taken seriously as an interlocutor, potential friend, or lover, as will be explained in later chapters. Whereas a man seen to behave as a macho might enter these circles with relative ease, men in this group would perceive a sissy's gender nonconformity as a liability.

Distance without return to the homeland encouraged Guerrero to express his affection toward his family, particularly his mother. "Ha cambiado" (It has changed), he responded to my question of whether and how his relationship with his mother evolved after his migration:

Cuando nosotros íbamos creciendo, nosotros nunca tuvimos esa forma de expresión hacia nadie porque nosotros teníamos mucho dolor. Pero ahora que yo tengo tanto tiempo aquí, yo veo como que una gente se

When we were growing up we never had that form of expression toward anybody, because we had too much pain. But now that I have lived here for so long, I see how one can miss somebody. I tell her each time that I

extraña. Yo se lo digo a ella cada vez que yo la llamo. Yo la extraño mucho. Yo quiero estar allá. So es más abierta ahora.

call her. I miss her very much; I want to be there. So [our relationship] is more open now.

For Guerrero, openness with his family did not relate directly to disclosure of his sexual identity. Guerrero's consistency as a worker and helper of his family from a distance gave him a voice to express affection and even express opinions. It also gave him decision-making power, if not oversight, within the household. Because of his reliance on his family and his limited prospects of upward mobility in the United States, one reward of migration was that it located him in the role of provider with a degree of power within the family.

::: Surviving AIDS in an Uneven World: Mejía's Story

Whereas informants like Guerrero connected migration to the renegotiation of family dynamics due to geographical distances, other informants migrated to survive by tapping the supports available to them. Many scholars, policymakers, and average citizens of the United States imagine people with AIDS (PWAS) who are immigrants as carriers of disease.[11] The narrative below offers another way of looking at immigrants living with HIV/AIDS. This is a narrative of a person who successfully mobilized the resources he needed to survive what Paul Farmer and others have called the "structural violence" of a world where resources are distributed unevenly.[12]

I knew Arturo "Latoya" Mejía before I decided to write about immigrant Dominican homosexual men.[13] Mejía moved to New York for HIV treatment, and his move coincided with the beginnings of my graduate school career. We met the day we began to live in the house of a common friend—"the asylum"—where I rented a room. I had known HIV-positive people before, but I had never lived with a person dealing with this disease on a daily basis. In the process of getting to know Mejía, I began to understand some of what it means to continue living after seroconversion.

A tall, soft-spoken, well-educated black Dominican living with HIV, Mejía travels back and forth between New York and Santo Domingo to see his doctor and to obtain refills for his treatment. I know few people with more zeal to live and enjoy themselves. Mejía's gargantuan appetite for food matches his appetite for sexual adventures and the manic charm with which he tells stories. When I asked him about a trip he made to the carnival in Rio de Janeiro, he replied with his idiosyncratic, ribald sense of humor: "I had a great time sweeping semen off the streets." Mejía's allure, refinement, and wit made him the center of attention. He was a force to be reckoned with.

However, Mejía was also my most elusive informant. I learned about Mejía's life through him and the friends that connected us. Members of this group included the man who hosted him in the United States and the men who arranged for his travels. All these men were either HIV professionals or well connected within HIV research and activism in New York and the Dominican Republic. Despite appearing to be quite open, Mejía was a reserved person. He agreed to let me write about his experiences, but my attempts to schedule interviews with him during the two years that followed our meeting each other failed miserably. Once he saw me bring out a tape recorder—we were about to start "the interview"—while he was speaking to someone on the phone. After hanging up, he looked at me and asked, "Will you fuck me?" Realizing that this was a joke, though I did not quite know where it was going, I said no.

"Well, you won't fuck me but the man I just hung up with will. So see you later," and he walked into the bathroom to take a shower. That was the end of that try.

Mejía's rhetorical tactic to keep control of the interview situation was to apparently tell everything; to be explicit and aggressively open, as if there was nothing else to say ("Well, that's that!"); and, at the same time, keep away from the interview structure. "I'll tell you my life, but I am in control of how and what, and the way I see it is the way it is, and that's that," he seemed to say. Whereas Sommer talks about withholding and reticence, Mejía's tactic of control or distance was the opposite—apparent openness.[14]

When I did not structure our conversations as "interviews," I learned the most about Mejía. He was resistant to talking about being HIV-positive with me while being candid about his life in general. If I wanted to learn about him, I learned that I had to understand how much more there was to him than HIV. I knew that as Mejía's friend, but it took me a while to learn it as an academic.

By the time the interview finally happened, I knew Mejía quite well. There were questions I could ask him now that would not have occurred to me before. I realized that my earlier attempts to interview him had been motivated by an interest to understand him not on his own terms but, rather, as belonging to a particular group of people: people with AIDS. In looking at Mejía in this way, to what extent was I reproducing the epistemological traps of public health and the AIDS-research industry, where the thrust of the effort has been to regulate the behavior and "risk" represented by PWAS? Are there ways to think about the survival of PWAS beyond counting their viral load and CD4 cells? Are there ways to understand the life of someone like Mejía without falling into the therapeutic listing of all the good things HIV/AIDS brought him?[15]

Looking at Mejía in these particular ways situated what I was doing at the time firmly within the purview of the public health research I had been taught to conduct. This is a research practice rooted in eliciting information about patterns of behavior as a way to understand the contextual variables that might (or might not) alter health outcomes. The possibilities for behavior modification generally operate strictly at the individual level in terms of the sought-after outcomes, even though the predominantly behavioralistic impulse in public health in the United States has been the object of much ongoing discussion and dispute.[16] Though the production of the portrait being elaborated here is, admittedly, part of a research project, the shifting of priorities and focus in the questions I began to ask moved the focus away from the calculation and calibration of behavioral variables and began to attend to elements that may be seen as "in excess" of what regular public health research documents.[17]

This previous way of "looking" failed to recognize and respect Mejía's humanity, and I suspect that was partly why he avoided the official-sounding name "interview" whenever I uttered it. What I learned about Mejía's struggle against HIV reveals both his extraordinary accomplishment and the difficult field within which he pooled resources. After testing positive on his HIV antibody test in 1997, Mejía heard from a doctor that there was little the Dominican health system could do for him:

Ya para decidirme a venir a vivir para acá, fue el haber salido positivo en las pruebas del HIV. O sea, me enfermé. Me dio hepatitis. Hepatitis B. Crónica. Allá en Santo Domingo. Y a través de eso, me hacen todas las pruebas, entonces determinan que soy HIV-positivo. Me combaten la hepatitis. Duro un tiempo en	What made me decide to come live here was when I tested positive for HIV. In other words, I got sick. I got hepatitis. Hepatitis B. Chronic. There, in the Dominican Republic. And through that, they do all the tests, and then they determine that I am HIV-positive. They start treating the hepatitis. I stay for some time on

tratamiento—bastante caro, por cierto. Me dicen que hay opciones, que ya existe el famoso cóctel, que no me puedo desesperar. Pero que es un poco caro. Calculo por cuánto me sale el tratamiento allá, y veo que me sale en un mes lo que yo gano en un año. Y sin la garantía de que los medicamentos lleguen porque no los venden tampoco. Hay que pedirlos en los laboratorios y que lleguen a través de alguien que se encargue de llevártelos. Entonces, fui hasta España, incluso, a ver (porque mi pareja era española) a ver si allá los conseguía y me quedaba por allá. No se pudo. Tomé la determinación de que Nueva York era la única vía factible para conseguir la medicación y el seguimiento médico.

treatment—very expensive, by the way. They tell me there are options, that there is a famous cocktail and that I shouldn't get desperate. But it's a little expensive. I calculate how much treatment costs run there, and I see that I have to pay in a month what I earn in a year. Without the guarantee that the medicines will get there, because they are not sold there either. You have to order them from the labs and have them get to you through someone in charge of bringing them. I went to Spain even, to check (because my partner was Spanish) if I could get them there and I could stay there. We couldn't do it. I decided that New York was the only feasible way to get the medicines and the medical follow-up.

Faced with inequalities in the distribution of medications around the world, Mejía did not have much of a choice. People in his situation either figure out a way to access the resources available elsewhere or face possible death.

Mejía contacted friends and used his visitor's visa to move to New York, where those friends connected him with an experimental treatment program. After spending a year in the United States, Mejía returned to live with his family in Santo Domingo in late 1998. He currently visits his doctor in New York roughly every three months.

That first year was not easy. By the first time he saw a doctor, Mejía had lost weight due to the damages caused by hepatitis B, and he was diagnosed with AIDS after the first set of laboratory tests. Soon after he started taking medications, however, it became apparent that Mejía would recover. His CD4 count shot up, and his viral load diminished. Though Mejía spent a few days sleeping or feeling drowsy, his recovery was nothing short of spectacular. The hardest part of living in the United States was being far from his family and job. The work he found in New York was mostly temporary.

He decided to return to Santo Domingo once he had recovered enough to arrange visits to his doctor a few times per year.

What resources enabled Mejía to survive the AIDS epidemic in the way he has? First, the friends Mejía sought help from after finding out about his HIV status were generally light-skinned, middle-class or upwardly mobile Dominican men who identify as gay, who migrated to New York from the Dominican Republic as adults, and who worked on HIV/AIDS prevention or were aware of the available resources. Additionally, Mejía's health may have been in decline at the time he first entered the United States. But his ability to mobilize markers of a middle-class status (e.g., evidence of earlier visits to the United States and Europe) helped him pass as a tourist to what was then the Immigration and Naturalization Service (INS). Finally, the condition of Mejía's immune system and the fact that he had not been treated at all—in a twisted but happy turn of circumstance—made possible his recovery. Mejía obtained the medication he needed for free as part of an experimental treatment program targeting people living with HIV who had not yet received treatment.

Once his medicines were taken care of and he recovered his health, how did the people around Mejía understand and handle his being HIV-positive? How does his status shape his interpersonal relationships? Sex may not constitute the center of Mejía's life, but it is an important part of it. Sharing an attraction for other men is also what has brought Mejía together with many of his friends in the United States and in the Dominican Republic. Sex is also what sets the tone of much of what Mejía talks about in public, giving a bawdy edge to much of his commentary among close friends. Aware of the unease that knowledge of his active sex life generated among the friends we had in common, I asked if living with HIV influenced the way other people interacted with Mejía:

Mira, influye mucho. Mis amigos están muy atentos a con quién yo tengo relaciones para correr la voz de que nadie tenga relaciones con esa persona. Aún ellos sabiendo que yo practico el sexo seguro, siempre han estado pendientes. Y eso a mí me ha hecho daño porque he tenido que aprender a mentir a ellos de	Look, it influences a lot. My friends pay a lot of attention to the people with whom I have sex to let everyone know that nobody should have sex with that person. Even though they know that I practice safe sex, they have always paid a lot of attention. And that has caused me damage because I have had to learn to lie to

qué hago. O a dejar de hacer lo que quiero hacer para que ellos no sigan comentando. Porque cada vez que yo les digo, conocí a alguien, lo primero que me preguntan es, "¿Tú le dijiste que tú eres HIV positivo?" O sea, como que tengo decírselo. Entonces yo le dije "No, porque si yo cada vez que conozca a alguien, por el simple hecho de conocerlo, aún no tenga sexo, le voy a decir que soy VIH positivo, mejor pongo el letrero y así no tengo que hablar." Y eso sí me ha pasado. Y creo que le pasa a todo el mundo . . . Mis amigos sí, viven pendientes de eso . . . a nivel de que si yo lo manoseé, ni lo topan. Es como que le cayó la plaga. Entonces desde que me ven con alguien, ¿Y tú te acostaste con él? Pero no "¿Tú te acostaste con él?" para preguntarme las preguntas que se hacían antes: ¿Cómo lo tiene? ¿Lo tiene grande? ¿Te dio el culo? ¿Le gusta meterlo? No. "¿Tú te acostaste con él?" para saber si ya los demás se pueden acostar o no.

them about what I do. Or not do what I want to do, so they don't continue gossiping. Because every time I tell them that I met someone, the first thing they ask me is "Did you tell him that you are HIV-positive?" In other words, as if I have to tell him. Then I said, "No, because if every time I meet someone, just by the simple fact of my meeting them, even without having sex with them, I have to tell that I am HIV-positive, I should have a sign, and that way I don't have to talk." And that has happened to me. And I think it happens to everyone. My friends, yes, they pay attention to that . . . to the point that if I touched the person they won't even touch him. As if the person caught the plague. Then as soon as they see me with somebody, "Have you slept with him?" But not "Have you slept with him?" to ask me the questions that were asked before: How big is he? Does he have a big one? Did he give you his ass? Does he like to fuck? No. The question of "Did you sleep with him?" is to know if the others can or cannot sleep with the person.

Mejía's seroconversion caused a shift in the way others interacted with him. In close personal relationships built on a mixture of intimacy and complicity, his seroconversion made others keep him under surveillance. Indeed, their expectation was that Mejía would not engage in a sexual encounter unless he prefaced each encounter with the disclosure of his status. Given that disclosing an HIV-positive diagnosis would be taken by a potential sexual partner as a sign that Mejía "tiene la plaga" (has caught the plague), Mejía's friends expected him not to have sex at all. It is sad, for instance, to notice the dramatic change in focus of the questions his friends asked him when he talked about sleeping with someone. The questions asked before, as Mejía explained, were the questions of friends. The questions friends now asked helped them decide whether or not to avoid sleeping with the person Mejía was talking about.

The insistence on getting Mejía to disclose his HIV status, even to strangers and even if he did not intend to sleep with the person in question, suggests that Mejía's friends were invested in having him keep himself under surveillance. The result of this was withdrawal and silence.

The insistence of Mejía's friends was wrongheaded. He was the "out" HIV-positive person they knew, and they excluded him because of this, but they ran a risk if they assumed he was the only person around them who was infected. The preoccupation of Mejía's friends with keeping him away from the pool of possible sexual partners suggests that, like many policymakers concerned with keeping HIV-positive individuals under surveillance, community members are also focusing on the HIV-positive body as a vector of disease.[18]

As wrongheaded as it may be, the reaction of Mejía's friends is also understandable. Here was someone living and struggling with being HIV-positive every day and wanting to enjoy life as much as possible despite the challenges he faced. His visibility as an active and vibrant person produced tensions in other men who loved and nurtured him but who, at the same time, could not let sexuality and sociality mingle in their exchanges with him as they may have done in the past.[19]

This is by no means the way all of Mejía's friends felt about him. Some people might be tempted to interpret the difficulty Mejía faced within this circle as evidence of the problems faced by "ethnic" homosexual men. Yet this anxiety was expressed by many of the same men who provided Mejía some of the resources, love, and support that have helped him continue living.

The details of Latoya Mejía's life reveal the possibilities and limitations of the transnational social field within which he has circulated. Circulating through these fields, especially as an HIV-positive person, is not something everyone can do. Privileges of access to well-informed and connected persons, at least in this case, structured the possibilities of survival available to Mejía. These possibilities may be unavailable to other people. Mejía can circulate in this field because of certain attributes and resources he could mobilize. He would not have known that protease inhibitors were available for free were it not for the friends he had in the United States who were up to date on medical trials. His ability to tap into his friends was critical to thinking that migration might be the means to succeeding in his struggle against HIV/AIDS. Finally, the ability to mobilize class markers in front of an immigration officer makes the difference between entering New York as a "visitor" and risking one's life to reach Puerto Rican shores via La Mona Canal.

Looking at HIV/AIDS from the perspective of someone who already has the disease compels us to consider the notion of risk management beyond the idea of contagion, which drives so many efforts against the disease. For Mejía, getting infected was not the risk; rather, the risk was dying from a disease when there are medications available that will help fight it. This case study illustrates the political and economic structures related to the global management of AIDS that are the larger context within which Mejía tried to survive. I have also been interested in showing how one person made decisions about his health given conditions of extreme inequality that he had little control over. Finally, this section narrates aspects of the life of one HIV-positive person that are in tension with the way his own group organized and disciplined the affective and sexual ties of each one of its members. Wanting to have sex may be Mejía's way of expressing how fiercely he clings to life, but the unease around him and the investment of his friends in regulating him suggest an ongoing negotiation of the slippage of intimacy, complicity, and pleasure with discipline and regulation.

::: Run, *Loca*, Run! Sábato Vega

When I interviewed Sábato Vega, he was thirty-six years old, had a relatively secure job as a civil servant, and was finally beginning to enjoy the rewards of finishing his undergraduate degree. Although he was single, Vega's relationships and sex life were deeply intertwined with his family life and with the friendships he forged and sustained with men and women since age fifteen, when he left his parental home. Vega and I met years before I came to live to New York. Once I moved to the city and got to know him better, I learned to relish Vega's incorrigible humor, his ability to laugh at others and himself, and his generosity.

Vega illustrates the ways an individual can be displaced, can survive, and can grow without choosing between biological and queer families. Vega's dealings with his parents and siblings were far from easy. But he struggled for respect within his family, creating spaces supportive of the men and women who are part of his life.

In our interview, Vega described his family as one of "nómadas" (nomads) who migrated wherever there was "comida y papeleta" (food and money). The displacements of the Vegas began in Santo Domingo before they ever stepped on a plane: "Íbamos de barrio en barrio [se ríe] porque siempre nos íbamos debiendo dos años de luz, tres años de agua, año y medio de renta" (We went from neighborhood to neighborhood [he laughs] because we always left owing two years of electricity, three years of water, a year and a half of rent). Vega was the sixth child in a family of eight children; his mother was a housewife and his father a public servant. He remembered his father being affectionate toward all the children, including the young Sábato. However, this affection waned as it became evident to the father that Vega was not as "masculine" as his brothers. Vega remembered that tensions between himself and his father rose as the Vegas' marriage soured, once it became known that the patriarch had mistresses who bore him two children. Even though these children eventually came into the Vega household and were raised by Vega's mother, the dissolution of the marriage was accelerated by Mrs. Vega's migration with her elder children to the United States. It took several years for Vega to obtain his residence in the United States. At age fifteen, he was the only one who stayed with his father in the Dominican Republic:

Así que fui el único que me vi forzado a quedarme. No tenía, todavía, los papeles para salir del país. Yo me quedé criando—cuidando a mis dos hermanitos junto con él [el papá] y me convertí en una niñera sin sueldo.

So I was the only one who was forced to stay. I still did not have the papers to leave the country. So I stayed raising—taking care of my two little siblings with him [the father], and I became a nanny without a salary.

It soon became obvious to Vega that being effeminate bothered his father enough to want to restrict the young man to the role of nanny for the younger siblings. Mr. Vega forbade Sábato from stepping out of the house. However, his rebelliousness grew in spite of the blows it earned from his father:

Mi papá me ponía de castigo, pero	My father would ground me, but I
ya yo me iba. Sabiendo que me iban	would go out anyway. Knowing that
a dar una pela. Bueno, una pela, no.	I was going to be punished. Well,
Una paliza era lo que me daban a	not punished, no. More like treated
mí [se ríe]. Es decir, ya yo no le tenía	to blows is what happened to me
miedo a los golpes.	[laughs]. In other words, I was not
	afraid to be beaten anymore.

By age fifteen, Vega had begun dating and having sex with several men, many of whom were non-Dominicans. He has rarely dated Dominicans before or after leaving the Dominican Republic because, as he put it, "No sé bregar mucho con el machismo del dominicano" (I do not know very much about how to deal with Dominican machismo).[20] Vega saved many of the small romantic cards and some of the money his partners gave him in a locked closet in his room. In addition, Vega saved cards from the various motels where he met his partners as souvenirs of their encounters, together with cigarettes and marijuana, which he had begun smoking. The tensions with his father escalated to the point that one day Vega walked in to find his father demanding that Sábato give him the key to the closet. "Yo le pasé la llave" (I handed over the key to him), Vega recounts,

Pero me mandé a correr en una	But I began to run before he opened
sola carrera antes de que él abriera	the closet. When he opened the
el clóset. Cuando él abrió el clóset y	closet and began to see all that was
comenzó a ver lo que había ahí, nada	there, he only said, "Find her!" [we
más dijo ¡Búsquenla! [nos reímos]	laugh] and the girl [Sábato addresses
y la muchacha [Sábato refiriéndose	himself in the third person] went
a sí mismo] iba lejos. Las paticas le	far. She was going so fast her legs
pasaban por las orejas mi amor: huye	brushed against her ears, honey: run
huye huye huye.	run run run.

Vega's account of what must have been a pretty difficult moment in his life gives a humorous spin to the coming-out narrative. Indeed, the humor of the story is partly due to the retrospective position from which it was told and from Vega's caricature-like description of his escape from his father's wrath. However, the humor of this particular anecdote also resided in his use of feminine pronouns to characterize what his father discovered. Inside Sábato's closet, Mr. Vega found precisely what Aníbal Guerrero's "straightjacket" masculinity masks: the symbolic woman (or *loca*) inside. One wonders, in the end, whether what seemed most outrageous to Mr. Vega was (1) that his son was gay or (2) that he was collecting souvenirs of his encounters with men.

It may be tempting to make an imaginative leap here and make Vega's story into a story of forbidden desire within a traditional family. However, the twists and turns of Vega's life do not allow for the reproduction of the tale of the queer exiled from the homophobic family. Yes, Vega ran, but only across the street, where he was protected by a gay neighbor. Vega continued to interact with his brothers, sisters, and mother, even though most of them were abroad and even after the patriarch stopped talking to Vega. Concerned about Vega's homosexuality—a secret he first shared with his oldest sister, who then passed on the information to everyone else—one of the brothers took Vega to a psychologist to see if there was something to be done to "fix" the young man. After the evaluation, Vega recounted that the psychologist said to the brother, "que yo estaba claro en lo que quería, que el problema lo tenían ellos en aceptarme o no, que ellos son los que tenían que cambiar su actitud" (that I was very clear about what I wanted, that they were the ones with the problem of whether to accept me or not and that they were the ones who had to change their attitude). The psychologist recommended that all the relatives undergo therapy to accept Vega.

Despite the commotion caused by Vega's departure from his paternal home and by the revelation of his homosexuality, Vega continued to date men until meeting the man who became his first partner. Vega was seventeen. His partner was a foreign man ten years older than Vega, who made a living as a writer and gave Vega financial and emotional stability, in addition to teaching him about culture and the arts. They moved in together, and it was while living with this man that Vega grew discontented with what the Dominican Republic could offer him. He was also increasingly frustrated by the ease with which someone like him could end up in jail just for being perceived as a homosexual or for the friends he had. "En el '86" (in '86), Vega recalled, "hubo una elección en Santo Domingo, y gana Balaguer. Ahí yo digo, 'No, mi amor. La niña se va. Yo me voy de aquí aunque sea para Haití, pero aquí yo no me quedo'" (there were elections in Santo Domingo, and Balaguer won. At that point, I said, "No, honey. This girl is leaving. I am getting out of here, even if it is to go to Haiti, but I am not staying"). The first logical possibility for Vega was the United States, because his mother had obtained her green card and migrated, along with most of his siblings.

However, because she had been sponsored by a sister and had not included her children in the initial application, Vega had to apply for a U.S. green card on his own. Like his brothers and sisters, Vega attended an appointment with the U.S. embassy for his green card. Unlike any of them, Vega was asked to take an HIV test before a decision could be made. In the end, his residence was denied even though the test results came back negative. Vega and his closest relatives were sure that the first rejection took place because of the influence of a malicious relative who denounced Vega as a homosexual to the U.S. consulate.

Because migrating to the United States through his mother's sponsorship was impossible, at least for a while, Vega looked into other possible places to go live. Taking advantage of the fact that it was possible for Dominicans to travel to Italy without visas at the time, Vega left with a friend and obtained the support of his partner to do so. "Así que la loquita" (So the little queen), says Sábato, "ella . . . echó sus tres pantis, mi amor, cuatro brasieles, tacos y arrancó, mi amor" (she . . . packed her three panties, honey, four pairs of bras, high-heeled shoes and left).

Vega lived six months in Italy and then in Spain, working for Dominican sex workers in these countries, doing sex work, studying design, working in bars, having sex with men and women, doing drugs, and so on. As he recalled of his time in Spain, "¡Qué ricura! ¿Qué hice en España? ¡Qué no hice! [se ríe]" (How splendid! What did I do in Spain? What did I not do? [he laughs]). A second opportunity to have his U.S.-residence case considered by a consul brought him back to the Dominican Republic for a short time. Upon his return after an absence of two years, Vega found that AIDS had hit his circle of friends hard. Despite the fact that, as he recounts, "yo llevé una vida totalmente desorganizada de lo que era sexualmente activa y sin precaución" (I lived a completely disorganized life as far as being sexually active, without precautions), bumping into so much death upon his return was shocking to Vega. However, he knew that the living conditions in the country, especially for homosexuals, were not likely to improve with Balaguer still in power. After obtaining his green card, Vega immigrated to the United States and began to live with his mother.

The next few years of Vega's life were nomadic and tumultuous, as he traveled between Providence, Rhode Island, and New York. Vega dealt with bouts of depression, a drug habit, a relationship that continued long distance but that was falling apart, and financial instability. As soon as he broke up with his partner in the Dominican Republic, Vega began to pull himself together. He settled definitively in New York, kicked the drug habit, and found steady employment. Once he was in a position to do so, Vega helped those close to him who needed it with the tools that he found at his disposal. He began by getting his U.S. citizenship and marrying an old neighborhood friend still living in the Dominican Republic as a single mother. Apart from giving his last name to her child, Vega helped his friend obtain her green card. Additionally, he began to make his house available to any and all of his gay and lesbian friends who came to New York to visit or try out living in New York. He did some volunteer work at Alianza Dominicana, a community-based organization in Washington Heights, and got involved in gay activism and HIV research. He returned to school and finished his undergraduate degree. He even made amends with his father before Mr. Vega died. Through the difficulties he experienced, Vega counted on the unconditional support of his mother, brothers, and sisters, who integrated Vega's romantic partners and closest friends into their family.

However, it would be a mistake to think that the "families" Vega participated in were open to anyone. Vega may not be himself be an upperclass person, but he was aware of the relatively higher social status that his level of education and his appreciation of culture conferred upon him relative to other Dominicans in New York. His critical attitude toward things Dominican manifested itself in his view of himself as a "Dominicano del mundo" (Dominican of the world), or someone who happened to have been born in the Dominican Republic but whose vision of himself stood a certain distance apart from the limitations of national and ethnic belonging. There is no question that Vega's light skin contributed to the relative ease with which he adopted this view, even though Vega bumped into others who thought of him as any nationality but Dominican. Thus, although he wanted to distance himself from certain aspects of *dominicanidad*—marked by racial and class difference from where Vega located himself—Vega did not want a definitive rupture with his Dominican identity. Though Vega's friends included homosexual men and some heterosexual women from a range of backgrounds, many of them share Vega's rejection of elements associated with the working classes in the Dominican Republic and in New York. Finally, lesbian—and particularly butch-identified—women were generally marginalized members of these groups because of Vega's open distrust of them. The distrust of butch-identified lesbians was one of the few points where there appeared to be a consensus among the informants. Many of these men, when asked about why they had these attitudes toward butch-identified lesbians, revealed in comments like "es que se creen más hombres que yo" (they think they are more of a man than I) that beyond the question of gender nonconformity, these women threatened their male privilege because they demonstrated something painfully obvious to these men: it takes more than having a penis to be a man.[21]

Vega's dealings with family, migration, and homosexuality show that he depended on family and friends to the point of not departing definitively from them. Apart from illustrating the degree to which Vega's homosexuality shaped his relationship with his father, mother, and siblings, his narrative illustrates the degree to which Vega's homosexuality excluded him from the project of family reunification in the United States.[22] However, although it excluded him from family reunification at one point, Vega found ways of creating his own definition of family, adding his lovers and friends to the mix and making legal structures work to benefit the people he loved. His story stands at a certain distance from narratives of the atomized and individualistic queer subject. Apart from convenience, Vega shows that fighting for recognition and respect within the family can give people the entitlements of membership without compromising their sense of who they are.

::: Straddling Worlds

The portraits of Aníbal Guerrero, Arturo "Latoya" Mejía, and Sábato Vega do not exhaust the variety and range of negotiations narrated by the men I interviewed. Subsequent chapters will introduce other men and address the specificities of their lives and negotiations of families and other relationships. Nevertheless, the selections from these interviews I have discussed demonstrate the degree to which, as immigrants who experienced downward class mobility and hardship after migration, the informants did not have the choice of departing definitively from the worlds and attachments that made it possible for them to get to New York in the first place. Migration as definitive departure from the world of the known was not what they sought.

New York appears in these narratives not as a final destination but as another site for relationships that are multisited. The city was a protagonist in these narratives not because it was where these men continued to live (Mejía lives in Santo Domingo) or because it was the only place where they lived (all of them have lived in other parts of the United States, Mejía has traveled to Spain and other parts of Latin America, and Vega lived between Italy and

Spain before finally settling in New York). New York was important in these narratives as one site for these men's encounter with me, which produced retrospective life histories to an important degree inflected by the location where we were (*estábamos*) when we completed the interview.

There are other elements that make New York important to these and other of the men with whom I spoke. In particular, and as the next chapter shows, the proximities that I have documented throughout this chapter (within and outside of queer groups, within families, and toward fellow Dominicans in the Dominican Republic and in New York) will be explored further for the ambivalences and uncomfortable attachments they produce.

It is possible to view Guerrero, Mejía, and Vega as protagonists in small-scale epic narratives for recognition, dignity, and respect as they moved through the worlds where they have been. It may well be in those opportunities they took during the interview to rewrite or recreate family politics (Guerrero), articulate the pain they felt when facing hypocrisy and sex-negativity (Mejía), or underline ongoing struggles to integrate the worlds within which one lives (Vega) that these men showed how much of who they were exceeded our recorded encounter. As the witness to these faces and mouths as they moved to produce sound, I am like Roland Barthes staring at the eyes that had looked upon the emperor's brother—amazed. But my amazement does not stem from being privy to the way these men arrest their own histories through speech. Rather, I am amazed and gratified by the impurity of these heroes and their ability to resist and reproduce the mechanisms that they need to survive and thrive.

To migrate is not to leave.

To live in—that's more like it.

CHAPTER 3

Desencontrando la dominicanidad
in New York City

Sólo la cultura salva a los pueblos.—PEDRO HENRÍQUEZ UREÑA

Ser cultos para ser libres.—JOSÉ MARTÍ

Para volver al progreso tenemos que llegar de manos de la cultura.
—LEONEL FERNÁNDEZ

: : :

I discovered these three quotes, which adorn the austere façade of the Secretaría de Estado de Cultura (Ministry of Culture), located in Avenida George
Washington and facing the Caribbean Sea, while jogging during a recent
visit to Santo Domingo. It was early in the day, and I had passed by this
area twice before since my arrival earlier in the week. Maybe I had been
distracted by the heavy traffic during my morning outings, which rendered
crossing the street a complicated project. I may also have been distracted by
the pollution accompanying multitudes of cars, which made getting a whiff
of air from the sea a challenge, even in *el malecón,* where people in this city
would most likely come to view and smell the Caribbean Sea. Once my eyes
found the words of Henríquez Ureña, Martí, and Fernández, however, I
made a mental note to return with a pad and pen to copy them verbatim—
after all, "ser culto" (being learned) was not exactly what I was sweating for
that morning—and began to savor the density of the juxtapositions at the
corner where the Ministry of Culture was located.

The building of the Secretaría de Estado de Cultura shared the intersection with one of the signature monuments of the Trujillo regime: *el obelisco
macho.*[1] But my mind was not as taken by the phallic symbolism of Trujillo's
urban planning as it was by two structures that bear links to my childhood
and coming of age: the Parque Eugenio María de Hostos and the Asociación

de Scouts Dominicanos, both of which are on the block immediately to the west of the corner of the Ministry of Culture.

Parque Eugenio María de Hostos was a public park with an open-air theater, named in honor of the influential Puerto Rican independence leader, intellectual, and educator. It was closed off to public access for renovation at the time of my visit. The theater was used for various events, but it stands in my recollection for its connection with Dominican wrestling during the early 1980s, when I was growing up in Santo Domingo. Indeed, the Parque was where the ongoing feuds between the "good guys"—led by bearded Jack "Veneno" (Poison)—and the "bad guys"—led by bald and goateed "Relámpago" (Thunder) Hernández—were resolved every Sunday evening. I did not know this because I went there, but because I was addicted to the Saturday matinee television show where leaders and members of each side boasted of past victories and announced new physical tricks they would try on each other. Matches were part of the show, and my brothers and I imitated the tactics of submission we saw on one another—all except the ones that involved flying or long-distance jumping. "Todos los caminos conducen al Parque Eugenio María de Hostos" (All roads lead to Parque Eugenio María de Hostos), the announcer said several times each Saturday, sandwiching announcements of each match between commercials for Salami Induveca and Forty Malt, "un brazo de poder en cada cucharada" (one powerful armful per spoonful). I never went there on Sundays, partly because my dad had little interest in a bunch of burly guys in their forties touching one another on national television. All the *manoseo* (groping, manhandling), *juegos de manos* (hand games, touching), beer bellies, and poorly staged wounding and hurting suggested to him that the wrestlers were not serious men.

I often visited the northern side of the Parque, which was right around the corner from the wrestling theater and was where the Asociación de Scouts Dominicanos was located. My official troop, Grupo 9, was based in my old neighborhood of San Juan Bosco, a good half-hour walk north from here. However, camping trips that involved more than one troop tended to meet at the national headquarters. We also came down for special events, promotions, and one rather unhappy occasion during which I and other high-ranked teens (I could not have been older than fourteen) sang Beethoven's "Ode to Joy" with full-throated (and, if my memory serves, rather tone-deaf) abandon.

The conjunction of my recollections with the layout of this corner may say more about my own history than it does about the space itself. Yet the juxtaposition of the lofty words of Henríquez Ureña, Martí, and Fernández, lacing "cultura" to "salvation," to "freedom," and to "progreso" (with a symbol of Trujillista power and two sites of cultural practices connected to my own working-class childhood on George Washington Avenue) is striking. I offer this vignette (1) to illustrate the cohabitation of the past in the present and of the present in the past in my narration of the moment when I faced these words, and (2) to underline my inability to engage them without remarking on the proximity of the modernizing impulse of late-nineteenth- and early-twentieth-century intellectuals in the Hispanic Caribbean with the richness and heterogeneity of quotidian cultural practices and with the looming presence of the United States in Dominican life, past and present. This chapter is about the way history, nationalism, and empire inflect projects of self-making.

As the previous chapter illustrated, the migration and settlement of the informants in New York City involved the creative utilization of resources at their disposal. Some of these men accessed help made available by kin and non-kin relations linked to their biological families. Others availed themselves of resources through the assistance of other self-identified gay or bisexual men, and a third group moved between groups. In other words, migration, settlement, and survival for them depended strongly on straddling various worlds, with all of their requirements for membership and unspoken bases of connectivity and stability. There was no deciding between blood families and "families of choice."[2] Instead, these men accessed all of the support available being cognizant of multiple and contradictory exigencies of belonging.[3]

Given this ongoing association with fellow Dominicans before and after moving to New York, and given the relevance of things Dominican to their daily lives, it might be tempting to conclude that ethnic and national affiliation was a source of pride to the informants. While pride was part of what their nationality elicited in them, I was at first surprised to realize the extent to which this was also a source of unease, ambivalence, and even profound rejection. Scholars who study queer populations might explain the criticisms and negative attitudes documented in this chapter as stemming from the troubled relation queer subjects have with heteronormative nation-state projects. As my analysis will show, that explanation is far from complete. Although there were criticisms directed at Dominican society in general for its homophobia, many of these men created their own positionalities by establishing distance between the person they constructed in the course of the interviews and their perceptions of Dominican society and of Dominicans in New York.[4]

For this discussion, I will treat *dominicanidad*, or Dominican identity, as a contested repertoire[5] of meanings, practices, and institutional arrangements that the informants associated with being Dominican.[6] By emphasizing the *contested* nature of this repertoire, I point to its mediation and reworking in figurations and their valences in production, exchange, consumption, and distribution—in this context, not centered in the traditional artifacts engaged in cultural critique but rather centered in the perceptions that emerged in research interviews.[7] The findings discussed here echo Silvio Torres-Saillant's observation that identity constructions such as that of the *Dominican-york* have to be engaged and understood as created in circuits of representation largely shaped by the desire of the Dominican Republic–based middle and upper classes to discredit New York–based Dominicans.[8] Ideas about the alleged pathologies of Dominicans in New York pointed to men's racial and class anxieties as they experienced downward class mobility after migration. Nevertheless, stereotypes of the Dominican-york were only part of the story.

A useful way to think of the range of views expressed by the men interviewed for this book is along the lines of what Néstor E. Rodríguez argues for Dominican literature of the 1980s: these interview excerpts are evidence of the informants' *desencuentros*, or failed encounters, with dominicanidad in New York.[9] First, Rodríguez explains that beginning in the 1980s, Caribbean literatures charted transformations in the regional ethos through local negotiations of global restructuring. Then he suggests that appreciating the intervention of Dominican authors who interest him requires rethinking the definition of literature and its role in untangling cultural identity. Instead of models that align literary production with the rearticulation of the nation-state, "se trata de la redefinición de la literatura como espacio de desencuentro entre ciertos relatos normalizadores de la nacionalidad y modelos más lábiles de identidad cultural" (the task at hand is to redefine literature as a space of desencuentro between some normalizing narratives of [Dominican] nationality and more flexible [slippery, fragile, unstable] models of cultural identity).[10] Though the archive that emerges from my interviews can be interpreted in general as a space of desencuentros akin to those Rodríguez suggests could redefine literature, I am more narrowly interested in characterizing the views the informants expressed as desencuentros with existing models of Dominican identity. Instead of seeing the interview material to be discussed here as windows into the realities of the informants, I treat this material as a series of interventions that illustrate the various paths of self-fashioning these men took during the interview encounter.[11]

Migration, settlement, and ongoing interactions with Dominicans and other populations in New York set in motion processes of recognition, evaluation, and self-fashioning premised on the vibrancy of and need for transnational support and the informants' growing awareness of themselves as racialized subjects and modern gay men within a sphere that historically has been dominated by imperial designs of the United States. Geographical displacement and the immediacy of racial and class subordination in the United States provoked a desencuentro with dominicanidad in New York. Whereas in many ways the negative light these men cast on Dominican identity made it antithetical and irreconcilable with gayness and modernity, the language of race mediated a strategically ambiguous engagement with the possibility of being Dominican and modern in ways that rejected nationalist phobias and that made some of these men "Dominicans of the world."[12] Regardless of (1) the ambivalence they expressed about their proximity to the "pathological" sides of dominicanidad (represented by the figure of the drug dealer in New York, for instance), (2) problematic aspects of official representations of Dominican society "imitated" in the United States (e.g., racism, authoritarianism, homophobia),[13] and (3) the ignorance and "backwardness" of their compatriots, these men voiced discomforts and critiques to bolster their self-fashioning as modern gay men and cosmopolitan Dominicans. Much of the material that follows reveals that expressions of the advancement (social, symbolic, and material) experienced through migration resorted to comparisons between a "here" (United States = full of possibilities) and a "there" (Dominican Republic = full of limitations). Nevertheless, the discursive work the informants did through their commentary on fellow Dominicans reveals the ways in which the "there" interpenetrated the "here" they described, critiqued, questioned, rejected, and ultimately reworked in interview exchanges.

Furthermore, these men deployed, critiqued, and reworked perceptions, categories, and understandings that have a long history in Dominican national (and, more recently, transnational) cultures. Thus, despite their critical engagement with dominicanidad in New York, many of the men I interviewed drew from a collective repertoire of understandings that were, themselves, embedded in Dominican cultures as well as globalizing "gay" discourse. Much attention has been given to the effect of transnationality and mobility in nurturing bases of distinction and hierarchies of inequality between migrants and nonmigrants, especially in the context of the return of displaced persons to the Dominican Republic.[14] Through its focus on the way Dominican immigrants view the New York where they arrived and negotiated their relationships with other immigrants, this chapter suggests that their collective understanding and investment in structures of inequality preceded their geographical displacement. Indeed, the informants produced themselves as they remade dominicanidad in New York.[15]

::: The Unsettling Proximity of the Same

The men with whom I spoke offered a range of perspectives on Dominican identity and presence in New York. Most of them coincided in stating that many practices, institutions, and ways of thinking they associated with Dominican society appeared in New York. Though a source of comfort and pride for some informants, expressions of dominicanidad were a source of ambivalence and rejection in others. But the pride, ambivalence, and rejection that appear in the comments in this chapter illustrate a critical engagement with dominicanidad, including the historical disjuncture between the aspirations of the Dominican intellectual elites and (1) the composition of the Dominican population; (2) the influence of the settlement in New York; (3) Dominican classism, sexism, racism, and homophobia; and (4) Dominican ethnic and nationalist insularity in the face of a changing world.

Many informants expressed an overall sense that they saw echoes of Dominican society in New York. A more contentious issue was the degree of "imitation" involved and what this meant to the person who shared that view with me.[16] When I asked him about what contrasts he found between life in the Dominican Republic and in New York, Pablo Arismendi responded: "Encontré gran similitud a la República Dominicana por la gente . . . Y era como lo mismo. Las bodegas: allá son pulperías, colmados. Eran como ver lo cotidiano" (I saw great similarity [between Upper Manhattan] and the Dominican Republic because of the people . . . It was basically the same. The bodegas: over there [in the Dominican Republic] they are *pulperías, colmados*. It was like seeing what you see every day). Like other informants, Arismendi located comfort in the presence of other Dominicans and of working-class institutions such as the bodega in Upper Manhattan. But that was a comfort that he indexed as *lo cotidiano* (quotidian experience). In suggesting that there was no contrast between daily life in the Dominican Republic and

New York, Arismendi emphasized the recognition that sprung from view-ing bodies and institutional spaces reminiscent of the life he lived before migrating. In other words, his response stressed the repetition of a "there" (Dominican Republic) in the "here" (United States) where he was located (*donde estaba*).

But even in this initial example, it is clear that the here did not *repeat* but rather *interpenetrated* the there. This was signaled by Arismendi's move-ment between words to describe a grocery store. There (in the Dominican Republic), as he explained, grocery stores were called *pulperías* and *colmados*, whereas here (in New York) they were bodegas.[17] *Bodegas*, in Arismendi's usage, did not just signal the way New York City–based grocery stores "imi-tated" those that could be encountered in the Dominican Republic. Aris-mendi's use of *bodega* also signaled the Spanish and Hispanic Caribbean influence in New York. The issue may appear to be one of simple transla-tion, because for Arismendi, after all, the three words referenced the same institution. Two aspects of his observation interest me: first, Arismendi's recognition of lo cotidiano, and his comfort in that recognition despite the changed setting, and second, that what Arismendi named pointed to the cross-national encounters and proximities that characterize immigrant life and institutions in New York. To be (*ser*) a colmado or bodega depended on where they were located (*estaban*). Names given to quotidian institutions in-dex dense historical and cultural encounters; shuffling between names sig-nals Arismedi's recognition of the conjunctures of site, space, and temporal-ity that obtain from the words one uses to describe quotidian institutions.

That Arismendi finds comfort in visiting working-class institutions, such as bodegas, may be partly connected to his own working-class background. Thus, his perspective is crucially marked by a commonality of class elements that Arismendi recognized in New York. Others found signs of working-class Dominican life in New York distressful, not comforting.

Aníbal Guerrero, himself also coming from a working-class background, explained that he distanced himself from other Dominicans after arriving in New York. Comfort was anything but what he associated with being near his compatriots. As he shared, "Yo nunca tuve dominicanos amigos aquí, en Nueva York. . . . por la sencilla razón de que cuando yo vivía en Santo Do-mingo, la forma en que ellos le hablan a los dominicanos que son homosex-uales, you know, el racismo y todo eso. Pues yo pensaba que el dominicano de aquí iba a ser lo mismo" (I never had Dominican friends here, in New York. . . . for the simple reason that when I lived in Santo Domingo, I saw how they spoke to other Dominicans who were homosexuals, you know, the racism and all of that. I thought Dominicans here were going to behave the same way). Guerrero mobilized the word *racismo* to point to the mistreatment of homosexuals (that is, interactions that presumably involved teasing, derogatory comments, and hate speech), and not to signal the specifics of racial discrimination in the Dominican Republic. Instead of "correcting" his usage, I view the displacement and relocation of "racism" in this instance as Guerrero's way of suggesting the entanglements involved in discriminatory practices (race, class, and sexual identity) and their effectiveness in creating and sustaining social inequalities, as it is evidenced by his commentary on the Dominicans he met in New York. Furthermore, *racismo* constituted the matrix through which he understood homophobia. This means that Guerrero came to conceptualize and name homophobia in the United States through the language of race—a conceptualization informed by a context in which racism is the medium through which he and other immigrants come to understand all other discriminations. The deployment of *racism*, then, revealed the expansion of Guerrero's discursive repertoire, his cannibalization of a vocabulary of struggle and marginality in the United States.

Guerrero mentioned that his sense that fellow Dominicans would mistreat him made him shy away from friendships and romantic and sexual entanglements with them. By the time we had our interview, however, he mentioned that he had begun participating in gay Dominican events and that he noticed that Dominican gays "se están como instruyendo más de cómo son las cosas aquí y viven una vida más abierta" (are better educated about the way things are here, and they are also leading more open lives). "Instruyéndose" (becoming educated), as Guerrero saw it, did not just signal adapting to a new environment; it also involved adopting U.S.-based conceptualizations to make sense of one's experience and that of others. Indeed, it was in this regard that Guerrero pointed to the limits of his fellow gay compatriots. He had not been heartened by some of the gay Dominicans he met: "Por el sistema de vida en que yo he vivido y que todavía tengo en mi mente de que son más racistas de que son personas que me van a juzgar más y he tenido la mala suerte de que sí, de que personas dominicanas con las que yo me he juntado siempre viven llevándome la vida . . . siempre viven . . . como con esta envidia de que yo soy más que tú y que mírame la ropa que yo tengo" (based on my experience, I still think that they are more racist, that they will judge me more, and I have been unlucky to find that to be the case. The Dominicans whom I've met have always kept close track on my life . . . they live . . . with this envy that I'm more than you, look at the clothes I have [and you don't]). Guerrero's usage of the word *racismo* in this passage points to his effort to find adequate language to capture the degree to which forms of hierarchy building, which he associated with Dominican society, presented themselves in his relationships with other self-identified gay Dominicans in New York.

However, his observations rested on seeing his recollections of life in the Dominican Republic set against the experience of the relocation of hierarchical categories through bodily displays. His comment about the way people judged his choice of brand-name clothes to signal distinction illustrates the way that, in his mind, being near other Dominicans involved continuing engagement with the mechanisms Dominicans used to establish and sustain boundaries and distinctions (of class and race) among themselves. By *racismo*, then, Guerrero indexed a range of practices of social hierarchy construction and marginalization that exceed the literal meaning of the word. In other words, this remark pointed to Guerrero's recollection as an epistemological and empirical resource, which he used as a barometer against his present interactions with fellow Dominicans.[18] In this discussion, Guerrero addressed class distinction specifically. But his insights make clear that American concepts to analyze racial discrimination provided Guerrero with the language, perhaps for the first time, to analyze and critique other discriminations, or discrimination *tout court*.[19]

Other informants described existing relationships with Dominicans in New York and expressed admiration for the hard work of Dominican immigrants. At the same time, they highlighted that there were important generational differences between waves of Dominican immigrants. Javier Acuña pointed out that he had stayed in touch with the people from his hometown who migrated to New York, but that some attitudes in more recent waves of immigrants distinguished them from the first Dominicans Acuña met. "Ahora hay otra generación ya que es mucho más agresiva," he said:

En el sentido de que quieren . . . profesionalmente establecerse aquí y ese tipo de cosas. Antes la gente era como muy pasiva. Llegaba aquí con un estilo de vida un poco—que yo jamás he pensado que es mejor que vivir en RD, ¿tú ves? De tu casa al	There is another generation now that is much more aggressive in the sense that they want . . . to establish themselves professionally and things like that. Before, people were very passive. They would arrive here with a lifestyle a little—that I never

trabajo y del trabajo a tu casa . . . Pero yo soy dominicano cien por cien y yo adoro a mis dominicanos . . . Pero ahora hay un movimiento de dominicanos fascinante, ¿me entiendes? Hay una comunidad dominicana con más carácter, yo diría, con la cual yo me siento también más cómodo. thought would make living here better than living in the DR, you see? From home to work and from work to home . . . But I am one hundred percent Dominican and I adore my Dominicans . . . But now there is a fascinating movement of Dominicans, you see? There is a Dominican community with a stronger character, I would say, and I feel more comfortable with them too.

Acuña's view of his fellow Dominicans—personal and collective pride combined with disagreement with their so-called lifestyle choices—illustrates the difference in class position and material conditions that gave someone like him (from an upper-class background in the Dominican Republic, and a college-level counselor at the time of the interview) choices that others did not have. In other words, what may have been for him a matter of "lifestyle" choices may not have been a choice at all for the target of his critique, especially given the material conditions which many Dominican immigrants face daily.

Yet Acuña was not alone in expressing connection with fellow Dominicans while criticizing them for their inability to commit to their social advancement in New York. Informants often referenced this particular failure of their compatriots by voicing a critique of the ideology of return to the homeland. As Claudio Báez put it, for example, "Los dominicanos tienen un deseo de triunfar increíble. Y son capaces de hacer lo que haya que hacer, desde matar y asesinar hasta tener dos y tres empleos en un día para hacerse de un dinerito para irse a vivir en la República Dominicana, a pasar trabajo sin agua y sin luz" (Dominicans have an incredible desire to succeed. And they are capable of doing whatever they need to do, from killing someone, to having two or three jobs so they can put together savings to go back to the Dominican Republic, to a hard life without water and electricity). What this informant saw as a problem was not Dominicans' drive to success but their investment in signs of material wealth in the homeland. As we will see below, it was not a coincidence that this informant referenced the lack of water and electricity to accentuate the futility of return. Unavailable drinking water and electricity demonstrated the incapacity of Dominican society to provide its citizens with the bare minimum amenities for civilized, modern life. It was for this reason that returning was futile.

The degree to which the return to the homeland is central to Dominican immigrant life in New York gave many informants pause. These men argued that the lives of some Dominicans were organized around this longing in a way that did not allow immigrants to focus on living and advancing in the United States. For these informants, longing for the homeland was a negative distraction from the more urgent need to settle in the United States. Alfredo Perales, a forty-year-old health professional and community activist, illustrates this view. Perales was critical of an aspect of Dominican immigrant life touted by scholars of transnationalism: the coordination of life between the homeland and the receiving society.[20] Apart from belonging to a family of professionals—and enjoying the benefits of a financially comfortable upbringing—at age fourteen, Perales started traveling to the United States several times per year. At the time of the interview, he enjoyed a degree of mobility that was uncommon even among the men I interviewed. Although he had not acquired full validation of his medical training—Perales tried but did not succeed in passing the required examinations—he worked in the health field. He also shared an apartment in downtown Manhattan with a white lover of many years.

Thus, Perales's critique of holding on to the homeland was shaped by his background in the Dominican Republic, his aspirations of upward mobility in the United States, his ability to travel as a permanent U.S. resident, and the facility with which he moved within middle-class circles in the Dominican Republic and the United States. As Perales explained,

Yo veo esto desde este punto de vista: yo estoy en Estados Unidos; yo debo pensar y debo hacer lo que hacen en Estados Unidos. O sea, yo no vivo aquí pensando en que yo me voy a retirar para Santo Domingo. Yo vivo aquí pensando que esta es mi vida, esta es la pareja que yo escogí. Aquí es que yo estoy. Yo me siento bien, me siento contento, y yo voy a seguir.

I see it from this point of view: I am [estoy] in the United States; I should think and should do what people do in the United States. In other words, I do not live here thinking that I am going to retire to Santo Domingo. I live here thinking that this is my life; this is the partner I chose. Here is where I am [estoy]. I feel good, I feel happy, and I am going to go on. I

Yo pienso que la mayoría de nosotros, aunque estamos aquí, lo que pensamos es en allá. Ese es el principal problema de por qué nosotros no nos estabilizamos realmente en este país. La gente me pregunta a mí, "¿Cuándo tú te vas?" "Yo no me voy. ¿Por qué, si yo estoy bien aquí? Mi vida ha estado muy bien. ¿Por qué me voy a ir?" Y me hace falta, o sea, mis amistades en Santo Domingo, me hacen falta muchísimo. Cada vez que yo voy me da nostalgia, pero yo decidí mi vida hacerla aquí y ya, la tengo hecha aquí. ¿Por qué la voy a dañar? ¿Por qué la voy a destruir?

Hay mucha gente que lo ve como algo positivo, el que la gente viva en dos mundos. ¿Cómo lo ves tú?

Cuando tú vives en dos mundos, tú no te estabilizas en ninguno de los dos. Tú no tienes paz interior, sobre todo. O sea, yo lo miro desde ese punto de vista. Si yo estuviera aquí y viviera también en Santo Domingo, yo no tuviera. O sea, estuviera allá y aquí y allá y aquí—y eso no puede ser. O sea, una dualidad como esa lo que hace es que te descentraliza de tu vida, de tu carrera, de todo. O sea, tú estás aquí o estás allá. Que tú quieras ir todos los días allá: perfecto, pero tú estás aquí. O sea, yo entiendo que las dualidades nunca son buenas.

think that the majority of us, even though we are [*estamos*] here, we keep thinking of life over there. That is the central problem of why we do not really stabilize ourselves in this country. People ask me, "When are you going back?" "I am not going back. Why? I am fine here. My life has been in good shape. Why am I going to go [back]?" And I miss it, you know, my friends in Santo Domingo, I miss them very much. Every time I visit I feel nostalgia but I decided to have a life here and that's it, I have it made here. Why am I going to damage it? Why am I going to destroy it?

There are many people who see it as something positive, people living in two worlds. How do you see it?

When you live in two worlds, you do not achieve stability in either of the two. You don't have internal peace, above all. In other words, I look at it from this point of view. If I was [*estuviera*] here and also lived in Santo Domingo, I wouldn't have . . . In other words, I would be [*estuviera*] there and here and there and here and there—and that cannot be [*ser*]. A duality like that decentralizes your life, your career, everything. In other words, you are [*estás*] either here or there. If you want to visit over there every day: perfect, but you are [*estás*] here. In other words, I believe those dualities are never good.

Perales suggested that psychological orientation should match geography. This was something that, throughout this excerpt, he stressed through repeated use of the *estar* form of the Spanish "to be." Defining who one is or who one might become depended on an explicit engagement with where one was located. The model presented is not assimilation in the sense of letting go of the homeland; Perales's model involved a psychological reorientation of energies, a channeling of objectives and practices through the exigencies of where one is (*está*). It required focusing on building a future in the United States, the physical location where he is (*está*). Like Perales, some informants viewed a longing for the homeland as an obstacle when it went beyond certain limits. It was one thing to travel to the Dominican Republic whenever possible, eat plantain products, dance the merengue, go to Dominican parties, and discuss the current political situation in the homeland. It was quite another to walk around with a copy of the *Listín Diario* under your arm and to make living "there" the referent of your daily existence in New York.[21] This orientation toward the homeland was particularly disturbing when it interfered with a person's mastering English, getting a decent job, or changing a legal status (from undocumented to documented).

Fundamentally, Perales suggested that making the homeland central to immigrant life was an obstacle to upward mobility in the United States. Working-class and undocumented participants were also critical of members of their circles who "stayed" (psychologically or emotionally) in the Dominican Republic. As Guerrero's comments demonstrated, however, the concern with moving away from ways of thinking associated with the homeland also involved putting distance between themselves and the mechanisms they associated with being marginalized or rejected by others in the Dominican Republic. But the participants most troubled by the retention of the homeland as center of immigrant life were those who perceived themselves as upwardly mobile. This tended to be the case even in situations in which the speakers' aspirations of upward mobility and competencies were incommensurate with their accomplishments in the United States, or where downward class mobility invalidated the cultural and social capital they enjoyed or accumulated in the Dominican Republic, as part of middle- or upper-class families, or through educational and professional accomplishments of their own. Holding on to the homeland, as many of these men saw it, was in conflict with their aspirations.

Perales argued that lives lived "between worlds" did not offer those who lived them psychic stability and inner peace. For him, there could be no peace in juggling two worlds at once, even though he acknowledged how much it pained him to be away from his family and friends in the Dominican Republic, or how much his frequent visits to the homeland were his way to travel back and forth between these physical and psychic locations. Other informants went much further than Perales by arguing, in no uncertain terms, that immigrating to New York was not just about moving geographically. For them, it was about changing the way one viewed the world. And, in this sense, many of them observed that their fellow Dominicans also fell short.

::: *Progreso*

To move to New York affords the displaced person the possibility of pursuing something valuable to the informants and to Dominican communities everywhere: *progreso* (progress).[22] Some informants pointed to the disjuncture between their aspirations to tap into progreso and their impressions of other Dominicans in New York. Indeed, some of the harshest critiques of Dominicans appeared in this context—critiques that established boundaries between the person speaking and their compatriots through the mobilization of categories that have a long history in Dominican culture.

An initial articulation of an ideology of progreso in Dominican history, informed by nineteenth-century liberalism,[23] occurred in the late nineteenth and early twentieth centuries during the emergence of a generation of young intellectuals who sought to reinvigorate the project of the nation-state by infusing it with a forward-looking orientation. As the historian Teresita Martínez-Vergne explains, these thinkers were part of a self-proclaimed "intellectual leadership" of the country who intervened in ongoing debates about the present and future of the nation while authorizing themselves on the basis of the knowledge they contributed. They were mostly young men and a few women who did not enter elite circles in power and politics because of their family lineages but because they received elite educations, had contact with European high culture, and began to write and pursue professional careers as intellectuals.[24] The generation preceding them had demonstrated reluctance or inability to sustain national autonomy in the face of the possibility of reestablishing the colonial order (through annexation to Spain, the United States, or Haiti) as *the* requisite for progress. In contrast, this new group of leaders sought to create a comprehensive agenda for what the country was and would become. Like other self-proclaimed intellectual elites in the Americas, these Dominicans believed themselves capable of formulating the path toward the progreso they idealized. But unlike other countries, in which intellectual leaders idealized the past for the sake of the march of the nation toward a future, the Dominican project of progreso turned away from the tumultuous past toward what Martínez-Vergne calls "a common destiny."[25] Rather than dwell on the fits and starts of Dominican nineteenth-century history, "political writers . . . chose not to revisit the past but rather to dwell on the advantages of a change in outlook."[26] They agreed that the key elements to fulfill the promise of progress were "education, employment, democratic government, national sovereignty, freedom of the press, and private property,"[27] yet their ideals confronted the reality of a racially heterogeneous and immigrant population (which included blacks from the West Indies who arrived in the country attracted by the boom in the sugar industry). They also had to confront the regional hegemony of caudillos as well as the difficulty of substituting collective landholding practices ("terreros comuneros," as they were known) for privatized properties for agricultural cultivation and exploitation.[28]

A consequence of the perceived disjuncture between the aspirations to progreso of the intellectuals and the realities of the populations to be enlisted in this project was a "civilizational" discourse focused on refashioning the behavior of the population. This was a discourse of reconstitution or reconstruction anchored in ideas about proper racial mixing (to produce lighter-skinned children) and a reduction of the "inferior races," which these thinkers perceived as an impediment to modernization. But the social engineering, which also expressed itself in Hispanophilia, focused on a racialist discourse that concentrated on quotidian practices, expressions of religiosity, and politics by average members of the society.[29]

Ideas of progreso were undeniably important for the regimes of Rafael Leónidas Trujillo Molina and Joaquín Balaguer in the twentieth century. Still, the discourse of progreso in their careers and state projects sustained key features of the ideologies articulated by late-nineteenth- and twentieth-century intellectuals: disdain for the population's African heritage and racial mixtures, Hispanophilia, and need for the support of peasants combined with extreme suspicion of them.

Despite the best efforts of intellectual elites in the Dominican Republic to modernize the nation, this work was undertaken under the political influence of the United States. As Hoffnung-Garskof has argued, the constitution of New York as the logical conclusion in the teleological narrative of progreso through migration, is not surprising in light of the asymmetrical yet intimate e███████ts between the two countries.[30] The massive exodus of Domi██ ███████ ███65 may have helped the Dominican and U.S. states resolve th█ ██████ █f political dissent caused by the changes following Trujillo'██████████ █, the Cuban revolution, and the April revolution (1965), as Ramona Hernández argues,[31] but the mobility experienced by working-class and poor Dominicans as a consequence of migration, and the way some of them have used that to reconceptualize progreso, is an unexpected consequence of the entanglements of empire: "Ironically, the United States, no historic friend of social advancement or political power for the Dominican poor, became a place for unprecedented social mobility and even for a measure of democracy."[32]

The informants engaged progreso in ways that resonate with the first articulation outlined above (the "civilizational" view of progreso), but some of these men transformed it as they mobilized this view for their discursive work during the interviews. For some informants, the settlement of Dominicans in New York replicated distinctions between "civilized" and "savage" Dominicans that have regional valence in the Dominican Republic. Rogelio Noguera, the light-skinned child of a landowning family in the Cibao region, for example, put it eloquently: "No me gustan los dominicanos [como vecinos] porque son muy asquerosos. Irresponsables. Personas que se creen el centro del mundo. No son muy sociables. No saben vivir en sociedad" (I don't like Dominicans [as neighbors] because they are filthy. Irresponsible. People who think themselves the center of the world. They are not very sociable. They don't know how to live in society). He drew a key distinction between geographical settlements of Dominicans in the New York metropolitan area. As he explained,

La mayoría, por ejemplo, de los emigrantes de aquí, yo los divido en dos áreas: los de Queens, Corona, que son de los sitios míos—Santiago, del Cibao. Entonces los que viven aquí, en el alto Manhattan que son muchos del sur, de la capital y de otros sitios. Y los dos tienen formas diferentes. Porque el cibaeño, por ser

The majority, for example, of the immigrants here, I divide them into two areas: those from Queens, Corona, who come from my places—Santiago, from el Cibao. Then the ones who live here, in northern Manhattan, many of them come from the south, from the capital and other places. And they behave differently.

campesino, es un poquito más respetuoso que el de sur. Los del sur, yo considero esa gente como semi-salvajes. Vienen de sitios peores todavía que los campos del Cibao. Donde la gente se hace caca en la calle. Yo no sé si tú te has ido por Neiba, por esos lados para allá, del sur, San Cristóbal—esos lados. La capital—imagínate, ni se diga. De los arrabales donde la gente vive en casas de cartón. Donde se hacen pupú detrás [de las casas de cartón]. Donde tiran los orines por la ventana.

Because the cibaeño, being a peasant, is a little more respectful than people from the south. Those from the south, I consider those people semi-savages. They come from places that are even worse than the countryside of el Cibao. Where people shit on the street. I don't know if you have traveled around Neiba, around those places in the south, San Cristóbal—those places. The capital—imagine, let's not even talk about it. They come from shantytowns where people live in houses made of cardboard. Where they shit behind the house. Where they throw urine out the window.

Rogelio Noguera's view was extreme. However, it was not that unusual for informants to manifest perspectives bordering on disdain and repulsion directed specifically at Dominican presence in Washington Heights. Another informant, for example, did not apply regional markers to distinguish settlements of Dominicans in New York, but he held a negative view of what has happened with Dominicans in Washington Heights. Dominicans, according to him, have "arrabalizado" (ghettoized) that part of the city.

What interests me about Noguera's perspective is the degree to which it suggested, yet again, the ways informants filter their impressions of their fellow Dominicans through the use of categories drawn from an existing Dominican discursive repertoire that distinguishes in explicitly racialized terms between people who come from the Cibao and those who hail from the southern part of the country. Noguera came from a rural background. He made a distinction between the "more respectful" (and generally, lighter-skinned) *cibaeño* and "almost savage" (also more strongly mulatto and black) *sureños*. In this way, he used place to index racial distinctions. At the same time, and in a way that parallels Guerrero's cannibalization of discursive registers (albeit for different purposes), Noguera mobilized homeland categories to dominicanize the geography of New York. It was significant that he referenced urine and excrement being thrown out of windows, or made anywhere except on a toilet, to emphasize the point that the Dominicans he was talking about were far from the person he imagined himself to be. While it is evident in his comments that the distinction between cibaeños and sureños still mattered to Noguera, the proximity of these groupings in New York—and the fact that he could be (and probably often was) confused with one of the "wrong" Dominicans—gave urgency to the distinctions he made in the interview. Furthermore, Noguera's invocation of "shit" points to the affective (and uncomfortable) proximity of that which he must symbolically excrete to produce himself.

One of the striking elements in Noguera's description of his relationship with fellow Dominicans was his unease at feeling that categories and ways of thinking about social difference and hierarchy that mattered to him did not matter to the gay men with whom he interacted. Like Guerrero, Noguera noted the growing importance of the consumption and display of material signs of progreso in New York.[33] But he had concerns related to the way people, whom he once knew were of humble backgrounds, forgot where they came from. "Estamos en la fiesta ahí," he recalled about a party he attended,

Y llega la loca ésta, "Ay. ¿Y esa camisa, dónde la compraste?" Digo, "en Conway." Pero que es un dominicano que yo lo conocía en Santo Domingo y vivía en unos arrabales de Santo Domingo, este, son de los que sufren del síndrome de que quieren ser pero que no pueden ser . . . *So* este, y mal vestido de to' la manera. Yo no sé. Aquí se ha arreglado un poquitito más. Parece que está copiando de otras locas y me dice . . . delante de to' el mundo, "Ella compra en Conway." Digo yo, "bueno, pues llevame a Macy's, que ahí es que tú compras." Pero mirándolo lo mal que estaba vestido y todo el mundo "uuuu" (haciendo bulla).

So this queen comes in, "Hey, where did you buy that shirt?" I say, "in Conway." But this is a Dominican whom I knew in Santo Domingo and he lived in one of the ghettoes in Santo Domingo. One of those who suffer from the syndrome of wanting to be but not having what it takes to be [elevated socially] . . . And he was badly dressed too. I don't know. He's improved a little bit over here. Maybe he's copying from other queens and he says . . . in front of everybody, "She buys in Conway." I said, "Well, take me to Macy's, then. That's where you shop." But I was looking at how badly dressed he was and everyone was like "oooo" (making a teasing noise).

After the commentary he shared earlier in the interview, it might appear odd for Noguera to be so forthcoming with this "queen" about shopping at Conway, knowing as he did that this admission exposed him to the derision of a person who wanted to establish distinction based on classed consumption practices. But Noguera's commentary about the exchange also indicated his perception that this "loca" (his use of this word here contains a strong element of dismissal of the person in question)[34] did not really know what it meant to be socially elevated. As Noguera said, "Yo nunca fui pobre. Pasé muchísima hambre, pero yo nunca fui pobre" (I was never poor. I starved many times, but I was never poor). In other words, Noguera's sense of his class position did not reside exclusively in material wealth; his family background together with his level of professional accomplishment made him socially elevated, despite the fact that Noguera may have "starved" once or twice in his life.[35] In contrast, this loca was someone Noguera suggested should have known better than to consider himself Noguera's social equal and possibly even his superior. In the views expressed by Noguera, migration to New York did not erase this person's origin, something that Noguera could only locate, or suggest, in his intimation that the loca dressed in poor taste. In other words, Noguera may have been the one shopping at Conway, but he knew what it took to be socially elevated. Presumably, Noguera was not afflicted by the syndrome that supposedly afflicted his rival in this exchange: that loca who did not know his place. Finally, there is a lack of certainty at the end of Noguera's commentary as to whether the loca returned to his place, or sense of classed and racialized subordination vis-à-vis his authentically socially elevated interlocutor, as a result of Noguera's reaction. The reaction of the group may indicate that they "got" Noguera's insinuation of his interlocutor's "bad taste" in clothes, but even if that part of the message was effectively communicated, it is not clear that everyone understood the background information about the loca's humble origins that informed Noguera's comment. Thus, Noguera's success was limited. The loca, on the other hand, may have been patently aware that for the purposes of the exchange at hand and given that all participants lived outside of the Dominican Republic, his humble origins did not trump the social-symbolic value of his consumption practices—especially since it was possible that Noguera and the loca were the only ones who knew of the latter's origins.

Some informants were troubled by the erasure of distinctions between good and bad taste, between rich or middle class and poor, between the educated and the uneducated, between acceptable and unacceptable consumption practices, and between licit and illicit forms of wealth accumulation, together with the erasure of spatial distinctions used in the Dominican Republic to index racial and class difference. Noguera clearly suggested, in his reimagining of spatial distinctions between Dominicans in Washington Heights and those in Corona, Queens, a way to mobilize Dominican social categories so as to indicate that cibaeños, even those in Queens, were way closer to behaving in a civilized way than were the "savages" of Washington Heights. For Roberto Panés, the problem was that the Dominicans who lived in Washington Heights did not have "culture." Panés was the twenty-eight-year-old white Dominican son of a doctor father and a factory-owner mother who had worked as a waiter ever since he arrived in the United States eight years before our interview. Panés was undocumented when we spoke. Yet his critique of Dominicans was also inflected by class bias, though he highlighted spatial divisions in the geography of Santo Domingo that disappeared in New York. When I asked what he meant when he said that Dominicans in Washington Heights "no tienen cultura" (do not have culture), Panés mentioned how "they" talked:

Yo nunca me imaginé que yo iba a llegar a un sitio y que se hable de droga delante de mí sin ningún problema en la esquina . . . Y yo veía a toda esa gente hablando así . . . que yo en Santo Domingo lo veía, si yo iba a un barrio. . . . Aquí no. Aquí yo tenía que convivir con ellos porque yo llegué a vivir en Washington Heights . . . El contraste fue horrible. Allá yo me codeaba con personas que iban a la universidad, que iban al colegio, que trabajaban . . . Aquí no. No es que yo me juntaba con ellos, pero cuando salía de mi casa tenía que verlos por obligación, ¿tú entiendes? Era como yo mudarme de donde yo vivía a un barrio de Santo Domingo. A Villa Juana . . . y decimos Villa Juana,

I never imagined that I would arrive at a place where people would talk about drugs in front of me, at the street corner of where I lived, without compunctions . . . And I saw all of those people talking like that . . . talk that I would witness in Santo Domingo if I went to a poor neighborhood. . . . That was not the case here. Here, I had to live with them because I came to live in Washington Heights . . . The contrast was horrible. There [in DR] I would surround myself with people who went to the university, who were going to school, who were working . . . That was not the case here [in the United States]. It wasn't that I would get together with them. The issue was that I was forced to see

mi amor, comparado con Washington Heights es que te digo, era un
palacio porque Washington Heights
es una mierda.

them as soon as I stepped out of
where I lived, you know what I mean?
It was like having moved from where
I used to live to Villa Juana . . . and
let me tell you, compared to Washington Heights, Villa Juana is a palace
because Washington Heights is shit.

The comparison of moving to New York with moving from the neighborhood where he was raised to a place that was in even worse shape than a
poor neighborhood in Santo Domingo underlined Panés's sense that he
paid a high price for migrating to New York. His first impressions of the
city illustrate the degree to which previously middle- and upper-class informants needed to rethink their relationship to the populations they encountered when they moved to New York. In this sense, Panés's effort to distinguish himself from "bad Dominicans" echoed the history of efforts by New
York–based Dominican entrepreneurs to claim middle-class respectability
for themselves in the Dominican Republic.[36] For Panés, the loss of social
status was located not only in having to interact with other working-class
Dominican New Yorkers. The people who talked about (and, presumably,
also sold) drugs and whose dealings he witnessed on a daily basis illustrated
Panés's sense that Washington Heights was "shit." Of course, there were
those who went to the university, to school, and who worked in Washington
Heights. As he pointed to the illegitimacy of the informal and illicit activities
carried out at the corner of his building, Panés did not concede that dealing
drugs was a form of work either. What was most troubling to him—and
this was something that his comments suggested strongly—was that these
less-than-respectable activities were being carried out where he could see or
hear about them. The erasure of the spatial distinction between privileged
and unprivileged Dominicans in New York troubled informants like Panés,
because they had to witness the activities others engaged in to survive. Activities like these were probably being carried out in his neighborhood back
in the homeland, but there he at least did not have to see them or hear them
talked about in polite company. The blunt and even cavalier quality of these
forms of economic exchange in New York challenged every form of respectability and decorum that Panés found acceptable.

After living in New York for more than three years, Panés moved to a city
in the southern United States. And it was in the context of living in a city

with a smaller presence of Dominicans that Panés found compatriots with values closer to the ones with whom he interacted before moving to New York. Although many Dominicans in New York were lured by the "street corner" (read: the drug trade) in his view, the Dominicans Panés identified in his new city were the ones who were "progresando" by working respectable jobs and pursuing a profession to make a living in respectable ways. When one is Dominican in New York, Panés observed, "inmediatamente te involucran con el que no trabaja, el que daña a la gente, el que tiene una bodega, el que vende droga en la esquina . . . aquí viene toda la basura dominicana . . . allá no. Allá ser dominicano . . . es simplemente ser latino" (others immediately connect you with the man who doesn't work, the man who ruins other people, the man who has a bodega, the man who sells drugs at the corner . . . here is where all of the Dominican trash comes . . . not there [in the city where he lives]. There, to be Dominican . . . is simply to be Latino). It is striking in this particular comment how different a working-class institution like the bodega looked to someone like Panés in contrast to my earlier discussion of Arismendi. Indeed, Panés viewed the bodega and the people who worked in them as precisely the kind of "trash" he associated with dominicanidad in New York and that he saw disappear into the label "Latino" in the southern city where he resided when we spoke. Given the collapse of categories of distinction used to establish racial and class boundaries in New York, Panés deployed spatial distinction yet again to illustrate the kind of Dominican with whom he identified. These were people, as he explained, for whom progreso was the most important project.

In addition, my translation of the masculine identification of the people with whom Panés argued he was connected with once in New York (as in "the man [el] who ruins other people, the man [el] who has a bodega, the man [el] who sells drugs at the corner") points to Panés's elaboration of his own respectable brand of masculinity vis-à-vis hypervisible masculinities in disrepute, such as that of the troublemaker, owner of the bodega, and drug dealer. The degree to which the object of both reviled and desired dominicanidad was a man will be explored in the chapters that follow. For now, the gendering of the dominicanidad that operated as the referent in this and other remarks by the informants points to the interarticulation of class, race, and gendering in the informants' self-making projects.

A final element that presented itself with insistence throughout the exchanges I had with informants went back to the idea that Dominicans in New York no tienen cultura. Panés elaborated his perceptions specifically in connection with his impression of Dominican involvement in the drug trade. Nevertheless, the discussion of cultura—itself also deeply implicated in past and present conceptualizations central to the way Dominicans imagine their relationship with the world—allowed some informants space to develop trenchant critiques of nationalist dominicanidad and offer avenues for the decolonization of Dominican society.

Many of the men who voiced opinions about their fellow Dominicans in New York, even those who expressed admiration for the hard work and dedication of their compatriots, agreed on being concerned over two issues: first, work as an end in itself, and second, consumption practices as the main way to show others one's advancement in society. In different ways, some of the informant perspectives touched on so far have already dealt with these concerns. But as encumbered as these critiques tend to be in establishing distance between the speakers and the working-class Dominican cultures that surround them, some of these informants located hope for themselves and for others in the collective project of breaking away from nationalist insularity. And education was a key instrument to embark on a project of this kind.

::: *No tienen cultura*

To work was not enough, and a few informants already pointed out that *progresar* involved much more than going from home to work and from work to home. I have already suggested that these perspectives generally came from informants who may have been better positioned than people who had to work two or three jobs to support their families. But a concern with the possible consequences of lives without aspirations—lived "passively," as Acuña put it earlier in the chapter—was a conformism that did not produce a worldview different from that held by Dominicans in the Dominican Republic.

In quotidian usage (one with which the men with whom I spoke were familiar) the concept of cultura is mobilized to indicate "a measure of national belonging but also a measure of class distinction."[37] This form of distinction is based on the cultivation of the self through education, and the concept has been historically associated with Dominican admiration or incorporation of European models to think about society and social hierarchy. Though the men in this study aligned cultura with education, professional advancement, and an appreciation of elite (European) arts, their deployment of the concept reproduced traditional middle-class disdain for the lives and values of working-class people while also, sometimes, turning the concept's historical valence on its head. Instead of simply mobilizing cultura in its traditionally racist and classist alignments with middle-class views of working-class people, some of these men appealed to cultura to stage sharp critiques of Dominicans' inability to deal with their African ancestry. Others appealed to cultura to signal an irreversible change in mentality, a newfound openness that jarred with the narrow-minded mentality of the people they encountered when they returned to the country to visit.

Panés was not alone in hoping to surround himself with people pursuing an education or people who reached a high level of education. Interestingly enough, Noguera mentioned during our interview that a lot of the people in his circles were gay, not only because he did not need to be guarded about his erotic preferences, but also because gay Dominicans tended to be better educated than the majority of Dominican populations. He found it difficult to have conversations with straight relatives about things other than baseball players, for instance: "A los maricones es que nos gusta la música, la danza o la pintura o leer un libro. Un heterosexual dominicano no se sienta como así a leer un libro, como eso es medio maricón, tú sabes . . . a mí me encanta leer libros y no me gusta sentarme con un individuo dominicano que no sepa . . . [con quien] tú no puedas hablar de nada" (We faggots are the ones who like music, ballet, painting or to read a book. A Dominican heterosexual [man] does not sit down to read a book—that's something faggots do, you know . . . I love to read books and I don't like to sit down with someone who is Dominican who doesn't know . . . with whom you can't talk about anything). In light of his earlier comments about the person with whom he had the exchange about buying clothes at Conway, the value Noguera placed on education was connected to his class-based vision of what were acceptable signs of progreso and achievement. Crucially, these were signs that needed to be on display. The clothes one bought at Macy's were not acceptable signs of progreso because they only adorned the body. What appeared more valuable about conversational exchanges informed by knowledge of music, ballet, painting, and reading was the display of an educated (evolved?) self. In other words, Noguera's observations suggest that faggots, unlike "normative" men who can talk only about baseball, represented the epitome of progreso insofar as their gayness allowed them to become hypermodern. They may not possess all the accoutrements of normative masculinity, but it is precisely because they appear eccentric to normative masculine ideals that they can open up their minds and eyes to something other than sports. The centrality of baseball to this presumably straight and ignorant interlocutor gave Noguera an opportunity to produce social elevation in the interview encounter by substituting and privileging cultivated knowledge of the arts over practices associated with popular and nationalist sports culture and masculinity. In a way that turned the tables on the unquestioned privileges that accrue to normative masculinity, heterosexuality, and nationalist sports, Noguera placed proud and straight male baseball enthusiasts in precisely the site of the ignorant dominicanidad that he wanted to keep at a distance.

Nevertheless, the realization of the value of wearing clothes and talking about books read or concerts attended with others happened in conversation, though the degrees to which they obscured the materiality of their own production were different: while displayed clothes were the direct result of one's consumption power (I bought what I could afford to buy), one's education involved material investments (e.g., buying the ticket for the ballet, purchasing the book) and a requisite level of appreciation, as well as the capacity to articulate that appreciation. As it is clear from Noguera's perspective, the ability to engage and sustain conversations of this kind was constitutive of groups of friends he valued.

The acquisition and display of accoutrements of cultural literacy was important for these men and definitely stood higher in the scale of value than what many of them viewed as the Dominican immigrant obsession with overtly materialistic displays of progreso. Aurelio Pedraza, for example, talked to me at length about advances of gay Dominicans in New York. During his response, he hailed me as his social equivalent and this book as part of my own project of *superación* (improvement, uplift) in the sense he was thinking about it:[38]

Muchos [gays] se han superado. Mira ahora: tú estás haciendo un proyecto que es para ti. Pero yo he visto que muchos andan por ahí . . . siendo un gay que está aquí en Estados Unidos porque su superación ha sido eso. Ya sea porque trabaja en un salón y tiene las manos llenas de anillos . . . y que cuando va a Santo Domingo va

Many gays have improved themselves. Look at yourself: you are doing this project for you. But I've seen many out there . . . being a gay person who is [está] here in the United States, because that has been their uplift. Maybe because he works in a beauty parlor and has his hands full of rings . . . and when he goes to

Centro Cervecero y se da el mejor	Santo Domingo, he goes to the Cen-
tíguere porque va con par de pesos y	tro Cervecero and fucks the hottest
lleva mucha ropa para repartir . . .	tíguere because he goes with a few
lo que les importa es tener un buen	dollars and a lot of clothes to give to
anillo y si usa peluca, comprarse una	friends . . . what matters to them is
peluca buena. Pero no se están apor-	to have a good ring and if he wears a
tando nada para ellos culturalmente.	wig, to buy a good wig. But they are
	not improving themselves culturally.

As someone who grew up poor but who worked his way up the Dominican social hierarchy through connections to the arts and artists, this informant located social distinction in the value that cultura has. But one element in his critique that was not as evident in Noguera's comments, but which may be relevant to both of them to some extent, was the value Pedraza placed on the possibility of individual self-improvement. In other words, while being vigilant about the class-inflected nature of what both these men said, the importance they placed in cultura exceeded its currency within circuits for the display and exchange of codes of distinction. In this sense, there were two key phrases he used: the first, which located the "achievements" of the men he criticized in the fact that they are (están) not in the Dominican Republic, and the second, when he suggested at the end that by buying gifts for friends and fucking tígueres when they returned to visit, the men he was talking about "no se están aportando nada para ellos culturalmente" (literally translated as "[they] are not contributing anything to their own cultural improvement"). In these two phrases, Pedraza located cultura and super-ación as lofty and valuable goals in themselves, as achievements that would contribute something to the life of these men. This is a sense of value he offered as counterpoint to distinctions and hierarchies fostered through life abroad (where living outside the Dominican Republic was, in itself, a person's only achievement) or returning to display that achievement through yet more material displays (the rings) or displays of financial power (fucking the tíguere).

Still, cultura amounted to something beyond a literacy one acquired in order to display progreso to others. More specifically, Pedraza's view of cultura as something one "contributes to oneself" suggests the possibility of reworking the concept in a direction that may still be ensnared in class bias but that challenges nationalist ideas of dominicanidad. In an interview exchange I quoted earlier, Claudio Báez praised Dominicans' desire to succeed and their extraordinary dedication to work. I did not mention then but will now address this informant's potent critique of what he perceived happened with Dominicans in New York. As he saw it, Dominicans lost the opportunity to rethink who they are politically:

Los dominicanos tienen una capacidad idiótica, fantástica . . . de calcar con un mapa los errores de su maldita vida social dominicana . . . tú te encuentras aquí con instituciones . . . que en realidad, manito, son un calco vivo y tendido de una sociedad trujillista sin Trujillo, balaguerista sin Balaguer, machógena, misoginista, racista, clasista— sumamente clasista . . . triunfar . . . para ellos es tener dinero para irse a vivir en la República Dominicana. Y esa capacidad de vivir en la Ciudad de Nueva York sin vivir en la Ciudad de Nueva York. Me explico: la mayoría de los dominicanos amigos míos, que yo conozco, straight o gay, no saben dónde queda el Guggenheim, no les importa un coño. Ellos sí saben que hay un sitio de pájaros en Queens que se llama Atlantis o que hay un parque con agua en Rye, Nueva York, que se llama Playland donde ir a hacerse pipí en la piscina. Pero ellos no saben dónde queda el Met, ni qué es el Met. Ni dónde quedan otros museos, ni lo que hacen. Entonces, esa necesidad que tiene uno en su país, tú sabes, de inmigrar, para venir a buscar una mejor vida—eso es muy bonito, eso es muy hermoso, como objetivo humano, de liberación, de

Dominicans have an idiotic, fantastic capacity . . . to copy[39] the mistakes of their fucked-up social life in the Dominican Republic . . . you find institutions here that are a loyal copy of a trujillista society without Trujillo, of a balaguerista society without Balaguer, a machista, misogynist, racist, and classist—very classist— society . . . to succeed . . . for them is to have money to go live in the Dominican Republic. And that capacity they have to live in New York City without living in New York City. Let me explain: the majority of the Dominicans who are my friends, the ones I know, straight or gay, don't know where the Guggenheim [Museum] is, and they don't give a shit. They do know that there is a place in Queens called Atlantis or a water park in Rye, New York, called Playland where they can go and piss in the pool. But they don't know where the Met is, or what the Met is. They don't know where the other museums are, or what they do. So, that need one has to leave one's country, you know, to immigrate, to come look for a better life—that's beautiful, wonderful, as a human objective of liberation, of social uplift . . . what we do here is work, work, work, be [estar] at home,

ascenso social . . . nosotros lo que hacemos aquí, manito, es trabajar, trabajar, estar en nuestra casa, ahorrarnos lo que podemos y después . . . irnos con diez maletas y pagar sobrepeso en American para traerle a todo el mundo un juguetito. save what we can and then . . . go back with ten suitcases and pay a fine for excess weight at American [Airlines] to bring everyone a little toy.

Like other informants, Claudio was distressed by signs that Dominicans did not see that progreso involved more than work and survival. Unlike others, this informant saw the retention, the *calco*, the imitation of what he called the "mistakes" of Dominican social life as the center of what held back Dominicans in New York. He was critical of New York–based Dominican institutions for retaining the more problematic aspects of Dominican nationalist culture: racism, classism, sexism, and homophobia. But he was also critical of the incapacity of Dominicans in New York to "integrate" themselves to life in New York—for him "work, work, work" amounted to "live in New York without living in New York." In a way that may be consistent with the class-inflected concerns already articulated by others, Claudio located cultural integration to New York in some of the more important and well-known bastions of mainstream Euro-American culture in the city: the Metropolitan and Guggenheim museums.

But Claudio was on to something more profoundly provocative in his critique, and offering more details from his narrative of grappling with being Dominican in New York will shed light on a key insight for him and other informants: to have the opportunity to live in New York was partly to enjoy the possibility of reformulating oneself, of becoming someone else and even, perhaps, of being Dominican in a different way, or even perhaps the possibility of "being" other than a mere "calco." In this sense, Claudio's desencuentro with dominicanidad points to the particular ways in which some informants looked at their proximity to other Dominicans as a constraint in the process of opening themselves to other influences, of becoming something (or someone) else.

Claudio explained to me that when he arrived in New York, he went to live in Staten Island, far away from the "manada" (herd) of Washington Heights. That experience of geographical distance from the spaces where Dominicans concentrated in the city allowed him to develop distinct perspectives on himself and his relationship to others. He mentioned that this "viaje interno" (voyage of introspection) involved understanding himself better through learning to appreciate contrasts with "the others" he found around himself as a worker, neighbor, and activist. During this painful process, Claudio recognized that he needed to rebel against dominicanidad, which, he argued, was "baggage," an obstacle to the new life he began to live:

Mis vecinos eran todos gente de color. Mis vecinos eran todos pobres. Mis vecinos eran todos, los que aquí, en este país se llaman, "the underclass" . . . un poquito más allá eran los proyectos. Entonces eso fue interesante porque eso me reubicó social y políticamente a mí. Me hizo recordar que yo no soy más que un maldito negrito en esta sociedad. Yo soy eso: un maldito negrito. Y eso puso todas las demás cosas en perspectiva para mí. Eso me dio a mí un eje en mi vida como inmigrante . . . Yo voy a vivir todos los días en esa batalla de . . . de borrar, de destruir la maldita dominicanidad con la que yo, por accidente, nací, y con la que yo no me puedo identificar porque ya yo te dije que es lo que la compone. Las cosas buenas que tiene la dominicanidad son tan pocas. Por ejemplo, el mangú y el merengue. Pero yo de mangú y de merengue no puedo vivir, Carlos. Dime, ¿cómo yo puedo vivir de mangú y merengue?

My neighbors were all people of color. My neighbors were all poor people. My neighbors were all those who are called, in this country, "the underclass" . . . a little farther down from where I lived were the projects. That was interesting because it relocated me socially and politically. It made me remember that I'm not much more than a fucking little nigger in this society. That's what I am: a fucking little nigger. And that put everything else in perspective for me. That gave my life a new center of gravity . . . I am going to live battling every day to . . . erase, destroy that fucking dominicanidad with which I was accidentally born and with which I cannot identify because I already told you what makes it up. There are very few things that are good about dominicanidad. For example, the mangú and merengue. But I can't live on mangú and merengue, Carlos. Tell me, how do I live on mangú and merengue?

Claudio's "viaje interno" resulted from the combination of introspection with experiences linked to his life in New York. First, he noted that he benefited from being geographically far from other Dominicans. That distance was beneficial insofar as it exposed him to the struggles and daily lives of people from other groups, all of which were "gente de color" who were also "pobre." The combination of distance from fellow Dominicans and of proximity with the plight of "the underclass" and inner reflection could have easily produced aversion and distance from those "others" who surrounded Claudio. But here is where cultura intervened in the mediating presence of James Baldwin, the African American gay novelist and critic, and one of Claudio's "prophets," as he claimed shortly after his remarks excerpted above. As someone who had studied modern literatures in the Dominican Republic and who could read in English, Spanish, and French, Claudio combined access and an appreciation of literary culture and university training with geographical dislocation even from other Dominicans. This combination of factors, training, and mediating presences produced a political awakening in Claudio, based on the realization that being in a new environment involved a new set of rules and a new opportunity to construct himself as a political subject. Furthermore, to become other than the "calco" of life in the homeland, which Báez saw as dominicanidad in New York, began by recognizing the blackness he shared with others in society. Race consciousness, sparked by the experience of migration and settlement, became the site from which to judge and critique other discriminations and the limits of dominicanidad as an education and self-forming practice.[40]

As he explained it, Claudio's new location and neighbors made him realize that becoming a subject was largely contingent on the conjunction of identification with location. For this reason, his statement of who he is (*quien es*) was based not on ontology but on the possibilities of political identification given his location (*donde está*). Claudio went even further when he suggested that dominicanidad was not something in which he was born, something internal. Instead, he viewed dominicanidad as something *with which he was born* but with which he could not identify. It is quite possible that he would have been able to distance himself from the elements of dominicanidad he did not identify with even if he had lived near other Dominicans. Indeed, distance from certain elements of dominicanidad characterized the perspectives of other informants whom I have discussed. Nevertheless, his trajectory was markedly different from others I have discussed throughout this chapter because of the importance to Báez's political awakening of his identification with literary culture, his high level of academic accomplishment, and the daily struggles of poor people of color in New York.

Claudio was specific about the elements of dominicanidad he rejected: these were those most closely aligned with the Dominican nation-state. Nevertheless, he found little value in what was left of dominicanidad (cultura popular) once stripped of the racism, sexism, classism, and homophobia of official nationalist cultura. When Claudio suggested he could not "live" on mangú and merengue, he echoed the ideas expressed by other informants—these practices may nourish, comfort, and even entertain, but they did not foster development of a different vision of what being Dominican could be. That "different" kind of Dominican was one who might open himself up to the "worldliness" of New York. That was a kind of Dominican who could be "nurtured" differently, who submitted his body and mind to different regimes of bodily production, and who literally moved to a different rhythm—to another mix of sounds and words.[41] Báez articulated a Dominican-inflected critique of a populism (represented by both the mangú and merengue as mechanisms to appease the population) that prevented a more authentic self-reflection. His antagonism, in this view, was directed not at Dominican authenticity but at Dominican imitation or calco. The mediating presence of James Baldwin and Báez's experiences suggest that he mobilized the rhetoric of Dominican antipopulist modernizers to underscore Dominicans' inability to reflect on their African heritage as emblematic of the other discriminations and injustices that make up their society.

Claudio's mention of mangú was not coincidental, for it signaled a distinction often made among Dominicans between food that fills your stomach and food that nourishes you. The plantain is a powerful signifier in this regard, associated with what is both most authentic and most "backward" about Dominican identity. According to this view, the consumption of elements associated with dominicanidad produces subjects unable to assimilate to modern life in the United States and to make strides within that society. Indeed, Báez's mention of mangú connects with the tradition of modernizing intellectuals who critiqued plátanos as the source of Dominican backwardness and obtuseness.[42] Contemporary versions of this view tend to emerge in a humorous vein among Dominicans. An example of this was the widespread criticism (in New York), during the time I conducted fieldwork, of then-president Hipólito Mejía's decision to change the breakfast of public school students from sandwiches to yucca. The general outrage over this decision sprang precisely from Mejía's rejection of the sandwiches and milk decreed as public school breakfast by New York–raised ex-president Leonel Fernández. Dominicans generally saw Fernández as a "modernizer" both in and outside the Dominican Republic. The criticisms and jokes provoked by Mejía's decisions were seen as part of a populist agenda meant to push the Dominican Republic *away* from modernity. Another example of the "outrages" of President Mejía's government was his offer to destroy a number of the highway projects developed by Fernández and plant those areas with sweet potatoes and yucca. Mejía was popular among poor and working-class Dominicans. However, Mejía's views disturbed Dominicans more attuned to Fernández's project of "making a little *Nueva York*" out of the Dominican Republic.

Mejía's populist project was incompatible with the vision of progress of some Dominicans. But their interpretation of his policies was incorporated into self-deprecating humor about food. Through these jokes, Dominicans could be critical of Mejía and express their ambivalence about the most authentic elements of Dominican national culture. Readers may be struck by the extent to which food consumption is a central feature of the expression of ambivalence about dominicanidad. Lauren Derby explains that metaphors of food and eating play on relations of power where boundaries between what is "foreign" and what is "internal" to Dominican identity have always been blurry. She suggests that "consumption has become a key arena in which anxieties over the dissolution of place in the transnational condition are expressed, and the boundaries redrawn."[43] Particular foods play central roles in jokes because "they hover on the borderline between metaphor and metonymy . . . foods are good to think with, but, given the right circumstances, they can also stand in for the thing itself."[44] When referring to a man who exhibits physical or phallic prowess without having much intelligence to accompany these attributes, Dominicans might joke that this person "es un plátano" (is a plantain) or "tiene un plátano en el cerebro" (has a plantain in the brain). The joke plays on the image of the plantain—a staple of Dominican diet—as phallic metaphor and as a metaphor for dumbness. The second meaning of the reference draws from the folk belief among Dominicans that plantains do not have nutritional value. In fact, many Dominicans believe that eating plantains makes you stupid and thus keeps you "backward" and underdeveloped and away from the modern. As Derby observes, "Dominican food is such a powerful conveyor of nationality that one could almost say that to eat Dominican is to be Dominican."[45]

An insight drawn from the work of Yolanda Martínez-San Miguel helps explain why many critiques of Dominican backwardness are articulated in a humorous vein.[46] Martínez-San Miguel's hypothesis is that the ethnic joke maps the limits between "self" and "other" in ways that project onto that other differences that threaten the coherence of the self (e.g., racial and class differences). Thus, in the case of the jokes that circulate about Dominican immigrants in Puerto Rico, tapping into the rich repertoire of jokes about Dominicans becomes one way of articulating a Puerto Rican identity.[47] I want to extend Martínez-San Miguel's insight by arguing that when Dominicans joke about their own backwardness, those jokes invite identification with dominicanidad while revealing the fractures of that identity along racial and class lines.

The informants elaborated ideas about the links of consumption and cultura not just in relationship to the modernity of Dominicans but also in relationship to generational differences among Dominican gay men in New York. Critiques of fellow Dominicans were not just articulated in terms of what may be holding them back from assimilating to American society, as shown in the discussion of Claudio's perspectives. These critiques were also articulated in terms of what may be holding Dominican homosexual men back from organizing as male homosexuals. One illustration of this was the view of Mauricio Domínguez, a self-identified black man of West Indian, or *cocolo*, ancestry,[48] an upper-class professional and community activist who has lived in the United States since the late 1970s:

¿Cuál dirías tú que es la distinción entre la generación quizás tuya o anterior a ti y esta generación que está subiendo ahora?	*What, according to you, is the distinction between your generation or the generation before you and this generation coming up now?*
La diferencia es, verdaderamente, única y exclusivamente [nos reímos] te lo voy a poner bien claro . . . bien claro . . . una familia americana se desayuna con cereals and milk . . . una familia dominicana se desayuna con plátano y salchichón. Estas loquitas dominicanas vienen subiendo comiendo plátano y salchichón, OK? Y si nosotros vivimos comiendo, comprando salchichón y hemos llegado al lugar donde estamos ahora, ¿qué tú	The difference is, truly, uniquely and exclusively [we laugh] I'm going to make it very clear to you . . . very clear . . . an American family has cereals and milk for breakfast . . . a Dominican family has plantain and salchichón for breakfast. These Dominican queens grew up eating plantain and salchichón, OK? And if we live eating, buying the salchichón and we have arrived where we are now, what can you expect from those

puedes esperar de estos que nacieron
aquí, que están criadas y que vienen
de esa producción [comiendo cereals
and milk]? Esto no va a ser fácil.

who were born here, those who were
raised and who come from this production [eating cereals and milk]?
They will be something else.

Domínguez's comment pointed to "plátano con salchichón" as emblematic
of what holds his generation back from organizing as a gay Dominican community, even while praising their accomplishments despite the "poverty" of
their dietary habits. To the extent that he drew on the dichotomy of the "internal" (e.g., plátano con salchichón) and the "external" (e.g., cereals and milk),
Domínguez's critique drew on language familiar to other Dominicans. "The
plantain today," Derby explains, "is often paired with the cornflake—held
to be the American national starch—as positively and negatively valued national parameters."[49] Domínguez saw the Dominican attributes associated
with the plantain in a negative light, one that men of his generation overcame to accomplish what they had accomplished in the United States.
Conversely, he saw the attributes of the "cereals and milk" or cornflakes
positively in their association with the United States and with the emerging generations of self-identified Dominican American gay and bisexual
men he admired. Progreso in the United States was possible for men of his
generation. Younger men will be even better able to organize because of
their integration into American society, symbolized by their different dietary
regime.

Self-deprecation was essential to Domínguez's critique of some of his
fellow Dominicans. However, he made a comment like this one in an interview with someone who was both a homosexual and Dominican. This suggests another nuance in the comment. As self-deprecating as it may be,
Domínguez's observation invited my recognition, co-identification, and
complicity. The extent to which I revealed my consent to Domínguez's invitation through my laughter reveals our mutual recognition as Dominicans.
Pointing to the "plátano con salchichón" thus relied on my understanding of their meanings. But the effectiveness of the exchange also relied on
Domínguez's expectation that I would identify with the class position from
which he made his comments. In other words, the exchange positions him
and me as upwardly mobile Dominican homosexual men. Dominicanidad,
then, is a discourse that is available to Dominicans to manipulate and joke
about. Whether Dominicans truly believe in the myths of the plátano or not,

Domínguez and I recognized each other as Dominicans by our ability to mobilize that discourse and manipulate it as such by a practice of *relajo*.[50] Derision and identification mingle in this instance to produce subjects who are Dominicans of a certain class position. Domínguez's comments suggest that dominicanidad, as seen by some informants, is incompatible with "progress." However, Domínguez also suggested that food and what is consumed can produce a certain kind of subject. Thus, men like Domínguez do not hold on to dominicanidad as a static, immutable reality. Indeed, Domínguez's comments reveal dominicanidad to be a process of becoming tied to specific social practices.

That capacity to become something else in opening oneself up to the world inevitably places the person who lives through such experiences at odds with Dominicans in the homeland, and it was upon return that some informants came to appreciate how much they changed and what those transformations meant to others. Sábato Vega captured this poignantly when he said, "Me siento las veces que he ido que ya no cuajo[51] . . . ya yo me considero un dominicano del mundo. Es decir, voy a ser un dominicano pero viviendo en el extranjero toda la vida" (I don't feel that I fit [make sense] . . . I consider myself a Dominican of the world. In other words, I am going to be Dominican but living my whole life abroad). But in explaining what he meant, Vega argued that what he experienced was not just a change of location but a fundamental change in mentality:

No me siento de que ya me identifico con la forma de pensar. Una vez, en una de mis clases de sociología, hablaron de Juan Bosch, de que Juan Bosch emigró y cuando volvió tenía tanto—veinte y pico de años—que no es que no era dominicano. Era dominicano, pero . . . su mentalidad había cambiado tanto y veía, tenía tantos conocimientos que el pueblo no lo aceptó. Y eso fue lo que él no entendió, que el público, que el pueblo se quedó estancado. Es que él creció intelectualmente, y que traía

I don't feel that I identify with the mentality. One time, in one of my sociology classes, there was a conversation about Juan Bosch, that he emigrated and when he returned he had been abroad for so long—more than twenty years—it's not that he was not Dominican anymore. He was Dominican but . . . his mentality had changed so much and he saw, he had so much knowledge that the people didn't accept him. And that was what he did not understand, that his public, that the people were stuck. He

ideas nuevas, pero que el pueblo no entendía nada de esa vaina. Eso mismo yo creo que es lo que pasa cada vez que yo vuelvo.

grew intellectually and he brought new ideas but the people did not understand any of it. That's the same thing that happens every time I go back.

Like other informants, Vega associated who he had become with a transformation that relies (to be effectively communicated) on statements of contrast between himself and other Dominicans. Clearly, Vega attributed a "fixity," an "estancamiento," to the mentality of Dominicans in the homeland that others have attributed to their fellow Dominicans even when everyone in question was an immigrant. By comparing himself with Juan Bosch (perhaps the most important twentieth-century Dominican intellectual, with a long history of left-leaning politics, life in exile, and international recognition), Vega revealed the capacity of cultura as intellectual growth to transform a person into someone who does not "cuaja" with a world closed off to new ideas, to new visions of the future. Clearly, Vega's was not a vision of cultura that was accessible to all, and he did not admit the possibility that being a "Dominican of the world" was achievable without leaving the geopolitical boundaries of the Dominican Republic. In this way, Vega's perspective was deeply rooted in his own experience of living in Europe and the United States, as well as in his own commitments to class differentiation.

Like all other informants, Vega pointed to a longing, rooted in the migratory experience and mediated by different forms of cultura, not necessarily to abandon dominicanidad but to rework a given repertoire to make it amenable to the Dominicans the informants constructed in the context of the interviews. Despite their eagerness to present themselves as different from the Dominicans in the Dominican Republic and the Dominicans in Washington Heights, the informants shared a perception of dominicanidad as a system of signs, as a repertoire, that was generally closed and insular in its nationalist and official guises but that they opened up in order to situate themselves in New York and the world. This process of self-fashioning often referenced rather stereotypical views of Dominicans in the service of constructing an individual self that was "up to date," as Aníbal Guerrero might have said, or "of the world," as Vega might have put it. Nevertheless, rejecting something is different than abandoning it altogether, and another characteristic that some of these men shared was having to reference that repertoire, whether they liked it or not.

The continuing engagement of the informants with their fellow Dominicans produced narratives of desencuentro with practices and meanings they
associated with dominicanidad in New York. Some of the men mobilized
figures of Dominican pathology and marginality to defend a professional or
middle-class status that was eroded by their proximity to their compatriots.
Others staged critiques of their fellow Dominicans that acknowledged their
hard work while voicing skepticism toward what the speaker perceived as
an immigrant overinvestment in the return to the homeland or an investment in forms of stratification and sociality associated with the homeland.
Despite where they stood on the benefits or drawbacks from Dominican
migration and settlement in New York, these men coincided in arguing that
while much remained the same, much had changed or needed to change in
the ways that they and their compatriots saw themselves in the world. What
was in dispute was the degree of change that was necessary.

An important means for these men to make intelligible and critique their
fellow Dominicans, the immigrant community in the United States, and
Dominican society was the language of race and race discrimination. The
use of this language suggested their strategic use of American discourses
of racial discrimination as a way to deal critically with Dominican society
and culture. In the most radical example, that of Claudio Báez, he activated
the language of race to inflect a critique of dominicanidad that may echo
the modernizing discourse of intellectuals of the late nineteenth and early
twentieth centuries in the Dominican Republic but that was most concerned
with the inability of Dominicans to deal with their African heritage. As
he saw it through his political critique of Dominican white supremacy, and
as others formulated through appeal to transnationality and cosmopolitanism, the point was to displace oneself physically and open oneself up to the
world.

Some of the men claimed blackness as constitutive of who they were
(e.g., Domínguez in connection with his cocolo heritage, Báez in connection
with his political awakening and coalition building with other poor persons
and people of color). However, the deployment of race as epistemological
entry point to a critical engagement with marginalization and injustice in
Dominican communities inside and outside the geopolitical boundaries of
the Dominican Republic is conceptually separate from quotidian engagements with African Americans. Although some of these men reported

integrating a few African Americans into their circles, expressions of distance, rejection, and racism toward African Americans surfaced in informal conversations and exchanges. This racist commentary, which was also directed toward Puerto Ricans on occasion, specifically targeted so-called pathologies associated with working-class populations—in many cases because they could tell that someone was Puerto Rican or African American, but in most cases because differences across ethnic and racial lines were hard to pin down, particularly among second-generation Afro-Latinos.[52] In this way, part of the discursive work of the informants conducted in the interviews involved negotiating slippages and similarities in the structural location of Dominicans, African Americans, and Puerto Ricans in New York.[53]

It might be tempting to draw comparative lessons from the scholarship on Dominican and Latina immigrant women and the alleged empowerment they achieve as gendered subjects as a consequence of migration or "becoming American."[54] Another tempting suggestion is that of "urban competency"—a conceptualization that valorizes and associates certain forms of American blackness with urbanity, modernity, and cosmopolitanism proposed by Ramos-Zayas in her research on second-generation Latinos in Newark, New Jersey.[55] Remarkably enough, however, "becoming American" in the sense of assimilating to the United States was not the end result of the progreso that the informants envisioned and narrated.

These men's mobilization of ideas of progreso and cultura drew from historical sources but also from coloniality vis-à-vis the imperial designs of the United States as a condition of possibility for their construction of themselves as modern and cosmopolitan. As the sociologist Ginetta Candelario has put it, the question to ask is not whether Dominicans are "really" black but rather how do Dominicans "face the 'black behind the ears' when confronted with both Haiti's and the United States' expansionist agendas and racial ideologies that would define them as black so as to legitimate Dominicans' subordination to their respective states and social orders?"[56] Candelario explains further that as "ethno-racial" minorities, Dominicans negotiate histories and local structures they do not control but "do so with a degree of agency and self-determination."[57]

Given the looming and continual presence of the imperial designs of the United States (which involved intervention, coercion, attempts at annexation, and investment of capital, etc., in the Dominican Republic through most of the twentieth century), it comes as no surprise that immigrants like the informants would level critiques of Dominican society from the vantage point of their New York locations. A stronger comparative example might be that offered by Harvey Neptune in his history of social relations during the occupation of Trinidad by the United States. In particular, Neptune explores the ways local women (particularly Afro-descendants) used their liaisons with American servicemen (many of whom were white) to challenge the racial hierarchies of the former British colony.[58] But this exercise of agency might be seen as one way marginalized populations negotiate the longstanding presence of the United States in the postcolonial articulations of Trinidad as a nation as a mechanism to challenge the gender and sexual status quo of British colonial and early postcolonial Trinidad. As Neptune explains, his account is concerned with exploring "the strong and varied U.S. presence, by a recognition, more specifically, that in the production of a postcolonial Trinidadianness, Americans featured as audience, actors, sponsors, and, always, behind-the-scenes forces sometimes powerful enough to cancel the entire drama."[59] Although located outside the geopolitical space of the nation-state, the informants' critiques of dominicanidad were issued from a metropolitan site of empire in United States–Caribbean relations, which also happens to be a key location for the formulation of metropolitan gayness. Like the Trinidadian women who engaged in transnational liaisons to tap into the possibility of upward mobility and trump local racial hierarchies, the transnational and the metropolitan operate for some informants as social locations from which they can level critiques at dominicanidad in its official and quotidian manifestations.

As will be shown in later chapters, however, the men I interviewed were only tentatively interested in gayness in its hegemonic guise because the white Anglo-American body (the unmarked ethnoracial body of American gayness) did not figure centrally in the affective, social, and erotic worlds of which these men partook. A key finding to be discussed later is that in the few interviews in which informants talked about sexual activity, other Dominicans and men of color were the central protagonists as sex partners. This tendency to make the Dominican male body central to discussions of erotic pleasures points to investments in dominicanidad beyond the nostalgic. It is also consistent with Manolo Guzmán's research and discussion of what he calls "homoracial" erotic investment among the Puerto Rican gay men he analyzed and suggested might obtain in other populations.[60] Later chapters will interrogate more fully informants' erotic investments in dominicanidad as what Candelario calls an "ethno-racial" formation—investments mediated by a cannibalization of gayness.

Given these articulations and hegemonic investments (which some of these men shared and illustrated earlier in the chapter), the range of critiques of dominicanidad presented throughout do not indicate a blind capitulation to what Doris Sommer has felicitously called "choose and lose," or the majoritarian mandate to leave the "old" culture behind and assimilate to the "new" culture.[61] The ways these men engaged, critiqued, and reworked dominicanidad in their narration of their lives point to the possibility of stretching and opening up dominicanidad as an identitarian, affective, and erotic site. "Choose and loose"—in the sense of opening up and relaxing choices and boundaries—moves beyond facile oppositions characteristic of majoritarian engagements with minoritarian voices toward strategic articulations of what might be possible with dominicanidad, figured no longer as a closed but as a porous, open body. The male gendering of the body of the nation, and the ways in which some of these men understand sex as a way to open up that body, will be explored in the chapters that follow. Just as I encountered (while jogging to stylize my body for displays of health and beauty), the conjunction of disparate historical and personal narratives and a juxtaposition of investments in high and popular cultural forms, so did the informants attest, even in their most uncomfortable juggling of Dominican worlds, the prices and pleasures of having it all, of not feeling that choosing one thing rules out the other.

PART II

BODY LANGUAGES

::::

My mother was in charge of teaching me how to be a man. Yet it was my dad who taught me most about the dangers in men's physical proximity to other men.

My father was my grandparents' youngest child. As grandchildren, we were expected to pay our respects to my grandfather at least once a year in family events, though he, his second wife, and his daughters were marginal figures in our lives. My grandfather was also largely absent from the upbringing of the Decena men, and "being a man" was something my father picked up on the streets. The rock of the Decenas was my formidable grandmother, a short and tough woman who raised my father and five other siblings all by herself, who married again and had two more children after my grandfather abandoned her (one of the stories I heard often as a child, told to emphasize my grandfather's disrespect for my grandmother, involved him walking by the front of their house carrying bed sheets he had taken from her house to go sleep with other women), and who raised a ninth child she adopted. Thus, my brothers and I were often told that my father had no paternal role models and that there were a lot of things about being a man we would need to pick up on our own.

I was devoted to my father. As a well-behaved child, I was also a welcome guest for long weekends at my older cousins' houses. During those stays, my relatives would ask me questions about my father's whereabouts, advice he gave me and my brothers, and interactions between him and my mother. Maybe it was because he was barely ten or so years older than they were, but there was always one joke or another among my older cousins that involved my father not really being a "serious" family man, his values not being right, or his behavior being "improper." Looking back, my loquacious and spirited advocacy of my father must have been interpreted as the naiveté of a child being raised by another child.

"Papi" tried teaching me how to play baseball once or twice, though his teachings did not awaken my interest in the sport. I was supposed to defend my younger brothers should they ever need defending. He did not teach me how to fight, though I remember being told that I threw punches like a "mujercita." I was also supposed to know how to dance merengue by watching him dominate the floor and impress everyone at family gatherings. At one of those get-togethers, one of my New York–raised cousins made sure everyone found out that instead of dragging my feet and moving my hips from side to side, I lifted my feet and stiffly held my hips. "He knows how to march, not how to dance," she said. That episode and others like it earned me the reputation of being an intelligent, if awkward (and effeminate), young person.

I understood early enough, however, that being close to my father would help me understand a thing or two about the man I wanted to become. My father's regular hangout was "la esquina," a street corner located six or seven blocks away from home. There was a barbershop where my brothers and I got our haircuts; after we sat on the makeshift "children's chair" the barber improvised by putting a flat piece of wood on the arms of their regular chairs. We always got short haircuts, but I visited the corner often because that was where my father hung out with his friends after work and on weekends. My mother knew he could be found there or, if not, that one of the people at the corner would know his whereabouts.

For a while, he used to take me to that corner to hang out with him. I generally sat under a tree or leaned against a wall while I listened to him argue politics with his friends. There was also commentary about female bodies passing by, but moments of heated conversation or *piropeo* were interspersed with observation of the surroundings, greeting of neighborhood acquaintances, and even silent witnessing of the passing of time. La esquina gave my father a space to be (*estar*), a location from which he could look and engage the world with people he trusted enough to have debates, share in laughter, and compete for the attention of women.

During one of these times I spent with papi in la esquina, I must have been in a clingy mood, for I held on to his hands, arms, or legs, or just hugged him while he tried to have a conversation with friends. It must have been a Saturday or Sunday morning, for I remember fresh air void of the humidity and sting of the heat of the afternoon. I could not have been older than eight or nine. I was an assiduous visitor of la esquina ever since I was officially allowed to cross streets and run errands on my own.

I was the only child in a circle of six to eight men, and my father indulged my touch until the collective dialogue came to a halt on its own. Then he leaned close to my ear and told me to go sit on my own by the tree near the corner. After I protested, he said I could go sit on a stoop by a door near where we stood, but that I had to stop touching him: "Do you see any of the men here clinging to one another the way you are clinging to me?" My recollection of what he said in Spanish lacks precision, though the word *manosear* (to handle or grope) stayed with me and pointed to the inappropriateness of my public expression of affection.

How ironic that it should be through being close to my father that I learned that there was something wrong with physical proximity between men. This is the way I recall being taught by my father to avoid touching other males.

The remainder of my schooling on the proper distance between male bodies took place in Colegio Don Bosco, the private school for boys I attended from second through tenth grade. There the Christian Brothers busied themselves imparting lessons in proper masculinity, together with evaluating our ability to multiply, add, and write calligraphy. "Juegos de manos, juegos de villanos" (Fighting Games, Villain Games), for example, was an adage meant to discourage roughhousing among the aggressive boys. Yet there was an element of homosexual panic involved in becoming a "villain," and the adage was most effective in disciplining overly physical children by making them fear that their aggressiveness would not be taken as a sign of virility but, instead, would cast suspicion upon it.

I was not an aggressive student, but a close friend of mine was. I give him the pseudonym Luciano Herrero. Though it was common in Don Bosco for students to call one another by last name (I was "Decena," which was quite confusing, because my two younger brothers were also at the school and were called by the same last name), Luciano Herrero was more often called by his first than by his last name. We must have become aware of one another because we were among the shorter students in each grade; thus, we stood near one another in the rows students formed by grade and section at the start of the school day to sing the national anthem and hear the school director's speech. We were also among the strongest students academically. Herrero had the added distinction of being a fast runner.

I knew Herrero for as long as I remember being a student at Don Bosco. We were close enough that we visited each other's homes after school. One day that I visited, he told me that he could not talk to me because his father had just died. I never saw him cry. In retrospect, that loss may have contributed to Herrero's combativeness with other students. He and I fought a few times, yet my recollection of those altercations casts them more as rough-housing than fighting per se. We must have stopped talking to one another occasionally too, though these enmities never lasted longer than a few days.

One of the few bits of wisdom my father imparted to me, which had a direct relation to the question of my manhood, revolved around being in-vited to go to the bathroom by another boy or by a man: "Women can go to the bathroom together. Men do not. If another boy asks you to go to the bathroom together, say 'no.'"

Our days at school, which ran from 7:30 a.m. to 12:30 p.m., were a combi-nation of class periods with two breaks of twenty minutes, during which stu-dents played outside, bought snacks at the school kiosk, or hung out in the school yard. My favorite activity was chatting with friends, and it was during one of these conversations that Herrero came and asked me to accompany him to the bathroom. Surprised at the request, I remember repeating what my father had said about men going to the bathroom together, perhaps to let other students know my awareness of the odd request my friend had made. Herrero and I did not talk for a few days after that, and that exchange never came up in our conversation. But together with my father's lesson about physical proximity between men, I passed on to Herrero an important mes-sage. He may have gone to the bathroom with other boys, but I never knew about it.

As tales of movement, contact, and self-making, the chapters in the pre-vious section set the stage for the questions that frame what follows. What languages do these men use to traverse the worlds they inhabit? How have they learned these languages, and how do they explore and exploit the ex-pressive potential of these languages in daily life? The chapters that follow analyze the informants' recollections of their socializations as men and their ongoing engagement with and investment in masculinity in daily life. What is central to their recollections of their childhoods and to the quotidian labor of legitimating themselves and cultivating close relationships with others is vigilance over (1) the way their bodies enter and move through the world and (2) the careful calibration of the codes and signs their bodies produce with the way those are read by the "others" who observe and evaluate them. The anecdotes that open this section point to various sites where masculinity was produced, evaluated, and validated in my own socialization. They func-tion as a counterpoint to the spaces and presences the informants connect most strongly with their socialization as men.

CHAPTER 4

Eso se nota: Scenes from Queer Childhoods

We can know more than we can tell.

—MICHAEL POLANYI, *The Tacit Dimension*

: : :

¿Qué decía la gente de ti?

¿De mi? Bueno. Cuando yo era más pequeño, yo era bien amanerado, que yo me acuerdo como ahora . . . Cuando tú eres niño, tú te acuerdas de muchas cosas que tú hacías . . . detrás del espejo, como dicen. Cuando yo no veía a nadie, yo era una persona completamente diferente. Yo era bien amanerado. Yo caminaba bien así, bien mujercita . . . por eso yo tenía miedo de participar en muchas cosas que hacían en mi casa. No me gustaba salir en videocasetes . . . porque cuando pasan los videos—ahí es que tú te das cuenta de lo amanerado que tú eres. Y tú sabes que siempre hay una gente que dice, "mira, mira eso." Yo era una persona bien amanerada. En la escuela no tenía tantos problemas porque yo tenía novia, pero como quiera no dejaban de decir los comentarios porque es que eso se nota, ¿tú entiendes? Ahora, después de grande, es que yo he ido como

What did people say about you?

About me? Well. When I was younger, I was very effeminate. I remember it as if it were today . . . When you are a child, you remember many things that you did . . . behind the mirror, as they say. When I didn't see anyone, I was a completely different person. I was very effeminate. I walked very much like a little queen . . . that's why I was afraid of participating in many of the things they did in my house. I didn't like to appear in videotapes . . . because when they run the videos—that's where you realize how effeminate you are. And you know there is always somebody who says, "Look, look at that." I was a very effeminate person. In school, I didn't have many problems because I had a girlfriend, but still, people did not stop making comments, because that's something that others can see, you know what I mean? Now that I'm an adult,

cambiando y he tratado de—y no es que he tratado porque yo no me considero ahora mismo que yo soy femenino, ¿tú sabes? Pero sí. Yo siento que yo cambié muchísimo y a mí no me da vergüenza decirlo: que cuando yo era más pequeño, yo era más femenino que ahora que soy un adulto.

I've been changing and I've tried to—it's not that I've tried because, right now, I don't consider myself feminine, you know? But yes. I feel that I changed a lot and I am not ashamed of saying it: when I was younger, I was more feminine than now that I am an adult.

Eugenio Heredia, twenty-nine years old at the time of our interview, responded to the question of what friends, relatives, and neighbors said about him as a child with recollections of the way he learned to manage a femininity that registered in his body, which was central to his socialization and which continued to frame his bodily deportment in the present, as something he "overcame." This was a femininity that Heredia projected onto a remembered childhood, a hypervisible movement through the world, a scandalous walking male body that, presumably, did not inhabit the corporal language he deployed in everyday life anymore.

Like other men I interviewed, part of Heredia's self-fashioning involved learning to produce a self that exerted some control over the ways people perceived him. Consistent features of informants' recollections focused on these men's initial confrontation (as children) with the intervening, evaluating eyes of others who pushed their earlier selves into movements, postures, and walking styles that avoided the appellation of "feminine" or "effeminate." Thus, their socializations involved support and acceptance with frequent doses of critique, evaluation, ridicule, and censure. As if styling one's body in ways considered "properly masculine" were not enough, the children the informants remembered also had to be mindful of the way they moved through local topographies shaped by "what people said" about children as well as specific grown men. Indeed, my interviewees revealed intense awareness of needing to avoid proximity with other bodies (e.g., when they knew of effeminate children in their neighborhoods) read by others as effeminate or otherwise "improperly" masculine. Nevertheless, the possibility of being marked as *la loca* loomed large in their childhood recollections.[1] This particular specter continued to play a role in their adult lives, revealed a deep investment in the privileges of masculine identification, and pointed to the spatial, contingent, and interpersonal sites of its materialization, circulation, and evaluation, which will be central to the analytical work of this chapter.

While the last chapter revisited the men's desencuentros with sites they associated with dominicanidad after migrating to New York City, here I flash back to earlier moments in their lives to set the stage for their current negotiations of sociality, the central concern in the next chapter. The moments when some of these men shared recollections of their childhoods reveal that they came to understand masculinity in particular (and gender in general) as a language they needed to master to navigate the world, their placement in it, and their relationships. To the degree that masculinity is made up of verbal and visual codes that these men engaged but did not originate (a discursive repertoire entangled, I will suggest, in the informants' ongoing engagement with dominicanidad), the stories of becoming men to be analyzed reveal the ways these participants became intelligible to themselves as men (and to me) through the language they used to remember that becoming.[2] To cite and orient one of Frantz Fanon's formulations on subject formations under colonial rule to the analytic work undertaken in this chapter, I will be concerned with mapping the circuitries that make "to speak [with the mouth, with the body] . . . to exist absolutely for the other."[3]

By analogizing gender to language, I foreground the body as a site of signification not by observing bodies in movement (e.g., through participant observation) but through an engagement with the words the informants used to describe and interpret their childhoods.[4] The attention paid to the hints of perception and the topographies of the social available through words woven into the fabric of interview exchanges may not offer a complete map of the worlds these men navigated, but positivistic purity is far from what I intend to accomplish here.[5] Instead, my focus will be the challenge of using words (and memory) to describe and map out what the body says, and what their bodies said.

There are limits to the descriptive power of language. Furthermore, we use words, movement, inflection, and other bodily codes to do things in the world other than describe who we are or who we were. The philosopher Michael Polanyi, author of the epigraph that opens the chapter, used the phrase "we can know more than we can tell" to point to knowledge that cannot be articulated verbally but that is important to the way one develops specific expertise. A piano teacher, for instance, cannot explain descriptively to a pupil how to achieve a certain sound, how to press a key to improve tonal quality, or the exact combination of pedaling and a held bass note that makes an ending feel like letting go of a lover's hand after a poignant goodbye. All the teacher can do is ask the student to "hear" the way the music should sound, and through a combination of demonstration and evaluation of the work of the student, to emulate the desired effect, arrive at that point where one hears the light caress of the silky fabric of the beloved's scarf as the bass figuration responds to the melody. This form of communication, which allows the student and teacher to access and exchange knowledge without having the specific words to name it, parallels the process through which these men learned to be men. The "others" who evaluated, criticized, and encouraged them to style their bodies in specific ways did not always name and describe what was desirable or not; instead, the process of becoming men hung on transfers of knowledge about body codes through demonstration, explanation by analogy, imitation, and critique. My posture throughout this chapter is skeptical of the descriptive and empirical potential of language and attentive to what these men's comments reveal about the way they constructed themselves in the present through their engagement with who they were as boys and who they were when we talked.

Though being seen as effeminate played a role in informants' recollections and negotiations of sexual practices, their investment in correct use of masculine corporal language points to the importance of their viability and legitimacy as subjects within the worlds they inhabited. I will have much more to say about the relationship of gender self-presentation to sexual practice and eroticism in the next chapters. For now, what is most relevant for this discussion is to separate sexual activity from the expression of gender conformity and nonconformity in daily life. Understanding the potential dynamism of this relationship is paramount to appreciate the way men like the informants transgress and remake heteronormativity in their lives.[6]

Much of the existing scholarship on the relationship between gender and sexual role performance (particularly among Latinos in the United States and Latin American populations) takes as a given that being read as a "sissy" means social vulnerability and sexual "passivity." Indeed, the conflation of male gender dissent with anal receptivity has only recently begun to be interrogated.[7] More common are assertions of a generalized understanding that to be seen as an effeminate man in Latin America (or in Latina/o communities in the United States) implies that the body in question is stigmatized because of its homosexuality, which registers as anal receptivity in sexual intercourse with other men.[8]

The informants' work of self-fashioning focused on what could be seen, and the possibility of the eruption of la loca in the visual field was ever present for them. Indeed, to the degree that this specter exerted an important force in their lives, despite their being directly or indirectly implicated with it, la loca will name figures, stylizations, and movements of the body and speech patterns *as performative utterances* that express dissent from the languages of normative masculinity in daily life. This is a dissent expressed not in the *desire to be a woman* (as many students of Latin American homosexualities and as many of the informants perceived men they considered effeminate), but rather in a male body that stages femininity through the deployment of stereotypes associated with women.[9] As a form of identification, in the psychoanalytic sense, la loca operates as the symbolic other through which the informants detour to inaugurate and sustain themselves.[10] Writing about the renowned Cuban author Alejo Carpentier's fashion articles for *Social*, a Cuban magazine for which Carpentier wrote under the pseudonym "Jacqueline" and that has been largely forgotten in literary discussions of the master's work, Ben Sifuentes-Jáuregui argues that the female-named "author" of the articles "is a pretension of what can be called a *gynographesis*, writing inscribed with the inventions of 'feminine' signifiers that address and inform questions for, by, and about women."[11] La loca, following Sifuentes-Jáuregui and borrowing his neologism to analyze corporal language use, is a *gynographic performative*, an "imagined form of femininity" staged as excess on a male body.[12]

An interpretation of la loca as figure and gynographic performative captures the profound ambivalence it provokes in the daily lives of the men I interviewed. La loca is not the abjected and repudiated identification for the production of coherence in the informants' subject positions. The philosopher Judith Butler has been influential in arguing that part of what repudiation and abjection achieve, in the constitution of subject positions, is a degraded or lost intersubjective connection, which results in illegible maps of power. "The question," she suggests, "concerns the tacit cruelties that sustain coherent identity, cruelties that include self-cruelty as well, the abasement through which coherence is fictively produced and sustained. Something on this order is at work most obviously in the production of coherent heterosexuality, but also in the production of coherent lesbian and gay identity and (within those worlds) the coherent butch, the coherent femme."[13] Informants like Eugenio Heredia argued that they needed to "overcome" their childhood effeminacy. But the discussion throughout this chapter and the next illustrates that the "coherence" resulting from that "overcoming" is unrealizable, for subject positions are the result of ongoing (and often quite tense) negotiations and struggles. La loca operates in disparate ways that give shape to the boundaries the informants established with others and to their sense of comfort or discomfort with their surroundings. Furthermore, the connections these men felt with the figure of la loca parallel the connections that Cruz-Malavé suggests link the town and the expelled homosexual figure of Trinidad's son in "¡Jum!," a short story by the renowned Puerto Rican author Luis Rafael Sánchez. Like the community that expels this particular member to secure its normative identity, the informants did not look to distance or expel from their self-making "the radically different but . . . the proximate other."[14] Still, la loca on the surface of my interlocutors' bodies was not an other that was proximate in the way that figure might be for the people who surround Trinidad's son; la loca constituted their authentic self in ways some of these men learned to negotiate by mobilizing codes of normative masculinity. To borrow from the title of a book of poems by Jorge Luis Borges astutely investigated in the work of Balderston and Quiroga, the dialectic at play here is not between self and other but between "el otro y el mismo" (the other and the same).[15]

::: Specular Circuits

Contextualizing and analyzing the interview excerpt that opens this chapter in relation to Eugenio Heredia's background and recollection of his childhood femininity will help situate the mediations, visibilities, and intersubjective exchanges the informants negotiated as children and as adults. My aim will be to identify and chart the structural parameters within which these men elaborated, interpreted, and contested the gendering of their bodies.

Born to a mother and father who had migrated to Santo Domingo from the cities of San Cristobal and Baní, respectively, Eugenio Heredia was one of the youngest children of the four boys and three girls Mr. and Mrs. Heredia raised. Heredia's father worked as a policeman, and his mother was a housewife. As Heredia recalled, growing up involved increased awareness of the ways in which he was different from other boys: "Según yo fui creciendo, yo como que . . . me fui ocultando porque ya eso iba desarrollándose, y yo cada día más me iba dando cuenta" (As I grew up, I began . . . to con-

ceal myself because that was developing and I noticed it more every day). Though it is tempting to venture that Heredia's effeminacy made up the "eso" (that) that he began to notice—and retrospectively, he would agree that he was a "muchacho femenino" (feminine boy)—the evidence he offered points to the various sites of gendering in daily life through which his own intelligibility to himself as a feminine boy became possible.[16]

In the course of this part of our interview, Eugenio probably had specific images of himself in mind. Yet his ability to convey what distinguished him from other boys obtained from descriptions of differences that were visible to him: characteristics of other boys and men who surrounded him. The boys most close to Eugenio were his older brothers, and through comparing and contrasting himself with them, he elaborated on his masculinity and theirs. Heredia remembered that though they all had girlfriends in school, his brothers seemed comfortable with girls, whereas Eugenio felt he had girlfriends out of obligation. Further, he preferred to stay home, whereas his brothers were out playing baseball and other games. Even if he wanted to go out and play, Eugenio felt he would not blend in with the boys: "Si vamos a jugar pelota, y yo hablo de una manera . . . y los modales míos son un poco diferentes. Si tú te pones a ver, tú te das cuenta cuando un niño es bien activo, es bien varonil . . . entonces yo me sentía como con esa debilidad de que yo no podía ser como mi hermano" (If we are going to play baseball and I speak in a certain way . . . and my manners are a little different. If you think about it, you can tell when a boy is very active, very virile . . . then I felt that weakness that I couldn't be like my brother). But how could he tell? How can we tell a boy is virile? Heredia *felt* "weak" compared to his brothers. His encounter with the evidence of his brothers' "active" dispositions, an imaginary (and generic) other boy whom you (implicating me and, through me, you the reader) sense was "varonil" produced a feeling of weakness, a sense that he could not be like them. These virile other boys, then, were another site of identification that Heredia moved through, symbolically and narratively, to express his growing sense of himself.

Heredia's brothers also followed what Eugenio remembered as the normative expectation that they would step out of the house, as adolescents, and bring money home through working in construction or other jobs associated with young working-class men: "A mí lo que me gustaba era estar en la casa. A mí lo que me gustaba era bailar, el arte, cosas así, y por eso es que yo veo la diferencia—yo puedo sentir y ver la diferencia de mis hermanos . . . nunca me llamó la atención como tener trabajo bruto" (I liked being

[*estar*] at home. I liked dancing, the arts, things like that, and that's why I see the difference—I can feel and see the difference [between me] and my brothers . . . brute labor never interested me). From the outset, Heredia's description of the normative heterosexual masculinity that was most relevant to his socialization implicated his brothers, who "had girlfriends," "looked active," and went out of the house to perform "brute labor." The perception of normality and virility that coalesced around them was already located not only in relation to Heredia's feeling and vision of that difference but in subordination to masculinities absent yet constitutive of the frame: those of subjects whose viability as "men" did not depend on "brute labor."[17] Part of what made Heredia "different" was his preference for being (*estar*) in *la casa* and his interest in pursuits that established distance between him and the interarticulation of class and gender evident in the masculinity of his brothers. This preference may have feminized Eugenio in the eyes of many, but it shielded him from having to produce the "rugged" expressions of masculine deportment expected of a construction worker. In ways consistent with how informants expressed affinity with cultura and education, the arts in general and dance in particular became a mechanism for Eugenio to express himself and eventually migrate to the United States.[18]

Heredia felt anxious about his masculinity as a child. This anxiety resulted from bodily deportment and boundaries that contrasted what he interpreted as the more easily normative working-class masculinity of his brothers. They liked being out in la calle, whereas he liked staying in la casa. They brought appropriate speech patterns and manners to playing baseball, whereas Eugenio was concerned that his manners would seem different. They liked "trabajo bruto," whereas he liked the arts. The differences between them were differences that Eugenio claimed he could feel and see.

For Heredia, that "eso se iba desarrollando" (that was developing) set distance between various ways of staging himself. He invoked the image of the mirror to establish that when located behind it, when he did not see anybody else, "era una persona completamente diferente." The image of Heredia as a young child sutured the mirror to the glance of others and being (*estar*) "behind" it as a requirement for him to be the "completely different person" he was: the effeminate, swishy little boy, the "mujercita." The challenge was that Heredia could not fully control the moments when the effeminacy appeared in front of the mirror—where he and others could see it. The young infant in the Lacanian mirror stage assumes a "specular image" of himself "in which the *I* is precipitated in a primordial form, prior to being objectified in the dialectic of identification with the other."[19] In contrast, the relationship between child and mirror Heredia recounted implicated others. There was no stage of self-recognition *prior* to sociality. Further, the sociality of Heredia's "eso" derived not from a dialectic between self and other but, more precisely, from a circuit where Heredia (and his others) recognized contextually specific images of himself. Even his narration of his identifications as movements through other figures distinguished from himself conjures a circuit. Heredia was *femenino* but not rugged like his "virile" brothers as a child; two images narrated to condense recollections and allow him to capture and communicate to me who he was. Heredia's understanding of what set him apart from other children located that difference as already within a *specular circuit* of which he and others partook, where he recognized the disjuncture between (1) the "I" facing the mirror and (2) the glance of others and the (presumably unacceptable) "I" behind it—unacceptable, of course, when presented to others but acceptable when Heredia was on his own. In addition, by slipping between his glance and that of others, Heredia pointed out the way he incorporated normative or shared frames into his way of looking at himself.

Heredia's narration of the person he was behind the mirror focused on ways of carrying the body that added up to the different person he was. Like several other men with whom I spoke, Heredia referenced the way he walked in order to address his effeminacy. But the insight of how effeminate he was in the past but not in the present suggests that Heredia viewed the swish as an improper deployment of masculine codes, a deployment that he had overcome.

The swish appeared in Heredia's recollection to stand in for stylizations of his body that his memory did not conjure in equally precise detail. What he conjured in a resonant manner was a scene where "eso" registered most disturbingly to him: in the family videotapes where he hated to appear and hated to hear someone else (presumably an adult) say, "look at that." In a fashion parallel to that of the Fanonian primal scene, Heredia's appearances in videos made scandalously evident to him just how different (in this case, effeminate) he was. But this is "evidence" available for his (and other's) evaluation when transformed into an object, a representation that dramatizes impressions that exceed Heredia's control. In Fanon's response to Lacan's "mirror stage," hearing the white child say "Look, a Negro!"

produced a sense of fragmentation within a circuit: "I existed triply: I occupied space. I moved toward the other . . . and the evanescent other, hostile but not opaque, transparent, not there, disappeared."[20] The production of the specular excess of blackness as object of scrutiny, morbid fascination, and fear in Fanon (perhaps analogous to the visual excess of la loca) points to the realization of the degree to which our bodies speak in ways we cannot fully control. Furthermore, the disappearance of the child who points, and the disappearance of the relative or neighbor who points to the "eso" that registered, visually reveal the parallel constitutions of whiteness and normative masculinity (and femininity, as many of the coaches and evaluators of male children's socialization were mothers) as disappearance. The excess of the black and the effeminate inaugurates the unmarked status of normative whiteness, maleness, and femaleness.

Heredia's "eso" could be captured in tape—objectified, circulated, and evaluated in settings where Heredia might or might not have been. This should have fueled additional anxieties in Heredia. It may have even provoked feelings like the "nausea" expressed by Fanon as he was hailed by the white child.[21] After all, anyone capable of reading normative codes and Heredia's deviation from them would have noticed.

But Heredia's description of the selves in front and behind the mirror suggest that he began to understand his own fragmentation as a condition of possibility for his own survival and not as evidence of a definitive abjection. When he was on his own, behind the mirror, Heredia expressed himself differently, in ways that other informants suggested characterized settings where they felt comfortable enough to "be themselves." Thus, the staging of self Heredia described involved the pain of realizing that he needed to calibrate his corporal language to deal with the possibility that his effeminacy would erupt visually in ways he could not control. The realization of the incommensurability of the authentic (private/behind-the-mirror) self with the one that needed to be produced to get through the world (public/in-front-of-the-mirror self) was foundational for Heredia as it was for other informants. But in his case, as with the others, he realized that being seen as a man was a collaborative process of becoming, which provoked efforts to measure up to standards that would make him a viable subject in daily life. His survival was at stake.

A second childhood recollection will highlight the importance of being seen as masculine in order for many of the informants to develop competencies in acting like men. Born in 1974 in Santo Domingo, Roberto Panés was one of five siblings of a troubled marriage. Panés and his siblings stayed with their mother after she and their father divorced. He did not get along with his father, who had four children before marrying his mother and who had two additional children with another woman while married to Mrs. Panés. Roberto Panés's recollection of being raised and taught to be a man from his mother emphasized an issue central to most men I interviewed: the question is not who he is (*quien es*) but rather the way he presents himself where he is (*donde está*). Again, the centrality of body stylizations to the configuration of the basic contours of the subject as always already gendered was crucial to the way Panés narrated his mother's work in making a man out of him:[22]

Yo siempre, desde chiquita, dije lo que iba a ser: una loca histeriquísima y mala . . . pero, imagínate . . . cuando uno era niño, no podía controlarlo de esa forma, sino que yo no sabía. Yo actuaba como yo me consideraba que debía actuar. . . . Yo era muy mariconcito cuando chiquito. Me partía mucho, y mi mamá me decía, "Tú tienes que dejar los ademanes." . . . Que yo no podía caminar así. Que yo no tenía que partirme . . . ella me lo disfrazaba porque yo era un muchacho, pero ella trataba de que yo lo entendiera . . . que yo no debía hacerlo así porque se veía mal.	I always, from when I was a little girl, said what I was going to be: a super hysterical and bad sissy, but you will imagine . . . when I was a boy, I couldn't control it because I didn't know. I acted the way I thought I had to act. . . . I acted very much like a little faggot when I was little. I acted very effeminate [*me partía*], and my mother said, "You have to stop the mannerisms." . . . That I couldn't walk like that. That I didn't have to act effeminate . . . she would tell me in other terms because I was a child, but she would try to make me understand . . . that I couldn't do it like that because it looked bad.

The scene of Panés being told by his mother to "stop the mannerisms" was layered on to the frame of his first statement; according to this informant, he had announced to the world from early on that he would be a "loca histeriquísima y mala." Panés offered narrative access to these scenes of exchange and feedback with his mother about the coordination of bodily deportment and the judgment of what "looks good" (that is, masculine) in the eyes of others. He signals their recurrence and repetitiousness, almost as an adage, by saying, "me partía mucho" and "[que mi] mama me decía." In other words, we do not gain access to one scene but rather to many scenes through one scene, which Panés attempted to capture retrospectively through his evocative yet temporally indeterminate retelling.

Furthermore, Panés's use of feminine pronouns ("chiquita" instead of "chiquito"; "una" instead of "un") and adjectives of stereotypical female excess ("histeriquísima y mala") points to the interview encounter as a site for the production of boundaries and intimacies. Panés made his language choices to implicate me (as interviewer, friend, and interlocutor in the relatively private setting of the research interview conducted behind closed doors) in the telling of the story. Because we had known one another for several years before I ever interviewed Panés, and because the setting of the interview lent itself to this particular framing, his language use (at least in the beginning of the anecdote) referenced the setting and the proximity of the relationship within which the exchange took place.

Like other informants, Panés pointed toward "la forma de caminar" (walking style) to underline the potentially scandalous (and discrediting) swish he had to control. But he also talked about his mannerisms in general. "Me partía mucho," he said. *Partirse* (literally translated as "to break") is a quotidian way of talking about situations in which a male lets out a signal of effeminacy (and possible homosexuality). A man "se parte" in a specific moment when he inadvertently acts in a way not considered proper of a heterosexual man. For *partirse* to register as a disruption of the presumably seamless trajectory of heterosexual masculinity in the visual field, others have to be present to voice that judgment. Thus, the pedagogical intent of the exchanges between Panés and his mother involved a calibration of the body language of the young Panés so as to produce a male body that would "not break."

The smooth and unbroken surface of normative masculine self-presentation here—constructed by negation, as that which Panés needed to approximate—is connected with what de Moya calls masculinity as "straightjacket" in the perception of many of the men I interviewed. *No partirse*, or to achieve an unmarked masculinity, generally involved styling the body in ways many of the men (even those who manifested most ambivalence about gender nonconformity) found restrictive.

As the son of a doctor and an entrepreneur, Panés was expected to become a man in ways consistent with the class background and aspirations of upward mobility of his family: apart from "acting masculine" in the requisite ways, Panés was expected to become a professional. As we will see below, *partirse* specifically references male effeminacy, despite the fact that other excesses and disruptions can also challenge one's access to forms of masculinity that have easy claims on power and legitimacy.

::: Masculinity—A Straightjacket

The informants are typical in their preoccupation with the construction and sustenance of masculine identifications. Indeed, much scholarship on masculinity has suggested that the "gender work" of its construction relies on men's ongoing evaluation of one another as men, regardless of sexual identification and erotic object choice.[23] Furthermore, scholars of masculinity have shown the way that homophobia and, more precisely, "homosexual panic" help constitute the masculine subject.[24] Thus, the informants negotiated and constructed a sense of self in relationship to masculinity and from the vantage point of their identification as gay or bisexual, but they were not alone in feeling anxieties about themselves as men.

Anxiety may be part of the constitution of masculinity within patriarchy, and Dominican masculine formations have specific histories that merit consideration. Christian Krohn-Hansen argues, for example, that masculinity is a "legitimate problematic," which he describes as a site of conflict produced by the unequal distribution of power and political legitimacy among men. The ability of individual men to authorize themselves and thus become viable in social life depends on how well they present themselves as men to others. But the centrality of masculinity to Dominican social life goes beyond enabling and sustaining relations among men. Krohn-Hansen argues that the "legitimate problematic" of masculinity helps construct a whole field of social relations within which power is negotiated: "Relations between leaders and followers, patrons and clients, are given meaning in terms of ideas about masculinity."[25] In this way, masculinity is central to what is politically imaginable in Dominican society.

Whereas the discussion of the last chapter emphasized the informants' negotiation and resignification of discourses of cultura and progreso that were once at the center of the aspiration of modernizing Dominican nationalist intellectuals, Trujillo (and the tradition of *caudillismo* he came to epitomize in the hegemonic imagination of Dominicans) is one of the models available to the informants. But unlike the models of tyrannical masculinity "on display" associated with Trujillo's presentation and projection of his own body, it was on the question of undisputed authority of father figures in the household where most informants saw parallels between their fathers and Trujillo. Even those who explicitly pointed out that their fathers were "from Trujillo's time" in their accounts remarked on the relative physical and emotional absence of male parent figures from the daily work of raising children or administering households. The work of sustaining and collaborating in the production of hegemonic males within the domestic sphere, as the examples discussed below illustrate, fell largely to mothers. Thus, whereas relationships with mothers tended to be central (albeit often emotionally complicated) anchors for informants' lives, emotional distance and resentment often characterized relationships with fathers. Strained relationships with fathers were quite common, and though the homosexuality or bisexuality of the informants caused some tensions and estrangements, tensions between children and fathers were generally connected with broader conflicts within the family (especially in the case where fathers had divorced and/or abandoned mothers).

Many of the informants experienced and narrated "becoming men" as the process of internalizing rules, mostly manifested as interdictions from others. In his work on the socialization of boys in the Dominican Republic, E. Antonio de Moya captures the restrictive nature of the masculine self-fashioning and the circuits of visibility and surveillance that produce and regulate these bodies:

> Mostly in the upper-middle and middle classes in the Dominican Republic, who are mainly concerned with social power, there is a relatively basic, clear-cut, stereotyped and paranoid (totalitarian) etiquette for gendering both the verbal and non-verbal behavior of young boys away from "femininity." . . .
> This spiral of no-no rules, this *panopticum*, is meant to avert any possible "femininity" in boys' body language. It works as a straightjacket that automatically warns them, as a thermostat, against any innocent gesture, movement, word or action that is not the best choice for prospective true males. . . . In this way Dominican males are socialized in a strongly restrictive and prohibitive environment, which surely cripples their spontaneity, authenticity and joy, and produces much hypocrisy and neurosis.[26]

De Moya's description of the etiquette that constitutes Dominican masculinity resonates with what many of the informants experienced growing up.

His use of the word *panopticum* (in a nod to the mechanisms of discipline described by Foucault) suggests that this "difference" can be located in the body. This difference registers as failure to cite proper masculinity when seen and evaluated by the informants themselves or their family and neighbors—in Eugenio Heredia's case, the onlookers crowded in front of the mirror. Since masculinity is so wound up with what is conceivable political agency, the problem is not a difference in sexual orientation per se but rather dissent that can be read onto particular bodies.

De Moya's suggestive use of the word *straightjacket* allows further elaboration on the masculinity of the "serious" man, or the unmarked site of masculine normativity in Dominican society. The restrictive bodily codes deployed to produce the effect of masculinity and legitimacy, as de Moya explains, reveal that what is opposed to masculinity on the surface of this body is not femininity per se, but *locura* (craziness). An expansive interpretation of locura, one that encompasses male effeminacy but that is also open to disruptions in the smoothness, seamlessness, and rationality of normativity, illustrates the ways in which power and legitimacy combine to produce masculinity as cover, as a straightjacket, for bodies imagined as always already excessive, prone to break, and feminized. This is a phallogocentric regime that requires masculinity to control, to shield a femininity imagined as essential and authentic excess.

An expansive interpretation of locura, then, helps situate languages that produce masculine "seriousness" in relation to all the other communicative practices that break that mold (which include male effeminacy but also, as I will explain below, tigueraje). In his research on masculinity in the Dominican Republic, Krohn-Hansen argues that the people he interviewed understood and negotiated masculinity around five interrelated ideas: "(1) of autonomy and courage; (2) of men's visibility in public spaces; (3) of the man as seducer and father; (4) of the power tied to a man's verbal skills; and (5) of a man's sincerity and seriousness."[27] "Seriousness" is particularly relevant in contrast to the figuration of la loca precisely because of its circulation as a gynographic performative centrally associated with *relajo*, or joking, in Dominican culture. In the next chapter, I will explain in more depth the connection that the informants made of eruptions of la loca, relajo, and their struggles to be legitimized. For now, I emphasize that the figuration of the serious man is restrictive; it does not contemplate having a sense of humor.[28] Krohn-Hansen elaborates:

People claimed that the serious man did not have recourse to the *relajo*; he didn't "joke" . . . men in La Descubierta claimed that joking could be dangerous. . . . A man did not know another man well enough to be able to joke with him unless they had already established some sort of friendship. One did not joke with a stranger. The *relajo* was, to some extent, based on a kind of *confianza*, or trust. . . . Stories about how a friendship between two men became destroyed by a *relajo* were commonplace among the villagers.[29]

The straightjacket projected onto these male bodies also spills over to a social world in which men develop close personal relations with one another based on mutual trust, interpersonal proximity, or kinship ties (such as those of *compadrazgo*) that work so long as every man involved remains mindful of the boundaries set by the other and the contexts of interaction (*donde están*). The disruptive potential of relajo constitutes the flip (or public) side of exchanges and homosocial intimacies between men that can cast doubt on their seriousness if aired in public. Two *compadres* may very well develop relationships shaped by inside joking and teasing; should one of the men attempt these jokes in the wrong context or in situations where strangers or people outside of trusted circles are also interlocutors, they could be jeopardizing the friendship. As we will see in the next chapter, parallel situations present themselves among the men I interviewed though, in their recollections, these questions (of proximity or intimacy with friends in public) are negotiated and worked through the figure of la loca.

::: *Tigueraje* and Other *Locuras*

Like the first two men whose recollections I have discussed, Diego Abreu recalled his socialization as a man in connection with becoming socially viable and, later, upwardly mobile. Nevertheless, being a man of a working-class background made la calle central to Abreu's socialization into manhood. His recollections help situate la loca and el tíguere (the Dominican tiger) as figurations in excess of the legitimacy accorded to serious men.[30] To the degree that it allows for the pragmatic negotiation and successful straddling of hierarchies of power not controlled by marginalized men (by race and class), tigueraje casts doubt on someone's seriousness but not on their status as heterosexual men in the way that acting out as a loca does. Nevertheless, tíegueres, like locas, operate as racial and class-specific performatives that subvert the legitimacy of serious men and that, insofar as they become identificatory sites traversed in the process of constructing male normativity, are ambivalently invested.

Of the men with whom I spoke, Abreu was by far the one who most closely identified with normative working-class masculinity. At the time of our interview, he was forty. Abreu characterized the color of his skin as "moreno" (black). He was born in Santo Domingo to a father who was a day laborer and to a mother who—like most of the mothers of the informants—took care of the household and children. He remembered that his parents had a good relationship and that his dad would bring his mother little gifts but that he was generally a man who spent a lot of time in la calle. "Pero siempre," he points out, "se preocupó por la comida . . . por la escuela de nosotros" (He always took care of our food . . . and made sure we went to school). One of the key jobs of the mother, as he remembers, was to make sure that the five boys she was raising "fuéramos varones" (acted and became boys)—she kept him and his brothers out of the kitchen and took care of washing clothes and cleaning: "Cuando llegué a Nueva York, yo no sabía cocinar porque los hombres no podían lavar ni cocinar. Lavaba ella" (When I arrived in New York, I did not know how to cook because men could not clean or cook. She did the wash).

Abreu remembered having been a masculine boy who had an easy time integrating into the street. He played baseball and basketball and even developed a code of honor with his brothers, which dictated that older brothers had to defend younger ones. Abreu remembered hitting someone with a baseball bat to defend his little brother.

Sustaining a masculine identity as a child involved presenting a tough image to other males in his neighborhood. As he grew up, however, Abreu channeled his image of childhood tíguere into community service and education. Abreu studied in the Dominican public schools and obtained a university degree in clinical psychology. While pursuing his studies, he became involved in various local causes, including fledgling national efforts to address HIV/AIDS. His work in this area led to his departure from the Dominican Republic.

He says, "Yo vengo de una familia . . . muy integrada. Muy *straight*, de papá y mamá . . . yo no quería estrujarle a papi una loquita o a mis hermanos una loquita" (I come from a family . . . that's very well adjusted. Very straight, with a mother and a father . . . I didn't want to force my father or brothers to face a sissy). Abreu shares with other informants the recollection of keeping distance from boys considered effeminate. Some informants expressed disdain for these neighborhood characters, but most men expressed ambivalence and even admiration of the daring it took to live and thrive as the neighborhood locas where they grew up. What is striking about Abreu's recollection of the distance he created between himself and these *loquitas* is that being close to them could bring shame and disrepute to his family and to the socially elevated people he began to spend time with as he pursued his studies. Though he came from a family of humble means, Abreu insisted that he had worked hard to build a reputation and that being associated with locas could undo his efforts to be upwardly mobile:

Yo con el asunto de la pajarería en Santo Domingo, yo era medio racista y medio clasista. O sea, el hecho de yo estar estudiando en universidad . . . eso me hacía juntarme con ciertas gentes. En Santo Domingo, la titulitis funciona mucho. Por eso me da . . .

¿¡Titulitis!?

¡Claro! Tú sabes: el doctor; el licenciado . . .

Exacto . . .

¿Tú ves? Eso funciona. Entonces, pues yo, aunque vengo de una familia humilde . . . Yo logré codearme con cierta gente que entonces . . . uno los avergonzaba, ¿tú sabes? Yo jamás me junté con la loquita del barrio. Jamás. Porque yo me levantaba temprano. Me iba para la escuela. Cuando tenía tiempo, me iba para la cancha o me iba para el play, ¿tú sabes? O estaba en el club

With the whole gay thing in Santo Domingo, I was a little racist and a little classist. In other words, the fact that I was studying in the university . . . that made me get together with some people. In Santo Domingo, titulitis works very well. That's why . . .

Titulitis?!

Of course! You know: the doctor; the licenciado . . .

Exactly . . .

You see? That works. So, even though I come from a humble family . . . I managed to get together with people that you . . . would shame, you know? I never got together with the neighborhood loquita. Never. Because I got up early. I went to school. When I had time, I would go to play basketball or baseball, you know? Or I was at the club giving a talk . . . Maybe I missed out, the little loquita or fooling around with the tígueres in back alleys. I

| dando una charla . . . Tal vez, me lo perdí, lo de la loquita o de estar jodiendo con los tígueres en los callejones. Yo no hice eso. Yo un día decidí acostarme con un hombre. Lo hice como un hombre adulto de veinte y pico de años. | didn't do that. One day, I decided to go to bed with a man. I did that as a man who was more than twenty years old. |

For Abreu, there was a connection between his reputation and proximity with neighborhood loquitas that mattered beyond his efforts to project normative masculinity. By staying removed from the space of the loca, Abreu sought to avoid shame on his family and on his reputation as a fledgling professional. This is all the more ironic given that Abreu was involved in HIV/AIDS work, which must have implicated those men in one way or another. But his articulation of the social location of la loca deserves further unpacking because of how consistent it is with the way most of the other men continued to establish distance between themselves and this image in daily life.

Abreu framed his discussion of the way he constructed himself around neighborhood locas first by underscoring the wholesomeness of his family, a characteristic anchored in normative patriarchy—after all, this is a *straight* family ("de papá y mamá"). This frame is crucial because it draws on the legitimacy accorded to the cohabitation of his parents in the neighborhood and in Abreu's own recollection. Despite that the father, as Abreu remarked, was a traditional Dominican male in his fondness for being in la calle,[31] that Mr. Abreu fulfilled his responsibility as male parent and stayed with Abreu's mother definitely locates this couple somewhere close to the center of a working-class version of what Gayle Rubin has famously called the "charmed circle."[32] Given that staying together made the Abreus a legitimate family,[33] Diego made clear the importance of not soiling that reputation by either acting out as a loca or being around them. In this way, Abreu established distance between locas and normative family arrangements, a physical and symbolic distance he further substantiated in his discussion of himself as a fledgling professional.

Becoming a student at the university, and later a man with professional expertise active in neighborhood causes, involved choosing carefully one's friends, colleagues, and associates. Abreu recalled being "clasista" and "racista"in his choices of those who would be near him, and he suggested that one of his basic criteria was to be close to people whose "titles," as marks of social distinction and professional accomplishment, would enhance his reputation. Abreu was one of the few men who made a point of telling me about how proud of his color he was: "Yo me considero un hombre moreno con mi narizota. A mí me fascina ser así: ese hombre rústico . . . más africano que español" (I consider myself a black man with my big nose. And I love being like that: a coarse man . . . more African than Spanish). Yet at the beginning of his discussion of pursuing a professional reputation, Abreu invokes "racismo" as a mechanism through which he distinguished between people with whom he wanted and people with whom he did not want to be associated. Thus, his pride in his color and features coexist with an understanding that becoming a reputable professional involved establishing distance between himself and a blackness he saw as intertwined with class marginality.

What is even more striking is that this is a discussion in which Abreu sought to establish his legitimate location in contrast to that of the loquitas. In order to do this, Abreu followed the discussion of his "clasismo" and "racismo" (as well as the "titulitis" that he said characterized the path to upward mobility in the Dominican Republic) with a discussion that centered him as a person who went to school, played when he had extra time, and made contributions to the edification of others. In other words, establishing himself as a reputable citizen in the research interview involved not only highlighting that his family was "wholesome" but that Abreu was an active and productive member of his world. The loquitas whose "fun" he may have missed out on were outside of his wholesome family and outside of spheres of domesticity, productivity, and upward mobility; they were in "back alleys, fooling around with tígueres." As a gynographic performative, *loca* refers to feminine excess that stands outside of the respectability and sanctity of the traditional domestic sphere. When used to refer to a woman, the word insinuates not only lack of seriousness in terms of life in general but also the sexual licentiousness and vulgarity that attach to stereotypical views of working-class, poor, and dark-skinned Dominican women.

The figurations of the loquita in Abreu's discussion are important because they echo the concerns that animate the way other men negotiated this figure in their lives. The loquita signals immaturity, a disinvestment in the practices and self-fashionings that produce upward mobility in the worlds the informants inhabited: competent deployment of normative masculinity, educational achievement, and the cultivation of circles that would enhance rather than diminish one's reputation.

But what about the tígueres, whom Abreu also located in the back alleys, "fooling around" with the locas? The location of the tíguere in the back alleys, instead of in public spaces of male comradeship and "seriousness," puts this figure in a marginal relationship with public men, "serious" men and father/providers symbolically located in the domestic sphere. An archetype of street-savvy masculinity, tígueres are men who tread on the edges of the licit. Krohn-Hansen explains that the tíguere "can be seen as the essence of any successful pragmatism. He is the type who acts according to the situation, is cunning, and has a gift for improvisation. In the southwest, the image of the *tíguere* represented both an everyday hero and a sort of trickster."[34] Lipe Collado further explains that the figure of the Dominican tíguere names a form of agile masculinity that developed to wrestle and "win" (tellingly phrased as "salir bien parado," or "come out standing") in adverse situations, most specifically poverty and political repression.[35] Although neither Krohn-Hansen nor Collado name it as such, the close relation that class marginality has to racial subordination points to a body that, apart from being poor, is predominantly dark skinned.

The furtive nature of encounters between tígueres and locas in back alleys does not point to structural equivalence of these marginal positions vis-à-vis serious masculinity. Nevertheless, their contact in the back alley suggests the coexistence, interaction, and exchange between these figures outside the "charmed circle" of the domestic sphere and the legitimized spaces of masculine (and white, upper-middle-class) hegemony. By locating the two characters outside spheres of familial productivity and civic-mindedness, Abreu sought not only to differentiate himself from them but to elaborate on his own genuine concern for the well-being of other community members as well as his own maturity (he *was* a tíguere himself and may still bring tigueraje to his social interactions, but he is looking out for himself and others).

To the degree that they are cast as creatures who look out for themselves and nobody else, who are gifted talkers and manipulators of adverse situations, and who tread in uncertain moral waters, tígueres represent part of the excess Abreu sought control in order to demonstrate to others and to me (through his own recollections) that he achieved legitimate masculinity. In ways that parallel Eugenio Heredia's "overcoming" of childhood effeminacy, Abreu's recollection demonstrates the way he overcame tigueraje.

::: ¿Mujer o maricón?

The examples discussed thus far focus on the collective effort of socializing boys, labor which usually falls on the laps of mothers. The final example to be discussed here helps explore how being identified as a feminine male has consequences for the socialization of an informant who identified as (male-to-female) transsexual. Karla Bassant was twenty-nine years old at the time of our interview. She was born in New York to parents from the El Cibao region and who ran transnational businesses (a furniture shipping company and travel agency). Bassant was one of four brothers, and she recalls that moving back and forth became a mechanism for the parents to discipline the siblings as they were growing up. Whenever one of them misbehaved in New York, they would be sent to spend time in El Cibao and vice versa. Nevertheless, the Bassant brothers were raised mostly in Santo Domingo.

Bassant recounted being an extremely androgynous boy, so much so that it caused a lot of tension with her father: "El miedo de mi papá era verme en la mitad, entre varón y hembra, because yo era bien femenino" (My dad's fear was of seeing me in the middle, between male and female, because I was very feminine). The father often used corporal punishment with Bassant. "'Si tú me sales maricón, yo te mato. Si tú me sales igual que un maricón, yo te mato'" (If you turn out to be a faggot, I'll kill you. If you turn out to be the same as a faggot, I kill you), she recalled. That the threat from the father came in two specific and repeated forms—"if you turn out *to be* a faggot" and "if you turn out *to be the same as* a faggot"—may be Bassant's slip but also may suggest that the father and other relatives recognized Karla's androgyny as effeminacy and became invested in having young Karla become something other than a "faggot."

Bassant's retrospective view of her socialization suggests that the family became invested in making her a girl. That Karla was widely seen as an androgynous boy had important implications for her socialization. As she explained:

Si iban gente a la casa, yo me preguntaba que por qué los hermanos míos podrían andar embromando con pasolas, jodiendo con los carros en el garaje y toda la cosa y hablando con los serenos . . . pero a mí me	If people visited, I wondered why my brothers could fool around with scooters, fuck around with the cars in the garage and all that and talk to the watchmen . . . but they always sent me to my room as soon as men

mandaban siempre para el cuarto desde que venían hombres a la casa . . . Mi mamá nunca me dejaba hablar mucho con los serenos. Nada más con las sirvientas de la casa. It was very weird to me . . . Era como que ellos sabían, pero a la misma vez no querían decirlo . . . a mí se me notaba tanto que yo hasta parecía una muchachita. Y siempre me preguntaban, "Are you a boy or a girl? Are you a boy or a girl?" Entonces yo llegué a un punto en que me cansé y yo decía, "I'm a girl." "Oh. Entonces tú eres pata because you look like a lesbian. ¿Por qué te pelan así?" Mientras que me digan que yo sea hembra, yo hasta aceptaba que me dijeran que yo era una pata, you know, just para que me dijeran hembra.

came to visit . . . My mother never let me talk to the watchmen for too long. Only with the female servants in the house. It was very weird to me. . . . It was like they knew, but at the same time they didn't want to say it . . . it was so noticeable in my case that I looked like a little girl. And people always asked me, "Are you a boy or a girl? Are you a boy or a girl?" At one point, when I got tired of it, I said, "I'm a girl." "Oh. So you are a dyke because you look like a lesbian. Why do they cut your hair like that?" As long as they said that I was a female, I even accepted being called a dyke, you know, just so they would consider me a female.

The importance of not becoming "a faggot" in her father's eyes resulted in a socialization that restricted young Karla's movements to the domestic sphere while she witnessed the freedom of movement enjoyed by her brothers. Most informants presented accounts of socialization where the pedagogical influence of mothers loomed large in the inculcation and evaluation of proper masculine codes. In addition, Eugenio Heredia's preference for la casa, as he recounted it in contrast with his brothers' preference for la calle, may have been a preference shared by his parents, even though he did not mention it. However, something altogether distinct occurred with Bassant: her recollections pointed to a femininity so noticeable that it demanded the restriction of Bassant's movement within the household and restriction of her contact with males outside the family. Though observing that she was generally restricted in movement when "men came to visit," the concern with her accessibility revolved specifically around men who worked for the family as servants and men who were watchmen. Thus, Bassant's family sought to keep her away from tígueres, men who might have been looking to take advantage of her in ways they would (presumably) not take advantage of her brothers.

Bassant offered evidence of her socialization as a transsexual partly in contrast to her male siblings. Yet her recollection of her father's fear her becoming "like a faggot" brought Karla to elaborate on what made her socialization different from that of a cousin of hers, a man with whom she had a "roce sexual" (sexual tryst) as a child and stayed friendly with despite the marked difference in the way they were raised. This cousin, who Bassant knew lived as a closeted gay man, endured physical punishment from Bassant's uncle and psychiatric treatment and eventually married and had kids to conceal his homosexuality. As she explained to me, the issue with this cousin was not his effeminacy per se but his attraction to other men:

Yo sé que él es gay . . . si no es gay es bisexual porque él no era afemi-nado, pero . . . ¿Cómo te [explico]? Era como tú . . . que tú no eres un hombre afeminado pero eres un hombre . . .	I know that he is gay . . . if he's not gay, he's bisexual because he was not effeminate but . . . How do I [explain it]? He was like you . . . that you are not an effeminate man but you are a man . . .
Gay . . .	*Gay* . . .
Ajá, ¿tú entiendes? Pero yo sé que tú tuviste relaciones con otro hombre porque yo te conocí novio . . . Así, y en la familia se sabía pero afuera no se sabía . . .	Yep, you see? But I know that you had relationships with another man because I knew your boyfriend . . . Like that, and the family people knew but outside, nobody knew . . .

Bassant's socialization and the multiple referent forms of masculinity (those of her brothers, father, and cousin) offer a view of a trajectory that is markedly different from that of most men I interviewed. Indeed, in their descriptions of socializations, most of these men were emphatic about being "feminine" yet not as effeminate as the neighborhood loquitas. In some cases, their use of the word *loquita* explicitly went beyond male bodies that carried themselves in feminine ways to talk about men who dressed as women or who understood themselves as women. Someone like Bassant would probably fall under what some of these men would consider a loca, despite the fact that many of these men took for granted the differences between variously positioned actors who fell under the loca category.

Like other informants, Bassant used the interview as a site in which to construct herself narratively. This retrospective life history interview with a self-identified Dominican transsexual woman produced her positionality partly through a dialogue with a childhood self and an engagement with the strict masculinity of the father, her mother's policing of Bassant's movement and the people with whom she spoke, her brothers' relatively "freer" movement through la casa and la calle, and the shame and pressure of the presumably gay cousin. Karla also implicated my readability as a gay interviewer in the production of her differentiation from the gay cousin. In this way, and like many of my interviewees at different times, Bassant referenced the interview encounter as a moment of self-formation, a project of self-making that depended on traversing and mediating various identifications (identifications with past versus present selves, fathers, brothers, cousin, other inhabitants and visitors to their house, Bassant, and me). Though she enlisted me and my gayness in the project of making her cousin's homosexuality intelligible, this was not a knowledge she thought resulted from being sufficiently acquainted with this cousin to be in the know about the fact that he had a boyfriend. In this way, Bassant alluded to bits and pieces of information she had picked up to locate this cousin on a family and social map.

Bassant's father became increasingly comfortable with her as she began to transition. During the interview, she talked about how much it pleased her father to be out in public with her:

Mi papá me acepta ahora . . . inclusive que le fascina andar conmigo en la calle y cuando yo voy a Santo Domingo le fascina andar conmigo because he likes to see the fact that I look happier . . . que ya yo tengo mis implantes de senos, que me hice mi nariz, que estoy viviendo en el rol de mujer . . . pero todavía yo le recuerdo que yo no dejo de trabajar ni de estar cerca de los muchachos gay. Él quería que yo me alejara completamente de la vida gay, y, en realidad, una transexual no puede hacer eso.

My father accepts me now . . . he even loves walking down the street with me and when I go to Santo Domingo, he goes around with me because he likes to see the fact that I look happier . . . that I have my breast implants, that I fixed my nose, that I'm living as a woman . . . but I still remind him that I am not going to stop working or being close to gay men. He wanted me to move completely away from the gay life, but in reality, a transsexual cannot do that.

It is clear here that the pride of Karla's father must have resulted from his sense that the transition brought her closer to being happy with herself as a woman. For a transnational family that still had strong ties to their hometown and to the same neighborhood in Santo Domingo, it would be inaccurate to suggest that the father's pride and display of his daughter obtained from a form of "passing" that stemmed from severing the family's connections to who Karla was as a child. Nevertheless, Bassant's awareness of her position as a leader in the Dominican gay male community has entailed educating her father about what it means to be a transsexual woman. As much as he may have wanted her to establish distance from the gay men she continued to interact and work with, perhaps in order to minimize the traces of her transsexuality, Karla was emphatic about the political import of her process of becoming a woman. For her, the point was to continue to work with gay men.

::: Beto Ludovico Vargas, a Few Tostones Later,
    or, Forget the Madeleine

L'enfance est un pays en soi.
—DANY LAFERRIÈRE, *Je suis fatigué*

Through the examination of moments when informants spoke about their socializations as children, this chapter set out to demonstrate the centrality of la loca in giving shape to the trajectory of each one of the young boys remembered. My overall aim has been to offer evidence to substantiate the claim that la loca is an ambivalently invested performative, one that I called *gynographic* in order to emphasize its association with stereotypes of black working-class Dominican femininity. A second claim substantiated throughout the chapter is that the work of socialization is collective and is undertaken through engagement with what I called *specular circuits*. "Becoming a man" involves the acquisition of knowledge and learning to style the body in "masculine" ways through a combination of critique, observation, evaluation, and coaching predominantly from mothers, though also from other relatives and neighbors. Feelings of inadequacy or anxiety surely held in the childhoods that informants remembered, but those feelings prompted efforts not only to become concerned and invested in codes of so-called proper masculinity but also in an understanding of effeminacy as an authentic quality of who these individuals were, especially when nobody else was looking and, as we will see in the next chapter, in situations in which the interlocutors feel they can trust and respect one another.

I want to end this chapter by conjuring the image of a sissy boy. Call him Beto Ludovico Vargas. He was eight at the time of this incident. I heard about a gathering of family and friends on a hot afternoon in Santo Domingo, a meeting that involved the boy's mother and many friends of hers, many of whom were self-identified gay people. There were other boys and girls present in the room, and all of them were playing with the host's toys. The conversation on that muggy afternoon revolved around catching up on gossip, reminiscing about the shared past among friends, and joking. The informant who told me the story said that at one point during the afternoon, young Beto Ludovico must have been trying to figure out how he was going to deal with the heat. As if talking to himself in front of the mirror in a pedagogical manner, the boy blurted out, "¡Y ahora me voy a hacer UN MOÑO!" (And now, I'm going to do my hair!).

I laugh and laugh every time I hear this story, and, over the years I play out the scene in my head. As the informant recalled, the party stopped for a few beats. Nobody knew how the mother would react, especially being that gay men were present, but it was possible she would talk to her son later. But for the time being, she let it pass, and the joking returned.

What makes me laugh about the story is that Ludovico's flamboyance was totally unaware, totally unencumbered with concern and investment in being perceived as a "virile" boy. I laugh with him with the hope that maybe his mother did not say anything because she had begun to recognize and accept him as he was, or maybe because this moment in her gathering, which lasted just a few seconds, slipped her mind. I know that chances are stacked up against my speculative resolution to this story, but I prefer to laugh with him and through him, conjure up a past, childhood as a country where boys like him move through the world aware that they are loved as they are before they are taught who they must become.

CHAPTER 5

Code Swishing

: : :

Tú sabes que a veces entre nosotros, en diferentes grupos de amistades, se usa mucho el femenino para referirse el uno al otro. Te cambian el nombre. Te lo ponen en femenino o te dicen loca o te dicen maricón . . . hay gente que se relaciona con otra gente así. ¿Eso es algo que tú haces con algunas de tus amistades?

Máximo Domínguez: Oh sí, sí. Sí 'tamo' en grupo. Depende adonde tú estés y la confianza que tú tenga' con el grupo . . . si tú eres de mi confianza pues tú dice, "mira e'ta loca y mira la Roberto o la Raúl." ¿Tú sabe'? Tú pones "la." Pero que hay una confianza. Pero si hay una gente que no es de confianza . . . pues tú no va' a 'tá' con ese relajo.

¿Ha habido alguna ocasión en tu vida en la cual alguien lo haya hecho contigo, te haya hablado femenino y que a ti no te haya gustado?

Oh sí, una vez cuando . . . hace muchos años un dominicano. Ese muchacho no era amigo mío, pero

You know that sometimes, among us in different groups of friends, it is common for people to use the feminine to refer to one another. They change your name. They call you in the feminine or they call you loca or they call you maricón . . . there are people who have interpersonal relationships like that. Is that something you do with some of your friends?

Máximo Domínguez: Oh yes, yes. If we are with the group. It depends on where you are and the trust you have established with the group . . . if you are someone I trust, well, you say, "look at this loca or la Roberto or la Raúl." You know? You put the "la" [in front of the name, to feminize it]. But there is trust. But if a person is not someone I trust . . . you can't start that relajo [joking around].

Has there ever been a situation in your life in which someone did that—addressed you in the feminine and that you did not like?

Oh yes, one time . . . a Dominican guy. That guy was not my friend but I had

yo lo había visto en Santo Domingo . . . y me saludaba. Me saludaba y depué' yo lo veía aquí y un día yo estaba saliendo con este muchacho y me dijo [el conocido] "mira tú, loca." Y yo no le contesté nada. Yo lo ignoré, y eso es lo peor pa' una gente. Yo como que no fue a mí. Y el muchacho que andaba conmigo ni se dio cuenta porque tú . . . si tú me ves con alguien a mí, por ma' confianza que haiga. Si 'tamo juntos pues 'tá bien o si 'tamo en el círculo que 'tamo' siempre. Pero si tú me ves con una gente extraña saliendo, ¿cómo tú me viene' a vocear a mí, "mira loca"? Y yo lo único que le hice al tipo fue que lo ignoré, y él no me pudo decir nada. Porque ya sabe que con eso le dije todo. No le contesté nada.

seen him in Santo Domingo . . . and he would say hello to me. He would say hello and later I would see him here (in the United States), and one day I was going out with this guy and this acquaintance says to me "hey you, loca." And I did not answer back. I ignored him, and that's the worst you can do to somebody. I acted like what he said had nothing to do with me. And the guy I was with did not even notice because you . . . if you see me with someone, no matter how much trust there is between us. If we are hanging out together, OK, or if we are in the group. But if you see me with someone you don't know, how can you shout out "look here, loca?" The only thing I did was ignore him, and he couldn't say anything. Because I said everything with what I did. I did not answer back.

We skipped adolescence. This was partly my fault. Questions like "What did it mean to be a man when you were growing up?" prompted recollections of infancy and young adulthood. Yet the anecdotes offered by the men I interviewed did not focus on the latter period explicitly. Instead, they identified moments in their socialization as children and then spoke about negotiating masculinity as adults. An important feature of these discussions of masculinity was that these men revealed an investment in it as a location of legitimacy necessary to be viable in daily life. A second feature of these discussions was that the figure of la loca played an important role in the way these men presented themselves as men to others, inside as well as outside of circles of gay- and bisexual-identified men.

The informants navigated the worlds in which they lived through the use of verbal and other bodily communicative practices to engage others as close friends, strangers, or mere acquaintances. The mobilization of the distinction between public and private worlds was operative in the way they mapped out their relationship to their surroundings. Nevertheless, that distinction was not mobilized in ways characteristic of traditional liberal conceptualizations of public and private. These men deployed these categories in a sense closer to that described by the anthropologist Susan Gal: "Public and private do not simply describe the social world in any direct way; they are rather tools for arguments about and in that world."[1] Moving beyond the perception of public and private as distinct "places, domains, spheres of activity, or even types of interaction,"[2] this chapter follows Gal's suggestion to understand public and private as "indexical signs that are always relative: dependent for part of their referential meaning on the interactional contexts in which they are used."[3]

The interview exchange that opens this chapter illustrates the way Máximo Domínguez described and enacted boundaries and proximities with others. Though it appears, at first glance, to describe dynamics remembered or projected to conjunctions of space, time, and bodies situated elsewhere, Domínguez also called attention to the interview encounter itself. In other words, Domínguez's words taught me the way he wanted to be addressed by others (including myself), regardless of their sense of proximity to him, and always in relation to a third party who might (or might not) be trusted. Once they appear in front of you, the reader, Domínguez's words also mediate social relations through a series of ethical rules about the way actors like him related (or did not relate) to one another. To the degree that informants like Domínguez explained and enacted the dynamics they narrated with their use of language in the interviews, these men "did things with words" beyond mere description.[4] The capacity of words and bodily movements to describe and do things (particularly in situations where a sense of belonging cannot ever be taken for granted, where "safe spaces" are not always safe, and where one's interlocutors are as multiply situated as one is) is central to the discussion that follows. As a gynographic performative, la loca was central to the way the respondents traversed the social sphere, negotiated boundaries with others while legitimating themselves, and nurtured an always contingent, often conflicted, and always tenuous sense of belonging.[5]

The informants' views of their connection to others and to larger collectivities cast them as social actors skeptical of "community" when survival is a more urgent (and generally immediate) stake in the social relations they encountered in daily life.[6] Furthermore, survival and legitimacy in the social sphere require careful evaluation of one's interlocutors, as well as the sites for the production of subject positions in power relations.[7] As with the Nuyorican/Puerto Rican children in the anthropologist Ana Celia Zentella's pioneering study, negotiating various languages and linguistic codes was a way to wrestle with adverse conditions of possibility for survival and social advancement for the men with whom I spoke.[8] In the previous chapter, I proposed to extend conceptualizations of "language" to encompass communicative practices of bodies as they traversed the social world in the childhood recollections analyzed. The task at hand is to broaden this analysis by accounting for the politics of intimacy, respect, and belonging among the men I interviewed. Although they clearly associated legitimacy in daily life with "masculine" deportment, these men were astute theorists of everyday survival, and they expected their interlocutors, friends, and close associates to share in their careful interpretations of social situations in order to sustain their connections without losing the respect of others.

Attention to the dynamic exchanges of verbal and bodily codes of multiply situated social actors in daily life demands an analysis of the political stakes in quotidian interactions and analysis of these men's collaboration with others in producing competent interpretations of the situations they faced and of their social locations. *Code swishing* names communicative practices the informants deployed to engage the worlds and the others who surrounded them. Like *code switching*, code swishing references the ability of speakers to mobilize and circulate specific and recognizable signs to communicate with interlocutors who possessed the requisite literacy to interact as speakers.[9] What makes this coinage useful here is that it implicates gender dissent—in the invocation of la loca or of the humor, or *mariconería*, associated with that performative—as a communicative practice with a polyvalent expressive potential in daily life.[10] La loca may be the target of ridicule but also often is a performative invoked to index proximity and affective intimacy. In this sense, then, this chapter stresses the poverty of models that uphold the abjection of the "sissy" as lending coherence to hegemonic masculinities (heteronormative or homonormative). Though still influential, these models miss the extraordinary elasticity of the figure of the sissy and other signifiers like it.

The word *swish*, as an intransitive verb, means "to move with a hissing or whistling sound, as a whip" or "to rustle, as silk." As a noun, it is "used as a disparaging term for a homosexual man."[11] To be more precise, swishes in the mid-twentieth-century United States were gay men "who appropriated female gender mannerisms as visible markers of their sexual identity."[12]

To move, hiss, whistle, rustle when one moves: the images and meanings associated with swishing suggest auditory and visual excesses, which may or may not be completely under the control of the person who produces a given code.[13] Switching codes suggests a somewhat mechanical turning on or off, an activation or deactivation of signification in social practice, though astute analysts of code switching like Zentella deftly develop their interpretations of the phenomenon as response, challenge, and engagement of specific sociopolitical conditions.[14] Apart from implicating the embodiments of gendered dissent in daily life, there is no such thing as sovereign intentionality in the practices of code swishing I analyze below. Like other linguistic practices, the happy reception of these codes, once mobilized, depends on accurate apprehensions of the interactional dynamics together with proficient assessments of the scene of interaction, or the conjunctions of bodies, temporalities, and situational dynamics that result in specific proper (or improper) readings of the social.[15]

:::

In his response to my question in the excerpt that opened this chapter, Domínguez outlined the circumstances for interactions where verbal cues allow interlocutors to express closeness or distance with other gay- and bisexual-identified male acquaintances and friends. Mobilizing codes with multiple inflections may be a way for these men to practice belonging, but Domínguez's observations stressed that specific interactional conditions must be met in order for these signifiers to produce desired linkages between men. Some of these insights, which are quoted below, prompt the extended analysis that follows. Together, they illustrate the conditions of possibility, interpersonal politics, and stakes in code swishing.

"DEPENDE DE DONDE TÚ ESTÉS."

Domínguez astutely pointed out that usage of code swishing did not depend on who you are (*quien eres*) but of where you are (*donde tú estás*). This was not a naive reference to a physical view of context but rather an allusion to the conjunction of temporality, spatiality, bodily contact, and shared affective resources that result in being (*estar*) somewhere—what I call the *scene of interaction*.[16] It might be tempting to assume that ambivalence about the figure of la loca would result in its avoidance. But part of the complexity of this figure is related to its centrality in the making of boundaries and intimacies among these men.

Loca had multiple meanings and uses. Some informants almost never used the word to talk about themselves or their close friends, but they used it to speak negatively about someone else. Older informants, for instance, might use *loca* or its diminutive, *loquita*, to signify crassness, lack of manners, low class, immaturity, and lack of direction in life. These were "defects" that stood in the way of one's upward mobility. When older men used the words, their commentary usually referred to younger, working-class and darker-skinned men who called attention to themselves as homosexual men in explicit terms by behaving in allegedly low-class, uncontrolled ways. The more middle-class an informant was, the less public he was in his expression of gender dissent.[17]

Loca also expressed intimacy. The word might operate as a put-down with words like *maricón* or *pájaro*. But in groups of older and younger Dominican immigrant men, these words also functioned as expressions of closeness among friends, depending on the context. In these situations, use of these words might have been accompanied by others, which were usually articulated in feminine form (e.g., *'manita* for *hermanita* or "little sister"; *mujer* for "woman"; use of the feminine article *la* in saying, for example, "la José").

La loca can express both distance (through its deployment as an insult) and intimacy (through its use as a term of endearment). This highlights that its performative force is happy (if it successfully distances or brings together speakers) or unhappy (if it is incorrectly mobilized or, as Austin might put it, "misfires") given the specificity of what Austin calls "the total speech situation."[18] But the expressive potential of *la loca* as a performative obtains from both the specificity of its deployment in a given situation and the history of usages it invokes. As might be explained by Judith Butler, *la loca* is a performative that "does" things in the world in the moment it is mobilized, "and yet to the extent that the moment is ritualized, it is never merely a single moment . . . [it] is a condensed historicity: it exceeds itself in past and future directions, an effect of prior and future invocations that constitute and escape the instance of the utterance."[19] Yet the "total speech situation" or "condensed historicity" of *la loca* were only partially available to interlocutors like the ones Domínguez described in his commentary. Like other social actors, then, Domínguez was aware of the history of multiple usages of terms like *la loca* in his life and in others' lives, but the exigencies of daily life demanded skill in the interpretation and response to specific scenes of interaction.[20] The accuracy and correctness of his (or his interlocutors') apprehensions of a given scene were manifested in what he and others considered (in)appropriate responses, practices that corroborated the correctness and felicity or incorrectness and infelicity of the performatives mobilized.

"TÚ PONES 'LA.' PERO [ES] QUE HAY UNA CONFIANZA."

As a gynographic performative, *la loca* materializes relations that connect various social actors through temporally, situationally, and interactionally specific and interarticulated subject positions. Domínguez explained that using feminine articles, feminizing male names, and using words in the feminine form depend on a trust, a *confianza*, established before all interlocutors understand these practices as appropriate in one another's presence. It cannot be taken for granted that the valence of these connections was always positive. Thus, not every one of the informants welcomed code swishing, these *jueguitos* (little games, referring to the feminization of words and names) or *mariconerías,* and even those who engaged in these signifying practices did so given certain conditions.

Most informants were conflicted about which situations made the use of these terms acceptable. When I asked an informant if addressing others in the feminine or using the word *loca* to address his friends were things he did, he replied angrily that he did not and that he considered men who called each other *loca* to be "lacras humanas" (human waste). Other informants reported not engaging in these exchanges at all, making a point of addressing even their closest gay-identified friends in the masculine. But a third group of people like Martín Piedra, a dark-skinned man with a professional degree in accounting, played those games only with people he considered very close to him. These games were most likely to take place in private contexts where his masculinity was unlikely to be compromised:

Por ejemplo, a mí eso que [me llamen] de Martina. Que nadie venga con Martina. Porque yo soy hombre. Soy homosexual y me gustan los hombres. Y soy hombre. Los otros, pues que se inclinan y que esto— bueno, se respeta, porque es parte de su vida. . . . En un grupo de apoyo . . . me dice un colombiano a mí . . . "Martin . . . ¿Y tu marido?" ¡Ay!	For example, that whole thing [of people calling me] Martina. Nobody should call me Martina. Because I am a man. I am homosexual and I like men. And I am a man. The others who have those inclinations— well, I respect them because that's part of their lives. . . . In a support group . . . a Colombian asks me . . . "Martín . . . Where is your husband?"

Cuando ese hombre me dijo eso a mí, yo me puse mal. Yo ahí, le digo, "Ven acá. ¿Qué marido? Yo no soy mujer. A la mujer es [sic] que tienen marido. Yo tengo un amigo. Así que no. Yo con ustedes singo. Hago todo con hombre. Soy macho. Soy hombre. Y me gustan los hombres. ¿Cómo que marido, ni que marido? ¿Yo soy mujer?" . . . La única que persona que yo le acepto porque los dos nos respetamos. A los dos no nos gusta esa cuestión, esa mariconería que dicen. Pero sí, entre los dos ha habido una química que lo aceptamos. Yo le digo a él la argentina, y él me dice la dominicana.

Ay! When that man said that to me, I was beside myself. Right there, I said to him, "Wait. What husband? I am not a woman. Woman is [someone who has a] husband. I have a friend. So no. With you, I fuck. I do everything with a man. I am macho. I am a man. And I like men. What's this husband thing? Am I a woman?" . . . There is only one person from whom I accept that because we respect each other. We both like that thing, that mariconería, like other people say. But yes, between the two of us there is chemistry that we accept that interaction. I call him the Argentine woman and he calls me the Dominican woman.

Piedra's comments reveal the importance of respect in expressions of closeness articulated as mariconerías. He presented two distinct situations to illustrate an inappropriate and then an appropriate deployment of practices associated with effeminacy. The first situation, in the focus group where the Colombian acquaintance asked where Piedra's "husband" was, resulted in Piedra's correction of the interlocutor for the sake of clarifying the relationship between them and in front of everyone else. It is possible that this Colombian person and Piedra had exchanges in the past that suggested that asking about Piedra's husband could be appropriate. Piedra's objection to the tenor of the question in the support group suggested that he was also interested in establishing boundaries of address with other people. By asserting that he was not a woman but a man who fucked men, Piedra made clear to other participants in the support group that they may not go beyond those boundaries he established.

The second situation was clearly distinct from the first, in that Piedra and the speaker (the Argentine woman) respected one another and felt close enough to code swish. Yet part of the distinctiveness of that situation is that it did not involve third parties. In other words, the playful engagement in expressions of intimacy, jueguitos, or mariconerías, was also dependent on an accurate reading of existing or possible relations among all present. Additionally, Piedra had exchanges of this kind with "the Argentine woman" because both parties had a high enough regard for one another to engage in this verbal exchange without feeling that any form of disrespect was in the offing.

"PERO SI HAY UNA GENTE QUE NO ES DE CONFIANZA . . .
PUES TÚ NO VA' A 'TÁ' CON ESE RELAJO."[21]

Like Domínguez, many of the men with whom I spoke revealed awareness of the need to discern where it was appropriate and where it was not appropriate to use mariconerías to interact with other people. If there is no trust, there is no joking; appreciating the conceptual frames that Domínguez brought to his evaluation of social interactions helps us understand his view of the operations of the social order and the way one connects with others within it. These are views echoed in the commentary provided by other interviewees, and they offer clues about the way some of these men understood and engaged the social sphere.

One's viability as a male subject in power-laden relations depends on projections of seriousness that garner the recognition and respect of others. In a classic article, the anthropologist Anthony Lauria argues that in order to command the respect of others, actors must project "proper demeanor" in ways that are publicly recognizable, in addition to demonstrating deference toward others. As he writes, "one shows that one has sufficient regard for one's self, to be allocated a self in society."[22] In this model of sociality, the self does not surface from an individual; it is not a projection of an internal, ontological "truth" of being. Rather, it is "allocated" to someone once an actor (demarcated in Lauria's reading as a man) demonstrates that he abides by a specific ethical (and normative) regard of the self. Apart from framing the discussion of *respeto* in Puerto Rico in terms of men's relations with one another, Lauria usefully posits it as "a quality ascribed to the properties," and later on as a "value" that Puerto Rican men "give each other."[23] Thus, social viability and mobility depend on negotiating power and the recognition of its locations in the social: a man must produce a presence that commands the respect of others, but this respect, this value, must be recognized and ratified by one's observers. The value is not inherent to self-presentation but is realized in relations of exchange.

Serious masculinity, the type that commands deference, is produced as a wholesome, ordered, discreet, and measured body in the social, and requires individual and collective recognition for its access to privilege within patriarchal regimes to be realizable. Theorists of seriousness posit it as a value realized through an ethical (and compulsory, I would add) commitment to existing social hierarchies.[24] For the philosopher Jorge Portilla, seriousness represents an ethical commitment to the future of the status quo in a given sociality: "La seriedad es el compromiso íntimo y profundo que pacto conmigo mismo para sostener un valor en la existencia" (Seriousness is the intimate and profound pact with myself to sustain a value in existence).[25] The particular value in question is not that which is upheld by an individual but rather that which is agreed upon and upheld by a collective. Nevertheless, this internalization of the "pact" (it is an "intimate" and "profound" pact, after all) sutures actors to the social order.

The flip side of seriousness or, to put it more precisely, its suspension, is what Portilla defines as *relajo*. As Portilla explains, the pause in seriousness is directed toward a particular value upheld by a group, and to work as relajo, requires the complicity of others:[26] "La conducta regulada por el valor correspondiente es sustituida por una atmósfera de desorden en la que la realización del valor es imposible" (The behavior regulated by its corresponding value is substituted by an atmosphere of disorder in which realizing that value is impossible).[27] The philosopher Jorge Mañach y Robato, in his *Indagación del choteo*, suggests that it is not a coincidence that the word *relajo* means both "to joke" and "to relax" (the body) in Spanish: "Pues ¿qué significa esta palabra sino ese, el relajamiento de todos los vínculos y coyunturas que les dan a las cosas un aspecto articulado, una digna integridad?" (So what does this word mean if not this relaxation of the linkages and conjunctures that give things the aspect of being fully articulated, a dignified integrity?).[28] By analogizing the "relaxation" of muscles and joints in the human body to the loosening, temporal disaggregation, and smoothness of the body politic, Mañach y Robato points to the capacity that relajo has to effect a momentary suspension of power of authority and, thus, to "level" unequally situated social actors.[29]

While seriousness is an important value of masculinity, and relajo effects a momentary affront or suspension of the smooth trajectories of normativity, mariconerías stage an assault and interruption of the seamless, wholesome, and apparently fully articulated contours of masculinity itself.[30] What makes mariconería a specific form of relajo is the explicit centering of practices associated with la loca—practices that call attention to the gendered dissent of the actor(s) who engage in them but that ultimately challenge the appar-

ently strict boundaries between serious masculinity and locura. Although same-sex desire is central to informants' negotiation of mariconerías, and although the appearance of these codes in Dominican popular comedy can cast suspicion on a comedian's sexual orientation, this is a form of relajo with effects that are not unilaterally stigmatizing of the sissy and that settle in any certain way the "truth" of a comedian's sexuality.

Nevertheless, the conditions of possibility for mariconerías in general impacted quite specifically the informants' negotiation of the social. For these men, there were requirements in situations for them to feel comfortable enough to practice this kind of humor. As Piedra explained above, mutual respect and trust are absolutely essential. Lauria writes that *confianza* "refers to an invasion of that social space surrounding the self which is demarcated by the ritual avoidances enjoined by the maintenance of generalized respeto."[31] Other informants helped elaborate and expand on characterizations of scenes of interaction by rendering the distinctions that mattered to them in spatial terms. Aníbal Guerrero, for example, mentioned that one of the advantages of interacting with men in "gay spaces" was the facility with which one could interact without fear of being singled out or shamed for acting effeminate. As he explained, "Si se me sale mi partidera y mi vaina nadie me va a estar, ¿tú entiendes? 'Oh. Look at este pato. Mira este pájaro.' You know? Porque si yo hago mis manerismos—yo no los hago, pero si por mano 'el diablo se me salen en un sitio straight, van a decir, 'Oh. Pero mira este maricón'" (If I want to behave in an effeminate way nobody will be, you know? "Oh. Look at this fag. Look at this fag." You know? Because I engage in mannerisms—I don't do them but if for some reason they slip out in a straight place, they are going to say, "Oh. But look at this faggot"). The distinction Guerrero posited was not between a space of absolute freedom of bodily movement versus one of absolute restriction of it. His argument was not anchored in a sense of complete mastery of the use of his body either, for it was clear to him that despite "not engaging" in mannerisms, they may "slip out" of him. What was at stake for Guerrero and for many other men I interviewed, in fact, was the ability to inhabit spaces where those slips were tolerated. In this way, "straight" spaces were imagined as restrictive of men's behavior to a degree that made many of these participants avoid them.

Guerrero preferred gay spaces because of their tolerance of the occasional "pluma" (feather) he may have let out every so often.[32] Still, there were limits to tolerance, even by gay-identified people in and out of gay spaces. Readers will recall that when I asked him to characterize the people with whom he

associated, Guerrero mentioned that he did not like "personas escandalosas" (scandalous people). I asked him to elaborate:

Escandalosas, ¿en qué sentido?	Scandalous, in what sense?
Like a flaming queen. Porque como yo me comporto como soy, que aparento ser straight pero no lo soy, a mí no me gusta andar con una persona que esté partiéndose al lado mío . . . cuando uno está caminando, uno no sabe quién lo está mirando y eso. Y a mí no me gusta que me estén . . . catalogando de que "¡Ah! Mira una loca ahí donde va." ¿Tú entiendes? Porque yo ande con él, a mí me van a catalogar de loca también.	Like a flaming queen. Because I behave the way I do, that I look straight but I am not, I don't like to hang out with someone who is acting effeminate [*partiéndose*] next to me . . . when you are walking, you don't know who is looking at you. And I don't like people . . . categorizing me: "Ah! Look at that queen there." You know what I mean? Because if I am walking with him, I will be categorized as a flaming queen too.

Guerrero distinguished between the relative tolerance of the gay bar and the street as a space of transit where one came across strangers.[33] This particular distinction was central to many of the other men I interviewed, and it captures their necessarily contradictory relationship to la loca: this performative allowed them to stage connection and belonging with others as long as it did not cast doubt on their public masculinity to the detriment of their legitimacy, as long as it did not make them vulnerable to physical or verbal insult, or as long as it did not make them erotically unappealing. Walking down the street with someone "letting out feathers," then, rendered Guerrero as someone who could be "catalogued" as a loca. To return to Domínguez's phrase, if there is not an already established trust among the actors in a given scene of interaction, mariconerías are unacceptable forms of relajo.

Undoubtedly, internalized homophobia has something to do with many of these men's conflicted relationship with la loca. Yet internalized homophobia has limited explanatory power. This categorization neglects a serious consideration of how astute these men are as theorists of their own realities. They recognized that in order to survive and thrive in a heteronormative and homophobic world, they had to be strategic in the way they carried themselves in settings where appearing as locas foreclosed access to the privileges of masculinity. Furthermore, they understood that recognition, legitimacy, and respect were contingent upon social actors' ability to exercise some control in the way they were perceived. While the men with whom I spoke recognized that they had limited control over their bodies' significations, we will see below that they generally did not give up on the effort to demand the respect of others.

"CON ESO LE DIJE TODO. NO LE CONTESTÉ NADA."

Although informants strove to exercise control of the way others addressed them, many of them were also aware of their ultimate inability to control language. In interview after interview, there were moments that echoed the exchange Piedra recounted earlier: a person acquainted with the informant used what the informant considered an inappropriate form of address. It may have been inappropriate because they did not really know each other as well as the speaker thought or because the speaker used the term in the wrong context. It was up to the person who heard the "incorrect" address (usually the person recounting the incident) to "correct" the acquaintance, to put the other "back in their place."

It might be argued that in addressing people with these terms, persons whose invitations to code swish misfired did not mean for them to be interpreted as they were. Informants mentioned walking away from someone who addressed them incorrectly. They also mentioned watching their friends walking away from them for having done the same. This tended to baffle the person who first engaged in the mariconería. "Pensaba que éramos amigos" (I thought we were friends), they said.

Returning to the specific situation Domínguez discussed in the excerpt that opened this chapter helps unpack the workings of power in specific scenes of interaction. Furthermore, underscoring Domínguez's deployment of silence suggests that the exercise of power resides not only in the one who issues a call but also in the scene of interaction in which the call is issued.[34] The man in question was a fellow Dominican, and Domínguez recalled having interacted with him in the Dominican Republic and then in New York City. On one occasion, which happened to coincide with a time when Domínguez was going out (on a date?), the couple crossed paths with this acquaintance, who shouted at Domínguez, "Mira tú, loca" (Look here, loca). Domínguez's response was silence, which neutralized the call, because Domínguez's date did not notice the interaction, which Domínguez also suggested hurt his acquaintance. As Domínguez set, through silence, a firm boundary between the couple and the acquaintance in this scene of inter-action, he also foreclosed the possibility of interaction and social legibility of the person issuing the call. Whereas Domínguez said everything with his silence (". . . con eso le dije todo. Ne le contesté nada"), his acquaintance was effectively silenced (". . . lo ignore y él no me pudo decir nada").

This scene suggests the importance of heeding J. L. Austin's advice that an examination of the scene of an utterance is crucial for a full grasp of a performative's success or failure in "doing" something in the world. In this way, Austin's view helps revise the Althusserian scene of interpellation. In Althusser's frame, subjects are inaugurated into subjecthood through the operations of ideology in the famous allegorical scene of the "call" issued by an authority figure (in the street scene, he offers the example of a cop) in the form of a "Hey, you there" that is recognized by the individual who (walking down the street and after hearing that call) "turns round, believing/suspect-ing/knowing that it is for him, i.e. recognizing that 'it really is he' who is meant by the hailing."[35] In her reading of Althusser, Butler suggests that it is not always necessary to "turn around in order to be constituted as a sub-ject" and that the power of the hail need not always stem from its being issued by a voice; this is Butler's attempt to disarticulate Althusserian in-terpellation from authority, which derives from what she calls the "divine voice."[36] That disarticulation of power from figures (the cop, the king, the fa-ther) or sites of authority (the state) is necessary to understand the multiple and multi-sited operations of power in the social. But that disarticulation is not enough. Attention to the performative aspects of the hail itself *as issued in the scene of interaction* suggests that Domínguez's silence trumps the hap-piness of this utterance.

In the situation that Domínguez presented, he clearly was "hailed," re-gardless of his nonresponse to the hail itself. He knew that he was the "loca" being called out by his acquaintance. This is consistent with Butler's reread-ing of Althusser. Yet Domínguez's "ignorance" of the hail and his silence before it further disentangle the power of hailing as a performative from the authority of the one who emits the utterance. In this situation, recognition of the hail did not equal capitulation to its potentially stigmatizing power, for nonresponse, a refusal "to turn back" after hearing the call, jeopardized the happiness of the call itself. What was staged here was not misrecogni-tion of the hail; after all, Domínguez heard and understood it as addressed to him. What he illustrated was that given a scene of interaction in which the alignments of power are not clearly derived from alignments with the state or its institutions (this was an acquaintance, after all, not a cop), a lack of acknowledgment or indifference before the call can suspend a potentially stigmatizing trajectory of power.

For these men, there was a lot at stake in the use of language in daily life, and part of their consistently tense and contentious engagements with one another stemmed from their being embedded in worlds where being respected by others was crucial to be viable (as a community member, worker, and family member). The sections below examine more closely what was at stake for the informants symbolically and materially in specific cases. They also underlined the challenge of boundary setting in a world where one could pay a high price for being perceived as effeminate. My aim throughout what follows is not to resuscitate "resistance" but, instead, to explore informants' sophisticated understanding of the operations of power and their ongoing vigilance and contestation of its workings in their lives.

: : :

At work, informants interacted with people outside of their families and close friends. Some men also mentioned interacting with heterosexual and lesbian women, transgender individuals, heterosexual men, and people of other ethnicities in the workplace. Thus, work was one of the few spaces in daily life where informants established connections and relationships with people cutting across sexual, gender, racial, and ethnic boundaries.

A minority of the men I interviewed were employed in settings with anti-discrimination policies. All of these informants had permanent residence status or working papers. The undocumented ones at some point could work as professionals, because they changed their immigration status or were in the process of doing so.

Informants who worked as professionals kept watch over their behavior at work as part of their projection of seriousness. Being serious, for them, was bound with their sense that masculine behavior legitimized them. Protections may have been available to informants working in professional environments. Still, some men reported doing the utmost to keep their personal lives out of the work environment. In some cases, discretion about one's life translated into keeping any reference to homosexuality or gender nonconformity out of the office. They may have abstained from making references to their personal lives in phone conversations and in exchanges with colleagues and friends. But some informants who held jobs like these managed to be out in the workplace and "soltar una plumita de vez en cuando" (let out a feather every once in a while) without suffering for it.

This does not mean that professional men were in the closet, however. Men who worked as professionals tended to be out in the workplace, though each man handled it differently. Some told their coworkers and supervisors, though most assumed that there was no reason anyone should know their business. They did not hide it, but when others tried to use their homosexuality against them in public, one common defense strategy was to make fun of naive and prudish attackers who thought they caused damage by revealing what was obvious to everyone else. Shaming the occasional attacker in this way discouraged others from confrontation with the informants over this issue.

Projecting seriousness was also of the essence to most informants who worked outside of areas connected with upward mobility. Informants struggled to legitimize their presence within the workplace, and gender identification played a role in these efforts. What an individual did to command that seriousness varied from person to person. For some men, being at work required leaving out most of their explicit connections with other homosexual men. This was especially true of informants who were in environments that included heterosexual men and women. Some developed friendships with heterosexual men by participating in discussions about women. Yet in many cases informants stayed silent about their personal lives, whereas their heterosexual coworkers shared their experiences. There were added pressures in the Dominican Republic for these informants to behave this way; men may have been even required to produce a narrative about "girlfriends" for the benefit of all around them.

The following example illustrates the way one informant struggled to be legitimized at work. Pablo Arismendi was a thirty-year-old, dark-brown-skinned Dominican man who came to the United States through Central America. He arrived in a rural southern state with a work permit granted to him through the sponsoring American couple for whom he worked. After working for this couple, Arismendi moved to New York. Arismendi's work history in the United States bears similarities to that of many other informants: he worked in factories; his jobs lasted while his supervisors ignored his immigration status; and Arismendi lost jobs after his immigration status became inconvenient to his employers.

What set Arismendi apart from other informants was that he was re-garded as a feminine man. Indeed, many other informants used the word *loca* to talk about Arismendi, and the use of the word carried much of the admiration *and* ambivalence described earlier. Apart from calling attention to himself through his behavior, Arismendi had characteristics the older informants associated with the younger Dominican gay men they criticized. He was dark-skinned, working class, and provocatively dressed. He dyed his hair, associated with transgender individuals and "children" of the houses,[37] and he behaved irreverently wherever he went.

In general, informants were concerned about the ways others perceived them. Living as a feminine man made Pablo Arismendi particularly aware of the way people saw him and addressed him in public. Would the people around him, moved by fascination and perverse curiosity with his behavior, scrutinize Arismendi for the limp wrist they could laugh at? Would people disrespect him?

What performance of masculinity was considered legitimate at work? This was a crucial question, for the degree of tolerance of gender noncon-formity in the workplace had a direct relationship to informants' comfort at work and to whether they could keep the job. Whereas for many informants the answer was a deceptively simple "act like a man," for Pablo Arismendi this question brought an added set of complications. How did a "feminine" man legitimize himself at work? The example of Arismendi's experience in two work spaces will illustrate that, apart from social, there were economic imperatives for someone like him to be mindful the ways in which his body was read.

Arismendi worked in various jobs in the Central American country he lived in: selling cosmetics and other merchandise informally, as a survey interviewer for a marketing research company, and finally as a housekeeper for the couple who brought him to the United States. Arismendi's job in a New Jersey factory was his first experience with manual labor. It was a shock to him, but he had to push ahead because he had lost a job and because he had been recommended for this one by a friend of his mother:

Al principio fue un poquito duro para mí porque yo nunca había bregado con martillos, destornilladores. Para mí, aquello era espantoso. Entonces	At first it was a little hard for me because I had never worked with hammers, screwdrivers. For me, that was horrible. Then I had to appear

ahí yo tenía que mostrarme más hombre de lo que . . . realmente no . . . Yo soy hombre pero, tenía que portarme más varonil porque era [el trabajo estaba conectado con] una amiga de mamá. La gente se presta para comentar y entonces, yo nunca había agarrado destornilladores ni taladros y . . . yo recuerdo la primera vez que yo agarré el taladro. Yo quise gritar, pero yo me refrené . . . a la primera semana, ya yo aprendí cómo dominar todo. Pero al principio, yo como que agarraba las cosas con miedo y con mucha delicadeza.

like more of a man than . . . I really do not . . . I am a man but I had to behave in a more masculine way because it was [the job was connected to] a friend of my mother. People make comments and then, I had never grabbed screwdrivers, drills and . . . I remember the first time that I grabbed a drill. I wanted to scream but I controlled myself . . . by the first week I had learned how to master everything. But at first, I grabbed things with fear and very delicately.

While discussing working at this factory, Arismendi mentioned that it mattered to him that others address him respectfully despite how different he appeared. The presence of a close friend of his mother (who lived in Santo Domingo) in connection with this job made Arismendi uneasy enough to master his fear of hitting nails with a hammer. Throughout the time he worked there, he knew he had to be cautious with male colleagues. There were some, Arismendi recounted, who were sincere in their camaraderie. But Arismendi had to "put others in their place" when they made inappropriate comments about Arismendi's behavior.

For Arismendi, a worker commanded authority by keeping others at a distance. One needed to command authority to be a successful worker, whether one worked at a factory or at the beauty parlor,[38] Arismendi's workplace at the time of our interview. By insisting on being treated as a man despite his gender nonconformity, Arismendi "marca[ba] la diferencia" (mark[ed] the difference) between himself and others. Legitimacy and viability were, for Arismendi, tied up in defending the integrity of his claim on respect, regardless of his appearance.

There was something else that Arismendi connected strongly with the way he was seen: the way others addressed him. Arismendi insisted on being addressed as "él" (he) in public environments, despite the fact that many people around him wanted to address him as "ella" (she) because of his gender nonconformity. This was difficult for Arismendi, and he found himself continually reminding friends, colleagues, and clients of the appropriate forms of address inside and outside his workspace:

¿Dónde está la diferencia en que te digan loca, 'manita . . . ?

What makes the difference in being called loca, little sister . . . ?

Porque es que uno tiene que . . . en tu trabajo tú tienes que dar una imagen de autoridad . . . o que te respeten. O sea, si tú quieres escalar en un trabajo, tú tienes que ser cordial con tus compañeros de trabajo, pero mantener la raya de que . . . mantener la línea de que sepan quién eres tú y . . . quién es el otro. Yo toda la vida, siempre he sabido cuál es mi puesto. Mira, yo sé hasta dónde traspasar y no . . . No traspaso los límites. Por eso he alcanzado y . . . y puedo decir que me siento una persona afortunada, porque yo he logrado muchas cosas precisamente por eso, porque si . . . siempre he mantenido, me he mantenido en mi lugar. . . .

Because one has to . . . at your job you need to project an image of authority . . . or get people to respect you. In other words, if you want to advance in your job, you have to be polite with your work colleagues but maintain a line that . . . maintain the line so they know who you are and . . . who is the other. All of my life, I have known what is my place. Look, I know up to what point I might step beyond or not . . . I don't step beyond the limits. It is for this that I have achieved and . . . and I can say that I feel I am a fortunate person because I have accomplished a lot of things exactly for that because it's like that . . . I have always maintained, I have always stayed in my place. . . .

Háblame un poquito más de la autoridad y del masculino vs. el femenino . . .

Tell me a little more about authority and the masculine vs. feminine . . .

Porque viene el irrespeto. Porque cuando tú estás en un trabajo—aquí en los trabajos uno va escalando. Tú puedes entrar y yo por lo . . . por lo menos en los trabajos que yo he tenido, desde ese país donde vivía hasta la fecha, yo he ido escalando. Yo entré en un trabajo, en ese país, como un simple encuestador y terminé siendo supervisor, precisamente por eso: porque demostré capacidad y

Because then people disrespect you. Because when you are at work—here you can begin to move up at work. You can begin and I . . . at least in the jobs I've had, from that country I lived in until today, I have been moving up. I started a job, in that country, as a simple interviewer and I ended up becoming a supervisor precisely because I demonstrated

distancia. . . . Entonces, uno siempre tiene que tratar de . . . tener una buena relación con los compañeros, pero manteniendo la línea dentro del trabajo. Aunque en la discoteca se relaje un poco y también con el límite porque yo soy alérgico a los escándalos. No me gustan.

¿Y cómo tú traduces esas reglas que tú tienes en tu ámbito de trabajo?

Precisamente . . . cuando yo comencé a trabajar en el salón. . . . un peluquero y después una peluquera, me dijo, "Niña, ven acá." Yo fui muy tranquilo. En un momento que estábamos libres dije, ¿Puedo hablar contigo? Le voy a decir, "Mira. Que yo sea gay y me gusten los hombres no es para que tú te refieras a mí, delante de todo el mundo, como una mujer porque no me gusta. Mi nombre es Pablo. Tú me llamas por ese nombre, y yo te hago to' lo que tú quieras. Y me respetas para que yo te respete. Porque no quiero mezclar una cosa con la otra. Tú eres dueño del salón. Tú eres socio del salón. Yo soy un empleado pero, si tú quieres que yo te respete, tú me respetas a mí." Jamás, en el salón, nadie me dice. Me llaman por mi nombre. . . . Y mira, que yo visto en el salón. Me pongo ropas cortas, pegadas. Me ando cambiando el color del cabello . . . Tanto los clientes como los . . . los peluqueros así lo tienen claro. Porque hay clientes que se le ha ido la mano y yo muy

capacity and distance. . . . Then, you always have to try to . . . have a good relationship with the work colleagues, but maintaining the line at work. Even if in the disco you can kid around a little and there also up to a certain point because I don't like it when people make a big fuss. I don't like it.

And how do you translate the rules you have to the workplace?

Precisely . . . when I started working at the beauty parlor . . . one male hairdresser and then a female hairdresser said to me, "Little girl, come here." I went up to them quietly. In a moment when we were free I told them, can I talk to you? I am going to tell them, "Look. Just because I am gay and I like men does not allow you to address me, in front of everyone, like a woman, because I don't like it. My name is Pablo. You call me by that name and I'll do everything you want. Respect me so I will respect you. Because I don't want to mix up one thing with the other. You are the owner of the beauty parlor. You are a client of the beauty parlor. I am an employee but, if you want me to respect you, you respect me." Never, in the beauty parlor, nobody calls me [names]. They call me by my name. . . . And look, I dress up at the beauty parlor. I put on short and close-fitting clothes. I am always changing the color of my hair. . . .

cordialmente, "Ven, vamos a hablar una cosa. Mira, tú eres mi amigo y todo pero, delante de las personas no te, cuando estemos en grupo, así en confianza no . . . no me digas manita, ni loca, ni nada así porque a mí . . . esos términos no me gustan." Yo te lo digo la primera vez suavecito. Te llamo. Si me lo vuelves a hacer, te hago pasar una vergüenza terrible. Y ya.

The clients and . . . the hairdressers have it clear. Because there are clients who have stepped beyond their boundaries and I, very politely, say "Come here, let's talk about something. Look, you are my friend and all but, in front of people don't, when we are in front of a group, even if we trust each other . . . don't call me little sister, or loca . . . I don't like those terms." I'll tell you the first time nicely. If you do it again, I embarrass you terribly. And that's it.

Arismendi's strategy countered that of informants who assumed that one could legitimize oneself at work only if one performed proper masculinity. Arismendi managed to legitimize himself in work situations *without* jeopardizing his gender nonconformity. While demanding to be addressed as a man and reproducing the link of masculine forms of address to seriousness, Arismendi showed that one can be a feminine man without subjecting oneself to the disrespect that effeminacy may invite. He fought back, given that certain conditions in his workplace allow him to do so.

Arismendi and many other informants experienced being addressed publicly in the feminine almost as a violation of the social boundaries they established with others. This was most evident in Arismendi's emphasis on social distance as a requirement for good working relationships. When he talked about the need to "maintain a line . . . so they know who you are and . . . who is the other," Arismendi suggested that good working relationships emerged from the interaction of legitimate individual subjects with clear social boundaries demarcated in their interactions. Subjects' legitimacy at work was established by the way they consented to being addressed by others. For Arismendi, being addressed as a man constituted a recognition and validation of who he was at work. When he was addressed in the feminine, Arismendi experienced humiliation and a violation of established boundaries. Fundamental to this sense of humiliation was feeling that the colleague forgot his or her place in Arismendi's work environment.

The workplace was by no means the only social space where informants associated masculine address with seriousness, formality, distance, and

legitimacy and feminine address with informality, blurred boundaries, and lack of authority. But the consistency with which they did reveals how attuned informants were to social structures that legitimated those who could claim masculine status and that systematically produced illegitimate subjects through their feminization. An informant who read this chapter in response to this statement said, "In fact, it is a common belief that only serious men can be promoted and taken seriously. Yes, they [employers] play the gay game [nondiscrimination policies] but they know that there is no remote possibility for a Latino fag in the workplace to be able to survive or succeed!" Arismendi demanded and succeeded in being addressed as a man at the "hegemonic female space" of the beauty parlor.[39] This success demonstrates the way some workplaces allowed informants to push others to see them as men and to expand on the meanings and practices colleagues and clients associated with legitimate masculinity. As Arismendi said, everyone who interacted with him understood how to treat him, even if "I dress up at the beauty parlor . . . put on short and close-fitting clothes . . . am always changing the color of my hair."

However, that Arismendi had to remind others—sometimes kindly but other times rudely—of what he considered appropriate ways of address shows that this was far from a settled matter for him and for the people surrounding him. Pablo Arismendi's masculine persona (articulated here through the "proper gendering") had to be continually legitimized. He could dress in the way he wanted at a beauty parlor, but this way of dressing would probably not be acceptable in other spaces such as a barbershop or a factory. This means that his success in commanding the respect of others was tied as much to Arismendi's attitude toward his effeminacy as it is to whether his workplace allowed for these negotiations.

: : :

In the public contexts in which I have heard it, the term *loca* mediated important divisions and tensions within groups of Dominican gay- and bisexual-identified men. At a Gay, Lesbian, Bisexual, and Transgender Pride event held in Washington Heights during the time when I conducted the research for this book, men appeared segregated by age and gender self-presentation. The following is an excerpt from my ethnographic observations:

> There were three distinct groups. There were men whose ages ranged from mid-twenties to their thirties. Many of them seemed to integrate "gay" styles

of self-presentation in their attire—seemed to be going to the gym and wearing clothes to display the results. There was a group of men who seemed older—in their forties, perhaps—and who could be distinguished from the first group by their more conservative clothing and demeanor. These two groups tended to mingle amongst themselves but there was less interaction with the third group. Many of these were even younger men—teens, early twenties?—generally several shades darker-skinned and engaging in pretty flamboyant behavior, which seemed to disturb the older folks. They were separated from the other groups and dispersed, playing games such as volleyball. The distinctions I am drawing may well be a function of the cliques—since the older guys seemed as gossipy and cliquish as the younger ones. But in a conversation with one older guy, the issue of the younger guys came up. "Son bien fuertes" (They are quite rough), he said, in the sense that they were really daring, irreverent.[40]

I pointed out earlier that the word *loca*, when used by older men (those in my sample) to describe younger ones, tended to capture a view of these younger men as "crass," "low class," and so on. However, the older men sometimes had a positive attitude toward the younger men. A word like *fuerte* used by an older man to talk about a younger one—literally meaning "strong" but also meaning irreverent, daring, and bold—signaled a secret admiration *and* apprehension about the way the younger men carried themselves. This admiration and apprehension were also present in the use of the term *loca* throughout the interviews.

The behavior of men aged eighteen to twenty-five did not always seem outrageous to the older folks. Younger men who abided by the standards of white, urban, middle-class gayness (i.e., "straight acting," gym body, fashionable clothing, etc.) generally did not have problems establishing friendships with older men, and this was also evident during the above episode. This may be partly because these young men were perceived as attractive and upwardly mobile in ways consistent with the aspirations of the older men. The younger men who seemed outrageous to these older men tended to be those whose behavior and self-presentation were connected with working-class, United States–based sexual-minority subcultures. The comfort with which younger men displayed effeminacy, associated with trans individuals, and called attention to themselves through their participation in events, dancing (some of which included "voguing"), and their visible identification with other queers of color was a source of ambivalence for the older men present.

While revealing their uneasiness with the way younger men presented themselves publicly, some older men used the word *loca* in an admiring way to describe and celebrate defiant effeminacy, courage, or irreverence.

Still, admiration has limits. Older men may be impressed by younger men's gumption. Nevertheless, being seen as a loquita has a price. Diego Abreu located the loquita figure in the context of a larger description of the "styles" he could identify among fellow Dominican gay- and bisexual-identified men:

Háblame de las diferencias de estilos.

Tell me about the differences in style.

Dentro de la comunidad homosexual . . . yo pienso que hay como seis o siete diferencias de estilos . . . Están las dragas, por ejemplo . . . Estos hombres con estas tetas, con esta idea de creer que alguna vez fueron mujeres o que van a ser mujeres. O sea, está ese grupo. Está después otro grupo que es el de los muchachitos así muy partidos, pero que en realidad no quieren ponerse tetas, pero que son más hamaquitas que un columpio allí en el parque [de] mi abuela. Y que no le veo yo a ellos ni a ellas entonces la intención de una, de una vía de superación centrada en escuelas por ejemplo. Centrados en aprender inglés. Muchísimos de ellos son ilegal, todavía aquí con quince años ¿tú ves? Viviendo aquí . . . Después sigue el homosexual así un poquito más—el estilo tuyo, que no es la loquita ¿tú sabes? No es la hamaquita . . . Después sigue otro estilo ¿tú sabes? Por ejemplo el estilo mío [self-identified as masculine, straight-acting] . . . Pero que en verdad es un

In the homosexual community . . . I think there are about six or seven differences of styles . . . You have the drag queens, for example . . . These men with tits, with this idea, this belief that they were or will be women. In other words, there is that group. Then you have the group of the very swishy boys [*muchachitos así muy partidos*], but who in fact do not want to have tits, but who seem more of a hammock [*hamaquitas*, referencing the walking style] than a swing in my grandmother's park. And I don't see in them [*ellos y ellas*] the intention of finding ways to improve themselves through education, for example. Centered in learning to speak English. Many of them are illegal, though they have been here for fifteen years, you see. Living here . . . Then you have the homosexual who is a little more . . . your style, which is not that of the little queens [*loquitas*], you know? Not the little hammock [*hamaquita*] . . . Then you have the other style, you know? For ex-

pájaro más en el grupo . . . Hay una serie de, ¿tú sabes? de clasificaciones que yo personalmente hago de nosotros porque tú no eres . . . No eres tú solo. Tú ni eres la draga. Ni eres la ponkita. Ni eres la loquita. Ni eres el que esta fleteando [flirteando] por ahí así por así. Tú eres el de la relación estable. De un novio o de una carrera una serie de cosas. ¿Tú sabes? En ese grupo se ajusta un grupo de personas, ¿tú ves? Hay una serie de diferencias que sí están ahí.

ample, there is my style [masculine-identified, straight-acting] . . . But who, in reality, is another queen [*pájaro*] in the group . . . There is a series of, you know? Classifications that I draw among us because you are not. . . . It's not just you. You are not the drag queen. You are not the femme boy [*ponkita*]. You are not the little queen [*loquita*]. You are not the one who is out there flirting with everyone [*fleteando*]. You are the type who has the stable relationship. Of a boyfriend and a career and a bunch of other things. You know? And in that group there are some people, you know? There are differences that are really there.

When I followed up his discussion with a question about whether these differences in style made organizing these groups easy or difficult, Abreu replied that it made it difficult because men from one group would not want to associate with the other. Abreu's commentary is useful not because it is representative of what all the men thought but more because his classificatory impulse located loquitas in a circuit that was strongly embedded not just in gender dissent, but in the larger implications of that dissent for men who were quite preoccupied with prospects of upward mobility.

Abreu's preoccupation with his upward mobility, and his emphasis on locating locas outside of spheres of what he learned to see as legitimate as a child, were explored in the last chapter. The first striking feature of his commentary above is that he developed a classificatory scheme in which he put himself and me. Abreu may be "another queen in the group," as he claimed, but he stood a certain distance from both loquitas and from me, his interviewer. I may not have been as masculine as he was, but in Abreu's mind, the fact that I was not "out there" with the loquitas and the fact that I appeared to have a career (as evidenced by the project of interviewing him for this book) suggested that I was another "type," one he associated with a "stable relationship" and with other attributes of upward mobility. Whereas

the loquitas of Abreu's youth "chased after tígueres in back alleys," he emphasized that he saw limited prospects of upward mobility in the ones he knew when we spoke.

It is not a coincidence that Abreu located trans individuals (whose heterogeneity he glossed through the term *drag queen*) and loquitas in an attitudinally and structurally similar position. In its more expansive sense, the word *loca* names all varieties of gender-dissenting male-bodied individuals, including people of trans experience. They had in common more than the fact that they were "wasting time" chasing after men and being preoccupied with having been or becoming "women." What troubled Abreu and other men like him was that these individuals were not facing the challenges that, if overcome, could produce upward mobility in them. They were not pursuing an education or legalization; they were not learning to speak English. To Abreu and many of the informants, loquitas were creatures unable to overcome immaturity (partly indexed by their effeminacy), which translates into limited prospects to become the men they should become and to associate with the men with whom they should associate.

::: *Pisar fino*

Even though informants attempted to control the ways they were addressed, the ways they were seen by straight and gay others were another source of tension. For informants who identified as locas or whom others identified as that, gender nonconformity was more of a problem for the people surrounding them, who were anxious about being considered locas by association. This anxiety played out in interpersonal relationships, as those apprehensive about being associated with effeminacy policed the behavior of their friends. Latoya Mejía, a black Dominican professional, wrestled with his friends' anxieties about the way they were perceived, especially when they were with him in public spaces. Mejía's friends devoted a lot of their attention to controlling the way *he* appeared to others.[41] Indeed, Mejía's friends tended to be so scandalized by his behavior that they forgot that they were also being observed and evaluated:

¿Alguna anécdota que tú tengas de un momento donde alguien te dijo, "Fulano, contrólate"?	Any anecdote you may have where somebody said to you, "Hey! Control yourself"?

Oh, sí. A mí me ha pasado muchas veces. Yo . . . si no abro la boca, y estoy tranquilo, paso quizás por feo. . . . Pero me pasó una anécdota muy simpática con un amigo. Y fue aquí, en Nueva York. Pero me pudo haber pasado allá, porque allá [en República Dominicana] también me ha pasado. Íbamos a visitar a una prima de él y ese día íbamos todo un grupo de locas en el carro. Íbamos "cua cua cua" [hablando como patos] íbamos . . . estábamos primero de tiendas, y yo estaba ese día, aquí en Nueva York, imagínate, con todas mis plumas al aire. Y cuando íbamos ya llegando a la casa de su prima, me ha dicho "Tú, contrólate. Que te has pasado la tarde entera más partido que nunca. Y vamos para donde mi prima. Y aunque ella sepa que nosotros somos gay, va a haber otros primos y otros amigos que no tienen por qué verte con esa partidera." Y digo, "Hijo, pero déjame llegar porque . . . yo es porque estamos aquí en el grupo." "No, no, no, no, no, que a ti te encanta siempre estar como más sobresalido." Yo dije "Bueno. La más loca soy yo." Me quedé tranquilo. Llegamos a la casa de la prima. Pasamos el rato muy bien. Cenamos. Llegaron los demás invitados. Todo el mundo, un grupo de gente. Muchos desconocidos para el primo de la prima . . . pasó algo de repente, que la prima estaba haciendo un cuento del trabajo, que había una

Oh, yes. That has happened to me many times. I . . . if I close my mouth and stay quiet, I may pass for ugly. . . . But a very funny anecdote happened to me with a friend. And it was here, in New York. But it could have happened to me over there because over there [in the Dominican Republic] it has also happened to me. We were going to visit this cousin of his and that day all of the locas were going in the car. We were "quack quack quack" [talking like ducks] we were going . . . first, we were shopping and that day I was, as you can imagine, showing off all of my feathers here in New York. And when we were close to the house of his cousin, my friend said, "You, control yourself. You have spent the whole afternoon behaving like a sissy. And we are going to my cousin's house. And even though she knows we are gay, there will be other cousins and other friends who don't have to see you acting like that." And I said, "But let me get there because . . . I am acting like that because we are all here as a group." "No, no, no, no, no, you always like to stand out." And I said, "Well. I am the biggest loca here." So I was quiet. We arrived at the cousin's house. We had a good time there. We had dinner. The other guests arrived. Everybody, a group of people. Many of these people were strangers to the cousin of the

chica que era lesbiana. Otro muchacho decía, "No, ella no es." Y ella decía "Sí ella es. Lo que pasa es que ella . . . hace como de las dos cosas . . . es bisexual porque no le . . . no le conviene" qué sé yo cuánto. "Además, ella es como tú, primo, que eres gay." O sea, declaró al primo que estaba ahí . . . que era el que me había mandado a callar a mí por partida. Y fue él que quedó—todo el mundo supo que él era gay. O sea, estaba todo el mundo tranquilo, sin embargo a él lo descubrieron. O sea, de qué te vale a ti decir contrólate o no contrólate si todo el mundo sabe qué tú eres o qué no . . . O lo supo ahí, en ese momento . . .

Lo que a mí me pasó, allá. Estábamos un amigo mío, bien amigo mío, en el gimnasio, y me encuentro con otro amigo de nosotros y me dijo "Mira, ahí en el sauna están diciendo que tú y fulano son marido y mujer. [Risa ambos.] Y que tú eres el macho y ella la hembra." Claro él era el más partido. Sin embargo, cada vez que llegábamos al gimnasio, él me decía, "Contrólate. No te partas. Contrólate." Sin embargo, el que estaba desacreditado, como que yo era el marido de él, era él. O sea, ¿de qué te vale mandar a controlar tanto? O sea, contrólate tú. Fíjate tú en lo que tú estás haciendo . . . porque cada quién es como es. Entonces . . . yo siempre he dicho que en la medida que tú aceptas al otro . . . Yo nunca me he controlado

hostess . . . something happened suddenly, that the hostess [female cousin of Latoya's friend] was telling a story about work, that there was a girl there who was a lesbian. Another guy said, "No, she is not." And she said, "Yes she is. What happens is that she . . . does the two things . . . is bisexual because it is not . . . convenient" and this and that. "Besides, she is gay like you, cousin." In other words, she "outed" the cousin who was there—the one who had told me to shut up for being such a sissy. And he was the one who ended up— everyone found out that he was gay. In other words, everyone was quiet and he was, nonetheless, outed. In other words, what's the point to saying control yourself or don't control yourself if everyone knows what you are and what you are not . . .

Something else happened to me there [in the Dominican Republic]. I was with a friend, a very good friend, at the gym and I bump into another friend of ours and he said, "Look, in the sauna they are saying that you and this guy are husband and wife. [Both laugh.] And that you are the macho and she is the female." Of course, he is the more effeminate one of us two. Nonetheless, every time we came close to the gym he would say, "Control yourself. Don't act like a sissy. Control yourself." Then again, he was the one who was

en mi forma de ser. Nunca. Yo te lo puedo decir. Yo seré atípico. Pero nunca me he controlado. Yo hasta bailaba ballet cuando pequeño. Y cuando pequeño me voceaban maricón, mariquita . . . hasta me, me ponían el nombre de hembra. A mí me decían un apodo, Pepo, me decían Pepa. O sea, por el estilo. O sea que yo siempre he sido media rotica. . . . Ya grande, media rotota.

already discredited. Everyone said I was his husband. So what's the point of demanding so much that people control themselves? Control yourself. Look at what you are doing . . . because everyone is the way everyone is. Then . . . I have always said that to the same degree that you accept others. . . . I have never controlled how I am. Never. I can tell you. I may be atypical. I even danced ballet when I was little. And when I was little people called me maricón, mariquita . . . they even called me by a female name. My nickname was Pepo but people called me Pepa. So like that. So that I have always been a little sissy . . . Now that I've grown up, I am a big sissy.

Mejía claimed he had experiences like the first one in New York and Santo Domingo. Given that his circle of friends was transnational, being treated this way by friends in New York and Santo Domingo suggests that migration might not change social norms. The ways Mejía was treated also suggest that his friends continued to be invested in controlling his (and their) body in the United States. As they saw it, Mejía's effeminacy interfered with their legitimacy.

In both situations Mejía described, friends asked him (for different reasons) to "control himself" because they thought him already too "obvious." These men assumed that Mejía's gender nonconformity exposed him—and them, by association—to social rejection and vulnerability. In both stories, and in different ways, friends ended up being read or discovered as homosexuals by others in public spaces. The pressure for Mejía to "control himself" came from other homosexual friends, not from heterosexual friends or acquaintances. These anecdotes illustrate two approaches to gender identification: Mejía's effeminate style and the more manly style advocated (though not necessarily realized) by his friends. These approaches came into conflict. One may be more acceptable to Mejía's friends and to most people they encountered. But it was obvious to Mejía that something went wrong for his friends as they tried to legitimize themselves in public environments. Be it because of someone else's revelation or because of the "feathers" that slipped out, Mejía's friends were unable to fully control the practices through which their bodies became legible to others. Their bodies always said more than what Mejía's friends wanted to say.

Mejía's self-presentation was different from that of most men in his circle. These were men whose class background or aspirations of upward mobility pushed them to neutralize varying degrees of gender nonconformity in public environments. They contrived their movements, changed their tone of voice, or limited the use of the feminine in their address. Running jokes among some members of this circle involved the change in the tone of voice of some of the men when they were on the phone talking to presumably straight strangers and friends. Because these gay men's voices turned unnaturally huskier when they were on the phone, others joked that affecting a husky voice would give their friends cancer. The group as a whole was read as a group of homosexual men. But as far as Mejía's friends were concerned, Mejía was the one who had to keep his feathers under control.

Many informants strove to seem more masculine to others, but many realized that they could not completely control the way their bodies signified. One choice was to anguish over the small "feathers" that slipped out. Another was to let them all out as Mejía did, or find some way to be at peace with themselves despite the occasional interpretation they inadvertently provoked with their body language.

During interviews with the few men who traveled to the Dominican Republic with frequency, a discussion emerged about the challenges of visiting and spending time with biological families after living abroad for a while and spending a lot of time within groups of gay and bisexual men. Domínguez, for example, suggested that he experienced a "desdoblamiento" (unfolding or splitting) whenever he returned: having to adjust his behavior to a presumably more restrictive environment. Other men referred to these adjustments as "pisar fino" (step lightly), alluding to walking as an important way to signal masculine deportment. Although there seemed to be disagreement about whether or not men "changed" when they returned and visited, informants like Javier Acuña talked about the difficulty and tension they experienced when they returned. When he visited the Dominican Republic, Acuña spent time with his parents and siblings: "Hablo mucho con ellos y cosas . . . pero siempre tengo alguna actividad . . . que voy para casa de unos amigos" (I always talk with them a lot . . . but I always have something going on . . . meaning that I am going to my friends' house). Acuña described the tension he experienced when he was around his relatives as derived from his sense that there were limitations to his proximity with them:

Como nunca he tocado el tema con ellos entonces cuando yo estoy con ellos, tengo que estar muy consciente ¿tú entiendes? Que yo no vaya a decir, "Mira, maricón," como que es la costumbre. Cuando yo hablo con los amigos míos aquí—yo tengo aquí dos íntimos amigos—y así es que uno siempre se llama. Y es una costumbre tan y tan grande que a veces hablando yo con amigos straights les digo, "Pero mira, maricón" . . . con la familia . . . tengo que estar tan consciente de yo no soltar una pluma . . . eso es lo que hace como que yo siempre busque una excusa para tener algo más que hacer y así dejar el limpio.

Since I've never broached the topic [of his homosexuality] with them [relatives], I have to be very aware, you know? Of not saying, "look here, faggot," as I usually do. When I talk to my friends—I have two intimate friends here—and that's how we talk to one another. And that's such a habit for me that sometimes, when I talk to straight friends, I say, "But look, faggot" . . . with my family . . . I have to be so aware of myself to avoid letting out a feather . . . that I always find an excuse to have something else to do and leave.

In Guerrero's observations, which I discussed earlier, he distinguished between the relative tolerance he expected in "gay spaces" versus his inability to feel really comfortable in spaces where "letting out a feather" might be a social liability. Acuña projected the spatialization of zones of comfort and discomfort transnationally. For him, having to be around his relatives required his hyperawareness of his language, lest traces of code swishing create tensions. Because Acuña had not addressed his homosexuality directly with his relatives, he avoided creating potential tension for them or himself; because he had other places to be (*estar*) when he returned, Acuña shortened his visits with relatives to minimize the tensions he might have experienced himself.

Acuña's and Guerrero's preference for environments in which they can easily code swish with friends may point to the rewards of community, though Guerrero's own discomfort with locas, as well as the antagonisms, power differentials, and struggles informants noted within Dominican as well as the so-called gay community in general, demonstrates that they knew better. They knew better than to subscribe blindly to a romance of belonging when any sense of connection and intimacy they created and sustained with others were tenuous and contingent at best. They recognized that expressing love, proximity, and solidarity with one another was possible as long as it did not conflict with the exigencies of survival.

Claudio Báez articulated the stakes for many of these men in a trenchant critique of the gay community:

La comunidad gay es una falsedad. La comunidad gay no existe. Eso es un invento que nos hemos inventado nosotros mismos. . . . Ah, pero el hecho de que él mama güevo quiere decir que él y yo somos iguales. ¿Quién te dijo a ti? Ese cabrón vive en el Upper East Side. Anda con un maldito reloj Cartier, y se mete $150,000 en un bolsillo. ¿Cómo tú lo vas a comparar conmigo que vivo en el maldito Bronx, que cojo el maldito D train everyday, y que tengo que irle a comer mierda a la bruja en mi trabajo? ¿Qué nos une? ¿La vagina? ¡No! La vagina no da comunidad.

The gay community is a fallacy. The gay community does not exist. That is something we have invented ourselves. . . . Ah, but the fact that he sucks dick means that he and I are the same. Who told you that? That fucker lives in the Upper East Side. He wears a Cartier watch, and puts $150,000 in his pocket. How can you compare him with me, living in the fucking Bronx, taking the fucking D train every day, and putting up with the shit of the witch boss I have at work? What unites us? The vagina? No! Vagina does not a community make.

The stakes are clear for these men. To survive, they need respect, not community.

::: Conclusion

To be bilingual is to speak knowing fully that what is being said is
always being said in another place, in many other place
—SILVIA MOLLOY, "Bilingual Scenes"

The informants' investment in masculinity as a site of legitimacy has everything to do with their understanding that to wield power in patriarchy, they needed to access male privilege. By offering an interpretation of la loca as a gynographic performative with rich expressive potential in the social, and by offering the conceptualization of code swishing as a means to grapple with the way men like the informants practiced boundary setting and belonging, this analysis has confronted the political implications of effeminacy as communicative practice. The discursive life of performatives like la loca extends well beyond foundational narratives of homosexual abjection. While ever cognizant of the potential of this figure to return subjects to the trauma of homophobic injury, the reading I have offered here also attends to an expressive potential prompted by the significations of these performatives as they circulate within Dominican male networks of same-sex desire. Although I have stressed the conditions of possibility and politics of power that make accessing male privilege the way in which these men gain legibility and respect, the subsequent chapters explore the problematic nature of their complicity with patriarchy locally and transnationally. The aim will not be to pass judgment on their choices but rather to engage the contradictory logics of oppression and complicity in their lives.

Finally, this analysis has also argued that once the hail is taken out of Althusser's "little theoretical theatre" of subject formation,[43] and once we follow Butler's suggestion to disarticulate authority from the structural and institutionally sanctioned "voice" of the power that hails, interpellation emerges as a performative that can be "happy" only to the degree that a "turn" (or another form of acknowledgment) inaugurates a subject engulfed by its chain of signification. Nonresponse to and ignorance of the hail might not rupture its full reach, and the informants understood this all too well. But they also knew that ignoring the hail, acting as if they were not the ones being called, interrupted its trajectory, put on pause the others' ability to injure, marginalize, or express inappropriate proximities.

PART III

COLONIAL ZONES

::::

Santo Domingo, October 12, 2008. I got up early to go out for a jog. Given all the advice I received about security, I took only my keys to the apartment building and wore typical running gear, though I noticed then that the gray gym shorts were smeared with paint from when Alfredo had been patching up and painting the apartment in the Bronx.

I headed down to El Malecón. As I crossed one of the streets running parallel to Avenida George Washington, the young man I was about to cross paths with took off his glasses. He was dark-skinned and wore blue workout slacks, a *cachucha*, and a matching blue sports shirt. He turned my way as we came closer to one another, and he looked me straight in the eyes. He was cruising me. Though somewhat shocked at his directness, I kept walking. I had also been cruising him, but the last thing I expected was for him to look back the way he did.

I was having a hard time crossing Avenida George Washington before beginning to run. Too many cars were coming in both directions. As I searched for a corner that would give me a way to go across, I looked in the direction in which the guy had gone and noticed that he went around the block and was walking toward where I was. He was far enough away for me to notice but not react in any particular way to his approach, other than to keep looking to cross and go jogging.

Eventually I crossed and began jogging. The weather was agreeable. I encountered a few people exercising along the way and worked up a good sweat by the time I got to Avenida Máximo Gomez. I then walked back.

It must have been about 9–9:30 a.m. when I returned.

In the early afternoon, I went to the supermarket to buy a few things for the apartment. Free trade agreements and all, I was shocked to see the poor quality of most of the things in there. It was as if I had walked into a 99-cent store in the United States and bought some of the worst paper napkins and toilet paper. As I came near the cash register, I noticed a selection of condoms there—I guess those are in enough demand that the market figured, why not have condoms near each cash register, just in case people are in a rush or forget. But if the quality of the paper napkins and the toilet paper are any indication of the quality of the condoms, so-called safe fucking around here remains a high-risk profession and leisure activity.

In the afternoon, it rained for about forty-five minutes, after which I went out for a walk. It takes a short while to go through the main areas of the zona colonial, so by about 5:25 p.m. I was heading back home. I bumped into three of my friends, two of whom I had not seen in a decade. It was felicitous enough to encounter one another that we walked together for a while, and I ended up bringing them back to the apartment. While having drinks, one of them mentioned to me that I might as well take advantage of the time I was here alone and get myself a bugarrón to work my ass. I said that this was not exactly my plan, that I had writing to do, and he insisted that I consider it. I thought twice about putting music on—didn't want them to stay a minute longer than the time afforded by the two "jumbo" Presidente Lights we were having—and took Manuel's cell phone number before they headed out.

There was an *apagón*, but we hardly noticed because Alfredo and I have an *inversor* in the apartment. He told me that, basically, having a separate source of energy made us the *riquitos del barrio*. When my visitors and I figured out how to get down the staircase without killing ourselves, I said goodbye, and the neighbor across the way instructed me to turn off my lights to use up less energy in the apartment, in case the *apagón* took a long time to end. I thanked her for the advice, came back up, and had a snack. I had spoken to another friend about connecting and going out this evening, but it looked like meeting up with him was a no-go because his partner was sick. It was so dark throughout most of what I could see that I grew fearful of leaving the apartment. I spoke to Alfredo on the phone, and he persuaded me to go grab a bite and buy food for the next day. This was my first trip back in seven years, but I had to stop paying attention to all the talk about the increased insecurity of the streets of Santo Domingo.

I locked up as much as I could and headed to El Conde.

By now, activities on this street were in full swing. When I had taken my first afternoon stroll, I noticed what looked like African American male tourists in the area. Many appeared gay-identified, but I couldn't be sure. I walked into a restaurant where two groups of six to eight of these men sat. All I wanted to see was the menu, but nobody seemed overly preoccupied with giving me service, so I left. The men looked like there were thirty-five to fifty in age, and most of them looked chubby or overweight. So the contrast between them and the men they were looking for was quite stark. As I walked out, I noticed out of the left corner of my eye an exchange between one of these men and the young, fit-looking man who sat next to him. Other than the smiling and the hands that appeared to be wandering around the young man's pocket—or the place where he had just grabbed his dick to give the prospective sugar daddy a sense of what he was packing—linguistic exchanges seemed to be instrumental enough to have each party understand what they were getting into.

I eventually found a spot to sit and order some dinner, at a restaurant right across the way from the Cathedral, the very place where El Conde starts or ends. In the park, people of different ages sat, hanging out. Across from where I sat, a young man wearing formal pants and a white *chacavana* tuned a guitar while some old bolero music blasted from someone's boom box or car. It took me a minute and a few repeated visual encounters with this young man to realize that he was part of a guitar trio looking to play a song or two for a fee to the couples at the restaurant or near the park.

The good thing about sitting where I sat was that I had a decent view both of El Conde and of who passed by on their way to the restaurants in the Plazoleta España or thereabouts. Many good-looking young men and women, but with the exception of two or three very provocatively dressed women (one of whom sat next to me with a much older man who I realized was Italian from the bits and pieces of conversation and attempts at translation I could hear from my table), this seemed like a scene where a lot was going on but where men looking for sex with other men were a prominent feature. Now, don't get me wrong: I saw plenty of stark contrasts between white male bodies and dark-skinned women. And my own erotic subjectivity is deeply implicated in what did and didn't jump at me. But I did see well-dressed young women who looked more like they were hanging out, *paseando* with friends, than hooking.

The older gentleman who came to serve me at the restaurant disappeared after bringing me water. Several minutes passed, and I guess it was then that my eyes met those of a young man walking along with everyone else there, in the direction of the Plazoleta. Our eyes met, and, once again, I was the one who had to look elsewhere, surprised yet again by the way those eyes did not show the masculine defiance I associate with Dominican men—the ones I grew up around, anyway.

I finished the meal, paid, and headed back to El Conde, to look for the street and get to the apartment before it got too late. When I stopped to wait for a car to cross, barely one block away from where I had been eating, the young man I had cruised before stood next to me, also waiting to let the car go by. He must have waited for me to finish and began to walk and catch up with me. I looked his way, both flattered and uneasy because of all of the warnings I had received before getting here. He looked a few times in my direction as we walked and greeted people he saw at establishments on the street. A bugarrón, I thought, though this man looked a little more groomed than many of the other young men in the area. Unlike many of them, who wore tight-fitting shirts to show off sculpted bodies, this guy wore a comfortable dress shirt, slicked-back hair, and dark earrings. A *jevito*? He certainly looked the part. I stopped once or twice to let him go ahead and give me time to check him out. He did the same. As we came closer to my street, I feared he would follow me but didn't quite know what to do. I was attracted to him. He sat on a bench and opened a newspaper while I saw a white older person wearing a wig, who turned out to be what one might call a man of transgender experience. Actually, I'm not sure of what I saw. All I am sure is that this was a sight I had never witnessed in El Conde. When this person passed by me as I came closer to the bench where the young man sat, I couldn't repress a smile and blurted out, "Esto ha cambiado mucho" (This has changed a lot). "Si señor," he said. "Y eso, que usted no ha visto nada" (Yes, sir. And you have seen nothing).

Okay, that was stupid. Of all the things I might have blurted out, why did it have to be the one that revealed that I didn't live in the Dominican Republic? I realized that revealing that small bit of information could render me vulnerable, but I was curious enough to want to talk to the guy.

I sat down.

He told me that he lived in Gazcue, not too far from where we sat, and that he was going to meet up with some friends later for some drinks. He then asked where I lived, and I said, "Not too far," but that there was no electricity where I was staying. The exchange couldn't have taken more than a minute or two. Once I realized that there was a script here that I did not know how to follow, I said my goodbyes and looked for the corner. As I walked in the darkness of the night, I looked back hoping this man had not followed me. He hadn't.

I was safe.

What a shame.

CHAPTER 6

Virando la dominicanidad

: : :

At one point in our discussion of relationship dynamics, Javier Acuña and I touched on his preferences in sexual practices with a current partner. He said:

Él es una persona súper abierta sexualmente, ¿tú me entiendes? Eso es lo que más me gusta a mí de él, que uno va cincuenta/cincuenta [50/50]. Cincuenta/cincuenta: cualquier cosa que él quiera que yo se la haga, él está dispuesto a hacérmela a mí también, ¿tú entiendes? Que eso no pasa generalmente en la relaciones. Siempre aparece uno: "¡Ah, no! Yo no mamo. Yo no esto. Yo no lo otro." Pero entonces quieren que tú se lo mames, que tú les esto y que tú lo otro, ¿tú entiendes? Yo me encojono. Y se lo digo. Una pareja con la que yo estoy. "¿Tú no mamas? Yo tampoco. Porque, ¿por qué te lo puedo mamar a ti y tú no me lo puedes mamar a mi? ¡Explícame eso! ¿Por qué? No." ¿Tú entiendes? Eso lo hace uno con una pareja . . . ya que tú estás establecido . . . porque.también yo entiendo que el asunto del sexo es un proceso educativo.

Sexually, he is a very open person, you know what I mean? That's what I like the most about him, that we go fifty/fifty. Fifty/fifty: anything he wants me to do to him, he is willing to do to me, you see? Which is something that usually does not happen in relationships. There is always someone: "Oh no! I don't suck. I don't do this. I don't do that." But then they want you to suck them, to do this or that to them, you know? And I get pissed off. And I say it to that person. If I am with someone, "You don't suck? I don't suck either. Why should I suck your dick if you are not willing to suck mine? Explain that to me! Why? No." You know what I mean? That is something you do with a partner . . . with whom you are more established . . . because I also understand that sex is an educational process, where each one gets to know the other so you can enjoy it. . . .

Que cada uno se vaya conociendo	And that's something that happened
para que uno lo vaya disfrutando . . .	with this man.
Y eso pasó por ejemplo con este jevo.	

Like other informants, Acuña shared stories about sexual experiences and partners to engage his past and present and to put forward the values and ideals with which he wanted to be associated. Narrating their "erotic journeys,"[1] then, made evident some informants' investments in retaining and refashioning masculinity. What sets these narratives apart from others I have analyzed thus far is the way they illustrate the challenge that sexual practices, eroticism, and pleasure pose to traditional masculinity, stereotypical views of homosexuality, and Dominican identity. For the informants, sexual exchanges, practices, and pleasures carry the possibility of accessing modernity—a modernity haunted, I will argue here, by an intensely desired and reviled other: the Dominican macho. Although the figure of la loca is ambivalently invested in ways that make it productive for the establishment of intimacies yet potentially threatening to everyday legitimacy and survival (as I explained in the previous chapter), the Dominican macho represents the ambivalently and erotically binding ghost of a nationalist subject form.[2] I am invoking the idea of "bondage" deliberately, to draw a parallel between the informants' engagement with the hypersexualized and overdetermined figure of the Dominican macho and the hypersexualized Asian woman that Celine Parreñas Shimizu discusses in *The Hypersexuality of Race*: "Any Asian/American woman who must understand her identity and her possibilities must engage hypersexuality in representation. That is, sexuality imbricates them, so that Asian women must always engage it as a force for understanding the self and their relations with others who project hypersexuality upon them."[3] Given the striking predominance of Dominican men as sexual partners in these interviews,[4] this chapter will concentrate in the way these sexual narratives become yet another vehicle for the narrators to engage dominicanidad as an ethnoracial formation.

"Sex is an educational process," as Acuña said, because it affords each actor experiential knowledge and lessons from handling one's body and the body of another through touch, smell, taste, risk taking, and repetitive engagement. This is a form of sedimentation that gets reworked in different erotic situations. Acuña found this man ideal not because he knew everything about sex but because the partner was open to a presumably horizontal exchange of pleasures, as open to giving as to receiving from Acuña, free from sexual hang-ups. Sex with him excited Acuña because the eagerness they brought to each sexual encounter conjured up memories of past pleasures, but the quality that mattered most to Acuña was an openness to experimentation that obtained precisely because of the trust, intimacy, and creativity they developed over time.

By contrast, other partners offered preconditions and prohibitions that Acuña suggested trump the equality of the exchange—the achievement of that "cincuenta/cincuenta." Some wanted to have their dicks sucked but did not want to suck; some wanted to fuck but not be fucked. Although the unusualness of the partner he liked is presented in a generalization about this man's sexual philosophy of openness, Acuña viewed "closed" partners as a broader trend within his available pool of potential lovers. This backdrop facilitated Acuña's articulation of his own critique of that closed sexual philosophy, staged in his refusal to suck or fuck if reciprocation was not in the offing.

"Why should I suck your dick if you are not willing to suck mine?" Acuña asked, echoing the questions other men I interviewed voiced to inflexible imaginary partners whose contrived sexual performance suggested (to the men asking these questions, at least) an inability to give themselves fully to the potential pleasures sex provided. Here, informants like Acuña presented themselves as well-adjusted gay men fully willing to experience their own bodies and those of others, in contrast with men unwilling to open up their bodies and let go of their hang-ups. Asking this specific question (and voicing, through it, a demand for reciprocity) while having sex also underscores the fact that sexual exchanges were just as subject to negotiations of demands and expectations as were other social exchanges. Through voicing the question, Acuña was also voicing (to the sex partner who heard him and to the interlocutor with whom he shared memories of these episodes) the importance of reciprocity as a value to him, a value so important as to make him police the behavior of his sex partners.

To understand sex as an educational process, following Acuña's observation, helps to locate sexual exchange as another means through which men like the informants engaged, learned about, moved, and realized themselves in the world. To many of them, the accomplishment of a well-adjusted sexual life involved willingness to explore the potentialities of their bodies, to develop a flexible approach to partners and sexual practices that involved cooperation and equal exchange, and to police those boundaries.

It is tempting to cast this model developed by the informants as the sexual expression of an ideologically neoliberal ethos,[5] but I believe it to be more strongly connected with the way they engage dominicanidad through sex. In his provocative book *Gay Hegemony/Latino Homosexualities*, Manolo Guzmán argues for the necessity of engaging the erotics of sexuality and race together as they manifest in social life. This insight echoes ongoing efforts by younger scholars to attend to the intersection of these two areas.[6] Guzmán's extraordinary provocation, which I explore in the specific case of the informants in this chapter, stems from his call to study the homosexual and homoracial dimensions of erotic life. He explains:

> Ethnorace is produced not only in relation to well recognized economic, geographic, political, social and ethnic processes but also in the unfolding of erotic fantasy, desire and practices. That is, when you "do" a Puerto Rican, a white guy or an Asian you "do" more than that guy, you "make" Puerto Ricanness and whiteness, you achieve ethnorace itself in the sedimentation which erotic practices leave in their wake, sedimentations that are simultaneously psychic and corporeal.[7]

Following Guzmán, I argue that the informants engaged, and in some fundamental ways remade and regulated, dominicanidad in their sexual narratives. But the philosophy of openness that Acuña outlined at the beginning of this chapter suggests that ideal sexual scenarios *viran* (flip) dominicanidad in a fundamental way: the male body imagined as closed and impenetrable enters sexual modernity by becoming open, penetrable, and responsive to the other bodies it encounters.

Yet this is an idealized scenario, and much of the learning I will describe throughout this chapter, involved negotiating interpersonal dynamics, expectations, erotic investments, and obstacles that challenged the ideals the informants brought to sexual exchanges. The "flip" is never as complete or consistent as they might wish it to be. Only a small number of men shared descriptions about partners and sexual histories, but the few who did emphasized their increased flexibility and openness with sex as linked to experiences and challenges faced after migration. Their espousal of a model that emphasizes elasticity and versatility in sexual relations suggests that they politicized sex to the degree that it gave them access to ways of being with other men that establish some distance from dominicanidad without ultimately rejecting it.[8] Thus, these men understood sexual practices to be intimately tied to the full realization of oneself through the establishment and regulation of reciprocity and versatility as kernels of a modern sexual horizon and a resignification of the models of same-sex desire they associated with Dominican identity.

::: Machismo, Racialization, and the Ghosts of Dominicanidad

Critiques of Dominican masculinity were never far from the informants' views of Dominicans in general. When discussing interpersonal interactions, informants resorted to machismo to explain what differentiated Dominican gay men from men of other nationalities and ethnicities in New York City. *Machismo* refers to behaviors and attitudes of men whose masculinity is defined in and through the exercise of power over others. Manifestations of machismo the informants made reference to included hypermasculine styles of self-presentation, authoritarianism, possessiveness, aggressiveness, propensity to psychological or physical abuse, and so on. Their characterizations of machismo are generally consistent with social science research on Latin American and U.S. Latino machismo.[9] What distinguished the informants' critiques was that they suggested that machismo was central to the "backwardness" of Dominicans and particularly Dominican gay-identified men. Thus, informants critical of machismo saw it as another obstacle in their quest for upward mobility in the United States. Although current ways of thinking about homosexual identity and practice in Latin America played a role in the way informants talked about sex, their comments often did not only make sense of homosexual identities and practices. They also explained the meanings given to the dominicanidad from which these men sought to distance themselves.[10]

The relationship of sex to economic exchange is central here. E. Antonio de Moya and Rafael García argue that sex work and sex tourism are foundational to the social organization of same-sex relations in the Dominican Republic.[11] Their argument points to another nuance in the meanings of dominicanidad with which the informants wrestle. Machismo and the "activo/pasivo" dynamic may be expressions of traditional Dominican codes of gender and homosexuality.[12] But their viability as *authentic* aspects of dominicanidad is possible through the exchange value Dominican male bodies accrue as commodities. Thus, the connection between (1) sex tourism and sex work and (2) the social organization of homosexuality in the Dominican Republic suggests that the "authenticity" of local manifestations such as machismo and the activo/pasivo dynamic is already part of larger

transnational fields of circulation. In distancing themselves from these manifestations, then, the informants sought intimacies that exceeded the circulation of Dominican men's bodies as sexual commodities.[13]

"Bed" was one political space where informants engaged in relations that
had meanings that went beyond the sexual.[14] Some meanings were closely
tied to the distance they set between themselves and dominicanidad. The
racialization of the sexual identities and practices of the informants (and
perhaps other Dominican men) was conditioned by the commoditization
of images of "machismo." These were images that circulated through the
transnational circuits of desire that are part of New York's sexual cultures.[15]
Racialized sexualities such as that of the "macho" are caught up in histories
of power and desire that subjects to whom these categories attach have to
negotiate.[16]

A way to measure the success of one's distance from dominicanidad is
through what one informant called "democracy in bed," or the expectation
that both partners will play the anal penetrative role. This was an expectation some informants had for partners in committed and other types of relationships. "Democracy in bed" dramatizes the entrance of the ethnoracial
subject into the space of the modern homosexual, an alternative site of regulation not through the imperatives of hegemonic masculinity but through
those of a homosexuality they view as a reformulation of same-sex eroticism
compatible with openness, progress, and whiteness. Though it is tempting
to argue (following Guzmán) that the regulatory ideals upheld by the men
I interviewed represented their internalization of a hegemonic logic of gayness (and its investments in white supremacy), my discussion throughout
this book suggests that their adoption of that hegemonic model is selective.
Their adoption and idealization of a democratic ethos of same-sex relations
is a cannibalization, or selective appropriation and resignification, of elements drawn from hegemonic gayness.

Nevertheless, the informants' ideal was frustrated in practice by two
problems. A first problem was that Dominican partners continued to "hold
on" to their "machismo." A second problem was that the role of "macho"
(top) was the one that Dominican men were expected to play within New
York's sexual cultures.[17] Thus, bed was a site of pleasure and surveillance.
Informants looked for signs of "backwardness" in their Dominican partners,
signs that made sexual and romantic intimacy impossible. They also looked
for signs that the partner was interested only in sexual exchange with a macho, thus foreclosing the possibility of "deeper" pleasures and attachments.

Because the macho was frozen in history, an anachronism that jarred with the modern selves the informants fashioned for themselves, he was granted enormous erotic power but little human depth in these accounts.

Sexual exchanges included the stereotyped expectations that whites, Dominicans, and other men of color had of Dominican men. This suggests that nonwhite groups are complicit in the reproduction of eroticized otherness in sexual encounters. This complicity ensues from the need all these men have to work through complex sexual cultures.[18] To work through the contradictions means to have no option other than to be complicit. However, this means more than blind complicity with oppression. It points to the cost of living in a contradictory system within which one seeks what one wants, yet pleasure always comes at some cost or uneasiness.

In this regard, Rogelio Noguera's views are instructive. As he explained it, machismo posed a series of problems to Dominican men, even when they self-identified as gay:

Creo que tiene cierta importancia el hecho de que el dominicano gay, a diferencia de otros gays de otros países, tiene todavía un poco una mentalidad machista. También, ¿cómo te diría? La forma de comportamiento o de apertura que tienen los homosexuales dominicanos es diferente al tipo de apertura hacia la sociedad que tienen otros homosexuales de otros países. Quizás por el mismo pensamiento machista.

¿Cómo así?

Nosotros preferimos más fácil vivir en el clóset que el puertorriqueño, por ejemplo, y llevar esa doble vida, que el puertorriqueño. Exceptuando algunos dominicanos que sí han nacido acá . . . Diferentes tipos de valores morales . . . algunas veces es una contradicción. Claman mucho

I think there is some importance to the fact that the Dominican gay man, unlike other gays from other countries, still retains a machista mentality. Also, how can I explain? Also, the behavioral forms or the openness that Dominican homosexuals have here in the United States are different from the type of openness toward society that homosexuals from other countries have. Maybe that's because of that same machista way of thinking.

Can you explain?

We prefer living in the closet more than Puerto Ricans do, for instance. And we prefer this double life more than Puerto Ricans do. This with the exception of some Dominicans who have been born here . . . Different types of moral values . . . sometimes it is a contradiction. They claim they

a lo de la monogamia porque, a pesar de ser maricón, yo soy macho y a mí no me la puede pegar nadie. Pero, sin embargo, yo sí se la puedo pegar a otro, ¿tú entiendes? Porque la mentalidad del macho dominicano es: mi mujer no se acuesta con nadie, pero yo me puedo acostar con todas las mujeres. Entonces, esa misma formación tenemos los maricones. O sea, no podemos escapar de esa formación porque fuimos criados y orientados como varones. Entonces seguimos pensando como varones aunque seamos mujeres en la cama, pero te da ese permiso mental de que tú puedas hacer con todo el mundo, pero tu pareja no lo pueda hacer con nadie.

are monogamous but even though they are faggots, I am a macho, and nobody can cheat on me. But, on the other hand, I can cheat on someone else, you understand? Because the mentality of the Dominican macho is: my woman does not sleep with anyone but I can sleep with all women. Then, that is the same rearing we have as faggots. In other words, we cannot escape that way of being raised because we were raised and trained as males. So we continue thinking as males even if we are women in bed, but it gives you that mental permission that you can mess around with the whole world but your partner cannot do it with anybody.

As this participant observed, machismo constituted an aggregate of attitudes all Dominican men shared, regardless of their sexual orientation. It may seem puzzling to readers that informants insisted on viewing Dominican machismo as more troubling than that of other Latin American immigrant populations. Their relatively limited interactions with other Latino groups partly explain their views. Since Dominicans predominated in the circles to which these men belonged, their perspectives were limited by their insularity.

Pathologized images of Dominican masculinity in New York also contributed to the informants' perception of Dominican machismo as extreme. In New York, the archetype of the Dominican tíguere has morphed into the stereotype of the "jodedor" (drug pusher), whose emergence as a cultural figure has been shaped by the structural position Dominicans have occupied within New York's economy.[19] This image has also been shaped by the involvement of some Dominicans in the drug economy.[20]

The circulation of stereotypes of Dominican masculinity in New York needs to be understood in the context of the racialization of Dominicans in the city. This process has not occurred to Dominicans in isolation. The racialization of Dominican immigrants has taken place in relational tension with the symbolic spaces occupied by Puerto Ricans and African Americans, the two nonwhite groups with the longest historical linkages to New York. As Grosfoguel and Georas explain, because of this history of African American and Puerto Rican presence in New York, the racial stereotypes of African Americans and Puerto Ricans established a precedent that new "black" and "Latino" immigrants must encounter to the extent that they are frequently confused with African Americans or Puerto Ricans in the hegemonic imaginary.[21]

Since Dominicans can pass or can be confused with African Americans and Puerto Ricans, the slipperiness of their racialization also shapes informants' attitudes toward Dominican machismo. The porn films made by the Latino Fan Club, which feature African American, black Puerto Rican, and Dominican performers, suggest that the image of the "homothug" may be one of the latest incarnations of the tíguere. In this way, the homothug that appears in these films (who might be Dominican, Puerto Rican, African American, or a combination) constitutes a filmic expression of these proximities.

The proximity of Dominican homosexual men to Puerto Ricans in New York is particularly salient. The ambivalences of this relationship were expressed in views such as Noguera's. It was not a coincidence that Noguera mentioned Puerto Rican gay men as being generally more comfortable reconciling their homosexuality with their national identity. This view is reductive and stereotyped, let alone neglectful of the complexities of male homosexuality in the Puerto Rican/Nuyorican context. Still, informants invoked and compared this image of the Puerto Rican gay man comfortable in his skin with the "repressed" and machista Dominican homosexual.[22]

Dominican machismo is particularly problematic in sexual exchanges. The activo/pasivo scenario, as viewed by some informants, tends to be more the result of an imposition of power of one partner over the other than the exchange of pleasures during sexual intercourse.[23] The conflation of migration with narratives of progreso and upward mobility in New York City also manifests itself in expectations of intimacy in sexual relationships with other men. These expectations refused machismo or the activo/pasivo dichotomy as ideals. Aníbal Guerrero, for instance, was emphatic about this issue. In particular, Guerrero was troubled by the ways in which being a macho stood in the way of Dominican men's full enjoyment of sexual pleasure with other men:

Muchos de ellos son machitos y que quieren privar en que "yo solamente te lo meto a ti" y que, you know. I mean, somos maricones, ¿qué vaina es? Y eso es 50/50. Sí, a mí me gusta metértelo a ti y yo te lo quiero meter, ¿por qué no? You know, pero como que . . . ellos se creen como que la persona que es bottom es como que menos que la persona que es top y siempre se ve eso como que el machismo y la vaina no los deja a ellos, you know, bend over, para que se lo metan. So esas son cosas, esos son temas que, you know, quizás tú deberías preguntar el por qué ellos se sienten así de . . . se sienten como tan menores o se sienten como que son menos hombres si se lo dejan meter.

Many of them are machitos and they want to boast that "I only fuck you" and that, you know. I mean, we are faggots, what the fuck is the problem? And that's 50/50. If I like to fuck you here and I want to fuck you, why not? You know, but like . . . they think that the person who is a bottom is like less than the person who is a top and you always see that as if the machismo and all doesn't let them, you know, bend over, to get fucked. So those things are, those are themes that, you know, maybe you should ask about why they feel like that . . . why they feel so minor as if they are less men if they let someone else fuck them.

As Guerrero suggested, machismo was a problem not so much because it was incompatible with being a "maricón" as much as because it rendered Dominican men inflexible in sexual encounters. Guerrero pointed to anal intercourse as the moment that somehow "revealed" a person's level of comfort with their homosexuality. While he was critical of the relationship of receptive anal intercourse and notions of a lacking self-esteem, Guerrero expected that within relationships between maricones, "eso es 50/50" (that's 50/50). It is striking the way he displaced shame in this particular discussion: feeling "more" than the bottom became, according to Guerrero, a problematic expression of the degree to which machismo held these men back from being fully "normal" homosexuals.

Guerrero's statement is also striking because he talked about the macho in the third person. Like other informants, this participant distanced himself from the stereotype of the macho. The "we are faggots, so what the fuck is the problem" signaled not only the space of the "liberated" homosexual; it also made a sexual role preference troubling for a Dominican, though in someone else it might be just a sexual preference and anything but revelatory of deeper truths about a partner's attitudes. The discovery of the macho is tied to the differentiation of the self and the other in sexual exchanges. When using the third person to speak about the macho, then, the informants constructed their sense of who they were by reproducing and distancing themselves from the stereotype. To become the liberated homosexual "whitens" them in the sense of giving them access to the power of gay sexual normativity. That power was constituted through the reproduction of the stereotype of the macho in other Dominicans. The degree to which securing the "normality" of their sexual selves was mediated through identification and disavowal of the figure of the Dominican macho illustrate these men's homoerotic and homoracial investments. Working through, desiring, refashioning, and consuming an ethnoracial body as an impossible object of desire (alluring because of its stereotypical attributes while needing to disappear to allow for full modernity and humanity) illustrate that fucking was yet another way these men continued to engage dominicanidad. Bed became a space for pleasure and (potential) intimacy as long as partners adhered to the expectations of the liberated homosexual.

What complicates this scenario even further is that those "machitos" were precisely the kind of the men Guerrero said he preferred. In other words, he was troubled by Dominican machos, but desire ultimately bound him to them. The fact that the presumed partner of the macho "bottoms" for him suggested to Guerrero that only the one who "tops" enjoyed the body of the other. Nevertheless, I submit that scholars have dwelt for far too long in the indignities and stigma that accrues to the position of the bottom while neglecting a consideration of the pleasures and powers that derive from that positionality. It is clear from Guerrero's redistribution of stigma in the sexual scene that machos were the ones with the problem here: in his view, their machismo produced these men as sexually maladjusted, as victims of a self-hatred so intense that it arrested their development. It is because of their "problem" that he suggested I should ask them to explain to me what is wrong (with them), why they feel and act as they do. In chapter 2, "Moving Portraits," discussing Guerrero's extended migration narrative, I suggested that Guerrero inverted the position of his once-abusive father in the context of our interview exchange: the man who brought so much suffering to the Guerrero children (and to Aníbal's mother) became the man Guerrero avoided when he called his relatives. Whereas Aníbal demonstrated that he was able to secure employment, his father never held a job for long; instead of behaving like the man he was supposed to be (the provider Aníbal had become), Mr. Guerrero was trapped in futile immaturity. An inversion in projections of "normalcy" and "adulthood" to himself versus the self-stigmatizing figure of the macho parallels Guerrero's earlier inversion of the dynamics with his father—except that there is no specificity to the macho in question, and the inversion operates in the sexual realm.

Readers will recall that in the ethnographic narrative that opened this section of the book, a friend talked with me about how advantageous it might be for me to hire a bugarrón to come and "work [my] ass." Although getting fucked was not in my travel agenda, his suggestion of securing those services pointed to the position of travelers (Dominican-born or not) as consumers of the products and services offered by bugarrones. Why not get a dose of Dominican dick while visiting?

Guerrero's sexual desire for machitos, if these machitos were seen as emblematic of what was most authentically Dominican and what was backward about dominicanidad in New York, may be roughly analogous to the longing for the homeland Dominican immigrants express through the consumption of the plantain. Machitos and plantains may hold them back from being truly modern and assimilated to the United States. Yet the familiarity they provide continued to be essential to the lives of these immigrant men.

Seeing the mouth and anus as sites of consumption leads me to argue that bottoming for the machito transforms him into a "walking plantain": a consumable expression of dominicanidad, an object of affection that can provide fullness without substance, that can fill one's ass but not nourish it.[24] Like the plantain, the macho's dick may remind the bottom of what is most "authentic" and "backward" about being Dominican. This dick may comfort, fill, or thrill.[25] But it does not line up with these men's views of what being modern is supposed to be. This analogy points to the intersections of the anal and oral as forms of homoracial remembering and self-making.[26]

Keeping the macho at bay in themselves and in others was anything but easy for informants. Rejection of the machismo associated with the dominicanidad, that they saw as an obstacle to their upward mobility, may have been an attractive goal. But the informants had to deal with the erotic lure of the macho and the ways in which the racialization of Dominicans in New York attached to them in sexual and romantic exchanges.

::: Lessons in Pleasure

Informants who volunteered information about their sexual practices reported that they did not adhere to the activo/pasivo opposition consistently. Decisions to perform the anal penetrative or receptive roles varied according to the characteristics of partners, contexts, sexual chemistry, and ages. Most significantly, these preferences changed over time. Thus, the activo/pasivo opposition did not operate as *the* model for understanding sexual behavior among informants.

Nonetheless, activo/pasivo was central to some informants. Aurelio Espaillat was a forty-eight-year-old brown-skinned professional from working-class origins. He worked his way up the social ladder in the Dominican Republic and experienced downward mobility as an immigrant. For Espaillat, the activo/pasivo paradigm played a role in relationships. His account of sexual roles in his relationship parallels similar discussions found in scholarship on Latin American homosexuality:

En la cama, yo me sentía como hasta como una niña así como que ese hombre me estaba sofocando me estaba utilizando, pero no en el sentido violación, sino que yo era su . . . mujer de él . . . una niña que él se la estaba comiendo viva [cuando su pareja le penetraba]. Pero una vez por casualidad se le ocurrió a él decirme que le hiciese yo a él todo lo que él me hacía a mí que se supone que . . . que yo era la parte ¿Cómo se dice?

¿Pasiva?

Pasiva. Exacto. Cuando este hombre me ha dicho así. Dizque "Pero ven. Ven. ¿Y qué es? ¿Y tú no te vas a venir? Métemelo tú a mí." Que este hombre se me viró.[27] ¡Este hombre

In bed, I felt like almost like a little girl like that man was suffocating was utilizing me but not in the sense of violation but that I was his . . . woman of his . . . a little girl he was eating alive [when the partner penetrated Espaillat]. But one time it so happened he had the idea of asking me to do to him everything he did to me that it's supposed to be that . . . that I was the part, how do you say that?

Passive?

Passive. Exactly. When this man has said this to me. Like "But come. Come. What's up? You can't cum? Why don't you fuck me?" That this man has turned his back toward me. This big man! With whom I felt so much like a little girl in that bed [with]

tan grande! Yo que me sentía así como tan niña en aquella cama [con] este hombre tan grande. " . . . Pues ven métemelo tú a mí." Así. En esos términos. Y se me ha vira'o. Yo me senté en la cama y empecé a . . . llorar ahí y duramos como dos semanas que yo no dejaba que él ni siquiera me tocase. Y él tratando de hacerme entender . . . porque yo no me imaginaba como una vida "gay" así. Yo me lo imaginaba, porque yo viví eso mucho en mi familia. Yo veía a mis primas con sus novios. Mi hermana que se casó. La otra que se casó. Mi papá con mi mamá. ¿Tú sabes? Las niñas del barrio, todas tenían sus novitos. Entonces yo me enfocaba como ahí.

that huge man. " . . . Then you come fuck me." Like that. In those terms. And he turned his back toward me. I sat in bed and started to . . . cry right there and for the next two weeks, I would not even let him touch me. And he was trying to make me understand . . . because I did not imagine a "gay" life like that. I imagined it the way I lived it in my family. I saw my cousins with their boyfriends. My sister got married. The other one got married. My father with my mother. You know? The girls in the neighborhood all had their little boyfriends. Then I saw it like that.

Most of the elements present in scholarly discussions of activo/pasivo appeared in Espaillat's account: (1) rendering of the effeminate man as symbolic "woman" or "girl" and of the other partner as "the man"; (2) conflation of gendered self-presentation with sexual roles (e.g., the "man" as top and the "girl" as bottom); and (3) trauma caused by the flouting of the rules of engagement between these "opposites" by the top who wants to play the anal receptive role. The pattern of engagement in sexual intercourse in Espaillat's case remained somewhat consistent throughout the duration of this ten-year relationship.

It is striking, however, that what carried a negative valence in this episode was that the partner flipped the script. Existing accounts of active/pasivo suggest that being the "passive" partner stigmatizes that partner, yet stigma and abjection do not register in Espaillat's account.[28] Although that could be attributed to the fact that Espaillat's narrative voice might have suppressed recollections of stigma and abjection, paying close attention to Espaillat suggests how profoundly exciting and *normative* he thought himself to be by casting himself as a "girl" who had a boyfriend "like my sisters," a big man who "ate me alive." What was surprising to Espaillat was not his being able to have sex with a man per se but rather that the "being a man" of his partner—part of the "gayness" Espaillat did not have models to imagine—involved anal receptivity. Instead of a model where he simply emulated, as the girl he imagined himself to be, the relations he saw his sisters have with their boyfriends (presumably where penetration was unidirectional), his partner's flipping presented a new choreography of the flesh, one in which being a "big man" was compatible with being penetrated. Despite an initially adverse reaction, sexual relations between Espaillat and his partner continued.

Other informants suggested that their sexual repertoires broadened as a consequence of migration. For Pablo Arismendi, life in the Dominican Republic was limited to playing the anal receptive role in sexual encounters. One of the changes he experienced upon arrival in the United States was that opportunities to play the anal penetrative role became available to him. Mauricio Domínguez's experience was the reverse. While in the Dominican Republic and during his first years in the United States, he was almost exclusively the penetrating partner. His relationship of several years ended in the United States after he arrived, partly because the partner could not accommodate Domínguez's desire to play the anal receptive role.

The ways some informants talked about sexual relations with men show that the activo/pasivo paradigm held sway. The informants' ideas about sexual encounters *were* anchored in an understanding of activity/passivity that resembles what a lot of the scholars of male homosexuality in Latin America have documented. But their ideas of what activo/pasivo meant were also connected to sexual identities and practices they associated with the dominicanidad from which they aspired to distance themselves in New York.

These men may not be alone in associating their national/ethnic identity with a "Latin American" sex and gender system they rejected as immigrants. Research on Latino men who have sex with men shows that in sexual relationships with long-term romantic partners, many of these men expect "versatility" in bed.[29] This research also makes a distinction between a casual (or strictly) sexual partners and long-term relationships. Some informants expected versatility to be within the range of possibilities existing in a partner in a long-term relationship. The point was not that partners would penetrate one another in each sexual encounter; the point was that partners knew that penetrating one another was within the couple's erotic repertoire, regardless of when or how (in)consistently it happened. This may be far from what is at stake in sexual encounters that were not part of a romantic partnership.

Even within romantic relationships, versatility was conditional on both partners performing proper masculinity to mutual satisfaction. Otherwise, there may be conflicts over who penetrated whom. One informant reported having spent a day hanging out with his partner and friends "soltando las plumas" (letting out feathers). When he and his partner were about to have sex that evening, the partner would not bottom for the informant because the informant had spent all day soltando las plumas. They eventually had sex. Still, the partner warned the informant that if the latter wanted to continue playing the penetrative role in anal sex, he had to behave like a "man." The partner was not willing to be penetrated by someone who acted as a "sissy," even if joking. The performance of sexual roles in encounters cannot be completely detached from each partner's evaluation of the masculine self-presentation of the other. Thus, these men want versatility in sexual encounters so long as both partners approve of each other's gendered self-presentation, illustrating that investments in normativity are not only tied to legitimacy and viability (which I addressed in chapter 5, "Code Swishing") in social life. Investments in normativity are also erotic.

::: "Democracy in Bed" and the Walking Plantains

The expectation of sexual parity tended to be constrained by the way images of Dominican men circulated within local and transnational social fields. While illustrating that informants' criticisms of dominicanidad were often rooted in painful personal experiences, the case study below explores some of the frustrations this informant faced as he wrestled with the expectations other men had of him in New York.

Claudio Báez, a light-skinned informant from an upper-class background, should have been born in New York. However, the relationship between his parents had deteriorated so much that his mother decided to return and give birth in her hometown in the Dominican Republic. He was born there in 1958. He remembered having little to do with his father, whom he characterized as being "sumamente difícil. Lo que aquí en los Estados Unidos se le llama un asshole. Ese término lo inventaron para describirlo a él" (extremely difficult. What here in the United States is called an asshole. That term was invented to describe him). Báez described his mother with admiration for rejecting the indignities of life with his father. But his description of his childhood as a "mama's boy" in a household led by women revealed some of the claustrophobia he felt. Apart from being a powerful presence, Báez's mother shared authority with her mother and sister. Báez characterized these women as "powerful," as "overprotective" and as having an elevated sense of their position as self-appointed members of an "aristocracy" of the last years of the Trujillo regime. Despite the financial difficulties they faced—partly due to the irresponsibility of Báez's father—Báez remembered a childhood sheltered from the rest of the world.

Báez's father occupied a high-ranking position with an international profile during the Trujillo regime. He lost his rank and influence when the regime ended. Mr. Báez ultimately managed to stay connected to former colleagues and continued working as a consultant abroad. His contact with the family in the Dominican Republic was minimal. Being surrounded by overprotective adult figures became a problem for young Báez, especially as he grew up and began to see himself as an intellectual and to recognize himself as a homosexual: "La familia para mí era, realmente, una cárcel" (Truly, the family for me was a prison). Although he had already traveled to Puerto Rico and New York to visit with his father, Báez was always strictly supervised by accompanying adults: "Yo venía aquí, mi padre se ocupaba de mí. . . . Lo mismo en Puerto Rico. O sea, que yo no tuve contacto social con otros jóvenes y con otros niños aquí, ni en Puerto Rico" (My father would take care of me when I came here. . . . The same thing happened in Puerto Rico. In other words, I did not have social contact with other young people or with other children here, nor in Puerto Rico).

All of that changed when Báez left his parental home to live and pursue university studies in Santo Domingo in 1974. In the capital city, Báez expanded his horizons intellectually and sexually. His arrival coincided with what he characterizes as the "explosión de la homosexualidad" (homosexual explosion) during those years. The availability of spaces for socialization gave young Báez opportunities to experiment in ways that until then were unprecedented for him: "Aquello fue como un enlightenment para mi vida. Y ahí yo empecé, coño, a singar y a rapar y a coger y a fumar y a beber. . . . O sea, yo te estoy hablando de los diez y seis a los veinte, si yo iba a la universidad dos veces a la semana, era mucho" (That was an enlightenment for me. And then I started, damn it, fucking, fucking and fucking and smoking and drinking. . . . In other words, I'm telling you that from age sixteen to twenty, if I went to the university two times a week, that was a lot).

As Báez recalled it, this was also a period of intense conflict with the family he had left behind, for they kept him under surveillance from a distance. Once they had figured out what was going on with Báez, they pressured him to undergo psychiatric treatment to "curar mi homosexualidad" (cure my homosexuality). During seven months in 1977, Báez went through electric shock treatment. He saw his family and psychiatrists take control over his life. In 1978, Báez had a nervous breakdown.

Báez recovered quickly and began to date women, which he did until 1981. He avoided relationships and sexual contact with men during this period because the treatment had successfully traumatized him. He said that every time he began to get aroused at the prospect of sex with a man, "de inmediato de lo que me recordaba era del corrientazo. . . . Y por supuesto, eso inmediatamente me detenía cualquier deseo sexual que yo tuviera" (I would immediately remember the electric shock. . . . And of course, that immediately stopped any desire I had).

Family pressures also influenced Báez's initial choice of professions. His parents pressured him into pursuing a career in medicine, which Báez rejected when he rejected the life that the psychiatrists and his relatives had laid out for him. While pursuing a career in modern languages and literatures, Báez became associated with left-wing circles and socialist organizations in Santo Domingo. But his ideas about sexuality as politics caused controversy among his acquaintances. Soon enough, Báez became alienated from those circles: "A mí me expulsaron de la organización porque yo tenía una novia que tenía un novio y yo, juntos a la vez. O sea, nosotros nos metíamos en la cama los tres, y todo el mundo lo sabía" (I was expelled from the organization because I had a girlfriend who had a boyfriend and me, together at the same time. In other words, we would go to bed all three, together, and everybody knew it).

Eventually, migration became the only viable solution to Báez. He lived in London, Montreal, and New York. I have delved at length into his difficulties in the Dominican Republic because they inform Báez's critical attitude toward all things Dominican. However, some elements of the dominicanidad that he criticized also haunted him in New York.

Báez defined his migration explicitly as a departure and rejection of the racism, classism, and homophobia in Dominican society. For Báez, migrating to the United States was centrally about sexual dissent: "Yo no vine aquí a buscar el sueño americano. Yo vine a este país a buscar un bimbín negro: grande, bueno, con mucha leche" (I did not come here looking for the American dream. I came to this country to find black dick: big, good, with lots of milk). Báez believed that his critical perspectives on Dominican society put him at odds with the values of many Dominicans he knew in New

York. Báez thought these other people had a less critical relationship with the cultures of their homeland: "Yo con lo que no podía bregar, realmente, era con la opresión social y cultural en la Republica Dominicana. Y yo vine para acá a dejar mi vergüenza. Yo cuando salí de la Republica Dominicana, dejé mi vergüenza allá. O sea, que ahora yo soy lo que se llama un sinvergüenza" (What I could not deal with, frankly, was with the social and cultural oppression in the Dominican Republic. And I came here to let go of my shame. When I left the Dominican Republic, I left my shame over there. In other words, I am now what people call a man without shame).

Among the informants, Báez was the closest to what Manolo Guzmán has memorably called a "sexile," but Báez's dissent, clearly expressed through geographical displacement, was also a rejection of the value system into which he was socialized.[30] This is partly why his becoming a "sinvergüenza," or a person "without shame," so radically revises notions of shame that are in so much United States–based scholarship about homosexual subject formation; the armature of shame that Báez abandoned is central to the project of the Dominican nation-state and, specifically, to the project of upholding racial and class privilege in his family.

The circumstances in Báez's life forced him to politicize his sexuality in relation to his background: "En mí siempre ha pesado más la vagina que la nacionalidad dominicana. Y ha pesado más la vagina que la ascendencia de clase de mi madre y de mi padre" (In my case, the vagina has mattered more than my Dominican nationality. And my vagina has mattered more than the class origins of my mother and my father). His feminization and politicization of his anus as his "vagina," in his departure from his family and in his erotic pursuit of dark-skinned and working-class men, reveal that sex was a mechanism of political dissent for Báez.

But Báez was also deeply critical of the gay community, as readers might recall from the end of the last chapter:

La comunidad gay es una falsedad. La comunidad gay no existe. Eso es un invento que nos hemos inventado nosotros mismos. . . . Ah, pero el hecho de que él mama güevo quiere decir que él y yo somos iguales. ¿Quién te dijo a ti? Ese cabrón vive en el Upper East Side.	The gay community is a fallacy. The gay community does not exist. That is something we have invented ourselves. . . . Ah, but the fact that he sucks dick means that he and I are the same. Who told you that? That fucker lives in the Upper East Side. He wears a Cartier watch, and puts $150,000

Anda con un maldito reloj Cartier, y se mete $150,000 en un bolsillo. ¿Cómo tú lo vas a comparar conmigo que vivo en el maldito Bronx, que cojo el maldito D train everyday, y que tengo que irle a comer mierda a la bruja en mi trabajo? ¿Qué nos une? ¿La vagina? ¡No! La vagina no da comunidad.

in his pocket. How can you compare him with me, living in the fucking Bronx, taking the fucking D train every day, and putting up with the shit of the witch boss I have at work. What unites us? The vagina? No! Vagina does not a community make.

Báez was one of the informants most open about his own sexual history. Moreover, his perspective stood out because he explicitly articulated a connection of his sexuality to his nationality and his race and class politics. Sexual dissent, in his case, was not just dissent from normative dominicanidad. It was also sexual dissent from normative gayness.

Báez explained that at the beginning, in the years before his family forced a psychiatric intervention upon him, "Yo fundamentalmente fungía como lo que en éste país se llama bottom" (Fundamentally, I operated like what in this country is called a "bottom"). From the beginning, however, the crossing of racial and class boundaries was central to his erotic life. A light-skinned Dominican man, Báez explained, "a mí, sobre todo, me encantaba un tíguere, me encantaba un moreno, y me encantaba que me lo metiera" (I loved a tíguere; above all, I loved a black man and I loved to be fucked by him). Although he did not have sexual contact with men during the five or so years he underwent psychiatric treatment, Báez explained that having relationships with women taught him that he could perform well as the penetrating partner. Thus, his next long-term relationship with a man was

más o menos de igual a igual . . . pues yo metía y metíamos los dos. Por supuesto, él siempre quería metérmelo a mí más de lo que yo quería metérselo a él, porque para un homosexual dominicano, quien lo mete es el que manda. Entonces ese, por ese nivel de control y por ese nivel de, tú sabes, de yo soy el que manda, él me lo metía a mí.

more or less of equal to equal . . . because we both penetrated. Of course, he always wanted to fuck me more than I wanted to fuck him, because for a Dominican homosexual, the one who penetrates is boss. Then because of that, because of that level of control and because of that level of, you know, of I am the boss, he fucked me.

Once that relationship ended, Báez dated other men in the Dominican Republic. He explained that during this time, sexual roles varied from partner to partner. In most cases, partners performed both receptive and penetrative roles throughout the course of the relationship, with varying degrees of preference. Some partners were more interested in penetrating than in being penetrated or vice versa. Everything changed in this part of his life once Báez migrated to the United States:

Y ya cuando yo vine para los Estados Unidos, ahí todo cambió. Cuando yo llegué aquí, a Nueva York, yo me convertí en un pene. Yo me convertí aquí en un güevo dominicano, en un macho, coño, bueno, singón, que lo que yo hago es encaramar, y lo que yo hago es que yo busco gente que me den servicio, que me la mamen y que me la saquen. Y eso es—así es como yo aquí funciono. Ese es el código de funcionamiento sexual que yo tengo aquí, que es totalmente diferente al que yo tenía allá.

¿Por qué dirías tú que es diferente?

Bueno, yo pienso que aquí no hay . . . yo no he tenido espacio para explorar otra cosa. Cuando yo intento ser, ¿cuál es la palabra? Democrático, sexualmente, de inmediato la gente no quiere salir conmigo. Y desde que yo quiero que un tíguere que está bueno, con el que yo estoy saliendo, me lo meta, de inmediato el tíguere se desilusiona y no le interesa salir conmigo. O si yo, por ejemplo, tengo una situación sexual con un tipo, suponiendo un sex club o una vaina de esas, y yo quiero que haya, tú ves,

And when I came to the United States, everything changed. When I arrived here, in New York, I became a penis. I became a Dominican dick, a macho, damn it, a good fucker, that what I do is to mount, and what I do is look for people to service me, to suck me and get me off. And that's—that's how I operate here. That is the code of sexual functioning that I have here, which is totally different from the one I had there.

Why would you say it is different?

Well, I think here there is no . . . I haven't had space to explore something else. When I try to be, what's the word? Democratic, sexually, immediately people do not want to go out with me. And from the moment I want that hot tíguere, with whom I'm going out, to fuck me, the tíguere is immediately disappointed and he's not interested in going out with me. Or if I, for example, have a sexual situation with some guy, say in a sex club or something like that, and I want there to be, you see, equality, democracy in bed. Damn it, because in the end, if I believe in democracy,

equiparidad, democracia en la cama. Coño, porque a fin de cuentas, si yo creo en la democracia, yo tengo que practicarla y en la cama es uno de los mejores lugares para practicarla. Cuando yo trato, intento de que haya esa igualdad, pues inmediatamente el tipo ya no quiere tener nada conmigo. O sea, que yo pienso que hasta cierto punto a mí me han, ¿cómo te digo? a mí me han . . . eh . . . forzado, la comunidad, los estereotipos. Acuérdate que un dominicano es un macho. Un dominicano aquí es una de las cosas más calientes que hay en la Ciudad de Nueva York. Con . . . porque son parte de la fantasía de la . . . de la identidad gay que un latino, un dominicano, un macho, dominante, pasional, ¿tú entiendes? Incansable—esa es otra, incansable. Cuando yo me vengo y el bimbín no se me quiere parar más, la gente se encojona. Pero coño, yo no tengo una fábrica de viagra en las bolsas, no jodas [nos reímos] . . . o sea que tú ves, yo pienso que en ese sentido, a mí me han forzado las circunstancias.

I have to practice it and bed is one of the best places to practice it in.[31] When I try, try to have that equality, then the guy immediately does not want to have anything to do with me. In other words, I think that up to a certain point I've been, how can I tell you? Others have . . . eh . . . forced me, the community, the stereotypes. Remember that a Dominican is a macho. A Dominican here is one of the hottest things in New York City. With . . . because they are part of the fantasy of the . . . the gay identity that a Latino, a Dominican, a macho, dominant, passionate, you know? Indefatigable—that's the other one, indefatigable. When I cum and my dick does not want to get up again, people get angry. But damn it, I don't have a Viagra factory in my balls! [we laugh] . . . in other words you see, I think that in that sense, I've been forced by circumstances.

One fascinating thing about Báez's account of what others expected of him in sexual encounters was that *they* were the ones wanting to exercise control over the sexual exchange. This reverses the activo/pasivo scenario, for it shows that the one supposedly in control (the top) is not in control at all. Báez may be the top, but one cannot say that Báez has complete control over the dynamics of these exchanges. In some ways, then, this new scenario contradicts the Dominican sexual exchange where the top is boss—a scenario Báez pointed to in his discussion of his sex life in the Dominican

Republic. Performing the role of "Dominican macho" with partners in New York was about not being "el que manda" (the one who is boss) but actually subjecting himself to the "fantasy of gay identity" of his partners, becoming the "walking plantain" to be consumed by the anus of his partners. This shows the influence on Báez's sexual exchanges of the expectations of what a Dominican macho was supposed to be.

Circumstances and politics make Báez's perspective particular. But his expectation of versatility in sexual encounters partly resembles the expectation of an equal chance to play active and passive roles expressed by Aníbal Guerrero and Javier Acuña. Báez called it "using the bedroom to practice democracy," whereas Guerrero and Acuña talked about it as "50/50."

The experiences of informants with diverse class backgrounds and with perspectives on different aspects of sexual exchange in New York illustrate that the bedroom functions as a political space. The way in which these men described their experience with partners hints at the importance of the ideological "baggage" that was dominicanidad to their sexual experiences. Acuña's ideal Dominican partner was open to sexual experimentation. Readers will also recall that for Aníbal Guerrero, dominicanidad was present in his Dominican partners' refusal to "bend over" to be fucked by other men. For Claudio Báez, the ghost of dominicanidad appeared in the refusal of the dark-skinned men he dated to do something *other than* "bend over" to the "Dominican macho" Báez represented. In different ways, these informants pointed to some of the narratives of dominicanidad with which they had to contend and that they reformulated in their narratives. In addition, they illustrated the erotic productivity of ambivalence.

In all instances, partners' refusal to adhere to these informants' sexual ideal of versatility signified different truths. For Acuña, the demand of reciprocity from a partner offered the promise of an education in sexual modernity. For Guerrero, Dominican partners were challenging because of the shame they expressed in their refusal or dislike of the anal receptive role in sexual intercourse. Báez's difficulty in performing the anal receptive role since he has lived in New York suggests that stereotypes of the Dominican macho within "the fantasy of gay identity" frustrated his sexual ideal. In all of these instances, bed was a space of pleasure *given that certain conditions were met*. Pleasure was conditional on its relational tension with dominicanidad. In short, narrating the conditions of possibility for fucking (or not fucking) Dominican men, these informants demonstrate their erotic investment in the reification and reformulation of dominicanidad. It is clear that

Dominicans were not these men's only partners, and not all the men I interviewed talked about their erotic lives. But the degree to which Dominican men are at the center of the joys and pains expressed by the informants about their sex lives, these men narrated homoerotic and homoracial erotic investments.

The ways that the image of the Dominican macho shaped the expectations Dominican and other men of color have of Dominican men challenge us to grapple with the complicated terrain men like the informants navigate. We should recognize that the "Euro-American" sex and gender system is in relational tension with other "sexual systems." But this recognition should not blind us to the ways men of color, and even men belonging to those groups for whom these ideologies are principles of social organization, are complicit in their articulations and their reproduction. Those complicities, as they are located in the larger transnational field of circulation (that some informants manage to circulate in when they return to the Dominican Republic), are at the center of the analytic inquiry undertaken in the chapter that follows.

Claudio Báez's wish for "equality" did not exist outside the realm of sexual exchange, even though he gestured toward an understanding of the possibilities of intimacy within the local homosexual cultures. He did not isolate intimacy and mutually satisfying sexual relations from the fields of exchange in which they took place. He located the possibilities and obstacles for these relations *within* these fields. Thus, Báez's observations warn social analysts from imagining an "egalitarian economy" of homosexual relations and sexual intimacy as independent (or even outside) of sexual cultures partly constituted by the circulation of commoditized images and bodies. He challenges us to think about how much the realization of sexual fulfillment is implicated in the reproduction of imaginaries that equate migration with progress and the ability to circulate and objectify others with "freedom." Additionally, Báez's objectification of black men and his black partners' objectification of him point to the subjects' complicity, marked by otherness in the reproduction of eroticized racial and class dynamics and hierarchies. As sexy as democracy in bed might be, sexual pleasure and intimacy continue to be haunted by fear that the exchange will produce the abjected loca or the commoditized macho.

Until now, location is a neglected aspect of the sexual narratives I have explored. Though I noted earlier that several of these men discussed the broadening of their sexual repertoires as something that happened to them *after* moving to the United States, I have yet to account for the implication of this particular variable (in all its complexity) for this analysis. Location matters, and I have insisted throughout this book in drawing attention to scenes of interaction and the way they inform and constrain not only what people say but also the fact that when people speak, they do much more than string words together.

::: We Can Say More Than We Say

In previous chapters, I pointed out that it was important to keep in mind that the interview material analyzed in this study was collected in the United States. The lives narrated by these men were seen retrospectively from the vantage point of a social location that inflected the interpretive lenses these men (and I) brought to the analysis and theorization of personal histories, present relations, and future prospects. In their exchanges with me, these men felt a need to account for all they had to overcome in order to become the men with whom I interacted. These men revealed an ongoing struggle to contest, reinvent, or readjust to the parameters within which they came to understand who they were, who they must be, and who they wanted to be.

Articulating a sexual philosophy of openness and elasticity can then be seen as a further elaboration of their ongoing critical engagement with dominicanidad from the vantage point of men who are socially located in New York. Similar reformulations and challenges to the (homo)sexual status quo may still be ongoing in the Dominican Republic; I am simply drawing attention to the specificity of the informants' perspective as immigrant men to the degree that they explicitly articulated a connection between migration and changing views on sexual relations.[32]

It also matters that their interviewer was Dominican; the interview encounter between unequally situated members of a specific ethnoracial group may make a difference in the encounter, for it afforded informants the opportunity to engage the "problems" of the group more centrally than they might have with a non-Dominican interviewer. Far from claiming privileges of "native" status, I underscore that the interview encounter offered me and the informants the opportunity to address and engage homoerotic and homoracial investments. Moments of shared laughter about the centrality of *plátanos con salchichón* to Dominican breakfast, as well as code swishing that announced that the informant in question was going to become a *loca histe-riquísima y mala*,[33] are examples of the way already established connections and the commonality of a Dominican background shaped the direction of interview exchanges.

Dominican men may not have been at the center of the erotic universe of all twenty-five men. Dominican men may not be central *in general* to the erotic lives of Dominican immigrant men who have same-sex relations. Yet the productivity of the analysis here does not depend on its representativity. Rather, calling attention to the interview encounter itself as a scene of interaction helps explain why Dominican men were so central to the sexual stories recounted; the informants and I collaborated in further elaborations, critiques, and reformulations of dominicanidad.

As important as location is to the information obtained and the analysis developed here, my view of "locality" goes beyond simplest readings of context. In her pioneering *Black behind the Ears*, the sociologist Ginetta Candelario set out to explain the conditions of possibility for stronger identification as "black" among Washington, D.C.–based Dominicans than among those based in New York. Among the factors that Candelario cites to explain this difference are characteristics of the sending areas (in the Dominican Republic); time of migration and settlement in Washington, D.C.; patterns of residence and occupation in the local area; and contact with local Latin American immigrant and African American populations. Candelario concludes that the expression of black-identified Dominican identities in D.C. stems from the specificity of the combination of these factors: "In the context of a stratified, predominantly black-identified community in Washington, D.C., where black self-identification has been imposed by the local racial order, on the one hand, and has become a means of access to socioeconomic, cultural, and political capital, on the other hand, Dominicans have multiple incentives to identify as black."[34] Candelario uses these findings to explore the contextual specificity of identity formations. An additional layer in Candelario's conclusions concerns the specificities of a U.S. local history of adaptation that transforms the way this immigrant grouping imagines itself and other immigrant or local groups, resulting in identifications that set distance from the negrophobia of Dominican nationalist ideology.

The informants' espousal of an open sexual philosophy counters the homoerotic and homoracial investments that bind them to the Dominican macho. To the degree that they repeatedly bump into this figure (as that which they revile *and* desire and as that which other men desire Dominican men to embody), the sexual narratives stage encounters overdetermined by histories of sexuality and power that are constitutive of the colonial project that first rendered the Caribbean legible to the Western imagination. The next chapter will focus on the erotic afterlife of colonialism as it manifests in informants' narratives of return.[35]

CHAPTER 7

To Be Someone, To Be Somewhere:
Erotic Returns and U.S.-Caribbean
Circuits of Desire

::::

It was an evening in February 2001, during a visit to Santo Domingo. At the
zona colonial, I met up with a Dominican Republic–based senior scholar to
go over the dissertation proposal that evolved into this book. Apart from asking me to define the term *transnational* in a more precise way, my colleague
observed that it was important for me to be mindful of the exceptionality of
my "bourgeois" upbringing. It behooved me, I scribbled, "to open myself up
to visions of the world different from my own." Despite anything I may have
said to explain that I was hardly bourgeois simply by virtue of coming from a
working-class Dominican family that moved from Santo Domingo to Philadelphia in the late 1980s, the fact that I was educated at reputable American
universities and the fact that I could mobilize resources to conduct research
on Dominican issues definitely placed me in *his* bourgeois register.

After hearty helpings of dinner and critique, we walked through a few
barely lit streets and arrived at a bar that catered to bugarrones[1] and their clients, most of whom were tourists. As I entered the locale, I noticed a picture
on the wall of Elizabeth II, the English queen. Her stern glance and terse
smile presided over the bar.

It is tempting to decode the meaning of having a picture of the queen of
England displayed prominently in a sex worker bar on a rather muggy February evening. But the pictures that interested me most were ones I never
saw. They were taken while my scholar friend and I sat at the bar, mingling.
Because my companion worked for the Ministry of Health, he was known
as a researcher among the local male sex workers, as well as by the British
owner of the bar.

A local man arrived with a small group of men (maybe five?) who took pictures of themselves with him. Although in my notes and recollections I quickly jumped to call this man a bugarrón and these men his clients, this label was based on my observation of the location, the scenario, and the interactions. He was (*estaba*) with these men; thus, I supposed he was (*era*) a bugarrón, or at least, "estaba bugarroneando."[2]

As pictures were taken and smiling faces and bodies entered and exited the frame or took pictures of other smiles and bodies, most of the images had in common the guy I remember casting as "bugarrón," striking various poses from shot to shot, switching the angles of his blue baseball cap. Right after taking a picture, this man looked at the person holding the camera and shouted (loudly enough that his friends in other parts of the bar could hear him), "Voy pa' Nueva York" (I am going to New York). Although these words came out of his mouth with the lightness and sparkle of a joke, this man was only partly kidding. It was clear in his tone that he did not expect to migrate to the United States, but images of him were going to circulate in the United States, as mementoes of good times had by the travelers and as advertisements for his services to other men who came in contact with the travelers or the spaces where pictures were displayed. He would travel, indeed.

Other moments from that evening stick in my mind: My friend and I spoke with a white man whose accent I could not place (a Brit, an Aussie?). He told us that he had traveled to the Dominican Republic and Cuba and had encounters with sex workers in both countries. When I asked what he thought was the difference between sex workers in Cuba and the Dominican Republic, this man pointed out that, in Cuba, "You fuck intelligent people." There must have been other conversations I engaged in that evening. Yet it may have been my outrage at his response to my questions that pushed me to hold his words so centrally in my recollections of that night. Something about our presence and interaction with him suggested that this could be said. After all, my researcher friend and I were both light-skinned Dominicans, could pass for tourists, and did not look like we were turning tricks. We were also buying our own beers instead of having others buy them for us. The unsettling part of what he said was not so much its callousness but the way it situated my scholar friend and me in relation to this tourist and to the other men in the establishment.

I also had a conversation with one of the black guys at the bar. I cannot remember if he was one of the picture-takers or just hanging out with another group. He was somewhat heavy-set and probably in his late thirties. I asked him how he liked the Dominican Republic, and he said he liked it so much that he wanted to learn Spanish. He liked coming to the country to see "the culture" and "ruins" (by these last words I believe he meant the vestiges of the colonial city). He also liked the men. Men in Washington Heights, he observed later, were too Americanized. He hoped the Dominican Republic did not become too touristy. Puerto Rico was too touristy.

Shortly after my impromptu survey, the local police entered the bar. It was a raid, and my friend attempted to quell my growing panic. "Don't worry," he whispered in my ear as a few cars with sirens could be heard and more policemen entered the establishment. "Here, you and I are white." While cops grabbed the young Dominican men closest to the entrance to the bar, many of the black American men there pulled out their passports to make sure they were not confused with the locals. I trusted my friend, but my body did not, and I soon discovered my left hand buried in the left back pocket of the khakis I wore. My passport was there. My friend pointed out that sometimes cops were explicitly after tourists, but this night they appeared to be looking for money from the bugarrones. The tension that built after the removal of the Dominican men gave way to relief when some of them returned minutes later. They had probably paid a bribe. The ones who did not return, I learned, were probably jailed for the night for not having money.

::: *Regresos*

The return to the homeland is a recurring theme in Dominican cultural manifestations, institutional initiatives, social movements, and daily lives.[3] Return is also important to the men with whom I spoke, and the retrospective life history interviews we conducted afforded me glimpses of their narrative and symbolic returns to the homeland and to their pasts, mediated through the questions I asked, the answers they developed, and their voices.[4] Readers will recall that some of the men observed how self-aware they had to be of the way they carried themselves when visiting relatives or friends in the Dominican Republic. The return of other informants conjured images of themselves as children becoming men in a place where their movements were co-produced through observation, evaluation, and critique coming from mothers, relatives, and friends. Nevertheless, a major emphasis of mine throughout this study has been to illustrate the possibilities for challenging received wisdom about what it means to be Dominican, a man, or a homosexual given these men's negotiation of various sites for the production and intermingling of these subject forms. Living in New York City was particularly important for many of them. They continued to engage fellow Dominicans while also finding new referents for their own self-fashioning, critique and develop new ways of being Dominican, or use the perception of their accomplishments and success in New York to distinguish themselves from those surrounding them and from the friends and relatives whom they visited when they returned. "You can't go home again," as the phrase has it,[5] and this chapter will illustrate the degree to which that was true for two of the few men in this study who frequently traveled to the Dominican Republic. Nevertheless, "return" suggests the anteriority of a departure that was not as complete for the informants as it might be for many an epic traveler. If the multiplicity of referents harbored in a transnationalized formation allows people to invoke those contradictions in order to launch their individual or collective revisions/critiques of the nation-state, physical displacement to a site where those referents continue to have value in practices of belonging means that these men continued to transit through Dominican ethnoscapes.[6] They lived in the mental island. They couldn't go home again because they never left.

Recognition of these men's continuing engagement with dominicanidad after migration cannot blind us to the meanings that physical returns to the homeland have in their lives, however. And the gendering of return is crucial for an understanding of the narratives I will analyze in this chapter. A cursory glance at important venues for the commoditization of the Dominican Republic for Dominicans living abroad, such as the thirty-five-year-old weekly program *Santo Domingo Invita*,[7] which provides its viewers with a mixture of extended reports on tourist attractions, historical and cultural features, and profiles of small towns and cities throughout the country, suggests that the imagined returning viewer and visitor is a man. Much to the credit of the production team, the program often explicitly addresses the concerns of its female viewers. Nevertheless, some insistently recurrent phrases such as "pueblo de hombres trabajadores y mujeres bellas" (town of hard-working men and beautiful women) and advertising of resorts that invariably display the bodies of smiling local women suggest that the business of return to the homeland mobilizes the erotic allure of women for a (presumably) heterosexual male viewership.[8] Unlike many imagined viewers of *Santo Domingo Invita*, informants tended to be interested in the "smiles" of the hard-working men—or in their smiles as hard work, as demanding a form of labor for men, as it is for women whose happy faces populate the service sectors and tourist industry. But I will argue throughout this chapter that the informants' investment in male privilege, as manifested in their interpersonal dealings with other men and women when they returned to the Dominican Republic, points to how bound their returns are to what I call the *colonial zone*.

At the core of this chapter are relationships, positions, and identifications that interarticulate the local with the cosmopolitan, the *aquí* with the *allá*, and the mobile with the immobile. Thus, parts of my focus are questions concerning how the transnational is embedded in the local and how the "here" and the "there" co-produce one another. In her introduction to a special issue of the journal *positions*, Yukiko Hanawa explains that despite the attention given to the construction of sexualities across cultures and historical periods, there are multiple ways in which categories that refer to sexual identities mediate and are mediated by sexual practices.[9] The point, as she suggests, is not to seek "pure" alternatives to U.S. or European categories of sexuality but rather to attend to the contact of multiple epistemic frameworks, political-economic imperatives, and discourses of identification. She calls these *heterogeneous registers*, which inform cultural encounters of various kinds, "circuits of desire." Although teasing out these complexities is daunting, Hanawa argues that "it is . . . through such multiple possibilities that it becomes possible to imagine the meanings of sexual political subjects in global political economies."[10]

This chapter is an attempt at a mapping of "circuits of desire" that attends to the disjunctures, power imbalances, and erotics of sexual encounters complicit with longstanding colonialist fantasies of travel despite the fact that men of color are authors and consumers of the images and bodies that circulate in all of what follows. White gay men may have been pioneers in this trade,[11] and they may still benefit disproportionately from their place within global colonialist and white supremacist hierarchies of desire,[12] but all traders in the erotic here (consumers, entrepreneurs, and workers) are men of color.[13] What happens when returnees are also sex tourists?[14]

Identifying the unevenness of transnational social fields, and the actors, ideas, and commodities that inhabit, move, or stay still in them, demands that we grapple with the continuities between these relations and older colonial practices of leisure, travel, commoditization, and consumption. The Dominican Republic shares with other Caribbean island-nations a history of being perceived as natural paradises in the minds of European and (later) U.S. explorers, chroniclers, conquerors, and travelers.[15] Like other island-nations and peoples in the Caribbean, the relations of exchange that obtain from the transnationalization of Dominican society represent a new phase in an ongoing process of insertion into the latest incarnation of global capitalism. To distinguish my perspective from that of others who have rightly emphasized the new and emergent forms of agency in transnational social fields,[16] I will argue that it is necessary to better grasp the way subjects subordinated and marginalized in various national and local contexts experience mobility, relative freedoms, and power that are closely tied to the immobility of others. In this way, they perpetuate power relations with extended colonial histories.[17]

Grasping the continuities of the present with the past is a crucial first step toward untangling the operations of power to be analyzed below. Mimi Sheller's *Consuming the Caribbean* offers a compelling overview of the history of the way the Caribbean has been represented and consumed in Europe and the United States. Of particular importance to the work to be undertaken here is her conception of "binding mobilities," or the way the meaningfulness of the movement of some people derives from the stasis of others. Thus, the pleasures return migrants and tourists might enjoy during their sojourns depends on those who wait for their return, make ends meet with the remittances sent, or cater to the needs and desires of return migrants and tourists in what Mark Padilla has aptly called the "Caribbean pleasure industry."[18] Following Sheller and recalling the insights drawn from the work of Celine Parreñas Shimizu in the previous chapter, I begin to think through the bondages of movement and stasis or, as Sheller puts it, between "people-in-motion and people-who-stay-still."[19] But it is not just people who circulate or stay still. Being that much of existing transnational scholarship, as well as Sheller's own work, has stressed that the mobilities of persons, ideas, and commodities are intricately connected, I will stress at the outset the importance of teasing out these interconnections and their meanings.

Scholarship on sex and commerce in the Caribbean has investigated the continuity of present-day forms of racialized and sexualized labor with the history of colonialism in the region and its centrality in early articulations of global capitalism.[20] In the specific case of the Dominican Republic, the imperial reaches of the United States have been particularly important, and ongoing economic dependence (based on sugar in the earlier part of the twentieth century and based on tourism toward the end of it, and the beginning of the twenty-first century) has created the conditions of possibility for what we currently call transnational capitalism. As Amalia Cabezas puts it, "transnational tourism reactivates historical patterns of production," making it possible for "former colonizers and new transnational classes [to] travel to the Caribbean to consume the scenery, beaches, and, ultimately, brown bodies."[21]

People of color are as complicit as anyone else in the inequalities spawned by transnational capitalism. Yet understanding the subtleties of their presence, participation, and enjoyment of privilege demands an analysis that disarticulates consumption and power from a white (gay) male body and that sets some distance from the "self"-versus-"other" dichotomy that usually organizes analyses of relations of (sexual) exchange in transnational settings.[22] Balderston and Quiroga draw from Borges to argue that "el regreso es una manera de leer la historia personal enfocada en la relación entre *el mismo y el otro, o el mismo visto como otro (y viceversa)*" (return is a way to interpret one's personal history with a focus on the relationship between *the same and the other, or the same seen as other [and vice versa]*).[23] Instead of a self-versus-other dialectic, Balderston and Quiroga reframe the dialectic as "the same" and "the other" to stress the slippage, the transit between positions. Whether one is situated on either side of this dichotomy depends on where and how one looks.

I will follow Balderston and Quiroga throughout this text in suggesting that returns stage encounters between "el mismo y el otro." However, I also want to explore the gendered dimension of this return, for the complicities of men of color who are returnees and sex tourists have to do with male privilege. For this reason, I will modify the dialectical formulation that Balderston and Quiroga borrowed from Borges to argue that return in this analysis allows for encounters between "el otro y él mismo" (the other and he himself). The accent on the pronoun adds a small but significant nuance in the discussion, for it marks the masculinity of the subjects in question (a masculinity unmarked but tacit in the Borgian formulation).

::: *El otro y él mismo*: Colonial Zones and Scenes, Replayed

The opening of this part of the study and the opening of this chapter are ethnographic accounts of my transit through the zona colonial in two different moments in my life and in the life of this book. Because I am a return migrant, a visitor, and a gay-identified man like many of the participants, my project of producing knowledge is entangled with my own conflicted relationship to the Dominican homeland. Explaining the sources of my conflict is beyond the scope of this study (and it will take several careers to account for it!), but revisiting these scenes will help unpack the transit between el otro y él mismo that I will then take up in the return narratives of the informants. The point here is not to posit my experience or that of anyone else as being representative of what happens to everyone. Instead, these ethnographic narratives demonstrate that although basking in the joys of the Dominican "pleasure industry" is part of the agenda of return visitors like me, our habitation of circuits of desire and our enjoyment of the Caribbean pleasure industry cannot be anchored on hierarchies of power based on phenotype. Like Salvador Vidal-Ortiz, I use autoethnography to "place biography in context."[24] Any attempts at unpacking the collision, intermingling, and interarticulations of circuits of desire in return narratives must grapple with the location from which they are being produced. In ways that echo the critiques of Manolo Guzmán and Greg Thomas, I am profoundly suspicious of the gayness from which I speak, a social location that tends to overproduce itself in the academy as an avant-garde of the progressive left, often without self-reflexivity about its complicity with academic structures of power, its lack of racial and class innocence, its intellectual Europhilia, and the service and pleasure sector hierarchies that sustain its cosmopolitan pretensions.[25]

These ethnographic accounts produce a male body in motion through the streets of the zona colonial, a body that observed the labor of others but that was unburdened by the urgency of having to labor to survive. It was a body "on vacation." Indeed, my only indication of exertion, my only hint of labor, concerns the intensification of motion for the sake of regulating my body: jogging may provoke beads of sweat to exit the pores of my skin, but they did so to balance a dietary regime, not because I was accountable to anyone for accelerated movement or lower cholesterol. The observation and writing of these narratives are forms of labor as well, but my official fieldwork activities did not include trips to the Dominican Republic. In other words, my incorporation of autoethnography into this chapter came in the writing process itself and not in the gathering of my first impressions, which were notes of a travel diary I kept as part of my leisure activities.

But the walking body in these vignettes was not the unmarked male gazing body of the tourist or the "disembodied" social scientist rightly criticized by Veijola and Joniken.[26] I was observing others, but I was also observed, a fact that was evident to me in the first note when I jogged, cruised, and was surprised that the young man who crossed paths with me took off his sunglasses and looked back. It was also evident later that day, when I discovered that another young man I had cruised was following me. I learned to disabuse myself of the idea that I looked "foreign" to my fellow Dominicans when I first met my senior colleague in 2001. We agreed to meet across the way from the Parque Independencia, at the very beginning of El Conde Street. I had seen pictures of him and knew to look for a man with a goatee, but I did not know if and how he might be able to tell who I was. As he told me later that evening or another day, he expected someone older, and, apart from my youth, I looked "like another Dominican." Maybe having lived in the United States for so many years had made me inadvertently fall into the myth that living in *los países* actually "whitens" those who leave. Maybe I hoped to be read as white, but even the "whiteness" that ultimately distinguished my colleague and me at the scene of the bar raid was a specific form of it, conferring privilege less for reasons of racial purity or descent than the combination of lighter phenotype, a U.S. passport, and "inside" connections that could be flashed at the police if need be. Had all of these codes not been mobilized together and in the right conjuncture of space and time, I could have gone to jail.

While I strolled or jogged, others labored (or tried to labor) to service my needs and desires. Some of that work can be located in specific moments in the two accounts (the cashier of the supermarket and the waiter at the restaurant in the first; the bartender who served beers to my colleague, me, and others mingling at the bar raided in the second). Yet some forms of labor that I might have engaged through money or gifts would have been secured by tapping into spaces of liminality. The young men "looking back" in response to my cruise and following me may have been looking for work or "looking for life," as Padilla poignantly puts it,[27] but it is not clear if and how sex was implicated in these scenes. The smartest students of the conjunctures of sex and commerce in the contemporary Dominican Republic, Cabezas and Padilla are quick to point out that although many of the men and women who provide these services might identify as sex workers, theirs are *adaptive* (Padilla) or *contingent* (Cabezas) responses to social marginality.[28] Indeed, Cabezas argues that the term *sex work*, though important, "is difficult to apply to the new forms of flexible, contingent practices that may contain elements of partial commodification but that do not conform to rigid categories of commercial sex work."[29] Homoerotic contacts and linkages, then, need not have resulted in sexual exchange for activities like "looking back" at tourists, checking them out, or initiating dialogue with them to be part of the activities of these workers.

The example of the young man who asserted that he was "going to New York" in the pictures he had taken with the tourists at the bar that was raided helps further unpack the operations of what Cabezas calls "the affective economies of transnational tourism."[30] One interpretation of his statement may underscore its futility, but the changing poses before the cameras and the joking tone point to this man's intuition that once his body becomes a commodity, it exerts an erotic force that exceeds its instrumentality in sexual commerce. To the degree that the body of a sex worker is treated as a commodity, it stands to lose the qualitative specificity of what it offers (or what Marx would term its *use-value*). To paraphrase Marx, the embodied commodity, once "stripped off"(!), its use-value still has the property of being the product of labor, though "all its sensuous characteristics are extinguished."[31] Yet the fusing of use- and exchange-value is critical to the "affective economies of transnational tourism" within which this man was working.[32] Having pictures of himself circulate and maybe even adorn the living rooms of the men with whom he engaged in erotic relations (which may or may not include sex) may not just produce more business. It may do so in ways that are sustainable over time, and the works of Brennan, Padilla, and Cabezas suggest that this is a common practice among male and female sex workers (self-identified or occasional). The man posing with the tourists at the bar understood that his own body may not move but that its display (a form of labor) carried potentialities that may bring more business and may generate unforeseen and unanticipated desires. In her analysis of the commentary of one of her male informants in the Dominican Republic, Cabezas points out that "lasting bonds with foreigners may ultimately position Camilo as a lover and a friend and assist him in asserting and maintaining a subjectivity of resistance to the exclusionary practices of transnational tourism capital."[33] Similar to the self-making of the men whose lives Jaffari Sinclaire Allen documents in Cuba, what is at stake for men like the man posing in front of the camera in my account is capital accumulation and the possibility of repositioning himself as a cosmopolitan subject.[34] Like the "smiling women" in the advertising in *Santo Domingo Invita*, the pose was a product of this man's labor, a "freezing" of himself that, once detached from his own body, circulated in ways that extend his potentialities as a provider of pleasure industry services.

While these forms of labor and affect are hard to apprehend under traditional identitarian rubrics, the ethnographic notes point to an insistent effort on my part to grapple with empirical description through categorization drawing from what could be observed. I did not offer a social type to describe the man who cruised me while crossing the street toward El Malecón in the first anecdote, yet I rather quickly erred on the side of labeling when attempting to describe the second man as either a bugarrón, a jevito, or both based on the fact that we were (estábamos) walking and checking one another out in El Conde Street in the evening. In the anecdote about the bar that was raided, I also developed a description of the circuitry of the situation based on what I saw, where we were, and how I classified the actors involved and their potential motivations.

One place where the specifics of the way I cast the scenes matters is where it involved the black tourists who had their pictures taken with the man I viewed as el bugarrón at the bar that was raided. My recognition of the difference between this man and the men who had pictures taken with him followed my hearing the men speak English and their companion Spanish. Until then, their dark skins suggested that they were all possibly African American. This is the way I have written it. Nevertheless, it takes more than English language and black skin to make an African American, and it stands to reason that some of these men were African American but also West Indian immigrants or children of immigrants living in the United States and Afro-Latinos (including Afro-Dominicans). The certainty projected by my characterization and categorization of who I saw cannot be taken at face value, for the markers I employed to guide my memory into an accurate empirical reading of the situation could be off the mark.

Nevertheless, the impulse to categorize in these notes emerges from a sense of danger, proximity, and competition with the various men I encountered. My homoerotic subjectivity is implicated in my noticing only men in these accounts, despite the fact that I came across women during the course of all the events narrated. This way of seeing is implicated in whom I noticed and in the way I interpreted El Conde, but it also marked my entrance and sense of discomfort (or jealousy?) with the black men in the restaurant in the first anecdote (the ones sitting at the table and being served while nobody at the establishment seemed to notice that I had come in) or the men at the bar that was raided who were taking pictures with the young Dominican man who said he was going to New York. After all, here were other men of color who might have been visiting from the United States and who could engage in activities I knew would be hard for me to entertain and thematize explicitly in my life and work without attending to serious personal and professional consequences.

My brush with danger is rendered explicit in the anecdote of the bar that was raided, but it is present more as foreboding in the anecdote that opens this part of the book. I arrived in Santo Domingo in 2008 after seven years of assiduous avoidance of return, and the whole narrative is imbued with a sense of uncertainty and anxiety about the world I was reencountering. Though empirically accurate, I also traded in metaphors of blackness and underdevelopment: the *apagón* (blackout) as the quintessential symptom of the chronic problems with electricity and of the inability of Dominicans to be a fully modern and efficient society, the growing concern with crime, and so on. I encountered a strongly lit El Conde (lit for the tourists) and parted ways with the young man I exchanged words with before walking back into the darkness of the street where my apartment was located. This was the night of the Dominican poor and working class: a night without electricity. Once my eyes adjusted to the darkness, I walked back, passed by my apartment building, and stood confused in the middle of the block until my neighbor from across the street (the woman who told me to turn off the lights in the house to save the energy of the inversor we had in the apartment) called to me. "Carlitos, es ahí," she said, awakening me from my confusion and directing me to the door of the building, immediately to my left. I could see it. She could see me. I was home, already linked through her watchful eye and her hailing of me with the felicitous use of my name's diminutive (a familial, almost motherly gesture) into her existing relations in the neighborhood. She was looking out for me.

For several years I wrote my dissertation and pondered the details of what I witnessed at the bar that was raided with a measure of self-righteousness and moral condemnation (and, I will admit, a measure of perverse, national-ist, masculine sense of entitlement; it would be fine for me, as a Dominican, to trade money and gifts for sex and the attention of a bugarrón or to get one of them to "work my ass," as my friend in the first anecdote suggested, but not for the black tourists I met). But my attitude was disingenuous. My first years of return trips to the Dominican Republic were organized around a relationship similar to the long-distance romantic/sexual attachments that may have been caused by the circulation of the picture of the guy with the blue baseball cap.

I immigrated to the United States in 1989 and returned, for the first time, in the summer of 1994, between my junior and senior years in college. This first trip was supposed to be a "research trip"; I had proposed to create a documentary on "Dominican homosexuality." Although I was grossly unprepared to undertake as massive a project as a documentary, a scholarly and artistic project about my experience of return came out of this first return trip. In addition to remarking incessantly on how much smaller everything seemed (compared with what I remembered), I got busy on other forms of documentation involving one of the cooks at the hotel where I stayed. Impossibly enough, his name was Carlos. This was the start of a relationship that lasted two years and that revolved around my biannual visits, time spent together, phone calls, and a few one-directional exchanges of money. I even pursued briefly the possibility of helping my namesake immigrate to the United States. Admittedly, it is unsettling for me to think of this as a form of sex or "romance" tourism, except that the characteristics of the situation are similar to those documented in the Dominican Republic and elsewhere.

In addition, having someone from abroad establish and sustain long-term relationships with local men was familiar to me, given my childhood in the Dominican Republic. One of my father's best male friends, who was married and had two children with a local woman and who lived near my childhood home, received frequent visits from an older Puerto Rican woman who brought gifts for his children, befriended my parents, and also brought gifts to my siblings and me. I assembled G.I. Joe dolls, expensive toy trains, and planes with complicated instructions as a child; many of these came to me through this woman and this relationship, which ended only once my father's friend immigrated to New York.

Developing a critique of sex tourism from the vantage point of the return migrant or person of color who is a sex tourist is particularly urgent, because some emergent forms of transnational capitalism involve sex and people of color as the producers *and* consumers of these services. Recent examples of the "binding mobilities" that structure the travels of American men of color to the Dominican Republic come from the blogs of Monaga Corporation and New Wave Black Man.[35] These enterprises were responsible for Dominican Island Heat, parts I and II (circuit parties organized for men of color visiting the Dominican Republic).[36] Monaga also administers a small gay hotel in the zona colonial and has become a major reference site for discussions and news directed to a gay-man-of-color-traveling audience seeking accommodations and other services.[37] The Dominican Island Heat events and Monaga have also enjoyed support by Latino and Dominican gay organizations and gay male entrepreneurs in New York. Outraged at a homophobic outburst by the Catholic leader of the Dominican Republic (not atypical of Cardenal Nicolás de Jesús López Rodríguez), this is what New Wave Black Man, a marketing and real estate entrepreneur and events planner, commented in his blog:

> Well, well, well. It seems that if you are a homosexual you will not be welcome in the Colonial Zone of Santo Domingo if the very reverand [sic] Cardinal has his way. Truely [sic] amazing. He calls homosexuals, IN GENERAL, degenerates. No wonder gay people worldwide are leaving the Catholic Church in droves. Personally, we will see what the government does. People have been asking us about DIH3. There will be an event, however we are not sure if we want to return to the Dominican Republic with our guests. Perhaps it would be better if we take our hundreds of thousands of dollars to another country that does not follow the lead of such a man. Perhaps it is just a press opportunity needed to build up the morale of the religious right . . . God knows it has worked in other places but I for one take it as a personal insult to me as an American, a tourist and a man who has tried to help the City of Santo Domingo. I just hope the business [sic] of the Colonial Zone don't just sit down and take this. Stay tuned to the Monaga Blog . . . In the meantime, check out www.bahianheat .com for an alternative to your vacation in DR.[38]

A growing industry in points such as the Dominican Republic and Bahia, Brazil, is headed by and for men of color. What is noteworthy about this excerpt is not so much that the cardinal said something homophobic but rather that our blogger mentioned his potential withdrawal of his "guests" and of himself, a "man who has tried to help the City of Santo Domingo." Shouldn't the "help" extend to combating the homophobia of the cardinal? Just as multinational corporations pull out their millions of dollars when local governments do not make the expected concessions, here is another entrepreneur willing to walk out of the Dominican Republic with his business—except, in this instance, that the expectation is that the leader of the Catholic Church will participate in the project of making the country amenable to entrepreneurs like him and their business pursuits.

Granted, the collaboration of Monaga Corporation and New Wave Black Man with LGBTQ activists and entrepreneurs in the Dominican Republic and in New York is, perhaps, part of the "help" that New Wave Black Man is talking about. The convergence of forces and actors in the work of the Dominican Island Heat organizers can be seen in the support they received from community activists and entrepreneurs in New York and Santo Domingo. Indeed, during the events and in the present, the tendency has been for these actors to advertise one another's events and ventures on their respective websites or announcements.

Sex tourism is not necessarily far from other forms of "help" made available to Dominicans through these enterprises, and some of these entrepreneurs align themselves with educational or philanthropic causes. Some examples of this will suffice: some of these actors supported a house for children orphaned by AIDS, and, perhaps most bizarrely, some of these entrepreneurs have collaborated with the Batey Relief Alliance to provide tourists with a "different kind of tourism" by having them visit the *bateyes*, or living quarters of Haitian immigrants in the Dominican Republic.[39] The websites tend to feature tours and excursions to educate tourists on Dominican history and culture.

But as invested as entrepreneurs like the Monaga and New Wave Black Man are in making the Dominican Republic a more "gay-friendly" country, their ability to commodify the bodies of locals depends on the effectiveness of the homophobia of someone like the cardinal. After all, at the bar that was raided, wasn't that guy from Brooklyn looking for bodies produced by an environment unlike that of an "Americanized" Washington Heights or Puerto Rico? Are Dominican "ruins" and "culture" not part of a mapping of "tradition" that contains homophobia (and family-centeredness, secrecy, and Catholicism) as claustrophobic, yet foundational? Isn't this part of what makes sex with local men so exciting? And what of the bugarrones, primary object of desire of the gay sex tourists? How much "help" are they receiving if they can be regaled with money and gifts by tourists but cannot move after being insulted by the cardinal's homophobia? What if the cardinal's homophobia does not register as an insult to them because they do not identify as gay or because this is just part of the abuse they have to ignore to get through their everyday lives?

It is easy enough to be condescending and critical of New Wave Black Man and entrepreneurs like him. My point, however, is that as "good" tourists as these folks may want to be, tourist enterprises and the consumers of their services can always find themselves elsewhere. In my personal case, it did not matter how frustrating my relationship with my namesake was; I always had a plane waiting for me at the end of those two-week periods, while he was left to deal with a reality I never quite understood and was never willing to engage. I could always leave.

Maybe facing the realities of social marginalization and struggle in the Dominican Republic challenged New Wave Black Man's access to his sense of cosmopolitan, leisured gayness or his entrepreneurial activities. The reactionary rants of the archbishop interrupted the seamless trajectory of this person's strolls through the zona colonial as a man whose U.S. dollars and activities have "helped" Santo Domingo. Maybe that's the one distinction between the return migrant as tourist and the person of color who simply visits: New Wave Black Man may "walk away," but the guilt of leaving haunts the life of the return migrant/visitor.

Maybe the honest thing is to acknowledge that like New Wave Black Man, Monaga, and the other male tourists of color who visited Santo Domingo to participate in Dominican Island Heat and to establish erotic relations with men in the Dominican Republic, I may not have access to the highest location in global hierarchies of power, but I will access whatever power I can. This is no simple appeal to the transnational to trump the limitations of locality. Like the black men who flashed their U.S. passports when the cops raided the bar, I could not simply rely on the "whiteness" my colleague said he and I had. My body knew better than that, which is why I assented to his reassurance but still wanted to ensure I had the passport. Like the black men in the scene, I grabbed my passport but simply watched as other men of color were taken away by the cops. I did not protest. Nobody protested. So much for international queer solidarity. We may have been reassured and even comforted by that sign that we were people whose life could not be limited by state structures of the Dominican Republic, whose world was really somewhere else, who were somebody, and who could not simply be "taken away" without accountability of the United States. We were mobile metropolitan subjects. We could leave. But the men who went to jail, whom those of us who carried U.S. passports looked like and desired—they could move only as far as the money they made would take them. Some could not even afford to return after the raid and continue making a profit off their bodies.

Students of transnational processes have developed analyses of growing complexity to apprehend the mobilities and immobilities that structure the lives of people, irrespective of whether they stay or leave one location, region, or country to visit, stay for some time, or settle permanently somewhere else.[40] A challenge that remains is to appreciate the way those who move and those who stay make sense of their positions, their relationships with others in these social fields, and their links to one another. Understanding the way transnational actors perceive the stakes in their relations to others near and far is particularly important when, as in the case of the informants, their access to mobility is embedded in and also exceeds formal or informal mechanisms sanctioned by heteronormative state, community, or kinship structures. Under what conditions do some people, ideas, commodities, and other resources circulate? Under what conditions might these same people, ideas, commodities, and other resources *not* circulate? How is the mobility of some connected, or even implicated, in the immobility of others? What roles do desire and longing play in the intimacies and inequalities spawned by these movements?[41] These are some of the questions I will take up in the sections that follow through an engagement with the narratives of return of two of the informants.

The challenge before us is not to condemn these activities by appealing to a false sense of ethical purity, a higher moral ground that does not exist. Nobody is innocent in these exchanges, which means that a radical critique of sexuality that insists in the liberation and democratization of sex in an uneven world is (to put it generously) naive. The task at hand is to understand the ways power and inequality are mediated through the erotic, making contact and intimacy possible but never completely comfortable. The narratives to be presented and analyzed in the next two sections illustrate the way these two returnees framed their visits as opportunities to subvert the sexual status quo of their lives as gay men in the United States.

::: Playing with Bugarrones

Mauricio Domínguez, forty-five, was born into a family of professionals in a thriving town in the eastern Dominican Republic. His father was a judge, and his mother holds a medical degree; both were well-established personalities in his hometown. Mauricio migrated to the United States in the early 1980s and traveled to the Dominican Republic a few times a year. Important details in Domínguez's life, for our purposes, include his identification with and pride in his blackness, which he traces back to growing up in a family very aware of its connection to Afro–West Indian migrations to the Dominican Republic resulting from the boom of the sugar industry in his home city. In addition, Domínguez had been active in Latino gay politics in New York.

Domínguez was remarkably candid with me about his sexual history, and it is from the conjunction of this sexual history and his returns that I draw three pertinent moments. To offer a general frame for this sexual history, Domínguez narrated his increasing comfort with his sexuality along the active/passive axis: a life initially characterized by almost exclusively penetrative sex evolves by Domínguez's need to experience what he called the "excitement" of being penetrated by a man. For him, there was pleasure in both positions, but his interest in receptive anal intercourse grew largely in the context of relationships where he experienced intense love for his partners.

The expectation of versatility in romantic relationships as a constitutive element of a well-adjusted gay self makes Domínguez's views consistent with those of other informants. What set him apart from others is both Domínguez's experiences of return and his candor about the relationship between monetary and sexual exchange. My first two examples come from situations involving desire, sex, and monetary exchange.

In the midst of telling me about relationships he had with men in the Dominican Republic when he visited, Mauricio provided an account of a relationship he started with a bugarrón. As he explained, despite the fact that this man "al principio fue muy activo" (at the beginning played the active role during sexual encounters), now they have reached what Domínguez calls a "very human level":

Nosotros comenzamos la relación muy comercialmente. Vamos al sexo. Yo te doy quinientos pesos . . . Él me penetraba a mí. Él no dejaba que yo lo penetrara . . . cuando yo fui en el '99, yo pensé que iba a pasar lo mismo. Y una noche, él me enseñó un condón y me dijo . . . "¿tú te	At the beginning, our relationship was very commercial. Let's have sex. I give you five hundred pesos . . . He penetrated me. He would not let me penetrate him . . . when I went in '99, I thought we were in for more of the same. And one night, he showed me a condom and asked me . . . "Do

cercioras muy bien de que eso esté bien puesto antes de que yo te lo meta?" Dije "sí. ¿Por qué?" Me dijo, "cerciórate bien de que esté bien puesto cuando tú me lo metas." . . . A mí el güevo se me quedó sarazo . . . Yo no funcioné esa noche . . . Entonces, después de ahí yo como que cogí el mando. Y hoy en día la relación es paralela completamente. Él me pide que por favor que no se lo diga a nadie . . . nos hemos hecho amigos. Hemos compartido cosas.

you always make sure this is correctly put on me before I fuck you?" I replied, "Yes. Why?" He said, "Make sure to put it on correctly before you fuck me." . . . My dick went limp . . . I could not do anything that night . . . but after that, I took control. And nowadays the relationship is completely parallel. He tells me to please not tell anyone . . . we have become friends. We have shared things.

The newfound "humanity" (framed as horizontal relationship and literally referencing versatility in bed) had consequences for the forms of exchange that took place between Domínguez and this sex partner:

Al principio fue una relación bien de "Vamos a hacer sexo. Yo te pago." Después que comenzamos a joder con paralelismos sexuales las cosas han cambiado. Ya yo, por ejemplo, ya yo no le digo "Toma. Toma esto." Sino yo le digo: "¿Con cuánto tú te vas a desenvolver mañana?" "Mira: yo necesito doscientos pesos para la leche de la niña . . . yo no fui a trabajar esta semana y me hace falta tal cosa." ¿Tú me entiendes? Y a ese nivel yo brego mejor que con decirle "¿Cuánto tú cobras?" Yo no sé bregar con eso. ¡Ni quiero tampoco hacerlo!

At the beginning, it was very much a relationship in the sense of "Let's have sex. I pay you." After we began fooling around with sexual parallelisms, things have changed. Now I don't say, "Take this cash." Instead, I ask "How much do you need to get through the day tomorrow?" "Look. I need two hundred pesos for the milk of my baby girl . . . I didn't go to work this week, and I need this and this." You know what I mean? And at that level it is easier for me to deal with it than to ask, "How much do you charge?" I don't know how to deal with that. And I don't want to!

This growing "humanity" in the relationship is manifested in a specific sexual role performance and in a relationship between sexual and monetary exchanges. He pitted the "commercial" against the "human" to distinguish between articulations of connection and the place of monetary exchange within them. The "commercial" exchange had a level of directness that Domínguez found alienating, not just in the sense of producing a relationship mediated by a commodity (sex) but also in the sense of separating sexual relations from other (perhaps more meaningful?) entanglements.

There is utility in layering Domínguez's distinction between the commercial and the human as a distinction between the sexual and the erotic. What he experienced as "alienating" in the commercial exchange is the emphasis on the compartmentalization of the body and the focus on genitality as the be-all end-all of exchange. The human level that they reached points to a connection based on collaboration and a broadening of the geography of their pleasures and exchanges to a level of friendship, of camaraderie.[42]

The human level involves growing intimacy between Domínguez and his partner, which is expressed in the partner's willingness to perform the anal receptive role in sex, in the request that Mauricio "not tell anyone" that his partner bottoms, and in the projection of the monetary to the sphere of "needs" that Domínguez could help with. Money and exchange did not leave the picture; they were displaced onto spheres that made Domínguez not someone who paid for a service but the partner who helped because he had the stronger finances.

Domínguez noted that *paralelismo sexual* characterized his relationship. However, he put together the shock and inability to perform sexually (el güevo se me quedó sarazo) with a shift in the relationship characterized first with his "coger el mando" and *then* (only after these two other things happened in the relationship) did we see a completely parallel relationship. Here, the fact that each partner can top stood in for the sharing of power, though Domínguez understood it also as a shift that put him in a position of leadership in the relationship.

The "humanity" that Domínguez argued characterized one relationship coexisted with the way he engaged with other men he encountered in the Dominican Republic. Before he started telling me about this informant, Domínguez noted that he had started "flipping bugarrones" frequently in his travels to the Dominican Republic. "Esa es como la especialidad de la casa, virar bugarrones" (That's like the speciality of the house, to flip bugarrones), he said. He explained his flipping technique by way of the following two anecdotes:

Yo me he acostado con un bugarrón que se me paró de la cama. "¡Págame mis cuartos, que tú eres mas tíguere que yo!" porque lo cogí y le di esta chuleá.' Cuando le mamé aquello él como que me lo quería dar y no quería y como que se volvió loco y se me paró de la cama. "¡Dame mis cuartos! ¡Dame mis cuartos! Que tú eres más tíguere que yo. Tú lo que quieres es metérmelo." . . . Hubo otro [bugarrón] en la discoteca en la capital. Cuando entró todas las locas vinieron "¡Ay Mauricio: diez pulgadas!" Y yo: "¡Como que yo ando buscando pulgadas! Tráemelo. Ven." Lo ligué. Terminó mamándomelo como un desgracia'o. No hubo metedera. Como un micrófono. O sea, eso fue fabuloso. Me dice, "Tíguere. Yo hago esto y es por usted . . . Uooop!" "Mire. . . . yo no estoy acostumbrado a esto . . . Uooop!" Y yo ahí: "Uhum. Uhum."

I went to bed with a bugarrón who jumped out of bed. "Give me my money, that you are more tíguere than me!" because I grabbed him, and he really got into fooling around with me. When I sucked that [ambiguous because "aquello" that was "mamado" could be his dick or his ass; in Spanish, one translation of rimming is "mamar culo" (suck ass)] it was like he wanted me to fuck him, then he didn't want to, then he went kind of crazy and he just jumped out of bed. "Give me my money! Give me my money! That you are more of a tíguere than me. You want to fuck me—that's what you want." . . . There was another [buggarón] in a disco in the capital. I walk in, and all of the locas come to me to say "Ay Mauricio: it's ten inches long!" And I'm like, "As if I'm looking for inches! Bring him to me! Come here!" We hook up. The guy ends up sucking my dick like a crazy person. There was no fucking. He sucked me like it was a microphone. In other words, it was fabulous. And then he's like, "Tíguere. I do this for you . . . gulp!" "Look, sir . . . I'm not used to this . . . gulp!" And I'm like, "Uhum. Uhum."

Although "cogí el mando" coexists, in Domínguez's account of his relationship above, with his sense that his position and his partner's position were "parallel," that parallelism was framed in masculinist terms. The ability of both partners to play the anal receptive role in sex was presented as evidence of the level of intimacy and camaraderie that afforded Domínguez leadership and a role as economic provider. Thus, the "mando" here extended to both sexual relationships and other aspects of the life of Domínguez's partner. Importantly, Domínguez narrated this change as the result of his partner's request.

Something related yet different from this appears to be going on when Domínguez talked about "flipping bugarrones" as "specialty of the house." First, the transactional setup assumes not only that bugarrones will always play the active (penetrative) role in sexual encounters; it also assumes that they penetrate other men to make a profit, not because they like it. In spite of this, Mauricio subverted the standard logic of the exchange by introducing foreplay and pleasure with a destabilizing force for the bugarrones. The instrumentality of the sexual was subverted by the power of the erotic.

In the first situation, growing pleasure in the exchange caused the partner to panic and demand his money. Here, receiving money restored the sense of stability (and tigueraje) that Domínguez's bugarrón felt he might lose if he let himself be penetrated. The partner also responded to Domínguez's use of erotic foreplay as a trick associated with the wily ways of Dominican tígueres. He wanted his money because he perceived Domínguez to be more of a tíguere than he was. The threat here was not only that the bugarrón may have ended up being flipped but also that the logic of the exchange would be reversed in such a way that the bugarrón would not be able to claim money because, after all, he was the one who "enjoyed" the services Domínguez provided.

The second situation points to Domínguez's ability to subvert a sexual scenario to come out "on top," as tígueres tend to do. He presented the situation as one in which people he knew, not coincidentally named "locas" here, or "not tíguere enough" to do what he could, approached Domínguez and summarized the attributes of the bugarrón in question: "ten inches." Unimpressed, Domínguez told the rest of the narrative to emphasize his own ability to get this man to flip by ultimately fellating Domínguez. As he gave Domínguez a blow job, the man appealed to the informant's discretion and assured Domínguez that this was something he did not do with just anybody—details that the narrator presented while peppering his reenactment of the scene with the sound effects of this man sucking him off.

The third example I want to draw out of Domínguez's commentary during our interview did not address his sexual history directly, but it offered insight into his experience of return and its linkage to the way he understood and grappled with his experience of being in his hometown. Toward the end of the interview, while explaining how he ended up having to be more circumspect about being gay when he visited, Mauricio talked briefly about his frustration with gay-identified people in his town who refused to go out with him because Mauricio hung out with men who were too obviously gay. His cousin, a man known as gay in the town, refused to go out with Mauricio because of the company Mauricio kept. As he explained to me, some people have told him the reason they avoided Mauricio's company. "Tú te vas, pero yo me quedo" (You leave, but I stay here), they said to him. This was true even of the man with whom he had the "human" relationship he described above. Because Domínguez and the man were well known in town, they went out only at night, in order to avoid damaging the reputation of Mauricio's friend.

The situation that interests me concerns the conditions that shaped Mauricio's ability to present himself, during the interview, as someone who often mistook his own placement in his hometown with the fantasy of "freedoms" he experienced in New York. Here is the anecdote:

Una vez yo fui a la discoteca con mi prima, una amiga de mi prima, el novio de la amiga de mi prima, y un muchachito con el que yo estaba saliendo . . . Y la discoteca estaba casi vacía. Y a mí me encanta como ese niño baila. Entonces, mi prima—que ya sabe que yo soy gay, que va conmigo aquí a la Escuelita y todo—ella vivía allá cuando eso. En una, estamos así parados . . . suena una salsa y una jodienda. Y él está bailando y yo lo iba a sacar . . . yo me vi como en la Escuelita y yo lo iba a sacar a bailar y mi prima se metió en el medio y me dijo, "¿Tú eres loco?" Y todo el mundo sabe que mi amigo es pájaro en el pueblo. Y si yo lo hubiera sacado, . . . Yo me quedé así como que yo . . . yo como que volví en mí. Y

One time, I went to the disco with a cousin of mine, a friend of my cousin's, the boyfriend of this friend, and a young guy I was going out with . . . And the disco was almost empty. And I love how that guy dances. So my cousin—who knows I am gay, who goes with me to La Escuelita here and everything—she lived back in my hometown when this happened. At some point, we are standing there . . . the DJ starts playing a salsa. And he is dancing, and I motion to pull him to dance . . . I saw myself like in La Escuelita, and I was taking him out to dance and my cousin stopped me and said, "Are you crazy?" And everyone in town knows that my friend is gay. But if I had taken him out . . . I came back to reality. And this other time,

Y otra vez, me pasó que bailando con . . . otra prima. Tú sabes que bailando muchas veces yo bailo con amigos míos y a veces quedamos que tú me llevas, que yo te llevo . . . Y en una, yo le di la vuelta, la solté, y cuando caí de nuevo, yo caí como en la posición [hace la posición para que lo lleven] y ella me dijo: "Pero yo no te puedo llevar. Eres tú el que me llevas" [se ríe] y eso ella se lo encontró como tan fuerte. Yo dije, "Ah, es que yo estoy acostumbrado a bailar con varones." Ahí mismo se lo solté así, prah . . . Como el que caga y no lo siente.

something happened when I was dancing with . . . another cousin. You know that sometimes, when I dance with male friends, one or the other leads . . . At one point, she turned, I let her go and when we came back we came back in the position [for her to take the lead] and she said: "But I can't lead you. You are the lead" [he laughs] and she thought that was such a shock. I said, "Sorry, I'm just used to dancing with boys." I said it just like that . . . as if it was nothing.

All the anecdotes recounted exchanges that took take place in the Dominican Republic while Domínguez visited. But whereas the first two anecdotes have him transcend or transgress expectations for different purposes (a more human relationship, flipping a bugarrón) the third presents the challenges Mauricio faced when confronted with how much his ability to contest/transgress the status quo had to do with not having to face the consequences of his "freedom."

Despite recognizing and expressing pain at the disjuncture between his lack of concern with what others would say about his friends in town if they were seen with Domínguez, he offered examples that highlighted his insistent misrecognition of existing norms in his hometown. Even his ultimate disregard for proper dancing positions when dancing with his female cousin is a function of his sense that this may have been his hometown, but he was a visitor and not somebody who dealt with the implications of major or minor transgressions.

Domínguez claimed that everyone knew of his friend's gayness, but that still did not give Mauricio permission to dance with another man. The first dancing incident featured a man whose dancing style Domínguez liked, a cousin who had been out with him to La Escuelita in New York, and a Domínguez who was transported to a Latino gay bar in New York by the sound of salsa. His attempt to realize the fantasy of dancing with the man was interrupted by the cousin, whose "are you crazy?" signaled that they were in a place where two men dancing was not appropriate. The second dancing incident featured Domínguez and a second female cousin. When his cousin was shocked to find him wanting her to lead, Mauricio simply stated that his choices in the dance floor stemmed from the habit of dancing with men. He punctuated his disregard for flouting rules in this way by resorting to a turn of phrase that characterized this transgression as analogous to painless excretion. "Como el que caga y no lo siente," which literally translates as "like someone who shits and does not feel it," detaches excrement from the site of its production (Domínguez's ass). But the painlessness of "taking a shit" in this way, of flouting a rule as if it were not important, produced in Domínguez a sense of empowerment that depended on someone else having to clean up the mess that came out of his ass, on others who stayed in the hometown and dealt with the consequences of Domínguez's apparently blasé attitude toward rules. In both these dancing incidents, Domínguez presented disjunctures between fantasy and reality, New York, and his hometown. There were limits to his choices of dance partners, with some consequences to him but many consequences for those who stayed. He left; they stayed.

Individual volition in all the examples in this section cannot afford the luxury of radical atomization, even if Domínguez enjoyed more options than many of those surrounding him. Because his family was an important one in his hometown, he had to negotiate the exigencies of return and his erotic priorities without posing a threat to the conditions that made his family and friends legitimate social actors in this world that they could not leave with the facility that he could.

::: "When I'm there, I feel so free, you know,
    so open and so like, sexual"

At age twenty-nine when we met for our interview, Pedro Solano was known and respected as a leader in the Latino gay community. An activist and community advocate for more than a decade, Solano was known to work hard and tenaciously on behalf of the people and causes that mattered to him. His strong views tended to polarize the people who knew him, even those who admired his accomplishments. But regardless of how strongly some people reacted to him, most people recognized the merits of his activism.

Solano arrived with his family in the United States when he was fifteen, and his preference for English with occasional code switching in the interview was consistent with my recollections of formal and informal interactions I have had with him for the ten years or so that we have known one another.

Like Mauricio Domínguez, Solano was one of the few informants who spoke candidly about his experiences of returning to the Dominican Republic and their impact on his sex life. He explained that after his arrival with the family in 1985, Solano returned to the country for the first time in 1991. As he recalled, 1991 was a momentous year in his life: "Everything that happened occurred at the same time: coming out in June, OK, gay parade, and went for a month to the DR. Then college . . . by like the second week of college, I met my lover, saw him like for three years." He also began a life as an activist in 1991. Solano recalled that it was in the Dominican Republic during that month-long return trip that he identified his attraction for masculine men: "I'm not attracted to effeminate men. I'm not. So, you know, the masculine men are the so-called bugarrones, no matter what they do [in bed]." It is clear here and in what follows that Solano did not generally see this preference for bugarrones as contradictory of his sense of identity and activism in the United States. Instead, he presented this particular preference of his as part of his own erotic map, which he began to draw out in 1991.

Apart from helping flesh out more of the meanings that relations of exchange had for him and possibly other gay Dominican returnees, the way Solano narrated these and other relationships in his life and experience shed light on the benefits and privileges that derive from mobility. The discussion of excerpts from this interview will help illustrate that for Pedro Solano, return was associated with the development of meaningful relationships involving monetary exchange. In addition, return offered him opportunities to delve into erotic relations different from the ones he considered normative in the United States.

When he recognized and began to establish relationships with bugarrones, Solano recalled feeling uncomfortable with the exchange of money for sex and the "machismo" he expected would reign supreme in these relationships. "I was, like, 'if I go with them, they are gonna fuck me,'" he recalled. He then narrated his increased understanding of the conditions that put young Dominican men in positions where engaging in these activities was the thing to do. But like Domínguez, Solano began to locate his financial contributions in places other than the sexual-economic exchange itself:

"I started thinking, 'oh well, if you buy dinner for them . . . if you give them, like, a hundred pesos to take a cab, that's not . . . ?'" Independently of whatever explanatory power his reasoning had, Solano argued that his involvement in the lives of these men included but ultimately went beyond money. In this way, his insights paralleled those of Domínguez. As he stated,

> I started developing relationships with these guys . . . I don't want to call them friends—but we started becoming close, ¿tú sabes? Y yo comencé siendo amigo de ellos [you know? I started being their friend], understanding their issues . . . getting involved in their lives, you know, with their kids, with their wives, with their parents. . . . I went from there to . . . I was like, "Hold on. If I'm helping these guys out, I want to get something out of this too." Comenzó, ¿tú me entiendes? [And then started, you know?] the exchange of sex for money.

Solano did not offer a long description of the meanings he attached to these relations, though it is clear in the details that he recounted that the place monetary exchange occupied in these attachments troubled him. For this reason, he was rather emphatic about his own exercise of power:

> They normally would charge you five hundred pesos for a night . . . Yo, vamos a suponer [I, let's suppose], if I take one of them to a hotel, I wouldn't pay them that. I would pay them less. Yo sólo le doy doscientos pesos . . . le digo "Mira, esto y esto es así, ¿tú sabes? [I only give them two hundred pesos . . . I tell him, "Look, this is how it is, you know?] I'm paying you because I understand your situation, OK? I am as good-looking as you are, OK? I am as young as you are, and probably even younger, OK? . . ." And I will break it up for them. They'll be like, "Damn . . . loco, tú sabes ¡coño! Tú no me tienes que decir todo eso . . . Yo sé que tú eres bien aparente" or whatever the word [Damn . . . man, you don't need to tell me all of that, you know? . . . I know that you are good-looking]. Y con su tigueraje, ¿tú me entiendes? [you know what I mean?] "Eso es lo que nosotros hacemos . . . y si tú estás ahí, con nosotros, tú tienes que pagar" . . . [and then they start acting out like tígueres and say, "That's what we do . . . and if you are [estás] there, with us, you have to pay" . . .] when they get cocky, like that, I get cocky back.

Solano also explained that, apart from playing the provider role in exchange for sex, the relationships have been extended and sustained by Solano's willingness to bring gifts when he visited and to send money or items to help out the men with whom he was connected. As he elaborated, this gift giving had specific expectations built into it:

> Even though it's not sex for money . . . but in a way, that's kind of what it is because . . . they know that if I go over there and I ask them . . . they have to, in a way—that's not what I mean. But they do it. Without questions asked. Because I'm there for them, ¿tú me entiendes? [you know what I mean?]

Along with the expectation that his partners will be accessible to him when he wanted to have sex with them, Solano was aware of the specific monetary and affective dynamics of these relationships:

> It's like . . . es como una relación de dinero . . . como algunas relaciones que tienen las mujeres con los hombres, ¿tú me entiendes? Que si el hombre no tiene dinero, ¿tú sabes? La mujer, aunque supuestamente te quiera, te deja [it's a relationship based on money . . . like some relationships women have with men, you know what I mean? That if the man doesn't have money, you know? Even if the woman loves you, she leaves you] because . . . that's basically what they are looking for in those types of relationships. . . . The good part is that . . . at least with men, those two people [he was referring to specific relationships with men in the DR] have made me feel very special. They made me feel wanted. They made me feel as if I was "the number one and only," even if I knew I wasn't. I knew it. I mean, I know I wasn't. They make you feel like . . . you are basically a king, you know. Wow. You know, me loving—I mean, I love doing things for people. And then to have this type of relationship, you know, even if it's money, or love, whatever! . . . Que yo te digo, tú sabes, es bien, pero bien difícil, pero [That I am telling you, you know, it's very difficult, but] it's fulfilling. It's fulfilling.

It is possible that, in practice, Solano's feelings about these relationships were a little more ambivalent than he let on in this part of our interview. What interests me here is the importance of narrating sexual exchange not as trade of money for sexual access but as an act of generosity on the part of the consumer whose satisfaction comes from "providing" for someone else. In this example, we get a glimpse of the investment Solano made (together with Domínguez and others, including me) in occupying a "masculine" position in these circuits of desire. This particular position did not result from the sexual role performed or from bodily self-presentation. Rather, it resulted from one's relationship and access to capital. Solano's fulfillment came partly from being able to set the terms for his exchanges with the two men in question, a power linked to the provider role he came to play in these men's lives. Strictly speaking, then, sending money nurtured entanglements that went beyond mere instrumentality.

A second set of issues that surfaced during the interview with Solano resolved around his desire to have sex with women and the relationship of that desire to his movement between New York and the Dominican Republic. Early on, he explained to me that he had sex with women in the past. He continued to have sex with women at the time when we met, but only when he visited the Dominican Republic. I was not so much surprised by Solano's report that he has sex with women as by the association he made between sex and women in the Dominican Republic. I asked him to explain:

Why does it happen precisely then? [when he traveled back to the Dominican Republic]

Maybe because here, I'm so busy doing so many different things . . . I could see a girl in the street and be like, "Now, she's pretty. She's beautiful," and be sexually attracted to her. But I don't have the time . . . nor the drive . . . it's not something that I'm like, you know, looking for: "Oh my God! Look at her! I have to get her because I need to fuck her." You know me, I mean, it's not like that . . . [Both of us laugh] . . . When I am getting ready to go to the DR, the sexual drives start opening up . . .

He then talked about the way his friends in New York reacted to his joking reference to having sex with women in the Dominican Republic. "Tú siempre dices la misma mierda" (You are always talking the same shit), they responded. He continued to quote his imaginary friend:

"¿Cuándo tú vas a parar de hacer eso? [When are you going to stop doing that?] I mean, when are you finally gonna say that you are gay?" I say, "I am gay, you know. Just because I have sex with women sometimes don't mean anything . . . if you want to call me bisexual, fine, call me bisexual . . . you can call me anything you want. OK. I prefer men. But I still like women . . . and I am telling you . . . the sexual drives are opening up again . . . I don't know why it is. But when I'm there, I feel so free, you know, so open and so like, sexual."

I responded that his association of "freedom" with visiting the Dominican Republic and having sex with women reverses the perception of many who associate freedom with immigration to the United States, particularly among self-identified gay men:

> *Why is it, in your view . . . freedom about sexual things and the freedom of doing sexual things with women?*

> I'm going to DR. I know that I'm going to have all the time in the world to do anything I want, basically, with anybody.

> *Why not have the freedom to do what you want here? What's different about going to the DR—*

> —Let me tell you—

> *—than being here?*

> —Well . . . I have a reputation to look after [here].

People in Solano's professional circles did not know about his sexual escapades in the Dominican Republic. In addition, he noted that his acquaintances in the Dominican Republic were not connected to his profession, which made it possible for him to engage with women sexually without having those surrounding him assume anything about how he identified in the United States.

The excerpts drawn from the interview with Solano present a discussion that differs from the one I undertook with Domínguez in that Solano disentangled sexual role performance from his perceptions of what made a man a bugarrón. For him, it was the exchange of money for sex, irrespective of what these men did sexually. Yet it is clear from his own discussion that his was an evolved definition: when he first visited and began engaging these men, his view of the situation and his assumptions ("I was, like, 'if I go with them, they are gonna fuck me'") paralleled those of Domínguez. It was in the process of getting involved with some of these men that his conceptualization of the relationships changed, and this may have something to do with his definition of bugarrón.

The excerpts also suggest that, like Domínguez, Solano viewed money as part of what he had to offer men who interested him. Commerce, haggling, and power play were some of the dynamics he worked out in these relationships, as he recounted. His citation of a verbal exchange he had with one of the men in his life illustrated to me the way he handled these situations. Setting the terms of the exchange by "breaking it up for them," Solano rendered explicit that money may have been one of the glues of these relationships but that it entered the picture not because of Solano's desire to have sex with a younger person, but for his desire for a particular man and his ability to provide for that man's needs. The issue here is not so much the truth value of what he said to me or to that remembered man but rather the fact that Solano, when he "breaks it up for them," laid bare the scaffolding of power and inequality to respond to the masculinity, tigueraje, and "cockiness" of these men. He said it best: "When they get cocky, like that, I get cocky back."

As they recounted interactions with Dominican men when visiting, Domínguez and Solano narrated the way they negotiated the terms of engagement to uphold their male privilege. Like the clients of bugarrones that Padilla writes about, these two men engaged in receptive anal intercourse when they traveled, but they also appreciated the power of the resources they had and the power of their ability to provide for their partners. Unlike Padilla's informants, Domínguez and Solano used their status as providers to renegotiate the terms of sexual interaction,[43] which suggests that what is at stake for some Dominican tourists in sexual exchanges with bugarrones is not just the consumption of an other through receptive anal penetration but rather homoracial transnational erotics. Their use of the provider role to assert male privilege was partly about exerting influence in the lives of the men with whom they partnered beyond commercial sexual exchanges (which might have limited both Domínguez and Solano to the performance of anal receptive roles). They sought to mean more to their partners, which was expressed in their narratives in the projection of money to spheres of "need," in their becoming involved and supportive of these men, and in expectations of sex beyond commercial genitality. Power and money are important, but they cannot be severed from the sense of connection, solidarity, hierarchy, and support that they make possible. Solano was aware of the importance of the resources he provided and of their value, but he also put a lot of weight on how "difícil, pero fulfilling" those relationships were.

Pedro Solano explained that a lot happened to him in one year: he came out, returned to the Dominican Republic for the first time, began his life as an activist, and met his first lover. Right around that time, he also discovered his preference for bugarrones. I mentioned earlier that his disarticulation of bugarrón from sexual role performance is significant because it stressed the function of monetary exchange. But he also defined "so-called bugarrones" as "the masculine men" who interested him. He may have been referring to men *in general,* but my hunch is that he was referring to the men *in the Dominican Republic* who interested him.

Money likely played an explicit role in Solano's United States–based relationships, and this may be something his colleagues and friends gave him a hard time about. Nevertheless, his ongoing interest in sex with women surfaced more clearly in his discussion of sex and travel to the Dominican Republic (and in the opinions that it sparked among his associates and friends). Solano's friends' attempts to discipline his erotic life were also striking. Asking someone to finally "define himself as gay" is a commonplace critique of bisexual behaviors in gay communities. Nevertheless, Solano's answer to his friends ("if you want to call me bisexual, fine, call me bisexual . . . you can call me anything you want") points to a discrepancy between what they called him and what he thought of himself. In his commentary to his friends in New York about sex with women when he returns to the Dominican Republic ("the sexual drives start opening up"), Solano expresses an inversion of the colonialist travel sexual scenario, what Rudi Bleys so resonantly called "the geography of perversion."[44] Instead of "going south" as Jack Twist, the cowboy character in *Brokeback Mountain,* does by going to Mexico, "enter[ing] an alley full of Mexican men in the shadows"—a scene that Martin Manalansan astutely reads as counterposed to the pastoral beauty of Wyoming and to the "gay love" of the white cowboys—Solano went to the Dominican Republic to take a break from a life regulated by the gayness he defended so vehemently in New York.[45]

This is a significant reversal, for it presents gayness as lived by one of its strongest advocates in the Latino gay community as part of a highly regulated modern life. In this life, Solano had "no time" or "drive" to pursue sexual relations with women, a life that may be to some extent lived in expectation of the moments of escape to the Dominican Republic, where leisure and ample time allowed Solano to let his "drives" guide him without being accountable to anyone for what it may (or may not) mean. The conjuncture of colonialist travel fantasy with return to the Dominican Republic produces a cosmopolitan gay activist whose access to the privileges of travel, mobility, and leisure included his ability to project his eros somewhere beyond the reaches of gayness, some place where the bodies of men and women like him allowed him access to a piece of heaven. Ample time, open drives, and no reputation to nurse: to Solano, this was freedom.

> At twenty-three—would you believe this has never happened to me before?
> I want to tell him a lot of things. I want to say: I've held that job before . . . I
> want to tell him: This job will take you nowhere. But why kid ourselves when
> we're living proof of a bigger truth. This job will take you everywhere. . . . At
> twenty-three—would you believe I've never been with anyone like him be-
> fore. . . . What I mean by that, like him? Like *me* . . . At twenty-three—would
> you believe I'm paying him. . . . For what? To hold my hand. To escort me
> around to our favorite bars and discos. . . . To tell me he loves me. To conspire
> on a clean mattress.[46]

This is the way the narrator of Lawrence Chua's novel *Gold by the Inch*, a New Yorker who returns to Bangkok and then initiates a relationship with a local man in exchange for money paid by one of his traveling friends, attempts to make sense of this erotic entanglement. He starts by enlisting the reader in his own sense of bafflement; after all, how could a twenty-three-year-old pay to be escorted or to be told he is loved by another man? Shouldn't his beauty and youth be enough? But yet there is Chua's narrator, having a friend of his paying for attentions he was once himself providing others, before he departed, before he became the someone who comes back to the place of his birth, to bask in the joys of being at the consumer end of that circuit of desire. The body and attention being paid for are those of a proximal (not a distal) other—like the narrator's object of desire, like the narrator himself.

Through the close analysis of autoethnography and excerpts from the interviews undertaken with two of the men with whom I spoke, this chapter has developed a map of circuits of desire in which men of color (and Dominican returnees in particular) are producers, workers, and consumers. I have shown that taking white (gay) men out of the picture—as antagonists, exploiters, and objects of critique—does not undo a scaffolding of inequality and power that is erotically productive and that points to present negotiations of the legacies of colonial expansion. In the case of the informants and of Dominican transnational cultures more generally, the importance of U.S. influence to the very structure of these fields of circulation cannot be underestimated.

Figure 1. BUGGARON shirt advertisement. Image manipulation by Rider Ureña.

EPILOGUE

T-shirts coat the torso, membranes made up of combinations of cotton or other textiles to shield while adapting to one's figure, hinting at the possible rewards of the flesh they cover. Their outer surfaces are as often empty as they are graced with a graphic, text, or combination of the two in order to make a point, crack a joke, or signal the wearer's thoughts, preferences, or politics.

Still, the shirt with the word BUGGARON that is the face of this epilogue does not operate as a regular T-shirt, even though it was advertised in one of the sites catering to the needs of gay men of color traveling to the Dominican Republic. I was baffled to encounter it as I surfed on this site: baffled at the easy way in which this word was rendered equivalent to others in the shirts advertised (e.g., FAMOSO, MORENO), as if the significations of this first word made this shirt as wearable as the others. BUGGARON pride?

Who would wear this shirt, I wondered? The young Dominican sex workers? Their clients? Where would one wear such a garment? In the Dominican Republic? In New York? I could not imagine any of the men with whom I spoke wearing this shirt. But maybe I am missing something here.

I hope someone will explain what.

Something else captured my attention: BUGGARON is an Anglicism of the Spanish word *bugarrón*. I began to hear the sound modulations, the disappearing rolling of the *r*, and the doubling of the *g*. For a word that traveled from the French *bougre*, through the English *bugger* (bugger on?!), to the Spanish *bugarrón*, going back to the Anglicized pronunciation may be the completion of a cycle, one that returns the word to travel and to U.S. empire, even if the person who now pronounces it, who buys and maybe even wears the shirt, looks like the men this word is supposed to name. What a whirl of worlds in these words, all held together through this sliding through inflections, through commodities that can be bought but not worn, through connections that cannot be fully articulated. There is historicity in this motion and this straddling; capturing some of that has been at the heart of this study. In this way, *Tacit Subjects* has followed up on a crucial point made by constructivist perspectives on identity: if all identities are socially and historically constructed, then our transit through them stages encounters of disparate histories, investments, and political exigencies. This book developed concepts to think through that movement. Its conceptual apparatus shifts, attempting to grasp the nuance of the ways its protagonists understood and wrestled with their conditions, never settling on a consistent or unified view of who or what they were, and always seeking a measure of self-determination despite facing many obstacles.

I ordered a shirt.

Waiting for the shirt.

NOTES

::: Notes to Introduction

1 Contín Aybar, *Biel, el Marino*, 99. The translation here is mine, as are all other translations throughout the book unless otherwise indicated. All capital letters in original.

2 Mateo, "La poesía homosexual dominicana," 21.

3 Ibid.

4 The poet Víctor Villegas, who considers Contín Aybar a mentor figure for himself and for other writers of the "Generación del 48," exalts *Biel* as Contín Aybar's "más consumada criatura" (his most polished creature) (15). As a member of a generation of young poets who emerged under the tutelage of this mentor, "father," and co-director of the official journal *Cuadernos Dominicanos de Cultura* barely a decade after the inauguration of the Trujillo regime, Villegas recalls the contradictory role that Contín Aybar's presence played in opening up spaces for critical views of the regime voiced in and through artistic expression. As Villegas recounts, this contribution did not pass unnoticed by Juan Bosch and Pedro Mir, giants of Dominican letters exiled in Cuba at the time the *Cuadernos* were being published. Furthermore, Villegas argues that contradictions and paradoxes are fundamental to understanding the complicated world Contín Aybar navigated successfully. However, his success in dealing with these contradictions and paradoxes always involved controversy and polemic. As Villegas writes, the great "paradox" of the life of his mentor was not "la del atormentado Hamlet que carecía [de] la libertad de escoger" (that of the tormented Hamlet who did not have the liberty to choose) but "la del héroe, la del poeta y el artista que desatan [*sic*] sus alas para aplacar la ira o despertar gozosos los pájaros del sueño" (that of the hero, the poet and the artist who unfolds his wings to appease the anger or to awake the joyous birds of dreams) (8). In the end, Villegas suggests that as the "consummate poet," "Pedro René vivió en poesía, murió en poesía. Y dentro de ésta, un extenso arco de contradicción, pero para edificar, para crear" (Pedro René lived in poetry,

died in poetry. And inside poetry, he was an extended canvas of contradictions to edify, to create). See Villegas, "Semblanza de Pedro René Contín Aybar," 15.

5 This phrase is from George Ayala, who uses it to point to the problematic nature of the category "MSM" (men who have sex with men), as if all that were involved in those exchanges were sexual and narrowly genital choreographies. See Ayala, "Retiring Behavioral Risk."

6 The lifelong struggles of Gloria Anzaldúa and Cherríe Moraga, among others, with critical feminist political scholarship and art exemplify, in broadest terms, the genealogy that informs the work of this study: a critique that is vigilant of the seductions of identity, that insistently questions the boundaries and hierarchies created and the proximities established in everyday exchanges, and a critique that values Paula Moya's suggestion that "who we understand ourselves to be will have consequences for how we experience and understand the world." See Moya, "Reclaiming Identity," 8. See Moraga and Anzaldúa, *This Bridge Called My Back*. See also Anzaldúa, *Borderlands*, and Anzaldúa, *Making Face, Making Soul/Haciendo Caras*.

   The work in this study is also in dialogue with a tradition of critical and creative political work by black gay male thinkers and writers. The films of Marlon Riggs (*Tongues Untied* [1988] and *Black Is . . . Black Ain't* [1994]) and Isaac Julien (*Looking for Langston* [1989]); poetry of Essex Hemphill and Haitian-born Assoto Saint; pioneering editorial work of Joseph Beam; fiction writings of Melvin Dixon; and scholarship of Robert Reid-Pharr and my mentor, Phillip Brian Harper, have all stressed the contradictions, challenges, and possibilities for critique, contestation, and revision of any given sense of community or identity. I found my voice through engaging these writers and artists. See Beam, *In the Life*; Hemphill, *Brother to Brother*; Harper, *Private Affairs*; and Reid-Pharr, *Black Gay Man*.

7 Cruz-Malavé, *Queer Latino Testimonio*, xi.

8 I am borrowing this phrase from the title of the book, *The Puerto Rican Nation on the Move*, by Jorge Duany.

9 A classic statement on intersectionality is Combahee River Collective, "A Black Feminist Statement." Influential first statements and models of intersectional analysis can also be found in the work of Kimberlé Crenshaw; see "Demarginalizing the Intersection of Race and Sex" and "Mapping the Margins." Recent overviews of intersectionality can be found in Hawkesworth, *Feminist Inquiry*, and McCall, "The Complexity of Intersectionality."

10 Tony De Moya, personal communication, September 25, 2007.

11 "Unsovereign state": Atkins and Wilson, *The Dominican Republic and the United States*, 5.

12 Shakespeare's *The Tempest* has been a source of inspiration to Latin American

and Caribbean intellectuals, and the figures of Caliban and Ariel have been taken up to stage specific critiques of imperialism and capitalism (particularly from the United States) and to articulate specific visions of continental resistance and decolonization. For some examples, see Rodó, *Ariel*; Fernández Retamar, *Calibán*; Césaire, *Une Tempête*.

13 Moya, "Introduction: Reclaiming Identity," 8.

14 Quiroga, *Tropics of Desire*, 197. Italics in original.

15 "American" meaning from the American continent. My engagement with Kusch is limited. There are several monographs, essays, and edited volumes on Kusch. See Picotti, *Pensar desde América*; Picotti, "Resonancia y proyección del pensamiento de Rodolfo Kusch: A propósito de una obra reciente de Carlos M. Pagano," and "Voces interculturales en el pensamiento latinoamericano." See also Pagano Fernández, *Un modelo de filosofía intercultural: Rodolfo Kusch (1922–1979)*; Bordas de Rojas Paz, *Filosofía a la intemperie, Kusch*; Rubinelli, *Reflexiones actuales sobre el pensamiento de Rodolfo Kusch*; Azcuy, *Kusch y el pensar desde América*.

16 In a crucial turn away from the Hegelian *Aufhebung*, Kusch explains that his "American" dialectic does not assume transcendence or elevation in the European sense: "No cabe hablar de una *elevación,* sino más bien—en tanto se trata de un planteo nuevo para el occidental—de una distensión o, mejor, *fagocitación* del *ser* por el *estar*, ante todo como un *ser* alguien, fagocitado por un *estar* aquí" (It does not make sense to talk of an *elevation* but instead—if it is considered a new way of thinking in the West—of a loosening or, better, *phagocytosis* of *being* [ser] by *being* [estar], before all as the "to be someone" is phagocyted [loosened, distended] by a "being here"). See Kusch, "América profunda," 195. Italics in original.

17 Kusch, "América profunda," 5–6. The entire citation is italicized in original.

18 This discussion had wide-ranging repercussions in North American and European anthropology. Perhaps the most representative text of this moment in anthropology is Clifford and Marcus, *Writing Culture*.

19 Mignolo, *Local Histories/Global Designs*, 151.

20 Ibid., 151, 153.

21 The scholarship on queer migration has been growing steadily over the last few years. Martin Manalansan is a pioneer in this area; see *Global Divas*. Manalansan has also published numerous essays on the topic and a recent overview of the literature. See "Queer Intersections." Another important scholar of queer immigration is Eithne Luibhéid. See *Entry Denied*. Luibhéid has also edited two essay collections on the topic: *Queer Migrations* and *Queer/Migration* (GLQ). Lionel Cantú's work was also pioneering; see *The Sexuality of Migration*. My work is in conversation with that of Susana Peña. See her "'Obvious Gays'

and the State Gaze" and "Visibility and Silence." See also La Fountain-Stokes, *Queer Ricans.* Two important collections of essays on immigration and sexuality are Patton and Sánchez-Eppler, *Queer Diasporas*; and Epps, Valens, and Johnson Gonzalez, *Passing Lines.*

22 Ramona Hernández's interpretation of Dominican migration focuses on the larger state and geopolitical goals it sought to accomplish. See *The Mobility of Workers under Advanced Capitalism.*

23 There is a large body of literature on Dominican migration to the United States. A useful introduction to the literature is Aponte, *Dominican Migration to the United States.* The first book-length treatment of Dominican migration to the United States is Hendricks, *The Dominican Diaspora.* Other works include Georges, *The Making of a Transnational Community*, and the classic Grasmuck and Pessar, *Between Two Islands.* Recent contributions include Levitt, *The Transnational Villagers.*

   Recent works break away from early U.S.-based scholarship that looked at Dominicans only as quintessential transnationals. See Candelario, *Black behind the Ears*; Weyland, *Negociando la aldea global con un pie "aquí" y otro "allá"*; and Hoffnung-Garskof, *A Tale of Two Cities.* The work of Néstor E. Rodríguez has also strongly informed my own. See *Escrituras de desencuentro en La República Dominicana.*

24 This is the title of one of Torres-Saillant's critiques of transnationalism. See "Nothing to Celebrate." In another trenchant critique of transnationalist scholarship, Torres-Saillant suggests that the view of Dominicans as "quintessential transnationals . . . falsifies the immigrant experience of this group in that it unfairly uses the few [who can afford to migrate back and forth] to represent the many, which bespeaks considerable indifference toward the actual condition of the majority of these migrants" (29). As a critical response to the body of transnationalist scholarship that has developed around Dominican migration, Torres-Saillant suggests that analysts begin by "contain[ing] the compulsion to celebrate" Dominican mobility (35). See "Diasporic Disquisitions."

25 Noteworthy in this regard is the work of the activist and scholar Jacqueline Jiménez Polanco, particularly her groundbreaking edited collection of Dominican and Dominican American lesbian writings, *Divagaciones bajo la luna/Musings under the Moon.* Other indefatigable radical feminist and queer Dominican thinkers living and working outside the country include Yuderkys Espinosa and Ochy Curiel. See Espinosa Miñoso, *Escritos de una lesbiana oscura*, and Curiel, "Identidades esencialistas o construcción de identidades políticas."

26 My work takes as inspiration the challenges to nationalism posed by the migratory experience and convergence of various Latino/a groups in the United States, which Latino studies scholars have only begun to explore. Examples of

this emerging trend include Ramos-Zayas, *National Performances*; De Genova, *Working the Boundaries*; and De Genova and Ramos-Zayas, *Latino Crossings*.

27 Jasbir Puar's and Jacqui Alexander's work on transnational sexualities have been strong influences for the analysis undertaken throughout this text. See Puar, "A Transnational Feminist Critique of Queer Tourism," "Transnational Sexualities," "Circuits of Queer Mobility," "Global Circuits," "Queer Tourism," "Sexuality and Space," "Transnational Configurations of Desire." See also Alexander, *Pedagogies of Crossing*. Two recent contributions to transnational feminist scholarship are Grewal, *Transnational America*, and Mohanty, *Feminism without Borders*.

28 In my view, the most productive and inspiring works in this scholarship mobilize queer studies strategically to get at broader social dynamics. Two remarkable examples are Ara Wilson, *The Intimate Economies of Bangkok*, and Yolanda Martínez-San Miguel, *Caribe Two Ways*.

29 For a history of the development of New York as a "gay" city in the early part of the twentieth century, see Chauncey, *Gay New York*. For a discussion of AIDS-related organizing in the gay communities of New York, see Kayal, *Bearing Witness*. Two important narratives and critiques of gay life in New York are Delany, *The Motion of Light in Water*, and *Times Square Red, Times Square Blue*.

30 One of the many remarkable *crónicas* of the urbanization of Santo Domingo in the late nineteenth and early twentieth centuries, Rafael Damirón's *De soslayo* contains one of the earliest references to the Dominican *tíguere*.

31 One early commentator for this manuscript asked why I did not conduct repeat interviews with the informants. Although I was tempted to engage in this practice and others such as participant action research, I decided to concentrate on the challenges and limitations of interviews that took place only once, in order to emphasize the conjunctions of temporality, physical environment, and interactional dynamics that produce the condensed historicity of the present (or, as Kusch might put it, *el estar*).

32 See Hernández and Rivera-Batiz, *Dominicans in the United States*.

33 Ibid.

34 Kusch, "América profunda," 3.

::: Notes to Chapter 1

An earlier version of this chapter was published in the *Gay and Lesbian Quarterly*.

1 Danny, a Filipino gay male informant cited in Manalansan, *Global Divas*, 28.

2 Alicia B., a Puertorriqueña informant cited in Chavez Leyva, "Listening to the Silences in Latina/Chicana Lesbian History," 434.

3 Patricio, a Puerto Rican informant in Guzmán, *Gay Hegemony/Latino Homo-sexualities*, 88.

4 Latino gay male informant in Guarnero, "Family and Community Influences on the Social and Sexual Lives of Latino Gay Men," 16.

5 D. C., an African American informant in Johnson, *Sweet Tea*, 124.

6 Marcos, a Mexican male informant in Cantú, *The Sexuality of Migration*, 91.

7 Apart from the comments cited at the beginning of this chapter, the following scholars also address this question in their work: Hawkeswood, *One of the Children*; King, "Remixing the Closet"; and Carrillo, *The Night Is Young*. The work of Diana Fisher illustrates how playing with being in and out of the closet is relevant to other immigrant groups and to lesbian-identified populations. See "Immigrant Closets." Katie Acosta's dissertation offers examples of lesbian-identified Latina immigrants who negotiate their sexual identities and live in ways that somewhat parallel what I document in this chapter. Nevertheless, Acosta's research illustrates the added pressures experienced by Latinas because of their socialization as women and their generally close connections to and regulation by their families. Acosta, "'Amigas' and Lovers."

8 This is an all too common view of Latinos and other gay men of color in the United States. It is also common for members of these communities themselves to espouse these views. In some contexts, coming out is associated with "departing" the heterosexual world one has been reared in and with becoming integrated into gay communities. Thus, it is not surprising that migration is a strong part of gay histories and collective imaginings, especially for Latin Americans and Latinos in the United States. "For gays and lesbians from Latin America," one article reads, "coming out often means joining the sexual migration to the U.S. . . . The combined pressures of machismo, religion, family, and Latin society for gays and lesbians living south of the border and the allure of a more open life in the big gay cities of the United States—known as El Norte—draw many into a migration that is partly for material reasons, partly for personal ones, not unlike the migration of gays from small U.S. towns" (Kirby, "Coming to America to Be Gay"). As this excerpt suggests, migration as coming out is equivalent to a departure from locations associated with restrictive cultural norms and institutions: from south of the border and from the rural United States to urban "gay ghettos." Mapping gay and lesbian collective histories as "coming out writ large" has recently been criticized persuasively by the historian John Howard, among others. See *Men Like That*. E. Patrick Johnson, in *Sweet Tea*, presents oral histories of gay-identified African American men who grew up and continue to live in the U.S. South to challenge the view of the South as inherently restrictive of these men's lives. What is most relevant in the discussion of informants' internalized homophobia, as the chap-

ters that follow will illustrate, is that many of these men see an avoidance of mainstream models of coming out as one of the drawbacks that keeps Dominicans in general (and many self-identified Dominican gay men specifically) away from being truly modern Dominican gay men.

Although in the dominant narrative coming out to oneself, in the sense of owning a gay identity, implies movement *away* from home, coming out to others demands a *return* to the settings and relationships where this identity has to be revealed. And a refusal to "have the conversation" where one's homosexuality is not explicitly articulated is akin to denial. For example, Steven Seidman argues that the closet in black communities dehumanizes: "Given their more ambivalent relationship to the gay community, blacks may be more likely than their white counterparts to manage their homosexuality within the framework of the closet" (Seidman, *Beyond the Closet*, 42–43). According to Seidman, the problem is that blacks' racial identity weighs more heavily than their sexual minority identity: "In short, blacks—straight or gay—are heavily invested in their racial identity and in their membership in the black community in a way that is generally not true of whites" (43). Seidman's thinking about sexuality in relation to race and ethnicity also illustrates that coming out, for people of color, tends to be understood as a choice between sexual and racial identities, with relatively little space for both.

9 The historical trajectories of coming out—from launching point to revolutionary gay liberation to the shift toward "mainstreaming" in the 1980s and 1990s and the normalization of the contemporary moment—have been discussed in texts including McRuer, *The Queer Renaissance*; Vaid, *Virtual Equality*; and Crimp, *Melancholia and Moralism*.

10 Critiques of coming out include Butler, "Imitation and Gender Insubordination"; Samuels, "My Body, My Closet"; and Sifuentes-Jáuregui, *Transvestism, Masculinity, and Latin American Literature*. Recent critics of coming out have pointed out that its normative guise fits white gay male urban middle-class people but does not fit people in other positionalities. For two examples of insightful recent critiques, see Ross, "Beyond the Closet as Raceless Paradigm," and Perez, "You Can Have My Brown Body and Eat It, Too!"

11 While acknowledging the range of attitudes expressed by his informants about coming out, Hawkeswood found that "for many gay men in Harlem, coming out was not a major concern, because their homosexuality, and later their gay identity, had always been *assumed* by family and friends. There was no need to 'come out'" (*One of the Children*, 138; my italics). Martin Manalansan argues something similar for Filipinos: "Many informants . . . felt that they didn't have to come out because they thought that their families knew without being told" (*Global Divas*, 28).

12 I am aware of the potential problems that may derive from borrowing a grammatical concept for an antisexist and antihomophobic enterprise. This might be especially true in the case of Spanish grammar because the language is so gendered. However, one of the remarkable and useful characteristics of the "sujeto tácito" is that although one is able to ascertain the number and person of the subject, gender is not implicit in the verbal formulation. In other words, if I say "vamos a la escuela" (we go to school), it is not clear whether the "we" in this case is "nosotros" (masculine) or "nosotras" (feminine). I thank Carolyn Dinshaw for asking me to clarify this point.

13 I am using the word *tacit* in the sense of something "not openly expressed or stated, but implied; understood, inferred" (*Oxford English Dictionary Online*, http://www.oed.com). As the chapter will show, a tacit subject is a form of apprehending a social reality, person, or topic that materializes as implicit knowledge, speculation, or intuition.

14 This point is worth underscoring. I am interested in a middle space between polar opposites common in LGBTQ scholarship and activist thinking: between secrecy and outness/pride or, to put it in the discourse of public health, between secrecy and disclosure. In addition, I also seek to retain the elasticity of the concept: *tacit subjects* may be about sexuality or sexual identity, but it is not reducible to an ontological subject or to sexuality. In other words, the definitive "truth" of someone's identity might be part of what's tacit, but *tacit subjects* points to entanglements and complicities that cannot be fully known or told.

15 Polanyi, "Tacit Knowing," 601.

16 See Polanyi, *Personal Knowledge*, and *The Tacit Dimension*.

17 This is a slight paraphrase and alteration of Polanyi's phrase, "*we can know more than we can tell.*" *The Tacit Dimension*, 4. Italics in original.

18 Goffman, *The Presentation of Self in Everyday Life*, 2. Italics in original.

19 The argument advanced throughout this chapter *is not* a proposal for a "post-gay" or "post-closet" model of identity formation. Apart from the irresponsible neglect of ways of knowing and organizing one's identity that have been fundamental to the lives of the informants, such an argument would erase the larger historical context in which the informants lived their lives.

20 For a very useful discussion of the meanings of *sujeto* in Spanish and in the larger context of European philosophy, see Mariñas, "*Sujeto, subdito, sugeto.*"

21 *Diccionario de la lengua española*, s.v. "Sujetar," Real Academia Española (http://www.rae.es).

22 Gal, "A Semiotics of the Public/Private Distinction," 80.

23 Taussig, *Defacement*, 6–7.

24 See Acosta, "'Amigas' and Lovers."

25 Member of the Partido Reformista Social Cristiano, a right-wing party led by

Joaquín Balaguer. A lifetime bachelor who exercised power over the country's politics until his recent death, Balaguer was the most powerful influence on the twentieth-century history and politics of the Dominican Republic. Noguera suggested that it was because of the affiliation with Balaguer's party that the "loca" ran the bar.

26 Cambumbo was a television personality whose career began in Radio Televisión Dominicana and whose fame rested on his very public homosexuality and his ownership of a cabaret frequented by working-class patrons and people involved in Dominican military, arts, and culture. Cambumbo's space was considered a space of debauchery and transgression, even though effeminate homosexuals—other than Cambumbo and his staff—only began to be tolerated in the last years of the cabaret. Even then, in its last years of existence, the space was more open to drag queens and their "bugarrones" than to homosexual men. Thanks to Richard Camarena for giving me background information on Cambumbo.

27 I am thinking specifically of the work of Sifuentes-Jáuregui and Quiroga.

28 King, "Remixing the Closet," 68.

29 "To let out a feather or two" means to act in ways that are, in general, construed as effeminate.

::: Notes to Chapter 2

1 In this sense, migration stories have in common with other forms of storytelling (such as conversion and coming-out stories) the construction of a coherent self, presenting individual constraints, opportunities, and decisions as artifacts of a personal history fundamental to the making of that person's identity. The main goal of this chapter is to illustrate (through engaging selected aspects of specific informants' narration of their migration and settlement) their continuing linkages and investments in kin and non-kin relations, socializations, and forms of discipline before and after migration. However, this interpretation is informed by scholarship that calls attention to interviews as "dynamic social interactions" (Collins). See Collins, "Negotiating Selves." See also Taylor, "Identity Trouble and Opportunity in Women's Narratives of Residence"; "Narrative as Construction and Discursive Resource"; "A Place for the Future?"; "Self-Narration as Rehearsal"; Taylor and Napier, "An American Woman in Turkey"; Taylor and Spicer, "Time for Space"; and Taylor and Wetherell, "A Suitable Time and Place."

2 Here, I am specifically referencing pioneering work in lesbian and gay scholarship that maps individual and collective geographical displacements in relation to rural/urban movements. For two influential examples, see D'Emilio, "Capitalism and Gay Identity," and Rubin, "Thinking Sex."

3 This suggests that as a genre of empirical investigation where intersubjective

exchanges (or "inter" "views") result in data, the research interview offers glimpses of the work of subject construction through the reliance on historically, nationally, and geographically specific markers. Here, I borrow from Steinar Kvale's idea of the interview as "construction site of knowledge" forged through the exchanges produced by the flow of questions, answers, probes, and elaborations. See Kvale, *Interviews*.

4 Barthes, *Camera Lucida*, 3.

5 Spivak, "Can the Subaltern Speak?"

6 Sommer, *Proceed with Caution*, xi.

7 The occupation of a chofer is sometimes equivalent to that of a taxi driver in the United States. However, the majority of choferes are car owners or renters whose daily occupation is to transport as many passengers as their cars will fit along specific routes in town for a fixed price.

8 See Cantú, *The Sexuality of Migration*.

9 I am borrowing the metaphor of masculinity as "straightjacket" from the work of E. Antonio de Moya, but I will have much more to say about this way of understanding masculinity and about de Moya's work in the chapters that follow.

10 Establishing and sustaining relationships with foreign nationals surfaced in several of the interviews, but usually the foreign partners mentioned were of other Latin American nationalities, U.S. American or European. What makes Guerrero's relationship with a Filipino stand out from the rest of the relationships mentioned by the men I interviewed is not so much that the man was Asian but that they met in the Dominican Republic and that this man contributed to Guerrero's arrangements to leave the country.

11 The tendency to view HIV-positive immigrants as corrupting U.S. body politic can be discerned most explicitly in the resistance of U.S. immigration authorities to allow self-reported HIV-positive people into the country and to conduct HIV screening as part of the procedures for obtaining a permanent-resident status. Like marking "yes" in the question of whether one has ever been a member of the Communist Party or belongs to a terrorist organization, testing HIV-positive constitutes grounds for denial of the green card. Furthermore, the view of immigrant bodies as corrupting the body politics was particularly evident in the reaction to Haitians as the fourth *H* in the "high-risk" group designations provided by the Centers for Disease Control in the early 1980s. For a useful history of this connection in the United States, see Kraut, *Silent Travelers*.

12 I have borrowed the expression "uneven world" from Radhakrishnan, *Diasporic Mediations*.

13 An earlier version of the account of "Latoya" Mejía was published in Decena, "Surviving AIDS in an Uneven World."

14 I am grateful to Arnaldo Cruz-Malavé for the phrasing here.

15 This is not to undermine the importance of current research efforts on medication adherence in public health, for instance. My concern here is with the way that the focus of resources and the research it produces tend to obscure the effects of seroconversion on the rest of an HIV-positive person's life and, particularly, their networks, as will be shown below.

16 Although he is hardly the only person voicing this critique, Paul Farmer's single-authored and coauthored work might be characterized as consistently critical of the behavior-centered and individualistic impulse in public health. See Farmer, *AIDS and Accusation*, and *Infections and Inequalities*; Farmer, Connors, and Simmons, *Women, Poverty, and AIDS*.

17 It would be terribly naive and even disingenuous to absolve the project at hand of its complicity with certain forms of regulation. After all, this kind of complicity is a performative contradiction of most research despite any intentions an author may have to walk away from regulatory forms of knowledge production. Nevertheless, one distinction that might be tentatively useful here is between (1) "portrait" as necessarily partial result of conjunctions of space, time, and contact that produce a circuitry that results in the words you read, and which I claim come from the mouths of the informants, and (2) a "profile" as a calculated specification of behavioral patterns one might detect in a given population. While the portraits I offer here would theoretically resist generalization in the traditional social scientific way, profiles appear as generalizable attributes that can be detected within specific populations. For more on "sexual profiles," see Decena, "Profiles, Compulsory Disclosure, and Ethical Sexual Citizenship in the Contemporary United States."

18 In the case of Mejía, his gender nonconformity also troubled his friends, as I discuss in chapter 5.

19 What is perhaps the saddest commentary on the transformations in Dominican gay male sociality after one's friends learn of an HIV-positive diagnosis is that the few PWAS I interviewed mentioned their seroconversion as a moment when they changed their friendships and began to connect more with other men living with HIV instead of continuing to be social in predominantly Dominican gay male networks. Mejía was unusual; though he had other HIV-positive friends, he continued friendships with most of the same men he was close to before his seroconversion.

20 Beginning in the next chapter, I address the informants' conflicted relationship with Dominican identity and fellow Dominicans. This statement by Vega was one I heard with surprising frequency while conducting the research.

21 The investments in normative masculinity and the struggles of these men to fit that standard are central to the analytic work of the chapters in part II.

22 In this sense, Vega suffered from the policing of sexuality that has been part and parcel of U.S. immigration policy. For a detailed history of this policing, see Lubhéid, *Entry Denied*.

::: Notes to Chapter 3

1 Lauren Derby explains that "the obelisk, luminescent with marble dust and laced with gold-leaf aphorisms at its base" operated as a reminder "of the force of Trujillo's masculine powers, of the dictator as sexual conquistador." See *The Dictator's Seduction*, 119.

2 By invoking "families we choose," I reference the groundbreaking work of Kath Weston, *Families We Choose*. "Families we choose" is the term Weston uses to name formations and structures built and sustained by the lesbians and gay men she interviewed in San Francisco in the late 1980s and early 1990s. The "choice" sets these families in pointed contrast to biological families, which at the time were perceived to be under crisis and threat articulated in the right-wing "family values" movement. Although there are moments when Weston notes the overlap and intersection of these two, presumably separate, family forms (particularly in her discussion of working-class informants), her work and much of the scholarship that had come before and after it gave the impression that there was tension and much antagonism between emerging gay and lesbian identitarian forms and the family as a social institution. Though that is indeed the case for many people, the "choice" most of the informants made is to straddle these structures of belonging, not to sever connections with one to join the other.

3 "Choose and lose" is the way Doris Sommer describes hegemonic attitudes toward the shuttling between worlds characteristic of minorities and, in her study in particular, of bilinguals. Instead of viewing bilinguals as resourceful, intellectually agile, and innovative citizens precisely because of the strengths that come from negotiating various codes of communication, the assimilating impulse in countries like the United States demands "letting go" of the old language (and the old world) despite the many impediments to full assimilation in the new one. The assimilationist impulse can also be found in lesbian and gay scholarship, except that the tendency there has been to project a rural-urban orientation without fully engaging the continuity of economic, affective, and psychic entanglements in the lives of out lesbians and gay men. See Sommer, *Bilingual Aesthetics*. As we will see throughout this chapter, immigrants such as the informants echoed this discourse of "choose and lose" in their own observations of themselves and other Dominicans, despite their ongoing engagement with questions of self-fashioning that have long histories in Dominican culture.

4 Upwardly mobile Dominicans like the men I interviewed engage in strategies of self-fashioning in New York that rely, for their effectiveness, on the mobilization and complicity with stereotypes generated about working-class Dominican lives among elites in the Dominican Republic. These are strategies they share with other Latin American immigrants with middle- and upper-class backgrounds as mechanisms to cope and negotiate the sudden downward mobility and the erasure of class and racial boundaries that results after migration. As Ana Yolanda Ramos-Zayas explains in the Puerto Rican case, geographical displacement has challenged the modernist grounding of the nation in geography, though a more flexible, elastic concept of "cultural authenticity" has taken its place as part of an economy of value where being "from the island" is prized as an attribute coded and readable from the way "insiders" carry their bodies. See Ramos-Zayas, "Implicit Social Knowledge, Cultural Capital, and 'Authenticity' among Puerto Ricans in Chicago."

5 The philosopher José Medina explains this as intercontextuality. "The notion of *intercontextuality* captures well how past, present, and future contexts interpenetrate each other and become tied together in a nondeterministic way through our performances and ongoing negotiations. On my view, discursive agency involves a process of constant recontextualization or *echoing,* in which our discursive acts are constantly being oriented by histories of use and at the same time are constantly reorienting these histories as well." This is a useful formulation because it demonstrates that speech acts are connected to what he calls "histories of use" while speakers have the potential to transform or alter the course of those histories in their usage. My view of dominicanidad as a *contested* discursive repertoire points to the productivity of conflict and difference in the evolution of "histories of use." See Medina, *Speaking from Elsewhere,* xiii–iv; emphasis in original.

6 In a recent critique of attempts to develop what he calls an "ontological" view of all Dominicans, Rolando Tabar Manzur suggests that this particular tendency characterizes influential public and intellectual figures in their attempts to put forward totalizing characterizations that do not correspond with the views expressed by those who participated in his study. Through a survey of almost seven hundred university students from various parts of the Dominican Republic, Manzur shows that views of Dominicans as "deviant," "corrupt," and "sad," for example, were echoed only in a small portion of the sample. One of the conclusions of this research is that it is important to alter the tendency to generalize about Dominicans and develop more sophisticated engagements with the ways that average Dominicans view themselves. As we will see later in this chapter, countering hegemonic discourse about who Dominicans are with the heterogeneity of views expressed by Dominicans themselves responds to the need to address the influence that intellectuals have had in defining and

sustaining problematic views of dominicanidad. See Manzur, "Algunas caracterizaciones sobre los dominicanos."

7   I see a parallel between my effort to treat the views of the informants as representations of dominicanidad that demand engagement as representations and Roger Rouse's important engagement of the work of Jameson on postmodernism through the vantage point of the views expressed by his Mexican informants. Unlike Rouse, who locates his intervention in the quotidian experiences of people from Aguililla, Mexico, I am interested in the way the informants narrate their perceptions. More precisely, the challenge that plagues even sophisticated theorizations in the social science is the recognition and engagement with what populations say as "mediated" or constructed narratives of the world. Listening and transcribing what people say gives one access not to their experience but rather to their narration of that experience in the context of interviews. Rouse, "Mexican Migration and the Social Space of Postmodernism."

8   See Torres-Saillant, *El retorno de las yolas*. In this important book, Torres-Saillant is concerned with critically engaging what he characterizes as the (mis)representation of Dominicans in the United States, and he persuasively argues that many are the investments in constructing Dominicans abroad as deviant. This particular intervention was necessary, certainly, at a time when Torres-Saillant was the most trenchant and controversial critic of nationalist intellectuals in the Dominican Republic. Nevertheless, to the degree that he emphasizes the importance of distorted views versus the "reality" of the lives of Dominicans in New York and elsewhere, I tend to agree with Néstor Rodríguez in thinking that Torres-Saillant anchors his intervention in the rhetorical force of "real" (read: essentialist) dominicanidad. Rodríguez, *Escrituras de desencuentro en la República Dominicana*.

9   Rodríguez's work is in dialogue with that of Julio Ramos. See *Desencuentros de la modernidad en América Latina*.

10 See Rodríguez, *Escrituras de desencuentro en la República Dominicana*, 11.

11 A model that haunts my discussion here is, of course, developed in José Esteban Muñoz's pioneering *Disidentifications*.

12 I am using "strategic ambiguity" in the sense proposed by Ginetta Candelario. As she explains about her Dominican informants in New York and Washington, D.C., "strategic ambiguity allowed simultaneously for purposeful self-presentation strategies and for equivocation in dynamic interplay between the internalization and externalization of official identity discourses." See Candelario, *Black behind the Ears*, 33.

13 These can be seen as part of what Candelario calls "the ideological markings of official Dominicanidad: Negrophobia, white supremacy, and anti-Haitianism." See Candelario, *Black behind the Ears*, 3.

14 I am thinking here, specifically, of the work of Luis Guarnizo. See "The Emergence of a Transnational Social Formation and the Mirage of Return Migration among Dominican Transmigrants." Guarnizo's research in New York, Santo Domingo, Santiago, and San Francisco de Macorís illustrates the emergence of transnational social fields that relocate social inequalities instead of eliminating them. An important example from the existing scholarship, which Guarnizo challenges, is that migration is generally "empowering" to female migrants. But Guarnizo demonstrates that men—particularly men able to succeed as entrepreneurs in the immigrant enclave economy—tend to be the most benefited by what he calls "emergence of a transnational social formation." Women's choices to migrate to the United States or return to the Dominican Republic tend to be more bound to family structures and gendered expectations than are men's choices. In this article, Guarnizo also explores class tensions caused by the growing presence of return migrants in the home country, whose success has been sustained and has challenged the normative status of the traditional Dominican upper classes. My argument throughout this chapter is that the informants' views of other Dominicans are shaped by racial and class perspectives that precede migration itself.

15 Discussions of perceptions and tensions across Latina groups appear in the joint work of Nicholas De Genova and Ana Yolanda Ramos-Zayas, as well as in the classic book by Félix M. Padilla. Nevertheless, concern with the construction of Latino ethnic/national identities in specific local contexts is an important area of inquiry in the field past and present. An area that remains underexplored is the way Latinas and Latinos engage existing and emerging discourses about their national/ethnic identities within their own groups as they adjust to life in the United States. That is some of the work I seek to undertake in this chapter. In Dominican studies, the contributions of Ginetta Candelario represent an important advance in this regard—specifically as it concerns the complexities of Dominican racial formations. But in this chapter, I will be mostly devoted to the ways informants engage and debate the meanings of dominicanidad in the United States while remaining attentive to interarticulations of race, class, and other factors in its construction and sustenance. See De Genova and Ramos-Zayas, *Latino Crossings*; Padilla, *Latino Ethnic Consciousness*.

16 The question of Dominicans and Latin Americans as "imitators" of ideas and practices from Europe and the United States is a recurring source of concern for intellectuals in the region. The usual argument involves, as the literary and cultural critic Roberto Schwarz has pointed out for Brazil, a disjuncture between European and U.S.-American models, and national or regional "realities" that do not fit these models. Writing about academic trends, for instance, Schwarz notes that "the thirst for terminological and doctrinal novelty prevails

over the labor of extending knowledge and is another illustration of the imitative nature of our cultural life." Schwarz, "Brazilian Culture," 234. What is distinct and important about the "imitation" the informants critique is that the referent is Dominican society, not European or U.S.-American models in the way they have figured historically in discussions of Latin American "imitation." The echoes of that earlier discourse can be discerned in the social (and geographical) location from which these men articulated their views and developed their own appealing model of the modern. Like the earlier examples of Dominican intellectuals such as Pedro Henríquez Ureña, these men encountered "modernity" as they engaged the worlds that became available to them after migrating to New York. For a discussion of migration and "modernity" in Henríquez Ureña's encounters with New York, see Mendez, "In Zones of Contact (Combat)."

17 Like their counterparts (pulperías and colmados) in the Dominican Republic, bodegas are institutions important not only because they trade in foodstuffs and other commodities for a neighborhood-specific Hispanic market. Neighborhood bodegas are spaces of sharing of information about accessing resources (rooms or apartments being rented, informal jobs, etc.), commodities otherwise inaccessible (particular those in the informal economy), and information about neighborhood events or gossip. Arismedi's suggestion of familiarity through the image of the bodega also points to the importance of Dominican presence in that part of the informal business sector. Surprisingly, there is relatively little work on the bodega as an institution in Hispanic communities, though Reynoso points out that working in bodegas has been part of the economic activities of Dominicans in the informal sector to negotiate downward economic turns. See Reynoso, "Dominican Immigrants and Social Capital in New York City." For a study on the economic and cultural roles played by the bodega, see Kaufman and Hernandez, "The Role of the Bodega in a United-States Puerto-Rican Community." For a study of the colmado in the Dominican Republic, see Murray, *El colmado*.

18 The display of material signs of wealth as a "crass" working-class display of advancement has been widely criticized by Dominicans in New York and in the Dominican Republic, as will become evident from the observations of other men. As a working-class man, Guerrero felt uncomfortable with distinctions based on the display of brand-name clothing because he saw it as a sign of the retention of codes of distinctions among Dominicans, not because he felt himself to be above others. Middle- and upper-class informants noted the importance of these displays, but they presented their critiques from a sense of being "above" what they critiqued, regardless of the frequency with which they bumped into these ways to establish and bolster hierarchies within these groups. Because of the important role that capital accumulation and contribu-

tions to the Dominican Republic by Dominicans abroad has played in undermining the traditional bases for hierarchy in this society, middle-class observers and critics have generally shown the superficiality of these advancements to question their validity. In this context, the production and circulation of the category *Dominican-york* as a derogatory term to describe Dominicans abroad as illegitimate members of the nation-state because of the perceived illegality of their access to capital—in contrast to the presumably "legitimate" capital accumulation bases for upper middle and upper classes in the Dominican Republic—obtains.

19 My gratitude to Arnaldo Cruz-Malavé for the phrasing here.

20 One important critique of this tendency among students of Dominican transnationalism is Torres-Saillant, "Diasporic Disquisitions."

21 *Listín Diario* is a major Dominican newspaper. The reference in this sentence is to a young man who was part of the groups of men with whom I interacted while conducting this research. As a way to indicate his intellectual disposition toward the homeland while being unable to pick up English-language skills and look for jobs other than those available in restaurants, some of these men would simply remark (when asked about this particular member of the group) that he was "walking down the street with a *Listín Diario* under one arm" the last time they saw him.

22 The anchoring of this chapter in the interrelated notions of "progreso" (progress; in this section) and "cultura" (culture; in the next section) borrows from Jesse Hoffnung-Garskof's research on Dominican transnational communities in Cristo Rey and Washington Heights. See Hoffnung-Garskof, *A Tale of Two Cities*.

23 González, Baud, San Miguel, and Cassá explain that though progress had been central to "proyectos ilustrados desde las últimas décadas del siglo XVIII, fue en la segunda mitad del siglo XIX cuando esta concepción se articuló de manera consistente a un proyecto de construcción nacional estatal. Tocó al pensamiento liberal introducir la idea del progreso como valor colectivo, pero no fue de su patrimonio exclusivo. En esta idea se resumían, para la época, las aspiraciones a una sociedad moderna y libre; moderna, por cuanto tendía a asumir como referentes la civilización material capitalista y el espíritu científico del occidente europeo; y libre porque se proponía fundar una sociedad republicana, sin privilegios estamentarios, basada en la igualdad ante la ley, sin más diferencias que las derivadas del talento y las aptitudes de sus individuos." See González, Baud, San Miguel, and Cassa, "Introducción," 16.

24 See Martínez-Vergne, *Nation and Citizen in the Dominican Republic*. For an important social-psychological perspective on Dominican nationality, see Záiter, *La identidad social y nacional en Dominicana*.

25 Martínez-Vergne, *Nation and Citizen in the Dominican Republic*, 19.

26 Ibid.

27 Ibid., 15.

28 As Hoffnung-Garskof explains, "Dominican nationalist thinkers around the turn of the century generally lamented what they saw as the backwardness and barbarism of their rural countrymen. In particular, they detested rural traditions of communal land tenure, slash-and-burn farming, and open-range grazing. Progreso required that land be cultivated with export crops and that rural people begin work in tobacco, coffee, and sugar production." Hoffnung-Garskof, *A Tale of Two Cities*, 19.

29 González, Baud, San Miguel, and Cassá, "Introducción," 31.

30 Hoffnung-Garskof, *A Tale of Two Cities*, 68.

31 Hernández, *The Mobility of Workers under Advanced Capitalism*.

32 Hoffnung-Garskof, *A Tale of Two Cities*, 95.

33 This critique of poor people's consumption habits is common, especially when issued by the nonpoor, whose sense of safety in distance from the poor is shaken by the ability of capitalist consumption practices to level the playing field among people of otherwise disparate backgrounds. I am grateful to Edgar Rivera-Colón for this insight.

34 This is addressed more explicitly and thoroughly in the chapters in part II.

35 Jesse Hoffnung-Garskof explains eloquently the role that obtaining a university education played in the aspirations of upward mobility among Dominican youth during the 1970s. Although university education became available to Dominicans of various social backgrounds, these degrees did not catapult most of these new professionals into jobs or positions where their achievements were recognized: "It was perhaps the continual postponement of these hopes that rubbed so uncomfortably against the messages of progress projected by migrants, producing stereotypes that exaggerated the speed and shallowness of the migrant road to economic success" (38). Though educated in the 1980s, Noguera was likely part of a generation of professionals who saw their achievements and claims to legitimacy undermined by the material displays of others, particularly because he ended up having to migrate to the United States and live close to others who did not have his educational achievement. Hoffnung-Garskof cites Rafael "Fafa" Taveras's comments: "When 'an imposter with no education could come and show you those symbols of opulence, chains, cars, booze, and money to spend on women, it produces a reaction'" (Hoffnung-Garskof's interview with Taveras, cited on p. 38). See Hoffnung-Garskof, "The Prehistory of the Cadenú."

36 As Hoffnung-Garskof writes, New Yorkers who organized to combat stereotypes of Dominican New Yorkers in the Dominican Republic in the 1980s

"did not deny that there were corrupt Dominicans in the United States. They sought rather to distinguish between themselves and the few bad apples." See Hoffnung-Garskof, "The Prehistory of the Cadenú," 31.

37 Hoffnung-Garskof, *A Tale of Two Cities*, 12.

38 By using *hail* here, I link this moment in the interview exchange with the processes of interpellation described by Louis Althusser. In a way that reverses the usual scene of interpellation (where "the call" or "hail" is issued by a figure of authority, most famously a cop in Althusser's example), this informant flips the script of the power dynamic of the interview exchange, to a degree, by foregrounding the way the project he participates in constituted me as author. See Althusser, "Ideology and Ideological State Apparatuses," and Harper, "The Subversive Edge."

39 By *calcar*, this informant means imitation, but "calcar con un mapa" (copy or imitate a map) references the process of copying a map by putting a clean sheet of paper on top of the original and following with a pencil the traces of the original that can be seen more or less clearly through the page where the map will be "calcado."

40 Thanks to Arnaldo Cruz-Malavé for the phrasing here.

41 My gratitude goes to Edgar Rivera-Colón for the phrasing here.

42 López, "La alimentación y las razas."

43 Derby, "Gringo Chickens with Worms," 455.

44 Ibid., 456.

45 Ibid., 459.

46 See Martínez-San Miguel, *Caribe Two Ways*.

47 Ibid., 157.

48 Candelario, in *Black behind the Ears*, explains that contrary to the perception of Haitian immigrants and native Dominicans, "Dominicans of West Indian descent perceived themselves as superior to the Dominican natives, due in large measure to their ability to speak English with North American owners and managers [of sugar plantations], who put them in skilled and supervisory positions. . . . Unlike the Haitian experience, *cocolos* and *Ingleses* [as these immigrants were called] in the Dominican Republic have been able to sustain a unique ethno-racial identity that is positively perceived" (162).

49 Derby, "Gringo Chickens with Worms," 470.

50 Chapters 4 and 5, especially, deal with the question of joking.

51 Vega's felicitous use of the verb *cuajar* to talk about himself merits some discussion. Dominican usage of this verb is consistent with that noted in the *Diccionario de la lengua española*: the transformation of something liquid to something solid, or (if not solid) something denser than a liquid. A second usage of this term addresses situations that, due to a mixture of elements, come

together or concretize in particular ways. The fact that Vega phrases his experience of return and experience of being in Dominican soil as "ya no cuajo" suggests that the world changed him enough that he did not quite "come together" or "concretize" himself as a Dominican. Like in other language used by the informants, their emphasis is not on who someone "is" (*quien es*) but in who someone "becomes" when they are (*está*) in a specific location.

52 Although the differences between immigrant and 1.5- and second-generation Latinos will not be addressed extensively in this book, tensions between older and younger generations of Dominican immigrant and U.S.-born gay and bisexual men will surface again in chapter 5, "Code Swishing."

53 This is consistent with the argumentations put forward by Grosfoguel and Georas about Dominicans' ongoing negotiation of their positionality in New York vis-à-vis the distinct histories and colonial dynamics of the pioneering racial minority groups in the city: Puerto Ricans and African Americans. See Grosfoguel and Georas, "Coloniality of Power."

54 For a recent treatment of this question, see Decena, Shedlin, and Martínez, "Los hombres no mandan aquí."

55 Ramos-Zayas, "Becoming American, Becoming Black?"

56 Candelario, *Black behind the Ears*, 6. The title of Candelario's book references the line "el negro tras de la oreja" in Juan Antonio Alix's well-known poem, written in 1883.

57 Candelario, *Black behind the Ears*, 10.

58 Neptune, *Caliban and the Yankees*. In particular, see chapter 6, "Love American Style: Race, Gender, and Sexuality in Occupied Trinidad," 158–90.

59 Neptune, *Caliban and the Yankees*, 5.

60 Guzmán, *Gay Hegemony/Latino Homosexualities*. Guzmán explains that his discussion demonstrates "the extent to which race is not only the product of economic, political, and social relations but also the product of erotic activity that is not sexually but racially structured and organized . . . formations of homoerotic desire are also structures that structure the formation and maintenance of racial distinction" (3).

61 Sommer, *Bilingual Aesthetics*, chapter 1.

::: Notes to Chapter 4

1 *Loca*, which literally means "crazy woman," is a category used to describe effeminate homosexual men in the Dominican Republic and in other parts of Latin America. The category works as a powerful insult because of its gender connotations and associations with emotional excess and flamboyance. A loca is generally a homosexual man whose gender transgressions call attention to themselves. But it is a term that has multiple valences, depending on

its usages. The association with "crazy woman," for instance, is one usually referenced when categorizing a woman who should not be taken seriously. In its general usage, when referencing homosexual men, a loca is generally not considered someone worth taking seriously. However, how and where it is used largely determines the way the word is interpreted. Usage of the term by presumably heterosexual men and women is generally interpreted (with some exceptions, and usually in the case of women more than men) as injurious or insulting. Men like the informants might use *loca* to talk about homosexual men in general, to talk about themselves, to put down specific people through public usage, or to index intimacy and close friendship with others. As the discussion throughout this chapter and the next will show, however, usage of a term like this can be strongly contested, largely depending on how well interlocutors understand (or don't understand) their relations with others.

2 My investment in underscoring the degree to which these men use but do not own the languages they mobilize is informed by Judith Butler's work on speech-act theory and, in particular, her revision of Althusser and Austin in *Excitable Speech*: "If the subject who speaks is also constituted by the language that she or he speaks, then language is the condition of possibility for the speaking subject, and not merely its instrument of expression" (28). Particularly important for the purposes of this essay is the way Butler moves away from the voice of authority that structures (and, more importantly, dominates) the scene of interpellation in Althusser to offer an account of the more "conventional" (in the Austinian sense) usages of performatives for subject formation. Because the "others" who train the informants in the proper use of masculine codes may be their mothers and other relatives but are usually not figures of state or religious authority (like the policeman in the famous scene of interpellation in Althusser), it is important to keep in mind the regulatory powers that inhere and organize socialities internally, not just in relation to the "ideological state apparatus." See Butler, *Excitable Speech*.

3 Fanon, *Black Skin, White Masks*, 17.

4 My work throughout this chapter is informed by Goffman's symbolic interactionism, though my focus on the work of language in narrative constructions of the self—and, in particular, my engagement with speech act theory in relation to body language *as language*—puts me on antifoundationalist ground. In other words, what I analyze is not a "real world" where people accomplish or manage impressions but rather the mediations that offer access to the ways informants interpreted their pasts for specific purposes during the interview. See Goffman, *The Presentation of Self in Everyday Life*.

5 This chapter is informed by Susana Peña's exploration of the production of what I will call the *gynographic performative* of la loca in the context of the presence of homosexuals in the 1980s Mariel boatlift. One of the most useful

analytic moves Peña makes in this work results from the avoidance of taxo-nomic or positivistic renditions of what the figures of la loca may have been at this time. Insightfully, Peña thematizes the question of the specular excess of the "effeminate" Cuban male body vis-à-vis Cuban authorities in charge of designating them as eligible to leave the country and the U.S. immigration of-ficials who greeted and evaluated them before allowing them to stay in the United States as refugees. Peña's theorization of "the glance" in particular con-nection with the political work Cuba and United States sought to achieve with this boatlift focuses, importantly, in protocols of evaluation that needed to be carried out by officials whose job it was to assess a person's "homosexuality" through an evaluation of how well they played out the role of the effeminate male homosexual. This was particularly important in Cuban state protocols, which held a more definitive (and stereotypical) view of the populations they wanted to see depart from the country. See Peña, "'Obvious Gays' and the State Gaze."

6 In an essay taken to be a founding moment in queer studies, Gayle Rubin made an argument for the necessity of understanding the differences between oppressions related to gender and those related to sexuality. This argument was important at its time because of the need to develop a radical critique of sexual-ity that took seriously feminism's contributions to the analysis and resistance of gender oppressions while grappling with the limitations (and problematic poli-tics) around sex and sexuality that had developed within feminism. The version of that necessary analytical delinking of the politics of gender conformity and nonconformity in everyday life and sexual identification counters the taken-for-granted scholarly conflation, especially in the discourse of scholars who study sexuality in the Americas, of the figure of the sissy with social vulnerability and anal receptivity. The nexus between being read as a sissy and being anal recep-tive—or passive, as is usually presented in the scholarship—needs to be ques-tioned rather than assumed to be automatic. This chapter contributes to that discussion by engaging the politics of gender embodiment and socialization where it presented itself most often to informants: in their negotiations of their own bodies in the world, and in their establishment of relationships of distance and proximity with others. In the next chapter, I will suggest that embodiment matters in sexual practices but not in the functionalist ways presented in the scholarship. See Rubin, "Thinking Sex."

7 A notable exception to this trend in the literature written by North Americans is the work of James Green. See Beyond Carnival.

8 An example of that conflation is in the pioneering work of Roger Lancaster: "In Nicaragua, anal intercourse defines the cochón [effeminate homosexual]; what-ever else he might or might not do, a cochón is tacitly understood as someone

who engages in anal intercourse with other men . . . it is the passive role in anal intercourse that defines the cochón" (238). Lancaster develops an interpretation of cochón in the Nicaraguan context that, I argue, emerges from hegemonic sexual imaginaries that become inevitable referents for self-identified homosexual or same-sex desiring men. Thus, the conflation of effeminacy and passivity operates in a phallic economy in which same-sex desire is mapped onto a strictly male/female dichotomous choreography, where the body with the organ that penetrates is a "man" and where the open body is the "woman." This chapter and the next go to great lengths to demonstrate the degree to which that conflation of effeminacy and passivity, ideological though it might be, is untenable. See Lancaster, *Life Is Hard.*

9 The distinction between effeminacy as a means to express a desire "to be a woman" and effeminacy as I treat it throughout this and the next chapter, as the staging of stereotypes of femininity in male bodies, is crucial because many researchers of Latin American homosexualities have misunderstood the figure of la loca. As the anthropologist Don Kulick astutely remarks, "The conundrum [of the ostentatiously effeminate male homosexual] has been generated largely because researchers have assumed that gender is a cultural reading of biological males and females and that there are, therefore, two genders—man and woman" (231). My interpretation of la loca as a gynographic performative moves away from the paradigm that views effeminacy as a form of "theft" of femininity because it suggests that these stereotypes of female excess are not so much evidence of behaviors that characterize "real women" but rather are productions emerging from a patriarchal (and, generally, gynophobic) matrix. See Kulick, *Travesti.*

10 See Fuss, *Identification Papers,* 2, where she defines identification as "a process that keeps identity at a distance, that prevents identity from ever approximating the status of an ontological given, even as it makes possible the formation of an *illusion* of identity as immediate, secure, and totalizable." Emphasis in original.

11 Sifuentes-Jáuregui, *Transvestism, Masculinity, and Latin America Literature,* 57; my emphasis.

12 Sifuentes-Jáuregui explains that "excessive writing has long been a cliché of masculine representations of women's voices; the use of such an 'excessive' model to represent femininity or, moreover, women's subjectivity is commonplace, for example, the *modernistas* often oscillated between the contradictory representations of woman as either an empty receptacle for male subjectivity or woman as excess and frivolity; this presentation of the feminine as excess culminates in the West in Joyce's 'Penelope' chapter of *Ulysses,* of course." Ibid., 59.

13 Butler, *Bodies That Matter,* 115.

14 Cruz-Malavé, "'What a Tangled Web!'" For the story, see Sanchez, "¡Jum!"

15 This is the title of a collection of poems by Borges. See Borges, *El otro, el mismo.* I found the reference to it in Balderston and Quiroga, *Sexualidades en disputa.*

16 While conducting interviews, I compiled a list of characteristics the informants associated with "being a man" when they were children. Most of the answers they offered are consistent with the findings of E. Antonio de Moya. See "Power Games and Totalitarian Masculinity in the Dominican Republic." The consistency between many of the do's and don'ts I elicited and those of de Moya suggest that the informants were generally attuned to the ways of understanding and reading masculinity that the author found in informal conversations about childrearing practices with men and women of various backgrounds in the Dominican Republic.

17 Part of what Heredia recalled, then, was negotiating the prospects of upward mobility connected with specific masculinities. Heredia suggested that he felt anxiety about his masculinity, yet part of what may have made construction work unappealing to him may have been that the physicality required of each worker did not result from the exhibition of specific, cultivated craftsmanship but from routine and repetitive motion, which may require brawn but not skill, in Heredia's view.

18 A remarkable aspect of Eugenio Heredia's trajectory as a migrant is that out of all the men I interviewed, he was the youngest unaccompanied man (seventeen) when he moved to the United States. The circumstances surrounding Heredia's migration were directly related to his pursuit of dance as a career option. During the interview, he shared how important dancing was to his self-expression and first income-generating activities. Unlike his brothers, Heredia achieved enough notoriety through his dancing to be hired by the Ministry of Tourism as part of a folkloric dance group that appeared in carnivals, Independence Day, and other national celebrations. Eventually that work led to an invitation for the troupe to visit Puerto Rico to participate in a dance festival—an opportunity the young Heredia took to stay and then travel to New York. Once in New York, Heredia connected with relatives living in the city while working and living on his own. Surviving as a seventeen-year-old was hard, and those difficulties were only intensified by the isolation Heredia felt due to his lack of access to spaces in which to socialize and meet other men.

19 Clearly, Lacan refers to a much earlier stage in the development of children, characterized by immobility and dependence on the mother figure. See Lacan, *Écrits,* 76.

20 Fanon, *Black Skin, White Masks,* 111–12.

21 Ibid., 112.

22 It is hardly unusual that part of the household labor associated with moth-

erhood is gender socialization of male and female children. In her research among the Kaluli of Papua New Guinea, Bambi Schieffelin argues that "gender-appropriate behaviors are constituted and maintained by caregivers and others in everyday situations through what they do and what they say to each other and to young children" (203). From her observations, motherly tolerance of certain male behaviors suggests, to Schieffelin, the way boys are socialized as entitled to preferential treatment by their mothers, and the way the reproduction of the marginalization of young girls is incorporated into the way in which mothers address them. "Maternal attitudes and ideologies affect the ways in which boys and girls are socialized to be different—that is, to assume gender-based roles." See Schieffelin, *The Give and Take of Everyday Life*, 203.

23 In his ethnographic research on masculinity and male intimacy in urban parts of Hermosillo and rural Sonora, Mexico, Guillermo Núñez Noriega remarks on the ways in which local men tended to experience others' surveillance of their masculinity: "El cuerpo de los hombres está sometido a una vigilancia estricta en cuanto su expresividad pública: en el modo de hablar, de dirigirse a los otros, de caminar, de expresar emociones, de conversar y de bailar. Es tal y tan evidente esta vigilancia del cuerpo que un hombre me comentó que él nunca cruzaba la plaza cuando había gente, en cambio prefería rodearla. Otro amigo me narró un caso extremo acerca de un vaquero que el solo hecho de imaginarse atravesando la iglesia para casarse, lo hizo desistir de casarse, de hecho, cuando lo hizo, la boda se celebró en un rancho" (The body of men is under strict surveillance in its public expression: the way of talking, the mode of addressing others, the walk, the way of expressing emotions, the way of talking and dancing. This surveillance of the body is so intense and so evident that one man told me that he never crossed the plaza when there were people; instead, he preferred to go around it. Another friend told me of the extreme case of a cowboy who decided not to marry just because of his fear of walking down to the church to marry; in fact, when this man married, the wedding took place in a ranch) (my translation). See Núñez Noriega, *Masculinidad e intimidad*, 116.

24 An important introduction and overview of the masculinities literature is Connell, *Masculinities*. Two relevant essay collections are Adams and Savran, *The Masculinity Studies Reader*, and Whitehead and Barrett, *The Masculinities Reader*.

25 Krohn-Hansen, "Masculinity and the Political among Dominicans," 108.

26 de Moya, "Power Games and Totalitarian Masculinity in the Dominican Republic," 72–73.

27 Krohn-Hansen, *Political Authoritarianism in the Dominican Republic*, 138.

28 The importance of seriousness and the orientation of male socialization toward work also appear in Barbara Finlay's research among rural women and their childrearing practices in the province of Azua: "For sons, after the major

goal of education came the traditional male activity, work. For about half of the community sample and almost half of the workers, one of the most important things to teach a son was 'to work,' or 'to have a profession,' or (for example) 'to be a good farmer.' So, although the women put education above other things for both sons and daughters, they followed that with household chores for daughters and work skills for sons. . . . A few women mentioned such things as 'to be responsible,' 'to be serious,' or not to steal or drink too much. These last two items were never mentioned for daughters." See Finlay, *The Women of Azua*, 111.

29 Krohn-Hansen, *Political Authoritarianism in the Dominican Republic*, 146.

30 *El tiguere* is the Dominicanization of the word *tigre*, or tiger, in Spanish. Throughout this chapter and consistent with the informants' usage, I spell the word *tíguere*.

31 Though it is unclear from Abreu's description that his father had other female partners, his characterization of the father makes promiscuity in la calle a possibility.

32 Through the diagram of the "charmed circle," Rubin describes and theorizes the various sexual practices and bodily attributes that organize hierarchies of oppression and legitimacy around sexuality. Working-class couples (particularly male partners), whether or not they are legally married or monogamous, probably fit somewhat uneasily within Rubin's model, which makes monogamy and marriage requirements to be within the charmed circle. However, many of the other men I interviewed would most probably see Abreu's parents as exemplary not so much because (in Abreu's account) they were married or because the father had other partners but because they stayed together and seemed to have a relationship that was functional. See Rubin, "Thinking Sex."

33 The normativity of common-law marriage, or "unión libre," has also been noted in the description of Dominican rural communities. See Suero, *Barreras*.

34 Krohn-Hansen, *Political Authoritarianism in the Dominican Republic*, 148.

35 Collado, *El tíguere dominicano*, 11. Collado evocatively points to the rise of this figure with the urbanization of Santo Domingo and other cities throughout the country, at least since the 1930s. The basic premise of *tigueraje* is the need for men to win a game of cards where they do not have access to the deck, where the rules have already been established by more powerful men, and where traditional morality and transparency are incompatible with survival. The *costumbrista* writer Rafael Damirón eloquently, if damningly, casts the tíguere as an agent of moral corruption in emerging Dominican cities: "La cárcel, el prostíbulo, el tapete verde, la trata de mujeres y cuanto vil y por grosero resulta indigno de la piedad de los otros, lo hacen el más definitivo agente de prostitución." See Damirón, *De soslayo*, 106.

1 Gal, "A Semiotics of the Public/Private Distinction," 79.

2 Ibid., 80.

3 Ibid.

4 In this sense, the statements by the respondents were constantive (in that they described something) and performative (in that the description itself "did" something in the context of the interview) as proposed by the philosopher J. L. Austin. See *How to Do Things with Words*.

5 The informants' engagement with the figure of la loca is roughly parallel to Manalansan's account of his Filipino male informants' engagement with the *bakla*. As he explains, "Filipino gay men do not readily assimilate into modern gay personhood and instead recuperate the bakla as a way to assert a particular kind of modernity." See Manalansan, *Global Divas*, x.

6 Here I am referencing Miranda Joseph's critique of "the romance of community," particularly in her discussion of the complex interaction of this notion with capitalism. An especially valuable aspect of Joseph's work is her emphasis on the performativity of "community" as it is deployed in various contexts to produce specific desired discursive effects while also producing boundaries and limits between these and other (sometime marginal, often overlapping) formations. See Joseph, *Against the Romance of Community*.

7 The work and career of William Leap stand out as pioneering, courageous, and sustained efforts to attend to the specificity of language for the lives of gay men and other LGBTQ populations. Apart from the single-authored monographs and edited volumes he has produced, Leap has been the coordinator of the Lavender Languages and Linguistics Conference (a setting for the study of the intersections of LGBTQ identities, genders, sexualities, and languages) since 1993. See Leap, *Beyond the Lavender Lexicon*. See also his single-authored work, *Word's Out*, and Leap and Boellstorff, *Speaking in Queer Tongues*. Although Leap is a pioneering voice in the "linguistic turn" in LGBTQ studies, this is an area that has drawn considerable attention from scholars. Two useful overviews of this scholarship are provided by Cameron and Kulick, *Language and Sexuality*, and by Bucholtz and Hall, "Theorizing Identity in Language and Sexuality Research." A tension existing in this scholarship concerns recent critiques of the so-called identitarian investments in much of this work (and Leap tends to be a target of these criticisms) and advocacy for what Cameron and Kulick call "a focus on desire" (106). With an interpretation that emphasizes that communicative practices obtain from the interarticulations of positionalities in relations of power, the perspective advanced throughout this chapter is vigilant of identitarian essentialisms while concurring with Bucholtz and Hall

that "identity, sexual or otherwise, is most productive when . . . understood as the outcome of intersubjectively negotiated practices and ideologies" (469).

8 As Zentella explains, "Bilingualism was an integral part of family life and community identity, but children were less preoccupied with growing up bilingual than with growing up, surviving." See Zentella, *Growing Up Bilingual*, 1.

9 In his pioneering study of black gay men, Hawkeswood alludes to "codeswitching" to talk about the way his informants juggled living gayness and blackness together: "My initial assumption that gay black men would 'codeswitch' between being gay and being black was challenged by these men. While there may be some ambivalence about identity for black men in mainstream gay society, gay black men in Harlem choose to identify themselves as black men first, using the gay identity as a status marker within black society." It is interesting that this interpretation of code switching posits it as a kind of shuffling of identities, whereas those who have studied linguistic code switching generally focus more narrowly on the production of signifiers that might add up to something we could understand as "identity" but that are not reducible to it. My engagement with this literature is more along the lines of linguistic anthropological understandings of code switching, though Hawkeswood's use of the phrase suggests an antecedent to my usage in relation to quotidian and interactional self-making. See Hawkeswood, *One of the Children*, 11–12.

10 Manalansan stresses the importance of performance for the sake of survival. "The immigrant," he writes, "is continually made aware of the performative aspects of survival so much that he or she is continually compelled to move or 'travel' (albeit discomfittingly) between various codes of behavior." See Manalansan, *Global Divas*, 14.

11 *American Heritage Dictionary of the English Language*, 4th ed., s.v. "swish."

12 Loftin, "Unacceptable Mannerisms," 577.

13 My gratitude to Dorothy Hodgson for the conversation that helped me draw workable analytic distinctions between "code switching" and "code swishing."

14 About existing scholarship on code switching, Zentella argues that "the starting point of the past research has been on specific features of the language or on the switching between them . . . not on the context that gives rise to bilingualism and the ways in which children learn to switch. As a result, we have partial portraits of interlocutors, rules, and usage, but no in-depth understanding of the process of becoming bilingual in any Spanish-speaking community in the United States." See Zentella, *Growing Up Bilingual*, 4.

15 By "happy" reception, I am explicitly invoking J. L. Austin's criteria for the evaluation of whether or not performatives work given a specific scene of interaction. One of the least explored aspects of his contribution is the question of which conditions (other than the initial utterance of a performative) make for what he deems the "happiness" or "unhappiness" of performatives. Some

theorists are dismissive of "context" in theories of performativity inspired by Austin. My conceptualization of "scenes of interaction" grapples with this crucial aspect of the social life of performatives, as will be explained later in this chapter.

16 In defining scenes of interaction in this way, I take cues from the literature on context in linguistic anthropology, which parts ways from reductive definitions of it as physical environment to conceptualizations that account for the convergence of bodies, spaces, temporalities, and linguistic practices. For a discussion of the various meanings of context, see Goodwin and Duranti, "Rethinking Context."

17 In the Argentine context, Sívori observes that important class-based distinctions exist among men who frequent homoerotic environments but that they tend to be framed in moral terms: "Determinadas conductas son vistas como contrarias a lo que se considera un tránsito decente por el ambiente. Ciertos verbos como 'putanear' y 'loquear' son utilizados por personas gay para referirse a la manifestación de una conducta homosexual desvergonzada y moralmente contaminante, opuesta a una conducta carente de otra calificación, no marcada" (96). As a consequence of these divisions, which manifest within gay "communities," Sívori suggests that the analytic inquiry cannot simply oppose its investigation of a subculture on its antagonism to a given "establishment" but that it needs to investigate frictions and tensions internal to that specific group. See Sívori, *Locas, chongos y gays.*

18 Austin, *How to Do Things with Words,* 52.

19 Butler, *Excitable Speech,* 3.

20 Butler's reading of Austinian performatives is almost exclusively devoted to the injurious aspect of their social lives. As a counterpoint, this chapter stresses that views of performatives like la loca miss their richness if they attend only to their usage as injurious speech acts.

21 For a treatment of relajo among Mexicans rural immigrants in Chicago, see Farr, *Rancheros in Chicagoacán.* For a treatment of humor in Puerto Rican literature, see Reyes, *Humor and the Eccentric Text in Puerto Rican Literature.* A text that might also be of interest is Barradas, "Cursi, choteo, guachafita."

22 Lauria, "'Respeto,' 'Relajo' and Inter-Personal Relations in Puerto Rico," 56.

23 Ibid., 55, 56.

24 The distinction of various forms of the second-person singular pronoun (*you*) in Spanish (*tú, usted,* or *vos*) is indicative of complexities in regional usage and interpersonal relations that are central to colonial and contemporary histories of the language. For some discussions of comparative historical and regional differentiations in usage, see Gutiérrez Marrone, "Temas gramaticales"; Russinovich Sole, "Correlaciones socio-culturales . . ."; and Schwenter, "Diferenciación dialectal por medio de pronombres." For a rich history of legitimacy in

the Spanish colonial project in the Américas particularly concerned with the struggles of illegitimate children of elites to be recognized by fellow elites and by authorities in the metropole, see Twinam, *Public Lives, Private Secrets*.

A comparative example of the way that respect and deference are built into linguistic structures is what Duranti calls the "Samoan respect vocabulary." As he explains, "The Samoan hierarchical system, with its distinctions between untitled and titled individuals, chiefs and orators, ordinary and high-ranking title holders, is reified by lexical distinctions that faithfully and routinely remind everyone of who-is-who in the sociopolitical arena. At the same time, the availability of such a taxonomy makes such a simple task as lexical choice into an art, unconscious at times, cunning on some occasions, merciless on others." See Duranti, "Language in Context and Language as Context."

25 Portilla, "Femonenología del relajo," 19.

26 Admittedly, the conceptualization of relajo I use in this chapter can be extended to address ritual inversions of the social order that involve humor such as carnival. For a conceptualization of relajo in this register, explored through ethnographic reflections on the Santo Domingo festival in Managua, Nicaragua, see Linkogle, "*Relajo*: Danger in a Crowd."

27 Portilla, "Fenomenología del relajo," 25.

28 Mañach y Robato, *Indagación del choteo*, 7.

29 Mañach y Robato further explains that "una de las causas determinantes del choteo es la tendencia niveladora que nos caracteriza a los cubanos, eso que llamamos 'parejería' y que nos incita a decirle 'viejo' y 'chico' al hombre más encumbrado o venerable." *Indagación del choteo*, 7.

30 The legitimacy of masculinities in the context of intense racial and class antagonisms may be worked through the figure of the homosexual, as it is among middle- and working-class men in Argentina documented in the work of Gustavo Blázquez. According to the author, the usage and mobilization of different usages of the word *gay* in Argentinian Spanish effects a leveling effect between men of various class backgrounds (differences that are racialized to the degree that working-class and poor men are seen as "negros" by middle-class participants in the sites documented in this ethnography). The result is the mobilization of the terms *gay* and *gay panic* for the stabilization of masculinities in specific class and racial locations. See Blázquez, "Gays y gaises en los bailes de cuarteto."

31 Lauria, "'*Respeto*,' '*Relajo*,'" 62–63.

32 Within these groups, someone who "lets out a feather" every once in a while stands in a different position from someone who is always perceived as a loca. This is something that I explain at length later in the chapter.

33 Tolerance is relative. I have already suggested that effeminacy constituted a source of tension and distinction among these men, distinctions that were gen-

erally framed in terms of the way someone's gender dissent might make that person appear "without future," "crass," or "uncontrolled."

34 In this particular discussion, I will move through Domínguez's narration of his ignoring the acquaintance who called him out in front of a third party to offer a reading of Althusserian interpellation as performative, highlighting the importance to its happiness of what I call the *scene of interaction*.

35 Althusser, "Ideology and Ideological State Apparatuses," 174–75.

36 Butler, *Excitable Speech*, 31, 32.

37 By "children" of the houses, I am referencing young queer people involved in the house ballroom scene. In the words of some of the men with whom I spoke and who commented informally about Arismendi, his proximity to these populations at various community events raised eyebrows and confirmed their view of him as a loca. Pioneers in studying these communities in the United States include Marlon Bailey and Edgar Rivera-Colón. See Rivera-Colón, "Getting Life in Two Worlds."

38 As workplaces, the factory and beauty parlor are different, especially with regard to the ways in which a gender-nonconforming gay man can inhabit the space of the beauty parlor—usually associated with the stereotypically gay occupation of the hairdresser—and the factory, where the gender norms and expectations leave less room open for someone like Arismendi.

39 See Candelario, "Hair Race-Ing."

40 Thanks to Jimmy Ariza for clarifying the meaning of "fuertes" in this context.

41 Mejía's friends also insistently policed Mejía's behavior, as I explained in detail in chapter 2, "Moving Portraits."

42 Althusser, "Ideology and Ideological State Apparatuses," 174.

::: Notes to Chapter 6

The title of this chapter is inspired by and pays tribute to an essay by my mentor and friend Arnaldo Cruz-Malavé, "Para virar al macho." Given the history of antagonisms and tensions between Puerto Ricans and Dominicans, one informant who encountered the word *virando* in the title of this chapter suggested that (1) "virar" is more of a common expression among Puerto Ricans than among Dominicans ("se partió," he suggested, is closest to the way a Dominican would talk about a man being "flipped" by another) and (2) my usage could be interpreted by Dominicans as a "flip" where the person flipping ("top") is Puerto Rican and the flipped ("bottom") is Dominican. "Virar," as the title of this chapter, risks this interpretation but also points to the confluence, quotidian exchange, and ongoing history of connections between Puerto Ricans and Dominicans in each country, as well as in New York. It is also empirically justified by the usage among some men I interviewed, such as Mauricio Domínguez, whose specialty was "virar bugarrones" (flip bugarrones) when he visited the Dominican Republic, as I discuss in more detail in the next chapter.

1 I borrow this phrase from Gloria Gonzalez-Lopez's groundbreaking book, *Erotic Journeys*.

2 See Shimizu, *The Hypersexuality of Race*.

3 Ibid., 16.

4 This is consistent with Manolo Guzmán's findings in his discussion of interviews with Puerto Rican gay men: "The most striking finding to emerge from the interviews analyzed for this chapter is the extent to which some Puerto Rican homosexual men report a very marked and strong preference for the sexual company of other Puerto Rican men." See Guzmán, *Gay Hegemony/Latino Homosexualities*, 61.

5 For a discussion of the way recent developments in gay male cultures fit within a neoliberal sexual model, see Adam, "Constructing the Neoliberal Sexual Actor."

6 Examples of this scholarly trend include Ferguson, *Aberrations in Black*; Barnard, *Queer Race*; Muñoz, *Disidentifications*; and Somerville, *Queering the Color Line*.

7 Guzmán, *Gay Hegemonies/Latino Homosexualities*, 61.

8 Informants' notion of what may make sex "political" throughout this chapter does not ever extend beyond the sexual encounter itself. In other words, the politicization effected throughout their commentary tended to be narrowly mapped onto the privatized sphere of the sexual encounter with one partner. To the degree that they envisioned the politics of the erotic in this narrow (and rather circumscribed) register, theirs was a decidedly homonormative politics of the erotic.

9 The scholarship on machismo and on Latin American men and masculinities is vast. For some useful examples, see Gutmann, *The Meanings of Macho*; Gutmann, *Changing Men and Masculinities in Latin America*; and Mirandé, *Hombres y machos*.

10 For a discussion of the function of sex as mediator of ethnonationalist conflict, see Lambevski, "Suck My Nation." For a discussion of negotiations of coloniality through (anal) sex, see Ho and Tsang, "Negotiating Anal Intercourse in Inter-Racial Gay Relationships in Hong Kong."

11 de Moya and García, "AIDS and the Enigma of Bisexuality in the Dominican Republic."

12 Machismo is a component of the project of teasing out "radical differences" between the "European-American sexual system" and "Latin-American sexual system." As Tomás Almaguer argued in "Chicano Men," the difference is that "the Mexican/Latin-American sexual system is based on a configuration of gender/sex/power that is articulated along the active/passive axis and orga-

nized through the scripted sexual role one plays" (257). Generally speaking, much of this literature argues that, in the United States, who penetrates and who is penetrated does not make a difference, as both male partners would be considered "homosexual." Conversely, in Latin America, the active partner would be considered a "machista," "hombre," or "heterosexual," whereas "it is the passive role in anal intercourse that defines the cochón [male homosexual in Nicaragua]." See Alonso and Koreck, "Silences"; Carrier, De los otros; Lancaster, Life Is Hard; Parker, Bodies, Pleasures, and Passions and Beneath the Equator.

Research has drawn much attention to the symbolism that male-to-male anal sexual practices have in the popular cultures of Latin America. For instance, there has been debate about the connection of activity versus passivity to stigma. Roger Lancaster argues that the anal penetrative ("active") partner does not share the stigma that attaches to the anal receptive ("passive") partner. "The machista's honor and cochón's shame are opposite sides of the same coin." Other scholars, such as Anick Prieur, do not think there is much honor in being the penetrating partner in sexual encounters. Prieur cites as evidence the unwillingness of partners who play these roles to brag about penetrating sissies in the way they brag about sleeping around with women. See Prieur, Mema's House, Mexico City.

Recent critics have voiced skepticism toward this conceptual model. Some have even used it to investigate the colonialist traces in anthropological thinking, public health, and human rights. Examples include Braiterman, "Sexual Science"; Bustos-Aguilar, "Mister Don't Touch the Banana"; and Strongman, "Syncretic Religion and Dissident Sexualitites."

Though anthropologists like Joseph Carrier and Roger Lancaster have been targets of criticism surrounding the activo/pasivo model, Martin Nesvig correctly observes that many of these pioneering scholars relied on the work of the Mexican Octavio Paz (specifically El laberinto de la soledad) to formulate it. Paz's "propositions about the essential nature of Mexican sexual identity," as Nesvig suggests, "have cast a tremendous shadow over the historiography and ethnography of Mexican and Latin American sexuality." Nesvig, "The Complicated Terrain of Latin American Homosexuality," 691. In his study of ethnographic writing from 1750 to 1918, The Geography of Perversion, Rudi Bleys argues that "static notions of (male) 'homosexual identity,' largely a western creation, do not correspond to the cross-cultural realities of 'bisexual' practices and role-defined sexual identities during the era surveyed in this study. Often only the passive partner would be labeled and, eventually, stigmatized" (1). I find it striking that though Bleys offers a long-historical view of the development of these "sexual systems" as part of the of empire building and of the development of ethnography as a technology of empire, Bleys finds contemporary echoes of this "activo/pasivo"–like scenarios in "most parts of the Arab world and among lower classes in Latin America. On the level of speech, and to a lesser extent of sexual praxis, this pattern also remains discernible in rural Mediterranean Europe" (note 4, p. 13).

13 Mark Padilla's work supports this assessment: "Ethnographic studies of homosexuality and globalization have implicitly or explicitly framed the figure of the *activo* [or bugarrón, in this context] as a 'traditional' phenomenon that is in tension with, and may ultimately be eclipsed by, currently circulating notions of global gay identity. This framing, however, presumes a lack of integration of *active* sexualities into global cultural flows and economic interests, a presumption that can in no way be confirmed by the ethnographic evidence presented in this book." See Padilla, *Caribbean Pleasure Industry*, 105.

14 I borrow from an informant's use of the word *bed*. Nevertheless, *bed* does not function as a marker of the privatized sphere of sexual relations between two partners. The metaphor might lend itself to appropriation by sexually conservative sectors of the LGBT movement. Yet, this informant points to the bed when he wants to talk about the space of intimacy regardless of its being a sex club, a bathroom, or a park.

15 Hanawa, "Circuits of Desire."

16 Much work has focused on commoditization of bodies of people from "developing" countries, most explicitly in sex work. Examples in this vast area of study include Brennan, *What's Love Got to Do with It?*; Herold, García, and de Moya, "Female Tourists and Beach Boys"; Leheny, "A Political Economy of Asian Sex Tourism"; Meisch, "Gringas and Otavaleños"; Sanchez Taylor, "Tourism and 'Embodied' Commodities"; Sánchez Taylor, "Dollars Are a Girl's Best Friend?"; Padilla, *Caribbean Pleasure Industry*; Cabezas, "Tropical Blues." In the Dominican Republic, de Moya's work on male sex tourism and homosexuality is groundbreaking. His suggestion (with García) of the importance of commoditized sexual exchange to the social organization of homosexuality in the Dominican Republic *in general* points to an area of research that has been relatively neglected: the way the commoditization of bodies in sex work and other manifestations of the convergence of sexuality and commerce (e.g., pornography) shape perceptions of populations of color *regardless* of whether or not they engage in sex work. Mireille Miller-Young's pioneering dissertation on black women in porn, "A Taste for Brown Sugar," is a notable exception to this trend.

17 A classic essay on the representations of Asians in porn is the widely anthologized piece by Fung, "Looking for My Penis." Manalansan also discusses the way his Filipino informants dealt with stereotypes about Asian men in New York. See *Global Divas*, 140–47.

18 Despite the richness of fictional and semiautobiographical accounts of homoerotic lives lived in New York, one remarkable silence in the literature on sex
in the city concerns the extraordinary heterogeneity of contemporary same-sex
desires and cultures in New York. For important autobiographical treatments,
see Delany, *The Motion of Light in Water* and *Times Square Red, Times Square
Blue*.

19 The tíguere archetype is discussed at some length in chapters 4 and 5.

20 Concern with the disrepute of Dominicans in New York (and their connection
with illicit activities) goes back to the 1970s, as documented by Jesse Hoffnung-
Garskof. See his essay "The Prehistory of the Cadenú."

21 Grosfoguel and Georas, "'Coloniality of Power' and Racial Dynamics," 90.

22 "Puerto Ricans" are not signifiers that circulate without mixed feelings among
informants. As Arnaldo Cruz-Malavé has argued, the figure of the Puerto Rican plays an ambivalent role in Dominican transnational culture—as mediator
between "lo criollo" and "lo Americano," as abjected by his relationship to the
United States, and as a source of derision and envy for their "special status."
Cruz-Malavé, "En ese vuelo no me voy yo: Migration, Translation and Homosexuality in *Nueba Yol* and Junot Diaz's *Drown*" (conference presentation,
"Hispanic Cultural Studies: The State of the Art," Tucson, Arizona, 2002). As
the work of Grosfoguel and Georas shows, passing as Puerto Rican has been a
practice of Dominican immigrants in Puerto Rico and in New York. Anecdotal
evidence obtained during fieldwork suggests that this continues to occur.

23 Gender roles and expectations shape much of the attention the concept of
machismo has received by scholars, particularly in the literature on Latin
American homosexuality. The evidence provided by the informants demands
an engagement of gendered racialization. As Dominican immigrants in the
United States, the informants associated machismo with the dominicanidad
they needed to disavow for the sake of progreso. During fieldwork, machismo
emerged as a racialized concept, or a signifier connected to what informants
perceived as a difference between Dominican men and men of other racial/eth-
nic groups. At the end of the interviews, when I asked respondents if there was
anything else they thought I should ask, some of them pointed out that I had
to focus on manifestations of machismo among Dominican homosexual men.
After reading an earlier version of my chapter on gender and legitimacy in daily
life, one informant asked me why machismo was absent from my discussion
of gender dynamics. I explained that although we use the term *machismo* to
critique attitudes we find troubling among fellow Dominicans—and I included
myself deliberately—I did not use the word in the questions because I did not
want to bias participants' responses by putting the word in their mouths. I was
certain the word or concepts related to it would emerge, and I waited to see how
and when it would surface in conversations with informants.

The informants insisted on my dealing with machismo as a problematic of gender. But it was not about gender roles in any population, they also suggested. Machismo was part of the "problem" of dating Dominican men. This suggested to me over time that many of them used the label as a marker of gendered racial and ethnic difference, an element that distinguishes Latino/Latin American from European American men in New York. In other words, informants invoked "Latin American" and "U.S." sex and gender systems that were consistent with what I found in the literature. When it came to describing what distinguished Dominicans from other Latinos, informants did not suggest that other Latino groups were exempt from "machista culture." For them, Dominican machismo was a more extreme manifestation of a Latino/Latin American phenomenon.

The history of machismo and its genealogy within the social sciences attest to the role it has played in the construction of racialized and gendered "otherness" (Gutmann, *The Meanings of Macho*). My use of "machismo" to name gendered and racialized otherness by members of the populations it describes draws attention to two aspects of the term: first, the fundamental link many informants saw between machismo and dominicanidad, as described earlier, and second, their perceptions of the way they are racialized in New York. Machismo stands in for a part of the culture the informants find themselves wanting but not being able to abandon when they get to New York. Informants' use of machismo points to dichotomies that are juxtaposed to one another: self versus other, premodern versus modern, undemocratic versus democratic, imprisoned versus liberated, and so forth. The poles of these dichotomies do not stand in a horizontal relation to their opposites, however. These oppositions are gendered, classed, racialized, and nationalized at the same time. Machismo is usually understood as one side in these dichotomies. This is a side associated with being working class, dark skinned, and stuck in what some informants have called "the mental island," or the inability to let go of the homeland.

24 My invocation of "nourishment" here picks up on my earlier description (in chapter 3, "Desencontrando la dominicanidad") of the widespread Dominican perception of plantains as having no nutritional value.

25 Readers skeptical of the valence of the oral and anal analogy through consumption might be further persuaded by the routine way in which this analogy circulates in circuits of same-sex desire. One need only check the "men for men" section of Craigslist.com to find personal ads with language about "hungry asses" and "hungry bottoms."

26 Thanks to Edgar Rivera-Colón for pushing me to expound upon this point.

27 The reflexive phrasing ("se me viró") is more common than the active use of the verb ("viré al tipo"), though I heard informants use the verb in both ways.

28 One notable exception to this trend in the literature is James Green's remark-

able interpretation of the life of João Francisco dos Santos (Madame Satã), a visible thug and popular figure in early-twentieth-century Brazilian history who was widely known to be gay and who preferred to be anally penetrated. See Green, *Beyond Carnival*, especially 85–92.

29 Carballo-Diéguez, Dolezal, Nieves, Díaz, Decena, and Balán, "Looking for a Tall, Dark, Macho Man."

30 Guzmán, "'Pa' la escuelita con mucho cuida'o y por la orillita.'" An extraordinary document in the Cuban case is Cortez, *Sexilio/Sexile*. The complex sociopolitical conditions of the migration of queer Cuban men during the Mariel Boatlift are rendered with unusual verve, sensitivity, and sophistication in Peña, "'Obvious Gays' and the State Gaze."

31 Here, Báez provides a remarkably different framing of sexual citizenship than the one that predominates in current scholarship. While much of the sexual citizenship scholarship has been important in mobilizing a rights framework to talk about sexual identities, Báez suggests something that centers sexual practices as citizenship praxis. The privatized nature of these sexual exchanges and exercises/sharing of power make me skeptical of the framework's utility without adjustments and further elaborations, of course, but it is refreshing and provocative for him to center "fucking" in a discussion in which it has almost completely disappeared.

32 Undoubtedly, some of these men held ideals of sexual openness *before* they ever migrated to the United States. Nevertheless, the mediation of sexual philosophy through migration is central here to the degree that the men themselves made the connection a theme in their narratives.

33 See Roberto Panés's commentary in chapter 3, "Desencontrando la dominicanidad," and his commentary in chapter 4, "Eso se nota."

34 Candelario, *Black behind the Ears*, 130.

35 I am borrowing the phrase "afterlife of colonialism" from the subtitle of the collection of essays *Queer Globalizations*, edited by Cruz-Malavé and Manalansan.

::: Notes to Chapter 7

1 De Moya and García explain that a bugarrón is understood as an "anal insertor" in paid sexual exchanges. "This term," they write, "derives from the French word *bougre* ('bugger' in English). . . . In everyday usage, being a *bugarrón* is almost synonymous with being the insertive partner in paid homosexual relations. The overt, public motivation for this transaction is economic need, not choice or pleasure." See de Moya and Garcia, "Three Decades of Male Sex Work in Santo Domingo," 128.

2 The transit between *ser* and *estar* that I want to center in this chapter appears

in an interesting moment of awkward translation in Padilla's excellent ethnography of bugarrones in the Dominican Republic. At the end of a quote by one of his informants, Padilla offers this translation and then the Spanish original: "He's a bugarrón [*está bugarroniando*]." The translation neglects the operations of *estar* in the informant's phrase. *Estar bugarroneando* highlights the "doing" of *bugarronear*. Unfortunately, the translation simply casts this as a question of "being" a bugarrón. See Padilla, *Caribbean Pleasure Industry*, 117.

3 A quintessential manifestation of the ideology of return and the centrality of the homeland in Dominican transnational cultures is Angel Muñiz's hit film of 1995, *Nueba Yol*. The plot of the film revolves around the adventures of everyday hero Balbuena and ends with a happy return to the homeland and marriage to a nice New York–based Dominican girl who returns with him. For a discussion of *Nueba Yol*, see Valerio-Holguín, "Santo Domingo, Nueba Yol, Madrid."

4 Some of the most potent critiques of dominicanidad are being articulated by artists and critics living in the Dominican Republic and abroad whose works can be categorized as "queer" insofar as they launch trenchant examinations of the value systems upheld by nationalist Dominican culture. Though sexuality is often central in much of this work, these artists have a distinctive concern about dismantling Dominican hispanophilia and anti-Haitian xenophobia. Junot Díaz is perhaps one of the better-known representatives of this diasporic critical assault on traditions of dominicanidad, but he is far from alone. These artists include Josefina Báez, Waddys Jaquez, and Nicolás Dumit Estevez and the writers Rita Indiana Hernández, Rey Enmanuel Andújar, and Ana-Maurine Lara. For a thoughtful exploration of Jaquez's work, see Stevens, "The Politics of Abjection in P.A.R.G.O." Maja Horn's forthcoming manuscript, "Sounds of Silence," explores much of the work of these established and emerging artists. For a discussion of the politics of reception in the work of the Paris-based Dominican artist Nelson Ricart-Guerrero, see Horn, "Queer Caribbean Homecomings."

5 Wolfe, *You Can't Go Home Again*.

6 By using the word *ethnoscape*, I invoke the influential coinage by Arjun Appadurai: "By *ethnoscape*, I mean the landscape of persons who constitute the shifting world in which we live: tourists, immigrants, refugees, exiles, guest workers, and other moving groups and individuals constitute an essential feature of the world and appear to affect the politics of (and between) nations to a hitherto unprecedented degree." See Appadurai, *Modernity at Large*, 33. I want to point to the importance of the gravitational pull of the nation-state in the formation and sustenance of ethnoscapes; if it is no longer possible to sustain the nation-state (or the ethnic or religious group identity) from within the geo-

political boundaries of a country, mappings of ethnoscapes still have specific and privileged referents.

7 This remarkable program began as *Aquí, Santo Domingo* in 1974. Produced by Ramón Rodríguez (Negro) Santos, who also hosts the program, *Santo Domingo Invita* airs every Sunday morning in New York City. It is currently associated with the Telemundo Network. See the *Santo Domingo Invita* website at http://www.sdi.com.do.

8 I have been an assiduous viewer of this show for the last decade, and though I have not counted the number of times this phrase comes up, its appearance, including variations of it (men are sometimes "valientes," "grandes héroes," etc.), is constant. The only thing that women seem to do in these reports of towns and cities in the Dominican Republic is "ser bellas."

9 See Hanawa, "Circuits of Desire."

10 Ibid., ix.

11 An important account of the incipient white gay male sex tourism entrepreneurship in Latin America in the context of the radical first years of gay liberation is Balderston and Quiroga, "A Beautiful, Sinister Fairyland."

12 And benefit disproportionately they do. A particularly stark testimonial to this involves the outsourcing of reproduction as narrated in "Renting Wombs." More recent representations of the phenomenon of upper-class women "renting" the wombs of women of color to carry their pregnancies have appeared in mainstream U.S. television series like *Brothers and Sisters* (ABC). The subplot of the white Irish immigrant woman carrying the child of upper-class African American Wilhelmina Slater in *Ugly Betty* (ABC) is an inversion of this racialized narrative.

13 As helpful and important as it has been and continues to be to point to "white gay men" as beneficiaries of hierarchical arrangements that obtain within white supremacy and heteronormativity (Nast, "Queer Patriarchies, Queer Racisms," 874), "white gay tourism" (Alexander, *Pedagogies of Crossing*, 67), or, in a more general sense, cultures of "phallicized whiteness" (Winnubst, *Queering Freedom*), the time has come to grapple with the complicity of women and people of color in the reproduction of inequalities that may have everything to do with white supremacist legacies of colonialism but where responsibility cannot simply be wished away in the figuration of the gay white man in the room. I am by no means the first to voice discomfort with this pitting of "white (gay) men" against all "the others." Guzmán, for example, points out that in *This Bridge Called My Back*, "the abjected figure of the white heterosexual man is deployed, as negative figuration, to secure the coherence of the subjectivity of colored womanhood. . . . The [Combahee River] Collective envisions progressive political action as a 'collective process and a nonhierarchical distribution

of power.' . . . White heterosexual men are incapable of this form of political action because, unlike the members of the collective, they 'are the very embodiment of reactionary-vested-interest-power.'" See Guzmán, *Gay Hegemony/Latino Homosexualities,* 11.

14 This chapter brings together literatures that are almost never in dialogue with one another: immigration and sex tourism. It is encouraging, however, that artists have begun to grapple with what happens when the beneficiaries of sex tourism are not white men. The film by Laurent Cantet, *Vers le sud* (2005), is set in Haiti in 1978, where three female travelers from the United States and Canada find themselves sunbathing and "sampl[ing] the handsome young islanders' sexual talents" (summary on Netflix.com). Unlike films such as Kevin Rodney Sullivan's *How Stella Got Her Groove Back* (1998) that offer a euphemistic treatment of a relationship often characterized in the sex tourism literature as "romance tourism," Cantet's film explores with honesty the power dynamics and different stakes for the various characters involved.

15 Candelario's *Black behind the Ears* eloquently shows the political function of the travel narratives fashioned by European and U.S. travelers in the Dominican Republic from the late eighteenth to the early twentieth century. What distinguishes these narratives from many developed about the Caribbean region in general, as Candelario explains, is the fashioning of constructions of Dominicans that presupposed a comparison/contrast with neighboring Haiti. In most of these depictions, the portrayals throw a positive light on Dominicans and their country and a negative one on Haiti. Candelario suggests that partly as a consequence of the impact of these images—which Dominican intellectuals and institutions incorporated into their nationalist narratives and museum exhibitions—many Dominican identity projects play on the comparison/contrast with Haiti that is reminiscent of these travel narratives.

16 The work of Guarnizo comes to mind, though he is one of several scholars of transnationalism who have emphasized the agency and, in particular in his writings, the economic viability of transnational communities. See his "Los Dominicanyorks." Peggy Levitt's work generally places a stronger emphasis on the costs and benefits of transnational lives. See *The Transnational Villagers.*

17 The profound ambivalence that I narrate in the autoethnographic sections of this chapter echoes that articulated by Lawrence La Fountain-Stokes, though he and I view the relationship between sex and monetary exchange differently. In writing of his travels in Cuba as a queer Puerto Rican, La Fountain-Stokes notes that "we can say that (male-to-male) sexual tourism not only affects relations between Cubans and foreigners but also affects relations between Cubans themselves, favoring the maintenance of older models of payment for sex (especially for working class men) while possibly impeding the expansion of

other types of relations based on the establishment of stable, egalitarian bonds (a phenomenon evinced more clearly among middle class men and among lesbians of diverse class backgrounds)" (218). Isn't monetary exchange for sex always already involved (or at least implicated) in so-called egalitarian bonds? Indeed, does the "egalitarian" not presume that both partners bring similar amounts of capital (material, cultural, symbolic, etc.) to the exchange? I fundamentally disagree with the opposition in sexual and affective relations as either "egalitarian" or "payment for sex" that La Fountain-Stokes puts forward, for it neglects a consideration of the way exchange operates in all of these relations. See La Fountain-Stokes, *"De un pájaro las dos alas."*

18 Padilla defines "pleasure industry" as "the diverse informal sector of the Dominican economy devoted to providing a myriad of pleasure-related services to the more than two million foreign guests that visit the country annually." Padilla, *Caribbean Pleasure Industry*, x.

19 Sheller, *Consuming the Caribbean*, 31.

20 The work of Kemala Kempadoo is particularly important in this regard, as it offers a long-historical view of Caribbean integration into the world economy through sexual commerce. See "Freelancers, Temporary Wives, and Beach-Boys" and her two edited volumes, *Sexing the Caribbean* and *Sun, Sex, and Gold.*

21 See Cabezas, *Economies of Desire*, 53. Cabezas offers an overview of international tourism in the Dominican Republic on pp. 38–43. It seems ironic that for a country that has, in general, historically received so little scholarly attention from the U.S. academy, so much of emerging recent work is concentrated on the conjunction of sex and tourism. Maybe *ironic* is the wrong word here: the amount of attention may actually be *symptomatic* of the geopolitics of U.S. dominance as it informs what imaginable research topics are. See Brennan, *What's Love Got to Do with It?*, and Padilla, *Caribbean Pleasure Industry*. A work that addresses sex work as part of a larger discussion of globalization and politics in the country is Gregory, *The Devil behind the Mirror.*

22 Mark Padilla remarks on a crucial, if severely understudied, aspect of cultural exchange in Dominican transnational cultures: "Regular travelers, including Dominican gays residing abroad, often develop social relationships with local gays and establishment owners, facilitating the transmission of privileged gay knowledge and the shaping of Dominican gay culture. An important population in this regard is the queer 'Dominican-yorks' who come to Santo Domingo on family holidays or vacations, composing a hybrid queer diaspora that maintains both intimate links and tensions between the Caribbean and New York." See Padilla, *Caribbean Pleasure Industry*, 31. Although this chapter and this study address issues raised by Padilla, the ideoscapes of queer Dominican (and Latin

American) queer cultures have yet to be studied rigorously. A pioneering effort in this regard, and a model for what such inquiries might look like, is the work of Lawrence La Fountain-Stokes. See *Queer Ricans*.

23 Balderston and Quiroga, *Sexualidades en disputa*, 26, my emphasis.

24 Vidal-Ortiz argues that autoethnography highlights "my sexual orientation, class and skin color based experiences without assuming generalization of such experiences to a whole group of people" (181). His point in engaging the auto-ethnographic is "to question current identities, to dislocate their foundations. My purpose is *not* to add another political category, but to bring up inequality and stratification outside these rigid identity parameters" (186; emphasis in original). See Vidal-Ortiz, "On Being a White Person of Color."

25 As Guzmán explains, "I do not ground myself on gayness to know about other ways of organizing homosexual life. I ground myself on gayness, firstly, because I have no other choice, and, secondly, because I want to know about gayness itself, because I am suspicious of that gayness which both constraints and facilitates my voice." See Guzmán, *Gay Hegemony/Latino Homosexualities*, 44. Greg Thomas states his critique as follows: "It is as if it were enough to raise the subject [of gender and sexuality], and magically some moral superiority in politics ensues. Since gender and sexuality criticism is not exempt from radical criticism itself, simply because it is about gender and sexuality, it remains necessary to determine what is just, progressive, or radical about any instance of this criticism, particularly if it cannot analyze its complicity with the sexual politics of white Western imperialism—past, present, and, unfortunately, future." See Thomas, *The Sexual Demon of Colonial Power*, 155.

26 Veijola and Joniken present their "tourist notes" as conversations with fellow sociologists of tourism. Between helpings of leisure (sunbathing, walking, etc.) the authors have conversations with other (imaginary?) sociologists of tourism they encounter in their travels. Sitting at a kitchen chair, one of them states, "The main argument/narrative developed and researched in this paper deals with the *absence of the body* from the corpus of the sociological studies on tourism. So far the tourist has lacked a body because the analyses have tended to concentrate on the *gaze*. . . . Furthermore, judged by the *discursive postures* given to the *writing subject* of most of the analyses, the analyst himself has, likewise, lacked a body" (149; emphasis in original). It is fascinating how even in their "anatomical" mapping of the body of the tourist, the authors do not remark but rather *mark* the gender of the body in question. The body of the tourist and of the "scientist" who writes about tourism, and who is the target of their critique, is male. That awareness and critique of the maleness of this body is present throughout the conversations in this remarkable piece. See Veijola and Joniken, "The Body in Tourism."

27 Padilla's translation of "me la busco" captures the urgency of survival and the highly adaptive strategies for the accumulation of wages by young men wrestling with massive male unemployment, underemployment, and the rising cost of living in Dominican society: "Recent economic trends in the country demonstrate the rapid growth of informal-sector work among lower-class men, and many of these men are filling employment niches that include occasional, episodic, or career participation in the pleasure industry." Padilla, *Caribbean Pleasure Industry*, 47.

28 Padilla writes, "Dominican male sex work, then, is situated within an informal economy in which the ability to successfully manage diverse social networks is highly adaptive." Padilla, *Caribbean Pleasure Industry*, 61.

29 Cabezas, *Economies of Desire*, 21.

30 Ibid., 20.

31 See Marx, *Capital*, 128.

32 Cabezas, *Economies of Desire*, 20.

33 Ibid., 17.

34 In his discussion of the Cuban case, Allen argues that "tourism-related sex labor is one of a growing number of spaces in which common sense understandings of racial and sexual identity are re-presented and exploited toward related aims of material 'survival,' commodity acquisition and consumption, and *becoming* a cosmopolitan subject." See Allen, "Means of Desire's Production," 184.

35 For more information (and pictures galore) about Monaga, see his blog at http://www.monaga.blogspot.com. For information about New Wave Black Man, see his blog at http://zenbizness.blogspot.com.

36 Monaga collaborated with the companies ZenBizness, LLC and Urbane Concepts in the development of these parties. This is the way they advertised Dominican Island Heat 2: "ZenBizness, LLC and Urbane Concepts of NYC is [*sic*] pleased to present the DOMINICAN ISLAND HEAT 2 event. DIH2 will take place in Santo Domingo, Dominican Republic from March 1–6, 2005. Get ready for five non-stop nights of parties, adventures, culture and more." See the Dominican Island Heat 2 website at http://www.dih2.blogspot.com.

37 Another entrepreneur is LeeStudiosNYC (http://www.leestudiosnyc.com), headed by the photographer Ernest Montgomery and billed as "industry professionals as innovative, trendsetting and pioneering in the conceptualization of urban, exotic, and inner-city images of men of color. From the gritty streets of Harlem to the barrios of Santo Domingo, Dominican Republic, the stunningly picturesque men captured by the photographic brilliance of LeeStudiosNYC has already garnered the agency with an international stellar reputation." Of particular interest is his "Men of the DR" portfolio of photographs.

38 See http://www.dih2.blogspot.com.

39 The deplorable conditions of Haitians immigrants and their descendants in the Dominican Republic *in general* and in the bateyes in particular are evidence of the violence, indignity, and neglect that the Dominican state inflicts on those who inhabit its geopolitical boundaries. Although the work of Batey Relief Alliance is commendable and is part of the many ongoing efforts within and outside the Dominican Republic to bring attention to these human rights abuses, it was shocking to see the connection to one of the Dominican Island Heat events as one of the forms of tourism available to visitors to these parties. In light of the objectives of these circuit parties, this version of "alternative" tourism is, to say the least, problematic. For the work of a scholar based in the United States whose scholarship is part of his activist passion for social justice on this issue and who has worked on this topic for most of his career, see Martinez, *Peripheral Migrants* and *Decency and Excess*.

40 A recent development in the study of transnational phenomena is what Mimi Sheller and John Urry call the "new mobilities paradigm," which brings together scholars working on themes often not analyzed in proximity with one another (e.g., seasonal migration, transnational entrepreneurship, tourism). As "a set of questions, theories, and methodologies rather than a totalising or reductive description of the contemporary world" (210), Sheller and Urry's paradigm challenges what they cast as the "a-mobility" of the social sciences. In general, the authors recognize that much analytic effort has gone into the introduction and analysis of space from a social scientific perspective. Nevertheless, they suggest that much of this work has "failed to examine how the spatialities of social life presuppose (and frequently involve conflict over) both the actual and the imagined movement of people from place to place, person to person, event to event." See Sheller and Urry, "The New Mobilities Paradigm," 208. My juxtaposition of return migration with tourism, throughout this chapter, follows the call issued by Sheller and Urry.

41 My questions are informed by and echo the work of Sarah Ahmed, as well as Ahmed, Castañeda, Fortier, and Sheller. See Ahmed, *Strange Encounters*, and Ahmed, Castañeda, Fortier, and Sheller, *Uprootings/Regroundings*.

42 In setting out to make this distinction between the sexual and the erotic, I am following Guzmán closely. As he writes, "We want to make a clear distinction between a genitally based sexuality and the more encompassing erotic. The reduction of the erotic to the sexual can only lead to the reproduction of all those mechanisms . . . that have successfully bound the erotic, our pleasures, and our bodies, to the primacy of an erotically under-productive genitality." Guzmán, *Gay Hegemony/Latino Homosexualities*, 18.

43 Padilla explains further that "gay tourists' desire to be sexually dominated is perhaps best illustrated by the fact that they almost universally seek to engage

in receptive anal sex with Dominican sex workers, and only very rarely do they express the desire to be the penetrative partner or to engage in a variety of sexual roles." Padilla, *Caribbean Pleasure Industry*, 161.

44 Bleys, *The Geography of Perversion*.

45 As Manalansan argues, "The inevitable coding of Mexico as a space of deviance and as the antipodal location in relation to the Wyoming lair (filmed across the northern border in Canada) rests on the very construction of these lovers as classically tragic—virtually alone in their own pristine temporal and cultural space. Their romance is literally and figuratively elevated by the whiteness of the space and memorialized in an immaculate postcard. Mexico stands in contrast to the whiteness and serenity of *Brokeback*'s mise-en-scènes, which are full of light and visually expansive. Not only is it racialized as brown, it is chaotic, dirty, dim, narrow, and claustrophobic—brimming with history's detritus." See Manalansan, "Colonizing Time and Space," 99.

46 Chua, *Gold by the Inch*, 13–14; emphasis in original. I am grateful to Richard Morrison for referring me to Chua's novel.

BIBLIOGRAPHY

Acosta, Katie. "'Amigas' and Lovers: How First and Second Generation Latinas Negotiate Family, Partnerships, and Community in the United States." Ph.D. diss., University of Connecticut, 2009.

Adam, Barry. "Constructing the Neoliberal Sexual Actor: Responsibility and Care of the Self in the Discourse of Barebackers." *Culture, Health and Sexuality* 7 (2005): 333–46.

Adams, Rachel, and David Savran, eds. *The Masculinity Studies Reader*. Malden, Mass.: Blackwell, 2002.

Ahmed, Sara. *Strange Encounters: Embodied Others in Post-Coloniality*. New York: Routledge, 2000.

Ahmed, Sara, Claudia Castañeda, Anne-Marie Fortier, and Mimi Sheller, eds. *Uprootings/Regroundings: Questions of Home and Migration*. Oxford: Berg, 2003.

Alexander, M. Jacqui. *Pedagogies of Crossing: Meditations on Feminism, Sexual Politics, Memory, and the Sacred*. Durham: Duke University Press, 2005.

Allen, Jafari Sinclaire. "Means of Desire's Production: Male Sex Labor in Cuba." *Identities* 14 (2007): 183–202.

Almaguer, Tomás. "Chicano Men: A Cartography of Homosexual Identity and Behavior." In *The Lesbian and Gay Studies Reader*, ed. Henry Abelove, Michele Aina Barale, and David M. Halperin, 255–73. New York: Routledge, 1993.

Alonso, Ana María, and Maria Teresa Koreck. "Silences: 'Hispanics,' AIDS, and Sexual Practices." *Differences* 1 (1989): 101–24.

Althusser, Louis. "Ideology and Ideological State Apparatuses: Notes Towards an Investigation." In *Lenin and Philosophy and Other Essays*, 127–86. New York: Monthly Review Press, 1971.

Anzaldúa, Gloria. *Borderlands: The New Mestiza = La Frontera*. San Francisco: Aunt Lute, 1987.

———, ed. *Making Face, Making Soul/Haciendo Caras: Creative and Critical Perspectives by Feminists of Color*. San Francisco: Aunt Lute, 1995.

Aponte, Sarah. *Dominican Migration to the United States, 1970–1997*. New York: CUNY Dominican Studies Institute, 1999.

Appadurai, Arjun. *Modernity at Large: Cultural Dimensions of Globalization*. Minneapolis: University of Minnesota Press, 1996.

Atkins, G. Pope, and Larman C. Wilson. *The Dominican Republic and the United States: From Imperialism to Transnationalism*. Athens: University of Georgia Press, 1998.

Austin, J. L. *How to Do Things with Words*. Cambridge: Harvard University Press, 1962.

Ayala, George. "Retiring Behavioral Risk, Disease, and Deficit Models: Sexual Health Frameworks for Latino Gay Men and Other Men Who Enjoy Sex with Men." In *Latina/o Sexualities: Probing Powers, Passions, Practices, and Policies*, ed. Marysol Asencio, 274–78. New Brunswick, N.J.: Rutgers University Press, 2010.

Azcuy, Eduardo A., and Fernando García, eds. *Kusch y el pensar desde América*. Buenos Aires: Fernando García Cambeiro, 1989.

Balderston, Daniel, and José Quiroga. *Sexualidades en disputa: Homosexualidades, literatura y medios de comunicación en América Latina*. Buenos Aires: Libros del Rojas, 2005.

———. "A Beautiful, Sinister Fairyland: Gay Sunshine Press Does Latin America." *Social Text* 21 (2003): 85–108.

Barnard, Ian. *Queer Race: Cultural Interventions in the Racial Politics of Queer Theory*. New York: Peter Lang, 2003.

Barradas, Efraín. "Cursi, choteo, guachafita: Propuesta para una historia del humor caribeño." *Casa de las Américas* 230 (2002): 101–7.

Barthes, Roland. *Camera Lucida: Reflections on Photography*. New York: Hill and Wang, 1981.

Beam, Joseph, ed. *In the Life: A Black Gay Anthology*. Washington, D.C.: RedBone Press, 2008 [1986].

Blázquez, Gustavo. "Gays y gaises en los bailes de cuarteto: Humor, homofobia y heterosexismo entre los jóvenes de sectores populares de Argentina." *Sexualidades: Una Serie Monográfica Sobre Sexualidades Latinoamericanas y Caribeñas* 3 (2008), http://www.irnweb.org.

Bleys, Rudi. *The Geography of Perversion: Male-to-Male Sexual Behavior Outside the West and the Ethnographic Imagination, 1750–1918*. New York: New York University Press, 1996.

Bordas de Rojas Paz, Nerva. *Filosofía a la intemperie, Kusch: Ontología desde América*. Buenos Aires: Biblos, 1997.

Borges, Jorge Luis. *El otro, el mismo*. Buenos Aires: Emecé, 1969.

Braiterman, Jared. "Sexual Science: Whose Cultural Difference?" *Sexualities* 1 (1998): 313–25.

Brennan, Denise. *What's Love Got to Do with It? Transnational Desires and Sex Tourism in the Dominican Republic*. Durham: Duke University Press, 2004.

Bucholtz, M., and K. Hall. "Theorizing Identity in Language and Sexuality Research." *Language in Society* 33 (2004): 469–515.

Bustos-Aguilar, Pedro. "Mister Don't Touch the Banana: Notes on the Popularity of the Ethnosexed Body South of the Border." *Critique of Anthropology* 15 (1995): 149–70.

Butler, Judith. *Bodies That Matter: On the Discursive Limits of "Sex."* New York: Routledge, 1993.

———. *Excitable Speech: A Politics of the Performative.* New York: Routledge, 1997.

———. "Imitation and Gender Insubordination." In *The Lesbian and Gay Studies Reader*, ed. Henry Abelove, Michele Aina Barale, and David M. Halperin, 307–20. New York: Routledge, 1993.

Cabezas, Amalia L. *Economies of Desire: Sex and Tourism in Cuba and the Dominican Republic.* Philadelphia: Temple University Press, 2009.

———. "Tropical Blues: Tourism and Social Exclusion in the Dominican Republic." *Latin American Perspectives* 35 (2008): 21–36.

Cameron, Deborah, and Don Kulick. *Language and Sexuality.* Cambridge: Cambridge University Press, 2003.

Candelario, Ginetta E. B. *Black behind the Ears: Dominican Racial Identity from Museums to Beauty Shops.* Durham: Duke University Press, 2007.

———. "Hair Race-Ing: Dominican Beauty Culture and Identity Production." *Meridians: Feminism, Race, Transnationalism* 1 (2000): 118–56.

Cantú, Lionel. *The Sexuality of Migration: Border Crossings and Mexican Immigrant Men.* New York: New York University Press, 2009.

Carballo-Diéguez, Alex, Curtis Dolezal, Luis Nieves, Francisco Díaz, Carlos Decena, and Iván Balán. "Looking for a Tall, Dark, Macho Man . . . Sexual-Role Behavior Variations in Latino Gay and Bisexual Men." *Culture, Health and Sexuality* 6 (2004): 159–71.

Carrier, Joseph. *De los otros: Intimacy and Homosexuality among Mexican Men.* New York: Columbia University Press, 1995.

Carrillo, Héctor. *The Night Is Young: Sexuality in Mexico in the Time of AIDS.* Chicago: University of Chicago Press, 2002.

Césaire, Aimé. *Une tempête: D'après "La Tempête" de Shakespeare: Adaptation pour un théâtre nègre.* Paris: Éditions du Seuil, 1969.

Chauncey, George. *Gay New York: Gender, Urban Culture, and the Making of the Gay Male World, 1890–1940.* New York: Basic Books, 1994.

Chavez Leyva, Yolanda. "Listening to the Silences in Latina/Chicana Lesbian History." In *Living Chicana Theory*, ed. Carla Trujillo, 429–34. Berkeley: Third Woman Press, 1998.

Chua, Lawrence. *Gold by the Inch.* New York: Grove Press, 1998.

Clifford, James, and George E. Marcus, eds. *Writing Culture: The Poetics and Politics of Ethnography.* Berkeley: University of California Press, 1986.

Collado, Lipe. *El tíguere dominicano: Ensayo*. Santo Domingo: Editora Panamericana, 1992.

Collins, P. "Negotiating Selves: Reflections on 'Unstructured' Interviewing." *Sociological Research Online* 3 (1998): u18–u37.

Combahee River Collective. "A Black Feminist Statement." In *This Bridge Called My Back: Writings by Radical Women of Color*, ed. Cherríe Moraga and Gloria Anzaldúa, 210–18. New York: Kitchen Table, 1981 [1979].

Connell, R. W. *Masculinities*. Los Angeles: University of California Press, 2005 [1995].

Contín Aybar, Pedro René. "Biel, El Marino." In *Poemas*, ed. Victor Villegas, 99–114. Santo Domingo: Comisión Organizadora de la X Feria Nacional del Libro, 1982 [1943].

Cortez, Jaime. *Sexilio/Sexile*. Los Angeles: Institute for Gay Men's Health, 2004.

Crenshaw, Kimberlé. "Demarginalizing the Intersection of Race and Sex: A Black Feminist Critique of Antidiscrimination Doctrine, Feminist Theory and Antiracist Politics." In *The Politics of Law: A Progressive Critique*, ed. David Kairys, 195–217. New York: Pantheon, 1990 [1989].

———. "Mapping the Margins: Intersectionality, Identity Politics, and Violence against Women of Color." *Stanford Law Review* 43 (1991): 1241–99.

Crimp, Douglas. *Melancholia and Moralism: Essays on AIDS and Queer Politics*. Cambridge: MIT Press, 2002.

Cruz-Malavé, Arnaldo. "Para virar al macho: La autobiografía como subversión en la cuentística de Manuel Ramos Otero." *Revista Iberoamericana* 162–63 (1993): 239–63.

———. *Queer Latino Testimonio, Keith Haring, and Juanito Xtravaganza: Hard Trails*. New York: Palgrave Macmillan, 2007.

———. "'What a Tangled Web!': Masculinity, Abjection, and the Foundations of Puerto Rican Literature in the United States." In *Sex and Sexuality in Latin America*, ed. Daniel Balderston and Donna J. Guy, 234–49. New York: New York University Press, 1997.

Cruz-Malavé, Arnaldo, and Martin F. Manalansan IV, eds. *Queer Globalizations: Citizenship and the Afterlife of Colonialism*. New York: New York University Press, 2002.

Curiel, Ochy. "Identidades esencialistas o construcción de identidades políticas: El dilema de las feministas negras." *Ciudad de Mujeres*, May 4, 2006 (http://www.ciudaddemujeres.com/articulos/img/pdf/Ochy_Curiel.pdf).

Damirón, Rafael. *De Soslayo*. Santo Domingo: Editora Alfa y Omega, 1983 [1948].

Decena, Carlos U. "Profiles, Compulsory Disclosure, and Ethical Sexual Citizenship in the Contemporary United States." *Sexualities* 11 (2008): 397–413.

———. "Surviving AIDS in an Uneven World: Latino Studies for a Brown Epidemic." In *The Blackwell Companion of Latino Studies*, ed. J. Flores and R. Rosaldo, 276–88. Malden, Mass.: Blackwell, 2007.

———. "Tacit Subjects." *GLQ: A Journal of Lesbian and Gay Studies* 14 (2008): 339–59.

Decena, Carlos Ulises, Michele G. Shedlin, and Angela Martínez. " 'Los Hombres No Mandan Aquí': Narrating Immigrant Genders and Sexualities in New York." *Social Text* 24 (2006): 35–54.

De Genova, Nicholas. *Working the Boundaries: Race, Space, and "Illegality" in Mexican Chicago*. Durham: Duke University Press, 2005.

De Genova, Nicholas, and Ana Y. Ramos-Zayas. *Latino Crossings: Mexicans, Puerto Ricans, and the Politics of Race and Citizenship*. New York: Routledge, 2003.

Delany, Samuel R. *The Motion of Light in Water: Sex and Science Fiction Writing in the East Village*. Minneapolis: University of Minnesota Press, 2004.

———. *Times Square Red, Times Square Blue: An Inquiry into Some Modes of Urban Sociality*. New York: New York University Press, 1999.

D'Emilio, John. "Capitalism and Gay Identity." In *The Lesbian and Gay Studies Reader*, ed. Henry Abelove, Michele Aina Barale, and David M. Halperin, 467–78. New York: Routledge, 1993.

de Moya, E. Antonio. "Power Games and Totalitarian Masculinity in the Dominican Republic." In *Interrogating Caribbean Masculinities: Theoretical and Empirical Analyses*, ed. Rhoda E. Reddock, 68–102. Kingston, Jamaica: University of the West Indies Press, 2004.

de Moya, E. Antonio, and Rafael Garcia. "AIDS and the Enigma of Bisexuality in the Dominican Republic." In *Bisexualities and AIDS: International Perspectives*, ed. Peter Aggleton, 121–35. Bristol, Pa.: Taylor and Francis, 1996.

———. "Three Decades of Male Sex Work in Santo Domingo." In *Men Who Sell Sex: International Perspectives on Male Prostitution and HIV/AIDS*, ed. Peter Aggleton, 127–39. Philadelphia: Temple University Press, 1999.

Derby, Lauren. *The Dictator's Seduction: Politics and the Popular Imagination in the Era of Trujillo*. Durham: Duke University Press, 2009.

———. "Gringo Chickens with Worms: Food and Nationalism in the Dominican Republic." In *Close Encounters of Empire: Writing the Cultural History of U.S.-Latin American Relations*, ed. Gilbert M. Joseph, Catherine C. Legrand, and Ricardo D. Salvatore, 451–93. Durham: Duke University Press, 1998.

Duany, Jorge. *The Puerto Rican Nation on the Move: Identities on the Island and in the United States*. Chapel Hill: University of North Carolina Press, 2001.

Duranti, Alessandro. "Language in Context and Language as Context: The Samoan Respect Vocabulary." In *Rethinking Context: Language as an Interactive Phenomenon*, ed. Alessandro Duranti and Charles Goodwin, 77–100. Cambridge: Cambridge University Press, 1992.

Epps, Brad, Keja Valens, and Bill Johnson Gonzalez, eds. *Passing Lines: Sexuality and Immigration*. Cambridge, Mass.: David Rockefeller Center for Latin American Studies, 2005.

Espinosa Miñoso, Yuderkys. *Escritos de una lesbiana oscura: Reflexiones críticas sobre feminismo y política de identidad en América Latina*. Buenos Aires: Violeta Barrientos Silva, 2007.

Fanon, Frantz. *Black Skin, White Masks*. New York: Grove, 1967.

Farmer, Paul. *AIDS and Accusation: Haiti and the Geography of Blame*. Berkeley: University of California Press, 1992.

———. *Infections and Inequalities: The Modern Plagues*. Berkeley: University of California Press, 1999.

Farmer, Paul, Margaret Connors, and Janie Simmons, eds. *Women, Poverty, and AIDS: Sex, Drugs, and Structural Violence*. Monroe, Maine: Common Courage, 1996.

Farr, Marcia. *Rancheros in Chicagoacán: Language and Identity in a Transnational Community*. Austin: University of Texas Press, 2006.

Ferguson, Roderick A. *Aberrations in Black: Toward a Queer of Color Critique*. Minneapolis: University of Minnesota Press, 2004.

Fernández Retamar, Roberto. *Calibán: Apuntes sobre la cultura en nuestra América*. Mexico City: Editorial Diógenes, 1971.

Finlay, Barbara. *The Women of Azua: Work and Family in the Rural Dominican Republic*. New York: Praeger, 1989.

Fisher, Diana. "Immigrant Closets: Tactical-Micro-Practices-in-the-Hyphen." *Journal of Homosexuality* 45 (2003): 171–92.

Fung, Richard. "Looking for My Penis: The Eroticized Asian in Gay Video Porn." In *A Companion to Asian American Studies*, ed. Kent A. Ono, 235–54. Malden, Mass.: Blackwell, 2004.

Fuss, Diana. *Identification Papers*. New York: Routledge, 1995.

Gal, Susan. "A Semiotics of the Public/Private Distinction." *differences* 13 (2002): 80.

Georges, Eugenia. *The Making of a Transnational Community: Migration, Development, and Cultural Change in the Dominican Republic*. New York: Columbia University Press, 1990.

Goffman, Erving. *The Presentation of Self in Everyday Life*. New York: Anchor Books, 1959.

Gonzalez-Lopez, Gloria. *Erotic Journeys: Mexican Immigrants and Their Sex Lives*. Berkeley: University of California Press, 2005.

González, Raymundo, Michiel Baud, Pedro L. San Miguel, and Roberto Cassá. "Introducción." In *Política, identidad y pensamiento social en la República Dominicana*, ed. Raymundo González, Michiel Baud, Pedro L. San Miguel, and Roberto Cassá, 9–29. Madrid: Ediciones Doce Calles, 1999.

Goodwin, Charles, and Alessandro Duranti. "Rethinking Context: An Introduction." In *Rethinking Context: Language as an Interactive Phenomenon*, ed. Alessandro Duranti and Charles Goodwin, 1–42. Cambridge: Cambridge University Press, 1992.

Grasmuck, Sherri, and Patricia Pessar. *Between Two Islands: Dominican International Migration*. Berkeley: University of California Press, 1991.

Green, James N. *Beyond Carnival: Male Homosexuality in Twentieth-Century Brazil*. Chicago: University of Chicago Press, 1999.

Gregory, Steven. *The Devil behind the Mirror: Globalization and Politics in the Dominican Republic*. Berkeley: University of California Press, 2006.

Grewal, Inderpal. *Transnational America: Feminisms, Diasporas, Neoliberalisms*. Durham: Duke University Press, 2005.

Grosfoguel, Ramón, and Chloé S. Georas. "'Coloniality of Power' and Racial Dynamics: Notes toward a Reinterpretation of Latino Caribbeans in New York City." *Identities* 7 (2000): 85–125.

Guarnero, P. A. "Family and Community Influences on the Social and Sexual Lives of Latino Gay Men." *Journal of Transcultural Nursing* 18 (2007): 16.

Guarnizo, Luis E. "The Emergence of a Transnational Social Formation and the Mirage of Return Migration among Dominican Transmigrants." *Identities— Global Studies in Culture and Power* 4 (1997): 281–322.

———. "Los Dominicanyorks: The Making of a Binational Society." *Annals of the American Academy of Political and Social Sciences* 533 (1994): 70–86.

Gutiérrez Marrone, Nila. "Temas Gramaticales: El uso de 'tú,' 'vos' y 'usted' en Bolivia." *Signo* 50 (1997): 267–69.

Gutmann, Matthew C., ed. *Changing Men and Masculinities in Latin America*. Durham: Duke University Press, 2003.

———. *The Meanings of Macho: Being a Man in Mexico City*. Berkeley: University of California Press, 1996.

Guzmán, Manolo. *Gay Hegemony/Latino Homosexualities*. New York: Routledge, 2006.

———. "'Pa' la escuelita con mucho cuida'o y por la orillita': A Journey through the Contested Terrains of the Nation and Sexual Orientation." In *Puerto Rican Jam: Rethinking Colonialism and Nationalism*, ed. Frances Negrón-Muntaner and Ramón Grosfoguel, 209–30. Minneapolis: University of Minnesota Press, 1997.

Hanawa, Yukiko. "Circuits of Desire: Introduction." *positions: east asia cultures critique* 2 (1994): v–xi.

Harper, Phillip Brian. *Private Affairs: Critical Ventures in the Culture of Social Relations*. New York: New York University Press, 1999.

Hawkeswood, William G. *One of the Children: Gay Black Men in Harlem*. Berkeley: University of California Press, 1996.

Hawkesworth, Mary. *Feminist Inquiry: From Political Conviction to Methodological Innovation.* New Brunswick, N.J.: Rutgers University Press, 2006.

Hemphill, Essex. *Brother to Brother: New Writings by Black Gay Men.* Washington, D.C.: RedBone Press, 2007 [1991].

Hendricks, Glenn. *The Dominican Diaspora: From the Dominican Republic to New York City—Villagers in Transition.* New York: Teachers College Press, 1974.

Hernández, Ramona. *The Mobility of Workers under Advanced Capitalism: Dominican Migration to the United States.* New York: Columbia University Press, 2002.

Hernández, Ramona, and Francisco L. Rivera-Batiz. *Dominicans in the United States: A Socioeconomic Profile, 2000.* New York: CUNY Dominican Studies Institute, 2003.

Herold, Edward, Rafael Garcia, and Tony de Moya. "Female Tourists and Beach Boys: Romance or Sex Tourism?" *Annals of Tourism Research* 28 (2001): 978–97.

Ho, Petula Sik Ying, and Adolf Kat Tat Tsang. "Negotiating Anal Intercourse in Inter-Racial Gay Relationships in Hong Kong." *Sexualities* 3 (2000): 299–323.

Hoffnung-Garskof, Jesse. "The Prehistory of the Cadenú: Dominican Identity, Social Class, and the Problem of Mobility, 1965–1978." In *Immigrant Life in the U.S.: Multi-Disciplinary Perspectives,* ed. Donna R. Gabaccia and Colin Wayne Leach, 31–50. New York: Routledge, 2004.

———. *A Tale of Two Cities: Santo Domingo and New York after 1950.* Princeton: Princeton University Press, 2008.

Horn, Maja. "Queer Caribbean Homecomings: The Collaborative Art Exhibits of Nelson Ricart-Guerrero and Christian Vauzelle." *GLQ* 14 (2008): 361–81.

Howard, John. *Men Like That: A Southern Queer History.* Chicago: University of Chicago Press, 1999.

Jiménez Polanco, Jacqueline, ed. *Divagaciones bajo la luna/Musings under the Moon.* Santo Domingo: Omnimedia, 2006.

Joseph, Miranda. *Against the Romance of Community.* Minneapolis: University of Minnesota Press, 2002.

Kaufman, C. J., and S. A. Hernandez. "The Role of the Bodega in a United-States Puerto-Rican Community." *Journal of Retailing* 67 (1991): 375–96.

Kayal, Philip M. *Bearing Witness: Gay Men's Health Crisis and the Politics of AIDS.* Boulder: Westview, 1993.

Kempadoo, Kempala. "Freelancers, Temporary Wives, and Beach-Boys: Researching Sex Work in the Caribbean." *Feminist Review* 67 (2001): 39–62.

———, ed. *Sexing the Caribbean.* New York: Routledge, 2004.

———, ed. *Sun, Sex, and Gold: Tourism and Sex Work in the Caribbean.* Lanham, Md.: Rowman and Littlefield, 1999.

King, Jason. "Remixing the Closet: The Down-Low Way of Knowledge." In *If We*

Have to Take Tomorrow: HIV, Black Men and Same Sex Desire, ed. F. L. Roberts and M. K. White, 65–68. New York: Institute for Gay Men's Health, 2006.

Kirby, David. "Coming to America to Be Gay." *Advocate* 834 (2001): 29–32.

Kraut, Alan M. *Silent Travelers: Germs, Genes, and the Immigrant Menace*. Baltimore: Johns Hopkins University Press, 1995.

Krohn-Hansen, Christian. "Masculinity and the Political among Dominicans: 'The Dominican Tiger.'" In *Machos, Mistresses, Madonnas: Contesting the Power of Latin American Gender Imagery*, ed. Marit Melthuus and Kristi Anne Stolen, 108–33. London: Verso, 1996.

———. *Political Authoritarianism in the Dominican Republic*. New York: Palgrave, 2009.

Kulick, Don. *Travesti: Sex, Gender, and Culture among Brazilian Transgendered Prostitutes*. Chicago: University of Chicago Press, 1998.

Kusch, Rodolfo. "América Profunda." In *Obras Completas II*, 1–254. Rosario, Argentina: Editorial Fundación Ross, 1999 [1963].

Kvale, Steinar. *Interviews: An Introduction to Qualitative Research Interviewing*. Thousand Oaks, Calif.: Sage, 1996.

Lacan, Jacques. *Écrits: The First Complete Edition in English*. New York: W. W. Norton, 2006.

La Fountain-Stokes, Lawrence. *"De un pájaro las dos alas:* Travel Notes of a Queer Puerto Rican in Havana." In *Our Caribbean: A Gathering of Lesbian and Gay Writing from the Antilles*, ed. Thomas Glave, 202–32. Durham: Duke University Press, 2008.

———. *Queer Ricans: Cultures and Sexualities in the Diaspora*. Minneapolis: University of Minnesota Press, 2009.

Lambevski, Sasho A. "Suck My Nation—Masculinity, Ethnicity and the Politics of (Homo)Sex." *Sexualities* 2 (1999): 397–419.

Lancaster, Roger. *Life Is Hard: Machismo, Danger, and the Intimacy of Power in Nicaragua*. Berkeley: University of California Press, 1992.

Lauria, Anthony Jr. "'Respeto,' 'Relajo' and Inter-Personal Relations in Puerto Rico." *Anthropological Quarterly* 37 (1964): 56.

Leap, William, ed. *Beyond the Lavender Lexicon: Authenticity, Imagination and Appropriation in Gay and Lesbian Languages*. Buffalo, N.Y.: Gordon and Breach, 1995.

———. *Word's Out: Gay Men's English*. Minneapolis: University of Minnesota Press, 1996.

Leap, William, and Tom Boellstorff, eds. *Speaking in Queer Tongues: Globalization and Gay Language*. Urbana: University of Illinois Press, 2003.

Leheny, David. "A Political Economy of Asian Sex Tourism." *Annals of Tourism Research* 22 (1995): 367–84.

Levitt, Peggy. *The Transnational Villagers*. Berkeley: University of California Press, 2001.

Linkogle, Stephanie. "*Relajo*: Danger in a Crowd." In *Danger in the Field: Risk and Ethics in Social Research*, ed. Geraldine Lee-Treweek and Stephanie Linkogle, 132–46. London: Routledge, 2000.

Loftin, Craig M. "Unacceptable Mannerisms: Gender Anxieties, Homosexual Activism, and Swish in the United States, 1945–1965." *Journal of Social History* 40 (2007): 577–96.

López, José Ramón. "La alimentación y las razas." *Revista Dominicana de Cultura* 1 (1955): 75–112.

Luibhéid, Eithne. *Entry Denied: Controlling Sexuality at the Border*. Minneapolis: University of Minnesota Press, 2002.

———, ed. *Queer Migrations: Sexuality, U.S. Citizenship, and Border Crossings*. Minneapolis: University of Minnesota Press, 2005.

Mañach y Robato, Jorge. *Indagación del choteo*. Havana: Editorial Libro Cubano, 1955.

Manalansan, Martin F. IV "Colonizing Time and Space—Race and Romance in *Brokeback Mountain*." *GLQ* 13 (2007): 99.

———. *Global Divas: Filipino Gay Men in the Diaspora*. Durham: Duke University Press, 2003.

———. "Queer Intersections: Sexuality and Gender in Migration Studies." *International Migration Review* 40 (2006): 224–49.

Manzur, Rolando Tabar. "Algunas caracterizaciones sobre los dominicanos." *Estudios Sociales* 34 (2001): 25–44.

Mariñas, José Miguel. "*Sujeto, subdito, sugeto*: The Body of the Subject: Montaigne and St. Teresa." *Radical Philosophy* 138 (2006): 38–39.

Martinez, Samuel. *Decency and Excess: Global Aspirations and Material Deprivation on a Caribbean Sugar Plantation*. Boulder, Co.: Paradigm, 2006.

———. *Peripheral Migrants: Haitians and Dominican Republic Sugar Plantations*. Knoxville: University of Tennessee Press, 1996.

Martínez-San Miguel, Yolanda. *Caribe Two Ways: Cultura de la migración en el Caribe insular hispánico*. San Juan: Ediciones Callejón, 2003.

Martínez-Vergne, Teresita. *Nation and Citizen in the Dominican Republic, 1880–1916*. Chapel Hill: University of North Carolina Press, 2005.

Marx, Karl. *Capital: Volume 1: A Critique of Political Economy*. London: Penguin, 1990.

Mateo, Andrés L. "La Poesía Homosexual Dominicana." In *Antología de la Literatura Gay en la República Dominicana*, ed. Mélida García and Miguel De Camps Jiménez, 19–22. Santo Domingo: Editora Manatí, 2004.

McCall, Leslie. "The Complexity of Intersectionality." *Signs* 30 (2005): 1771–800.

McRuer, Robert. *The Queer Renaissance: Contemporary American Literature and the Reinvention of Lesbian and Gay Identities.* New York: New York University Press, 1997.

Medina, José. *Speaking from Elsewhere: A New Contextualist Perspective on Meaning, Identity, and Discursive Agency.* Albany: State University of New York Press, 2006.

Meisch, Lynn A. "Gringas and Otavaleños: Changing Tourist Relations." *Annals of Tourism Research* 22 (1995): 441–62.

Mendez, Danny. "In Zones of Contact (Combat): Dominican Narratives of Migration and Displacements in the United States and Puerto Rico." Ph.D. diss., University of Texas, Austin, 2008.

Miller-Young, Mireille. "A Taste for Brown Sugar: The History of Black Women in American Pornography." Ph.D. diss., New York University, 2004.

Mirandé, Alfredo. *Hombres y machos: Masculinity and Latino Culture.* Boulder, Co.: Westview, 1997.

Mohanty, Chandra Talpade. *Feminism without Borders: Decolonizing Theory, Practicing Solidarity.* Durham: Duke University Press, 2003.

Molloy, Silvia. "Bilingual Scenes." In *Bilingual Games: Some Literary Investigations,* ed. Doris Sommer, 289–96. New York: Palgrave, 2003.

Moraga, Cherríe, and Gloria Anzaldúa, eds. *This Bridge Called My Back: Writings by Radical Women of Color.* New York: Kitchen Table, 1981.

Moya, Paula. "Reclaiming Identity." In *Reclaiming Identity: Realist Theory and the Predicament of Postmodernism,* ed. Paula M. L. Moya and Michael R. Hames-García, 1–26. Los Angeles: University of California Press, 2000.

Muñoz, José Esteban. *Disidentifications: Queers of Color and the Performance of Politics.* Minneapolis: University of Minnesota Press, 1999.

Murray, Gerald F. *El colmado: Exploración antropológica del negocio de comidas y bebidas en la República Dominicana.* Santo Domingo: Fondo para el Financiamiento de la Microempresa, 1996.

Nast, Heidi J. "Prologue: Crosscurrents." *Antipode* 34 (2002): 835–44.

Neptune, Harvey. *Caliban and the Yankees: Trinidad and the United States Occupation.* Chapel Hill: University of North Carolina Press, 2007.

Nesvig, Martin. "The Complicated Terrain of Latin American Homosexuality." *Hispanic American Historical Review* 81 (2001): 691.

Núñez Noriega, Guillermo. *Masculinidad e intimidad: Identidad, sexualidad y Sida.* Mexico City: El Colegio de Sonora, 2007.

Padilla, Felix M. *Latino Ethnic Consciousness: The Case of Mexican Americans and Puerto Ricans in Chicago.* Notre Dame, Ind.: University of Notre Dame Press, 1985.

Padilla, Mark. *Caribbean Pleasure Industry: Tourism, Sexuality, and AIDS in the Dominican Republic.* Chicago: University of Chicago Press, 2007.

Pagano Fernández, Carlos María. *Un modelo de filosofía intercultural: Rodolfo Kusch*

(1922–1979): *Aproximación a la obra del pensador argentino*. Aachen, Germany: Mainz, 1999.

Parker, Richard G. *Beneath the Equator: Cultures of Desire, Male Homosexuality, and Emerging Gay Communities in Brazil*. New York: Routledge, 1999.

———. *Bodies, Pleasures, and Passions: Sexual Culture in Contemporary Brazil*. Boston: Beacon, 1991.

Patton, Cindy, and Benigno Sánchez-Eppler, eds. *Queer Diasporas*. Durham: Duke University Press, 2000.

Peña, Susana. "'Obvious Gays' and the State Gaze: Cuban Gay Visibility and U.S. Immigration Policy during the Mariel Boatlift." *Journal of the History of Sexuality* 6 (2007): 482–514.

———. "Visibility and Silence: Cuban-American Gay Male Culture in Miami (Florida)." Ph.D. diss., University of California, 2002.

Perez, Hiram. "You Can Have My Brown Body and Eat It, Too!" *Social Text* 84–85 (2005): 171–91.

Picotti C., Dina V., ed. *Pensar desde América: Vigencia y desafíos actuales*. Buenos Aires: Catálogos Editora, 1995.

———. "Resonancia y proyección del pensamiento de Rodolfo Kusch: A propósito de una obra reciente de Carlos M. Pagano." *Stromata* 55 (1999): 325–28.

———. "Voces interculturales en el pensamiento latinoamericano." *Stromata* 60 (2004): 307–12.

Polanyi, Michael. *Personal Knowledge: Towards a Post-Critical Philosophy*. New York: Routledge, 1998.

———. *The Tacit Dimension*. Gloucester, Mass.: Peter Smith, 1983.

———. "Tacit Knowing: Its Bearing on Some Problems of Philosophy." *Reviews of Modern Physics* 34 (1962): 601.

Portilla, Jorge. "Femonenología del relajo." *Fenomenología del relajo y otros ensayos*. Mexico City: Ediciones Era, 1966.

Prieur, Annick. *Mema's House, Mexico City: On Transvestites, Queens, and Machos*. Chicago: University of Chicago Press, 1998.

Puar, Jasbir. "Circuits of Queer Mobility—Tourism, Travel, and Globalization." *GLQ* 8 (2002): 101–37.

———. "Global Circuits: Transnational Sexualities and Trinidad." *Signs* 26 (2001): 1039–65.

———. "Queer Tourism: Geographies of Globalization—Introduction." *GLQ* 8 (2002): 1–6.

———. "Sexuality and Space: Queering Geographies of Globalization (Guest Editorial)." *Environment and Planning D: Society and Space* 21 (2003): 383–87.

———. "Transnational Configurations of Desire: The Nation and Its White Closets." In *The Making and Unmaking of Whiteness*, ed. Birgit Brander Rasmussen,

Eric Klinenberg, Irene J. Nexica, and Matt Wray, 167–83. Durham: Duke University Press, 2001.

———. "A Transnational Feminist Critique of Queer Tourism." *Antipode* 34 (2002): 935–46.

———. "Transnational Sexualities: *South Asian (Trans)nation(alism)s and Queer Diasporas.*" In *Q&A: Queer in Asian America,* ed. David L. Eng and Alice Y. Hom, 405–24. Philadelphia: Temple University Press, 1998.

Radhakrishnan, Rajagopalan. *Diasporic Mediations: Between Home and Location.* Minneapolis: University of Minnesota Press, 1996.

Ramos, Julio. *Desencuentros de la modernidad en América Latina: Literatura y política en el siglo XIX.* Mexico City: Fondo de Cultura Económica, 2003.

Ramos-Zayas, Ana Y. "Becoming American, Becoming Black? Urban Competency, Racialized Spaces, and the Politics of Citizenship among Brazilian and Puerto Rican Youth in Newark." *Identities* 14 (2007): 85–109.

———. "Implicit Social Knowledge, Cultural Capital, and 'Authenticity' among Puerto Ricans in Chicago." *Latin American Perspectives* 31 (2004): 34–56.

———. *National Performances: The Politics of Class, Race, and Space in Puerto Rican Chicago.* Chicago: University of Chicago Press, 2003.

Reid-Pharr, Robert. *Black Gay Man: Essays.* New York: New York University Press, 2001.

"Renting Wombs." *Antipode* 34 (2002): 864–73.

Reyes, Israel. *Humor and the Eccentric Text in Puerto Rican Literature.* Gainesville: University Press of Florida, 2005.

Reynoso, Julissa. "Dominican Immigrants and Social Capital in New York City: A Case Study." *Encrucijada/Crossroads: An Online Academic Journal* 1 (2003): 57–78.

Rivera-Colón, Edgar. "Getting Life in Two Worlds: Power and Prevention in the New York City House Ball Community." Ph.D. diss., Rutgers University, 2009.

Rodó, José Enrique. *Ariel.* Madrid: Cátedra, 2000 [1900].

Rodríguez, Néstor E. *Escrituras de desencuentro en la República Dominicana.* Mexico City: Siglo Veintiuno Editores, 2005.

Ross, Marlon. "Beyond the Closet as Raceless Paradigm." In *Black Queer Studies: An Anthology,* ed. E. Patrick Johnson and Mae G. Henderson, 161–89. Durham: Duke University Press, 2005.

Rouse, Roger. "Mexican Migration and the Social Space of Postmodernism." *Diaspora* 1 (1991): 8–23.

Rubin, Gayle. "Thinking Sex: Notes for a Radical Theory of the Politics of Sexuality." In *The Lesbian and Gay Studies Reader,* ed. Henry Abelove, Michele Aina Barale, and David M. Halperin, 3–44. New York: Routledge, 1993.

Rubinelli, Maria Luisa, ed. *Reflexiones actuales sobre el pensamiento de Rodolfo Kusch*. San Salvador de Jujuy: Universidad Nacional de Jujuy, 2001.

Russinovich Sole, Yolanda. "Correlaciones socio-culturales del uso de 'tú/vos' y 'usted' en la Argentina, Perú y Puerto Rico." *Thesaurus* 25 (1970): 161–95.

Samuels, Ellen. "My Body, My Closet: Invisible Disability and the Limits of Coming-Out Discourse." *GLQ* 9 (2003): 233–55.

Sánchez, Luis Rafael. "¡Jum!" *En cuerpo de camisa*. San Juan: Ediciones Lugar, 1966.

Sanchez Taylor, Jacqueline. "Dollars Are a Girl's Best Friend? Female Tourists' Sexual Behaviour in the Caribbean." *Sociology* 35 (2001): 749–64.

———. "Tourism and 'Embodied' Commodities: Sex Tourism in the Caribbean." In *Tourism and Sex: Culture, Commerce and Coercion*, ed. Stephen Clift and Simon Carter, 41–53. London: Pinter, 2000.

Schieffelin, Bambi B. *The Give and Take of Everyday Life: Language Socialization of Kaluli Children*. Cambridge: Cambridge University Press, 1990.

Schwarz, Roberto. "Brazilian Culture: Nationalism by Elimination." In *The Latin American Cultural Studies Reader*, ed. Ana Del Sarto, Alicia Rios, and Abril Trigo, 233–49. Durham: Duke University Press, 2004.

Schwenter, Scott A. "Diferenciación dialectal por medio de pronombres: Una comparación del uso de 'tú' y 'usted' en España y México." *Nueva Revista de Filología Hispánica* 41 (1993): 127–49.

Seidman, Steven. *Beyond the Closet: The Transformation of Gay and Lesbian Life*. New York: Routledge, 2002.

Sheller, Mimi. *Consuming the Caribbean: From Arawaks to Zombies*. London: Routledge, 2003.

Sheller, Mimi, and John Urry. "The New Mobilities Paradigm." *Environment and Planning A* 38 (2006): 207–26.

Shimizu, Celine Parreñas. *The Hypersexuality of Race: Performing Asian/American Women on Screen and Scene*. Durham: Duke University Press, 2007.

Sifuentes-Jáuregui, Ben. *Transvestism, Masculinity, and Latin America Literature: Genders Share Flesh*. New York: Palgrave, 2002.

Sívori, Horacio Federico. *Locas, chongos y gays: Sociabilidad homosexual masculina durante la década de 1990*. Río de Janeiro: IDES, 2004.

Somerville, Siobhan B. *Queering the Color Line: Race and the Invention of Homosexuality in American Culture*. Durham: Duke University Press, 2000.

Sommer, Doris. *Bilingual Aesthetics: A New Sentimental Education*. Durham: Duke University Press, 2004.

———. *Proceed with Caution, When Engaged by Minority Writing in the Americas*. Cambridge: Harvard University Press, 1999.

Spivak, Gayatri Chakravorti. "Can the Subaltern Speak?" In *Marxism and the Interpretation of Culture*, ed. C. Nelson and L. Grossberg, 271–318. Urbana: University of Illinois Press, 1988.

Stevens, Camilla. "The Politics of Abjection in P.A.R.G.O.: Los 'Pecados Permiti-dos' by Waddys Jaquez." *Symposium—a Quarterly Journal in Modern Literatures* 61 (2008): 255–65.

Strongman, Roberto. "Syncretic Religion and Dissident Sexualitites." In *Queer Glob-alizations: Citizenship and the Afterlife of Colonialism*, ed. Arnaldo Cruz-Malavé and Martin F. Manalansan IV, 176–92. New York: New York University Press, 2002.

Suero, Victor Avila. *Barreras: Estudio etnográfico de una comunidad rural domini-cana*. Santo Domingo: Editorial CENAPEC, 1988.

Taussig, Michael. *Defacement: Public Secrecy and the Labor of the Negative*. Stanford: Stanford University Press, 1999.

Taylor, Stephanie. "Identity Trouble and Opportunity in Women's Narratives of Residence." *Auto/Biography* 13 (2005): 249–65.

———. "Narrative as Construction and Discursive Resource." *Narrative Inquiry* 16 (2006): 94–102.

———. "A Place for the Future? Residence and Continuity in Women's Narratives of Their Lives." *Narrative Inquiry* 13 (2003): 193–215.

———. "Self-Narration as Rehearsal—a Discursive Approach to the Narrative For-mation of Identity." *Narrative Inquiry* 15 (2005): 45–50.

Taylor, Stephanie, and N. K. Napier. "An American Woman in Turkey: Adventures Unexpected and Knowledge Unplanned." *Human Resource Management* 40 (2001): 347–64.

Taylor, Stephanie, and A. Spicer. "Time for Space: A Narrative Review of Research on Organizational Spaces." *International Journal of Management Reviews* 9 (2007): 325–46.

Taylor, Stephanie, and M. Wetherell. "A Suitable Time and Place—Speakers' Use of 'Time' to Do Discursive Work in Narratives of Nation and Personal Life." *Time and Society* 8 (1999): 39–58.

Thomas, Greg. *The Sexual Demon of Colonial Power: Pan-African Embodiment and Erotic Schemes of Empire*. Bloomington: Indiana University Press, 2007.

Torres-Saillant, Silvio. "Diasporic Disquisitions: Dominicanists, Transnationalism, and the Community." New York: CUNY Dominican Studies Institute, 2000.

———. "Nothing to Celebrate." *Culturefront online* (Summer 1999): Article 5.

———. *El retorno de las yolas: Ensayos sobre diáspora, democracia y dominicanidad*. Santo Domingo: Ediciones Librería la Trinitaria/Editora Manatí, 1999.

Twinam, Ann. *Public Lives, Private Secrets: Gender, Honor, Sexuality, and Illegiti-macy in Colonial Spanish America*. Stanford: Stanford University Press, 2001.

Vaid, Urvashi. *Virtual Equality: The Mainstreaming of Gay and Lesbian Liberation*. New York: Doubleday, 1995.

Valerio-Holguín, Fernando. "Santo Domingo, Nueba Yol, Madrid: Migración e identidad cultural." *Cuadernos Hispanoamericanos* 637–38 (2003): 89–93.

Veijola, Soile, and Eeva Joniken. "The Body in Tourism." *Theory, Culture and Society* 11 (1994): 125–51.

Vidal-Ortiz, Salvador. "On Being a White Person of Color: Using Autoethnography to Understand Puerto Ricans' Racialization." *Qualitative Sociology* 27 (2004): 179–203.

Villegas, Victor. "Semblanza de Pedro René Contín Aybar." In *Pedro René Contín Aybar: Poemas*, ed. Victor Villegas, 7–15. Santo Domingo: Comisión Organizadora de la X Feria Nacional del Libro, 1982.

Weston, Kath. *Families We Choose: Lesbians, Gays, Kinship.* New York: Columbia University Press, 1991.

Weyland, Karin. *Negociando la aldea global con un pie "aquí" y otro "allá."* Santo Domingo: INTEC, 2006.

Whitehead, Stephen M., and Frank J. Barrett, eds. *The Masculinities Reader.* Cambridge: Polity, 2001.

Wilson, Ara. *The Intimate Economies of Bangkok: Tomboys, Tycoons, and Avon Ladies in the Global City.* Durham: Duke University Press, 2004.

Winnubst, Shannon. *Queering Freedom.* Bloomington: Indiana University Press, 2006.

Wolfe, Thomas. *You Can't Go Home Again.* New York: Harper and Row, 1998 [1934].

Záiter Mejía, Alba Josefina. *La identidad social y nacional en Dominicana: Un análisis psico-social.* Santo Domingo: Editora Taller, 1996.

Zentella, Ana Celia. *Growing Up Bilingual: Puerto Rican Children in New York.* Malden, Mass.: Blackwell, 1997.

INDEX

Page numbers in italics indicate figures.

Abreu, Diego, 126–31, 162–64

Acosta, Katie, 246n7

activo/pasivo, 181, 185, 189–91, 198, 273n12, 274n13. *See also* bugarrones

Acuña, Javier, 169; background and overview of, 24–25; on Dominicans, 75–76; family and relatives, 24–26, 28, 169; preferences of, in sexual practices, 177–80, 199; return of, to Dominican Republic, 168–69

African Americans, 103–4, 184, 215

Allen, Jafari Sinclaire, 283n34

Althusser, Louis, 152, 171, 261n2

ambiguity, strategic, 71, 254n12

anal penetrative role, 187; both partners playing, 182, 191–92, 197, 222–23; masculinity, dominance, and, 186, 190, 192, 196, 226, 263n8, 273n12; willingness and desire to perform, 189, 191–92, 197, 222–23, 285n43

anal receptive role, 186–88, 235, 285n43; and being a "sissy," 114, 192, 262n6, 273n12; both partners playing, 222–23, 225–26; effeminacy, gender dissent, and, 114, 186, 190–91, 226, 262n6, 263n8; shame, stigma, and, 187, 199, 224, 273n12; willingness and desire to perform,

189–92, 196–97, 222–24, 226, 284–85n43

Arismendi, Pablo: background and overview of, 154; coming out, 23–24; dealings with information about sexual identity of, 23–24, 28–29; family and relatives of, 23–24, 28–29; femininity/effeminacy and, 155, 157–60; involvement of, in gay politics, 29; on life in Dominican Republic vs. New York, 72–73, 191; sexual encounters of, 191; struggle of, for legitimacy at work, 154–60

Austin, J. L., 152, 268n15

autoethnography, 212, 237, 282n24

Báez, Claudio, 192–200; background and life history of, 192–94; critique of Dominicans and *dominicanidad*, 93–97, 103; critique of gay community, 170; on Dominicans' drive to success, 76, 92–93; family and, 192–94; migration of, to United States, 194–95; on sexual citizenship, 277n31; sexual encounters and relationships and, 193–200

Balaguer, Joaquín, 81

Balderston, Daniel, 211

Baldwin, James, 96–97

Barthes, Roland, 42

Bassant, Karla: family background and overview of, 132; as woman or "faggot," 132–36

bilingualism, 16, 170, 252n3, 268n14

bisexuality, 233, 236

blackness, 103–4, 202, 215. *See also* race

Blázquez, Gustavo, 270n30

Bleys, Rudi, 273n12

bodegas (grocery stores), 72–73, 88, 256n17

Borges, Jorge Luis, 116

Bosch, Juan, 101–2

"bottoms." *See* anal receptive role

bugarrones, 188, 206, 215, 219, *238*, 278n2; Anglicism of the word, 239; definitions of, 234–36, 277n1; playing with, 221–37

Butler, Judith, 115, 152, 171, 261n2

Cabezas, Amalia, 211, 213–14, 281n21

Cambumbo, 249n26

Cameron, Deborah, 267n7

Candelario, Ginetta, 104, 105, 202, 280n15

"Caribbean pleasure industry," 210

Carpentier, Alejo, 115

"choose and loose," 106, 252n3

"choose and lose," 106

Chua, Lawrence, 237

closet, 32, 246n7. *See also* coming out; outing

code swishing, 142–46, 151, 169, 171, 201–2; vs. code switching, 142–43

code switching, 142–43, 268n9

Collado, Lipe, 131, 266n35

colonial zone (*zona colonial*), 211–21; traveling in, 237

coming out, 29, 32, 38, 60, 246–47nn8–11; Arismendi's, 24; class

position and, 36–37; conventional U.S. views of, 18; Francisco Paredes on, 36–37; negotiations of, 22; neoliberal interpretation of, 18–19; tacit subjects and, 19; and taking ownership of one's life, 22. *See also* silence

confianza (trust), 126, 145, 147–51

Contín Aybar, Pedro René, 1–2

Cruz-Malavé, Arnaldo, 5, 271, 275n22

cultura (culture): "no tienen cultura," 86, 88–102. *See also* social class

"democracy in bed," 182; walking plantains and, 192–201. *See also* anal penetrative role; anal receptive role

de Moya, E. Antonio, 7, 124–25, 181, 264n16

Derby, Lauren, 98, 100

desencuentros. See under dominicanidad

Domínguez, Mauricio, 100–101, 222–30; background and overview of, 221–22; on Dominican gay men, 99–100; penetrating vs. receptive role in sexual encounters, 191; self-deprecation and, 100; on various generations of Dominicans, 99–100

Domínguez, Máximo, 22–23, 27–29, 147; boundaries and proximities with others, 139–41; deployment of silence, 151–52; involvement of, in gay politics, 29; on language and communication, 139–40, 143–45; power and, 151–52

dominicanidad (Dominican identity), 10, 97, 106, 199; *activo/pasivo* and, 181, 191; black-identified, 202; case material on, 63, 88, 91, 94–97, 100–102, 194, 199; conceptions, meanings, and nature of, 70, 92, 96,

102–3, 181; consumption of elements associated with, 97; critiques of, 89, 95, 103–4, 106, 192, 278n4; as discourse to manipulate and joke about, 100; distancing oneself from, 69–70, 91, 96–97, 180, 182; engagement with, 106, 113, 178, 180, 187, 201, 208; erotic investment in, 105–6, 199; expressions of, 72, 188; failed encounters (*desencuentros*) with, 14, 70–71, 94, 103; food consumption and ambivalence about, 98; gendering of, 88; ideal sexual scenarios *viran* (flip), 180; as incompatible with "progress," 101; jokes and identification with, 99; machismo, racialization, and ghosts of, 181–201, 272n12, 275n23; narratives of, 199; negative associations to, 88; "pathological" sides of, 71; pleasure and, 199; positive aspects of, 95; as process of becoming tied to specific social practices, 101; producing oneself while remaking one's, 72; race and, 103, 105, 178; rebellion against, 95; representations of, 252n7; sex and, 180, 187; sexual dissent and, 196, 199; and the unsettling proximity of the same, 72–80; what is "foreign" vs. what is "internal" to, 98

"Dominican macho," 178, 184, 187, 199–200, 202. *See also* machismo

Dominican Republic: contradictions of Dominican history, 7; visiting, 67–69, 78, 80, 90, 168–69. *See also* return

"Dominicans of the world," 63, 71, 101–2

Dominican-york, 70, 257n18

Duranti, Alessandro, 270n24

effeminacy, 15, 112, 114, 136, 146; apprehension about being associated with, 164; appropriate vs. inappropriate deployment of practices associated with, 146–47; in boys, 115–18, 124, 127–28, 131; as communicative practice, political implications of, 171; conceptions of, 263n9; passivity and, 190, 263n8; unease with, 50. *See also* Bassant, Karla; gynographic performative; *loca*; *locuras*; masculinity; "sissy" boy image

Espaillat, Aurelio, 189–91

ethnography, 212

ethno-racial formation, 105

ethnoscapes, Dominican, 204, 278n6

"families of choice," 69, 252n2

family knowledge about one's sexual orientation, 20, 26; case material on, 23–28, 34–36, 51. *See also* silence

feminine address, 115, 139–40, 145, 159–60. *See also* feminine language

feminine language, 60, 122, 144, 145. *See also* feminine address

femininity, 15, 112, 115; authority and, 157–58. *See also* Arismendi, Pablo; Bassant, Karla; effeminacy; gynographic performative; *loca*; *locuras*; masculinity

feminism, 262n6

Fernández, Leonel, 97–98

Finlay, Barbara, 265n28

"flipping bugarrones," 224–26, 228

Gal, Susan, 141

García, Rafael, 181

gay community, criticisms of, 170, 195–96

gay panic, 270n30. *See also* "homosexual panic"

Goffman, Erving, 261n4

Guarnizo, Luis, 255n14

Guerrero, Aníbal, 65; childhood of, 44–45, 187; father of, 44, 46–47, 187–88; in "gay spaces," 149–50, 169; on homophobia, 74; on machismo, activo/pasivo dichotomy, and sexual relationship challenges, 185–88; moving up in the family and, 43–51; overview of, 43; on "*racismo*," 74–75; relations of, with other Dominicans, 73–75; sexual desire for machitos and, 187–88; sexual relationships and, 199; social adjustment and, 48–50, 73–75, 149–50, 169–70; "straightjacket masculinity" and, 48, 60–61

Guzmán, Manolo, 105, 180, 182, 195, 272n4, 279n13, 282n25, 284n42

gynographesis, 115

gynographic performative, 115; *la loca* as, 115, 125, 130, 141, 144, 145, 170–71

Hanawa, Yukiko, 209

Hawkeswood, William G., 268n9

Heredia, Eugenio, 118–20, 131, 264nn17–18; childhood, 111, 112, 115–19; family, 116–19; femininity/effeminacy, 111–12, 115–20

Hernández, Ramona, 82

"heterosexual networks," 48, 49

HIV/AIDS, 6, 13, 58, 62, 251n19

HIV-positive diagnosis, disclosing, 56–57, 251n19

HIV-positive immigrants, 250n11. *See also* Domínguez, Máximo; Mejía, Arturo "Latoya"

Hoffnung-Garskoff, Jesse, 258n28, 258nn35–36

homophobia, 74, 123, 218–19; internalized, 18, 150, 245n8; "racism" and, 74

"homosexual panic," 123. *See also* gay panic

humor, 98–99

identities, 8–9, 263n10, 267n7. *See also dominicanidad*

Jokinen, Eeva, 282n26

Joseph, Miranda, 267n6

King, Jason, 33

Kirby, David, 246n8

Krohn-Hansen, Christian, 123, 125–26, 131

Kulick, Don, 263n9, 267n7

Kusch, Rodolfo, 9–10, 243n16

Lancaster, Roger, 262–63

Lauria, Anthony, 147

Leap, William, 267n7

legitimacy, 22, 28, 110, 126, 129, 141, 151, 168; being outed and, 29; investments in normativity and, 192; keeping one's sexuality in the tacit realm and, 36; "masculine" deportment and, 142; masculinity and, 38, 114, 123, 125, 131, 140, 150, 153, 155, 158–60, 167, 170, 270n30; power and, 125; restrictive bodily codes deployed to produce, 125; in workplace, struggle for, 154–60

lesbians: butch-identified, 63–64; Latina, 246nn7–8

loca, 61, 85, 116, 125–26, 129, 134, 142–43; as ambivalently invested performative, 136; connotations of the term, 85, 126, 128, 131, 148, 155, 161–

62, 260n1; declaring oneself to be, 121, 164–65; definitions, meanings, and uses of the term, 130, 144, 162, 164, 260n1; as gynographic performative, 115, 125, 130, 141, 144–45, 170–71; internalized homophobia and, 150; machismo and, 178, 200; as mediating divisions and tensions in groups, 160; reactions to being called, 50, 112, 128, 140, 145, 151–52, 157, 159; "total speech situation" of, 144. *See also loquitas*

locuras, 15, 125, 149; *tigueraje* and other, 126–31. *See also loca*

loquitas ("queens"), 127–30, 134, 144, 162–64

machismo, 272n12, 275n23; defined, 181; "Dominican macho," 178, 184, 187, 199, 200, 202; problems posed to Dominican men by, 183–84. *See also under dominicanidad*

"machitos," 186–88

male privilege, 28, 36, 91, 112, 151, 170, 211, 235; women threatening, 64. *See also* anal penetrative role

Mañach y Robato, Jorge, 148

Manalansan, Martin F., IV, 268n10, 285n45

mangú, 97

Manzur, Rolando Tabar, 253n6

mariconerías, 142, 145–51

maricones ("faggots"), 132–36, 139, 149, 186

Martínez-San Miguel, Yolanda, 98–99

Martínez-Vergne, Teresita, 80–81

masculinity, 113; authority and, 157–58; conceptions of, 125; "proper," 48–50, 109, 112, 125, 133, 136, 159–60, 192; as

straightjacket, 48, 60–61, 122–26. *See also* effeminacy; femininity; legitimacy; machismo; "serious" masculinity

Mateo, Andrés L., 1–2

Medina, José, 253

Mejía, Arturo "Latoya," 64–65; effeminacy and, 167–68; overview of, 51–52; self-presentation and, 167–68; social adjustment and, 164–68; surviving AIDS in an uneven world and, 51–58

Mejía, Hipólito, 97–98

Mignolo, Walter, 9

modernity, 14, 71, 98–99; sexual, 178, 180, 199

Monaga Corporation, 217–18

Neptune, Harvey, 105

New Wave Black Man, 217–20

New York City, 64–65; moving to, 10, 71, 87, 101, 191. *See also progreso*

Noguera, Rogelio, 84–86; confrontation and estrangement from his father, 30–32; on Dominican identity, 185; family background of, 29–30; on gay Dominicans, 90–91; on machismo, 183–84; negative view of Dominicans, 82–84; outing of, 29; relationship with fellow Dominicans, 84

Núñez Noriega, Guillermo, 265n23

outing, 29, 31, 36, 41, 166

Padilla, Mark, 213, 274n13, 281n22, 283nn27–28

Panés, Roberto, 86–90, 120–23

Paredes, Francisco, 32–37

Pedraza, Aurelio, 91–92

specular circuits, 116–23, 136
swish, 118–19, 122, 142–43; defined, 142.
　See also code swishing

tacit knowing, 20
tacit knowledge, 19–20
tacit subjectivity, 21
tacit subjects, 2, 19–21, 38, 248nn12–14;
　subjectivity and, 31
Taussig, Michael, 27
tiguere dominicano, El (Collado),
　266n35
"tops." *See* anal penetrative role;
　"machitos"
Torres-Saillant, Silvio, 11, 70, 244n24,
　254n8
tourism, 211, 214, 282n26. *See also* sex
　tourism
transgender persons, 164, 176. *See also*
　Bassant, Karla
transnational capitalism, 211, 214
transnationalism, 211–12
transnationalist scholarship, 210,
　244n24, 245n27
transnational phenomena, study of,
　284n40
transnational processes, 221
transnational social fields, 255n14
transnational social formation,
　emergence of, 255n14

Trujillo Molina, Rafael Leónidas, 1, 67,
　81–82, 107, 123–24, 137–38
trust. *See confianza*

Urry, John, 284n40

Vega, Sábato, 27–28, 63–65, 101–2,
　259n51; background and life history
　of, 58–63; family and, 26–27, 41,
　59–64; involvement of, in gay
　politics, 29; outing of, 41
Veijola, Soile, 282n26
versatility in sexual relations, 180–81,
　191–92, 199, 222–23. *See also* anal
　penetrative role; anal receptive role
Vidal-Ortiz, Salvador, 282n24
Villegas, Víctor, 1–2, 241n4

walking and masculinity, 168
"walking plantains," 188; "democracy
　in bed" and, 192–201
Weston, Kath, 252n2
whiteness, 120, 213, 279n13, 285n45
white supremacy, 103, 182, 209,
　279n13
workplace, 153–60; struggle for
　legitimacy in, 154–60

Zentella, Ana Celia, 268n14
zona colonial. See colonial zone

Carlos Decena teaches in the Department
of Women's and Gender Studies and in
the Department of Latino and Hispanic
Caribbean Studies at Rutgers University.
This is his first book.

: : :

Library of Congress Cataloging-in-Publication Data
Decena, Carlos Ulises, 1974–
Tacit subjects : belonging and same-sex desire
among Dominican immigrant men / Carlos Ulises
Decena.
p. cm.
Includes bibliographical references and index.
ISBN 978-0-8223-4926-6 (cloth : alk. paper)
ISBN 978-0-8223-4945-7 (pbk. : alk. paper)
1. Dominicans (Dominican Republic)—New York
(State)—New York—Social conditions. 2. Gay im-
migrants—New York (State)—New York. 3. Gay
men—New York (State)—New York—Identity.
I. Title.
F128.9.D6D333 2011
306.76'6208968729307471—dc22
2010049647